WOMEN AND EMBODIED MYTHMAKING IN IRISH THEATRE

SHONAGH HILL
University College Dublin

CAMBRIDGE
UNIVERSITY PRESS

University Printing House, Cambridge CB2 8BS, United Kingdom

One Liberty Plaza, 20th Floor, New York, NY 10006, USA

477 Williamstown Road, Port Melbourne, VIC 3207, Australia

314–321, 3rd Floor, Plot 3, Splendor Forum, Jasola District Centre,
New Delhi – 110025, India

79 Anson Road, #06–04/06, Singapore 079906

Cambridge University Press is part of the University of Cambridge.

It furthers the University's mission by disseminating knowledge in the pursuit of
education, learning, and research at the highest international levels of excellence.

www.cambridge.org
Information on this title: www.cambridge.org/9781108485333
DOI: 10.1017/9781108756327

© Shonagh Hill 2019

This publication is in copyright. Subject to statutory exception
and to the provisions of relevant collective licensing agreements,
no reproduction of any part may take place without the written
permission of Cambridge University Press.

First published 2019

Printed and bound in Great Britain by Clays Ltd, Elcograf S.p.A.

A catalogue record for this publication is available from the British Library.

Library of Congress Cataloging-in-Publication Data
NAMES: Hill, Shonagh, 1977– author.
TITLE: Women and embodied mythmaking in Irish theatre / Shonagh Hill.
DESCRIPTION: Cambridge : New York : Cambridge University Press, [2019] | Includes
bibliographical references and index.
IDENTIFIERS: LCCN 2019010370 | ISBN 9781108485333 (alk. paper)
SUBJECTS: LCSH: English drama – Irish authors – History and criticism. | English drama – Women
authors – History and criticism. | Women in the theater – Ireland – History – 20th century. |
Theater – Political aspects – Ireland – History – 20th century. | Feminism and theater – Ireland –
History – 20th century. | Women in literature. | Myth in literature. | Human body in literature.
CLASSIFICATION: LCC PR8795.W65 H55 2019 | DDC 822/.90992870941s–dc23
LC record available at https://lccn.loc.gov/2019010370

ISBN 978-1-108-48533-3 Hardback

Cambridge University Press has no responsibility for the persistence or accuracy of
URLs for external or third-party internet websites referred to in this publication
and does not guarantee that any content on such websites is, or will remain,
accurate or appropriate.

For Mary and David Hill,
with love.

Contents

Acknowledgements		*page* viii
	Introduction: A Creative Female Corporeality	1
1	Revolutionary Bodies: Mythmaking and Irish Feminisms	26
2	Unhomely Bodies: Transforming Space	65
3	Metamorphic 'Bodies That Matter': Process and Resistance	104
4	Staging Female Death: Sacrificial and Dying Bodies	135
5	Haunted Bodies and Violent Pasts	172
6	Olwen Fouéré's Corpus: The Performer's Body and Her Body of Work	213
Bibliography		237
Index		253

Acknowledgements

I have been very fortunate in having two wonderful mentors to guide me through the course of this book project. The work started as my PhD research at Queen's University Belfast supervised by Professor Anna McMullan. I developed my thesis into this monograph as a postdoctoral fellow at University College Dublin under the mentorship of Dr Cathy Leeney. Both Anna's and Cathy's scholarship has inspired this work, and I owe a huge debt of thanks to them for their critical rigour and intellectual generosity in helping to develop my work. I would also like to thank my PhD examiners, Dr Paul Murphy and Dr Clare Wallace.

I would like to express my gratitude to the Irish Research Council for awarding me a Postdoctoral Fellowship which enabled me to bring the book to fruition. During my time at UCD I have found many supportive colleagues in the Humanities Institute and the School of English, Drama and Film; in particular I would like to thank Danielle Clarke, Eamonn Jordan, Finola Cronin, Anne Fuchs, Valerie Norton and Ricki Schoen.

My passion in the research has been sustained through my membership of the Feminist Research Working Group of the International Federation for Theatre Research. I thank the members for their support, friendship and intellectual rigour which is inspiring and invigorating. Many friends have provided support along the way but in particular I would like to express my deep thanks to Trish McTighe, Brenda Winter, Richard Palmer and Margaret Robson.

Archival work in the Abbey Theatre Archives at The National University of Ireland Galway (NUIG) was facilitated through the award of a Moore Institute Visiting Fellowship 2017–18. I am very grateful to the Moore Institute for the Humanities and Social Studies at NUIG and I would also like to thank Dr Miriam Haughton for hosting me. There are many people whose archival assistance has been crucial to my research and I extend my thanks to: Eugene Roche in UCD Library Special Collections; Barry Houlihan in the Archives, Hardiman Library, NUIG; Estelle Gittens in

Manuscripts and Archives at Trinity College Dublin; Mairead Delaney at the Abbey Theatre; James Harte at the National Library of Ireland; Jen Coppinger and Rough Magic Theatre Company; Rebecca Geddes at PRONI; Dr Mary Clarke, Dublin City Library & Archive.

I would like to thank the following immensely talented artists for their generosity in discussing their work with me: Mary Elizabeth Burke-Kennedy, Paula Meehan, Olwen Fouéré, Kellie Hughes and Alma Kelliher. Permission to quote from private correspondence and conversations with Paula Meehan, Mary Elizabeth Burke-Kennedy and Alma Kelliher has been granted by the aforementioned.

I am grateful for the following permissions: extracts from Draft script, *Trojan Women/Greek Men* OB/526, dated 10 November 2002 and Draft script, *Trojan Women/Greek Men* OB/522, dated June 2002 by Edna O'Brien, reprinted by permission of Peters Fraser & Dunlop (www .petersfraserdunlop.com) on behalf of Edna O'Brien; quotes from MS 5048, Pos 8517, Pos 8518 and MS 21,440 reprinted courtesy of the National Library of Ireland; permission to quote from the Eva Gore-Booth pamphlet, 'Rhythms of Art' (PRONI catalogue reference number D4131/L/4) granted by Deputy Keeper of the Records, the Public Record Office of Northern Ireland; permission to quote from the unpublished script for the 2002 production of *Women in Arms* (ITA/258/01/11) granted by Dublin City Library & Archive; permission to quote from unpublished translation of *Sodome, My Love* granted by Olwen Fouéré. All efforts have been made to secure rights for material used in this book. If any material used here is credited inappropriately please contact me through my publishers.

I would like to thank photographer Colm Hogan for kindly granting me permission to use the image from *riverrun* on the front cover.

Parts of chapters have been previously published and I thank the publishers listed below for permission to reprint the material as follows. Material from Chapter 5 appeared in 'Ghostly Surrogates and Unhomely Memories: Performing the Past in Marina Carr's Portia Coughlan', *Études Irlandaises*, 37:1 (2012), 173–87; Chapter 3 (in a very early form) in 'Articulating the Abject: Metamorphosis in Marina Carr's The Mai', *Platform*, 4:1, Staging Gender(s) (Spring 2009), 44–59; Chapter 6 in 'Olwen Fouéré's Corpus: The Performer's Body and Her Body of Work', in *Radical Contemporary Theatre Practices by Women in Ireland*, ed. Miriam Haughton and Maria Kurdi (Dublin: Carysfort Press, 2015); Chapter 4 in 'Female Self-Authorship and Reperformance of the "Good Death", in Marina Carr's *Woman and Scarecrow*', in *Staging Thought: Essays on Irish*

Theatre, Scholarship and Practice, ed. Rhona Trench (Bern: Peter Lang, 2012).

I would like to thank my editor at Cambridge University Press, Kate Brett, as well as Eilidh Burrett, for their guidance and assistance. Thank you also to the readers for their comments and suggestions, and to my meticulous copyeditor Doreen Kruger.

Finally, I would like to thank my family for their support: my Mum and Dad, Sarah, Dee (my rock) and my little (but by no means less important) supporters Art and Etáin. Each of them has inspired me in their own way to stick at it. This book is dedicated to my parents for their unending belief in me.

Introduction: A Creative Female Corporeality

In the opening moments of *riverrun* (2013), Olwen Fouéré delivers a rallying cry: 'Calling all downs. Calling all downs to dayne. Array! Surrection.'[1] Fouéré's astonishing solo performance is an adaptation of the last section of James Joyce's novel *Finnegan's Wake*, and its significance lies in Fouéré's re-embodiment of the river, Anna Livia Plurabelle. Understanding the performing female body as a lived body which is fundamental to experience and the production of knowledge enables exploration of the creativity of the female body. Not only does Fouéré seize control of the frame of narration from one of Ireland's male literary giants, but the bodily meanings generated through performance recover that which has been erased by female iconicity.

Irish theatre has long been steeped in mythic narratives, an obsession which has hindered women's participation in the cultural fabric of society through the perpetuation of idealized and dematerialized tropes of femininity. Yet, women theatre makers have persistently and imaginatively engaged with and re-written these icons to refuse this silence. Anna Livia Plurabelle's 'Array! Surrection', or resurrection, through *riverrun* defiantly marks her corporeal resistance and the moment 'when the icons return to haunt the icon makers'.[2] Indeed, the icon *becomes* the icon maker as Fouéré awakens the audience to Anna Livia's desires and to the possibilities for female self-authorship and a creative female corporeality. *riverrun* is part of the rich tradition of women's mythmaking in Irish theatre that constitutes the focus of this book; a tradition which is invigorated by energetic opposition to inherited myths and thereby defined by the ongoing struggle

---

[1] James Joyce, *Finnegan's Wake* (London: Faber & Faber, 1939; repr. London: Penguin, 1992), p. 593. *riverrun*. Adapted, directed and performed: Olwen Fouéré. Co-Director: Kellie Hughes. Sound design: Alma Kelliher. Lighting design: Stephen Dodd. Costume: Monica Frawley (TheEmergencyRoom and Galway Arts Festival: Druid Theatre, Galway, opened 18 July 2013).

[2] Eavan Boland, *Object Lessons: The Life of the Woman and the Poet in Our Time* (Manchester: Carcanet, 1995), p. 197.

Women and Embodied Mythmaking in Irish Theatre

to dismantle cultural and material structures that support male power and privilege.

Fouéré reshapes the contours of Anna Livia's body to demand female expression; likewise, it is the intention of this book to forge a new paradigm, the genealogy, as a means of remodelling our understanding of the development of Irish theatre. Cathy Leeney describes 'the stubborn persistence of patriarchally-led definitions of what is canonical' in Irish theatre and argues that 'simply adding women to the mix is not enough'.[3] Leeney develops this argument in her contribution to *The Oxford Handbook of Modern Irish Theatre*; one of two chapters devoted to women in theatre.[4]

It is a pointed irony that her astute exposure of the difficulty of moving beyond the stage of the recovery of women's work to 'an integration of this recovery into canonical judgement, a disruption of the canon' appears seventeen chapters into the collection.[5] My proposal of the genealogy is an explicit engagement with the male-dominated literary canon and mythmaking of Irish theatre and masculinist scholarship which have served to replicate the marginalization of women's voices and experiences from the public sphere. I draw on feminist philosopher Alison Stone's use of the term genealogy which is not concerned with origins, purity and bloodlines, but rather advocates a coalitional politics whereby 'women are connected together in complex and variable ways, through historical chains of partially and multiply overlapping interpretations of femininity'.[6]

The mythmaking in the plays and performances discussed in this book comprise these chains of reinterpretation. Moreover, the non-linear genealogy indicates the 'progress' of women's history in twentieth and twenty-first century Ireland, characterized by periods where women's demands for equality have been met, only to be followed by regression. A linear canon of Irish theatre has served to reinforce the apparent silence of these stalled periods by severing the connections which form a tradition of women's theatre. Rebecca Schneider speaks to the process of reperformance: 'striking a pose partakes of reenactment, and reenactment defers its site in

---

[3] Cathy Leeney, *Irish Women Playwrights, 1900–1939: Gender and Violence on Stage* (New York: Peter Lang, 2010), p. 10.

[4] See Cathy Leeney's 'Women and Irish Theatre Before 1960' and Melissa Sihra's 'Shadow and Substance: Women, Feminism and Irish Theatre after 1980', in *The Oxford Handbook of Modern Irish Theatre*, ed. Nicholas Grene and Chris Morash (Oxford: Oxford University Press, 2016). There are forty-one chapters in the *Handbook*.

[5] Leeney, 'Women and Irish Theatre Before 1960', p. 269.

[6] Alison Stone, 'On the Genealogy of Women: A Defence of Anti-Essentialism', in *Third Wave Feminism: A Critical Exploration*, ed. Stacy Gillis, Gillian Howie and Rebecca Munford (Basingstoke: Palgrave Macmillan, 2004), pp. 85–96 (p. 93).

Introduction: A Creative Female Corporeality   3

multiple directions. What is cited extends not only into the past but also across complicated fields of possibility that undo any linearity that would give us, securely, forward and backward.'[7] The women in this genealogy 'strike a (mythic) pose' which defers in multiple directions to speak across the silences and create a (non-essentialist) body of work. In the chapters that follow, I develop the lines of confluence between these women to uncover the hidden veins of resistance and revolution embodied in their mythmaking.

The theatrical work explored extends from the start of the twentieth century, when the manipulation of myths of femininity was intertwined with the fight for an independent state and the subsequent development of the modern Irish state, to the present day where these myths linger on and have been moulded by other emergent forces such as neoliberalism and globalization in more recent decades, forces which have also spawned new myths of femininity. The performances analysed include the tableaux vivants performed by the Inghinidhe na hÉireann (Daughters of Ireland), plays written by Alice Milligan, Maud Gonne, Lady Augusta Gregory, Eva Gore-Booth, Mary Devenport O'Neill, Mary Elizabeth Burke-Kennedy, Paula Meehan, Edna O'Brien and Marina Carr, as well as plays translated, adapted and performed by Olwen Fouéré. Though the contexts differ, all the work studied in this book coheres around a self-conscious adoption of mythic narrative to critique idealized myths of femininity which support patriarchal structures and repudiate women's cultural participation. The performances interrogate the contingent and performative nature of myth and gender to articulate women's experience of exclusion, as well as uncovering the possibilities for expressing a creative female corporeality.

The Legacy of Mother Ireland

The stultifying legacy of idealized myths has occluded women's cultural engagement through confinement to iconicity. In her seminal work, *Women in Irish Drama: A Century of Authorship and Representation*, Melissa Sihra explains how, in Ireland, 'the social and cultural position of woman has historically been one of symbolic centrality and subjective disavowal as both colonial ideology and nationalist movements promoted feminized concepts of nation, while subordinating women in everyday

---

[7] Rebecca Schneider, *Performing Remains: Art and War in Times of Theatrical Reenactment* (London and New York: Routledge, 2011), p. 161.

life'.[8] The gendered narrative of representing woman as land can be traced back to the sovereignty figure: a pagan goddess of the land who conferred prosperity on a people through her union with their king.

This figure had several functions, representing war, fertility, sex and victory, but different aspects were employed and emphasized during different historical periods. The Morrígan, a goddess of war, had a dominant position in early Irish literature but this figure, and her sexual function, was later shunned in favour of the *aisling* figure.[9] This popular poetic convention flourished in the eighteenth century in response to the imposition of British rule following seventeenth century colonization. The narrative follows the dream convention as the poet falls asleep and has a dream-vision of a beautiful lady who tells him she is Ireland. However, the *aisling* was 'no longer a powerful or practical goddess, but a weak, melancholy maiden, romanticized and unreal'.[10] In the nineteenth century it was the more defiant figure of the *Shan Van Vocht* (The Poor Old Woman) who was favoured and appeared in political ballads.[11] The representation of women in myth during the early years of twentieth century Ireland was largely shaped by the political agenda of emergent cultural nationalism: the choice of myth was influenced by the need to represent Ireland's struggle for independence. This is epitomized in W.B. Yeats's and Lady Gregory's 1902 play *Kathleen ni Houlihan* in which the eponymous Kathleen is the symbolic Mother Nation figure who is dependent on the actions of men and serves to inspire them. The possibility of locating a feminist politics in this play is explored in detail in Chapter 1's discussion of the premiere production.

The enduring trope of Mother Ireland has defined women's bodies as the terrain over which power has been contested, while concurrently erasing the reality of their corporeal experiences. During the Revival years of the early twentieth century and the foundation of the Irish Free State, the Catholic Church contributed to the construction of an immutable Irish feminine identity through recourse to the Virgin Mother as role model. Ailbhe Smyth's description of 'the realities of Irish women's lives Mater-reality'[12] captures how this idealized figure became the 'reality' that shaped and supplanted the material realities of women's lives. The legacy of

---

[8] Melissa Sihra, *Women in Irish Drama: A Century of Authorship and Representation* (Basingstoke: Palgrave Macmillan, 2007), p. 1.

[9] Rosalind Clark, *The Great Queens: Irish Goddesses from the Morrígan to Cathleen ní Houlihan* (Gerrard's Cross: Colin Smythe, 1991), p. 8.

[10] Clark, *The Great Queens*, p. 6.   [11] Clark, *The Great Queens*, p. 169.

[12] Ailbhe Smyth, 'The Floozie in the Jacuzzi', *The Irish Review*, No. 6 (Spring 1989), 7–24 (p. 8).

Introduction: A Creative Female Corporeality

these attitudes is still felt in Ireland today. In March 2018 former President of Ireland, Mary McAleese, delivered the opening address at the 'Why Women Matter' conference in Rome, in which she lambasted the Catholic Church as 'an empire of misogyny'. McAleese spoke of the need for reform within the Catholic Church, fostered by gender equality: 'John Paul II has written of the "mystery of women". Talk to us as equals and we will not be a mystery.'[13]

The perpetuation of inequality through a mystified and idealized construction of 'woman' underpins the Eighth Amendment of the Irish Constitution, inserted in 1983, which effectively bans abortion and denies women their bodily autonomy. Instead, the reality of women's bodily experiences has been dealt with by evasion: between January 1980 and December 2016, at least 170,216 women and girls travelled from the Republic of Ireland to access abortion services in another country.[14] Following decades of campaigning, the Eighth Amendment was repealed by a referendum held on 25 May 2018. The resounding defeat of the amendment was evidenced by the voting figures; an almost exact reversal of the figures in 1983 when 66.9 per cent voted to insert Article 40.3.3 into the constitution, while in 2018 66.4 per cent of voters voted for its repeal.

In *The Second Sex*, Simone de Beauvoir delineates between the fixity of mythic 'woman' and the complexity of actual women: 'Thus, as against the dispersed, contingent, and multiple existences of actual women, mythical thought opposes the Eternal Feminine, unique and changeless.'[15] The central concern of this book is how women in Irish theatre in the twentieth and twenty-first centuries have employed mythic narratives to expose the gap between idealized myths of femininity and women's lived realities. I explore how these performances grapple with this tension through consideration of embodied experience, for, as Elizabeth Grosz explains: 'Far from being an inert, passive, noncultural and ahistorical term, the body may be seen as the crucial term, the site of contestation, in a series of economic, political, sexual, and intellectual struggles.'[16] Myth can impose limiting and inflexible representations which present female identity as timeless and unchangeable, yet it is through their attention to embodied

---

[13] Patsy McGarry, 'Catholic Church Resembles "a Male Bastion of Patronising Platitudes", McAleese Says', *Irish Times*, 8 March 2018, www.irishtimes.com/news/social-affairs/religion-and-beliefs/catho lic-church-resembles-a-male-bastion-of-patronising-platitudes-mcaleese-says-1.3419596 [Accessed 8 March 2018].

[14] www.ifpa.ie/Hot-Topics/Abortion/Statistics [Accessed 8 March 2018].

[15] Simone de Beauvoir, *The Second Sex* (Paris: Gallimard, 1949; repr. London: Vintage, 1997), p. 283.

[16] Elizabeth Grosz, *Volatile Bodies* (Bloomington: Indiana University Press, 1994), p. 19.

6   Women and Embodied Mythmaking in Irish Theatre

female experience that the theatre makers considered herein resist this illusion. The theatrical work discussed reveals the process of embodied mythmaking: how bodies bear the consequences of myths of femininity, while refusing the female body as passive bearer of inscription. The assertion of a creative female corporeality refuses the negative and essentialist alignment of woman and the body, and is central to repositioning women as the icon makers.

Embodied Mythmaking and the Writing Body

Embodied mythmaking considers the reiteration, reperformance and reinscription of myths on and through the body. Analysis of the theatrical work examined here attends to the ways in which bodies trace the residues of an inheritance of limiting myths of femininity, yet we can also look to the ways in which bodies might reinscribe meaning. This requires casting the body not simply as matter onto which meaning is imposed, but as the body–subject through which we experience and know the world. Maurice Merleau-Ponty's *Phenomenology of Perception* addresses the bias in Western philosophy towards René Descartes' privileging of the mind over body, a hierarchical binary which has been mapped onto man and woman, and instead suggests: 'The world is not what I think, but what I live through.'[17] Elizabeth Grosz describes the importance of Merleau-Ponty's work for feminism:

> His emphasis on lived experience and perception, his focus on the body-subject, has resonances with what may arguably be regarded as feminism's major contribution to the production and structure of knowledges – its necessary reliance on lived experience, on experiential acquaintance as touchstone or criterion of the validity of theoretical postulates.[18]

Feminist phenomenologists, including Grosz and Iris Marion Young, have explored the implication that the lived body is fundamental to both experience and the production of knowledge: 'The lived body is a unified idea of a physical body acting and experiencing in a specific sociocultural context; it is a body-in-situation.'[19] This approach is of vital importance to

---

[17] Maurice Merleau-Ponty, *Phenomenology of Perception* (Paris: Gallimard, 1945; repr. Oxford: Routledge, 2004), p. xviii.
[18] Grosz, *Volatile Bodies*, p. 94.
[19] Iris Marion Young, *On Female Body Experience: 'Throwing Like a Girl' and Other Essays* (Oxford: Oxford University Press, 2005), p. 16.

Introduction: A Creative Female Corporeality

this study in its acknowledgement of the specific material, and thus historical, contexts of corporeal being.

Remaining cognisant of context ensures that we acknowledge both the ways in which women are limited by, and simultaneously test, prescribed cultural limits. Young captures this tension in her description of 'the variable movements of habituated bodies reacting to, reproducing and modifying structures'.[20] Young examines how female embodiment within patriarchal society is defined by contradiction and ambiguity as a result of women's experience as both subject and object: 'as human she is a free subject who participates in transcendence, but her situation as a woman denies her that subjectivity and transcendence [. . .] [the] tension between transcendence and immanence, between subjectivity and being a mere object'.[21] Woman's contradictory experience is further developed by Rosalind Gill who examines the relationship between culture and subjectivity within the contemporary frame of 'neoliberal and postfeminist times'. Gill marks 'the shift from objectification to sexual subjectification',[22] whereby woman's subjecthood is defined by individualism and 'a compulsory (sexual) agency'.[23] Through my discussion of twenty-first century performances, I address this postfeminist fetishization of autonomous choice in order to examine our investments in the circulation of myths of femininity; for as Gill states, 'This is much more than a remoulding of the body; it is nothing short of a remaking of subjectivity.'[24]

The examination of embodied mythmaking through twentieth and twenty-first century Irish theatre enables the redress of Irish theatre studies' neglect of female bodies; both their creativity and their histories. The elision of female experience and of female bodies has been perpetuated by Irish theatre, and the study of it, as a predominantly literary theatre tradition; as Anna McMullan notes, 'the linguistic virtuosity of Irish theatre has a high textual value, and this very value encourages a primarily textual construction of Irish theatre history'.[25] Within the Irish literary theatre tradition, women's contribution has been marked by iconicity and, furthermore, the association of woman with the body has heightened the effects of a critical neglect of bodies within a theatre

---

[20] Young, *On Female Body Experience*, p. 26.   [21] Young, *On Female Body Experience*, p. 32.

[22] Rosalind Gill, 'Culture and Subjectivity in Neoliberal and Postfeminist Times', *Subjectivity*, 25 (2008), 432–45 (p. 437).

[23] Gill, 'Culture and Subjectivity', p. 440.   [24] Gill, 'Culture and Subjectivity', p. 440.

[25] Anna McMullan, 'Reclaiming Performance: The Contemporary Irish Independent Theatre Sector', in *The State of Play: Irish Theatre in the 'Nineties*, ed. Eberhard Bort (Trier: Wissenschaftlicher Verlag Trier, 1996), pp. 29–38 (p. 31).

8   Women and Embodied Mythmaking in Irish Theatre

tradition that affords prominence to the literary text. That said, Irish theatre studies has looked to the body with renewed interest; for example, in *Performing the Body in Irish Theatre* Bernadette Sweeney re-examines five Irish plays which have 'been suppressed in some way by the dominant discourse of dramatic, textual analysis'.[26] If, following Turner and Behrndt, we define dramaturgy as 'the composition of a work, whether read as a script or viewed in performance'[27] and extend this analysis 'beyond the performance itself, to include the context, the audience and the various ways in which the work is framed',[28] embodied mythmaking offers a dramaturgical framework through which to view the contributions of women in Irish theatre.

My intention throughout is to uncover a feminist reading of the work which displaces the privileged viewpoint 'of the ideal white, middle-class, heterosexual male spectator' and in his place locates a 'feminist spectator who can cast an eye critical of dominant ideology'.[29] Performance analysis is central to my discussion of embodied mythmaking in each chapter. Where I have experienced performances at first hand or had access to recordings of performances, I consider the contribution of text, direction, performance and creative design in interpreting meaning. However, there is scant archival material on some of the plays while others have never been staged, so in these instances I have worked with the performance text to uncover the potential for a feminist reading of the work and its embodied mythmaking.

My focus is on how these layers of meaning shape the body as a 'site of contestation'[30] to open up the gap between body and representation, between corporeal reality and mythic icon, thereby undoing the authority and apparent fixity of myth. Through performance, the women discussed in this book corporeally challenge and rewrite the myths imposed on them, and shift their role from bearing to creating and controlling meaning. The chapters which follow cohere around the body in process as it is presented before an audience: bodies that are revolutionary, unhomely, sacrificial and dying, haunted and, in (the final) Chapter 6, writing bodies. My approach draws on dance scholar Susan Leigh Foster's 'claim for a writing-dancing

---

[26] Bernadette Sweeney, *Performing the Body in Irish Theatre* (Basingstoke: Palgrave Macmillan, 2008), p. 2.
[27] Cathy Turner and Synne K. Behrndt, *Dramaturgy and Performance* (Basingstoke: Palgrave Macmillan, 2008), p. 4.
[28] Turner and Behrndt, *Dramaturgy and Performance*, p. 18.
[29] Jill Dolan, *The Feminist Spectator as Critic* (Ann Arbor: The University of Michigan Press, 1991; repr. 1998), p. 18.
[30] Grosz, *Volatile Bodies*, p. 19.

Introduction: A Creative Female Corporeality 9

body',[31] which enables examination of corporeal interventions in the cultural production of myths of femininity. Embodied mythmaking is thus concerned with how bodies are written upon but also resist forms of cultural production, and how these resistant writing bodies perform alternatives that negotiate female agency and expression.

Each of the chapters examines performances that offer bodies inscribed by an archive of myths of femininity but which also generate other possibilities. The revolutionary bodies in Chapter 1 offer the means of analysing the negotiation of change and the different feminisms at play at the turn of the twentieth century through discussion of the Inghinidhe na hÉireann's tableaux vivants (1901), Maud Gonne's performance in *Kathleen ni Houlihan* in 1902, Gonne's play *Dawn* (published in 1904) and Eva Gore-Booth's play *The Triumph of Maeve* (written in 1902 and published 1905). The discussion of theatrical form which emerges in Chapter 1 is further developed in Chapter 2 on unhomely bodies. I focus on Paula Meehan's *Mrs Sweeney* (1997) and Mary Elizabeth Burke-Kennedy's *Women in Arms* (1988 and 2002) to examine the tension between the body and the space it inhabits, and thus women's experience of a lack of accommodation within society and onstage, through alternative forms to realism.

The pursuit of alternative forms is advanced in Chapter 3's exploration of metamorphic bodies in Lady Gregory's *Grania* (published 1912) and Marina Carr's *The Mai* (1994). Metamorphosis as a process of transformation and corporeal change offers the means of refusing the unhomely experience and negotiating expression and accommodation. Resisting the curtailment of corporeal expression is central to Chapter 4's discussion of sacrificial bodies in Marina Carr's *Ariel* (2002), Edna O'Brien's *Iphigenia* (2003) and the dying body in Carr's *Woman and Scarecrow* (2006). These plays, to varying degrees, refuse the beauty of the female corpse and explore the trope of the 'good death' as a process of dematerialization and desexualization which erases female corporeal experience. Chapter 5's analysis of Mary Devenport O'Neill's ballet-poem *Bluebeard* (1933), Eva Gore-Booth's *The Buried Life of Deirdre* (written between 1908–12 and illustrated in 1916–17, although not published until 1930) and Marina Carr's *Portia Coughlan* (1996) explores the haunted body as a site of memory which enables the resurfacing of violent histories.

Central to all these chapters is analysis of the persistent theatrical efforts to articulate the female body in process as a means of dismantling the

---

[31] Susan Leigh Foster, *Choreographing History* (Bloomington: Indiana University Press, 1995), p. 19.

perfection of mythic icons of femininity: a corpus of work which traces the consequences of myths of femininity as they are felt through the body and which generates the possibility of rewriting them. Process and transformation underpin the discussion in all chapters of the book and culminate in the concluding chapter (Chapter 6) on Olwen Fouéré's *Sodome, My Love* (2010) and *riverrun* (2013). In this final chapter I draw on Jean-Luc Nancy's work in *Corpus* to advance a new framework for feminist critique of performance. His notion of 'exscription' addresses that which is beyond inscription and can be applied to the endeavour of reclaiming the unhomely female body which is outside of the symbolic frame. Both plays are male-authored texts – Fouéré translates Laurent Gaudé's script of *Sodome, My Love* and adapts James Joyce's novel in *riverrun* – but I would argue that Fouéré is the author who uses the female body as the primary text. Her performances champion a creative female corporeality and assert female authorship to question the dominance of a text-focused performance tradition. Expression of the female writing body serves to resist the imposition of myth and silence, as Hélène Cixous proposes: 'By writing her self, woman will return to the body which has been more than confiscated from her, which has been turned into the uncanny stranger on display.'[32]

The inheritance that the myth of woman as nation, another uncanny stranger, has bequeathed women writers is addressed by the poet Eavan Boland: 'What I found was a rhetoric of imagery which alienated me: a fusion of the national and the feminine which simplified both.'[33] Both are patriarchal constructs which deny the expression of women's subjectivity and renounce their bodies. My focus on embodied genealogies of women's performance serves to refuse the deathly silence imposed by the perpetuation of essentialist binaries on the female body. This genealogy of women's mythmaking constitutes a body of work animated by the suppressed realities of women's corporeal experiences; thereby enabling a dual reconsideration of patriarchal and conceptual frameworks of the female body *and* the canon of Irish theatre.

Mythmaking and Nation Building

A nation's heritage is one of its unifying components, offering a sense of the past and future through a created collective consciousness of its people. Mythologies are part of this heritage, traditional stories passed down

---

[32] Hélène Cixous, 'Laugh of the Medusa', *Signs*, 1:4 (Summer 1976), 875–93 (p. 880).
[33] Boland, *Object Lessons*, p. 128.

through the ages which serve to explain the world and its orders to society; as Richard Kearney notes, 'myth is closely bound up with tradition as a recollection, transmission and reinterpretation of the past'.[34] The ongoing reinterpretation of the past forms communities which result in the incorporation of certain experiences at the expense of excluding others. This was made manifest in October 2015 when the Abbey Theatre, Ireland's National Theatre, announced its programme to commemorate one hundred years since the Easter Rising – a rebellion against British rule. The 1916 Rising is part of the history and mythology of the modern Irish state and the intention was to 'interrogate rather than celebrate' the event, yet women were largely obscured from the programme: 90 per cent of the plays were male authored.

The marginalization of women theatre-makers and female narratives prompted an incendiary response in the form of the #WakingTheFeminists, campaign which has compelled arts organizations in Ireland to address gender equality at the level of policy and governance, and demands that we 'interrogate what stories are told, who gets to tell those stories'.[35] The pressing need to dismantle the mechanics of myth, as a central structure of the nation's storytelling, is the impetus for the performances discussed in this book.

The universal appeal of myth contains its repressive aspect as it attempts to freeze time and reaffirm a unified narrative of the past which supports the dominant ideology of the day. Laurence Coupe highlights the dangers inherent in mythic narratives: 'Thus the drive towards completion and unity can create not only powerfully imaginative stories but also systematic violence. Myth may imply totality, but "perfectionism" is to be resisted where it becomes totalitarian.'[36] In *Mythologies*, Roland Barthes reveals myth's capacity to naturalize the ideology of the dominant order. He examines myth as 'a type of speech' and 'a mode of signification'[37] in order to expose 'the very principle of myth: it transforms history into nature'.[38] Barthes focuses on uncovering the historical aspect of the signifying process to undermine myth's naturalization as 'myth has the task of giving an historical intention a natural justification, and making contingency appear eternal'.[39] Similarly, the performances discussed in this book

---

[34] Richard Kearney, 'Between Tradition and Utopia: The Hermeneutical Problem of Myth', in *On Paul Ricoeur: Narrative and Interpretation* (London and New York: Routledge, 2002), pp. 55–73 (p. 64).

[35] www.wakingthefeminists.org/about-wtf/how-it-started/ [Accessed 13 March 2018].

[36] Laurence Coupe, *Myth* (London: Routledge, 1997), p. 8.

[37] Roland Barthes, 'Myth Today', in *Mythologies*, revised edn (Paris: Editions du Seuil, 1957; repr. London: Vintage, 2009), p. 131.

[38] Barthes, 'Myth Today', p. 154.   [39] Barthes, 'Myth Today', p. 168.

Women and Embodied Mythmaking in Irish Theatre

seek to expose mythmaking as a historically contingent practice which embodies social structures, thereby dismantling the perfection of the Eternal Feminine.

The women discussed in this book look to two realms of mythic narrative for their inspiration and appropriation: Greek and Celtic myth. Indeed, Marina Carr melds both Greek and Irish mythic references to uncover and rewrite women's place within both traditions. The choice of either Greek or Celtic myth is interpreted by many critics as a deliberately reactive strategy adopted by a postcolonial nation. Declan Kiberd points to the tradition of classics in Ireland as revolutionary when the collapse of the bardic schools after 1600 gave the classics, together with Irish, 'the glamour of an outlaw activity'.[40] Furthermore, as the literature of civilization, Greek classics act as a rebuttal to the colonial construction of the Irish as uncivilized savages. This is evident in Lady Gregory's description of the aims of the Irish Literary Theatre in 'Our Irish Theatre' (1913): 'We will show that Ireland is not the home of buffoonery and easy sentiment, as it has been represented, but the home of an ancient idealism.'[41] Irish myth was deployed to assert a native culture, yet this 'ancient idealism' was shaped by the (gendered) ideals of early twentieth-century Ireland. Women's mythmaking did not always align with, and frequently opposed, these motivations so examining their purpose enables us to bring the tensions between nationalism and feminism into sharp focus: Chapter 1's analysis of performances from the start of the twentieth century reveals the complexity and range of feminist politics intertwined with, and obscured by, nationalist histories.

The Unhomely Experience

The patriarchal home, as regulated by the Irish Free State and Catholic Church, served as the framework for the project of national identity formation and rested on the purity of women. In *Ireland's Magdalen Laundries and the Nation's Architecture of Containment*, James M. Smith outlines the newly independent state's response to what it deemed to be 'problem' women and children: the construction of 'Ireland's architecture of containment', which 'encompassed an array of interdependent

---

[40] Declan Kiberd, 'Introduction', in *Amid our Troubles: Irish Versions of Greek Tragedy*, ed. Marianne McDonald and Michael J. Walton (London: Methuen, 2002), pp. VII–XIII (pp. VII–VIII).

[41] Lady Gregory, *Our Irish Theatre: A Chapter of Autobiography* (New York and London: G.P. Putnam's Sons, 1913), p. 9.

Introduction: A Creative Female Corporeality

institutions: industrial and reformatory schools, mother and baby homes, adoption agencies, and Magdalen asylums, among others'.[42]

The Magdalene laundries were founded in the eighteenth century and Dublin's Gloucester Street laundry (now Seán McDermott Street) was the last to close in 1996. The home as a space in which to contain women was bolstered by restrictive legal and ideological frameworks enshrined by the government of Éamon de Valera. Article 41.2 of the 1937 Constitution defined women's place in the home and granted the role of mother dominance over other models of femininity:

2.1. In particular, the State recognises that by her life within the home, woman gives to the State a support without which the common good cannot be achieved.

2.2. The State shall, therefore, endeavour to ensure that mothers shall not be obliged by economic necessity to engage in labour to the neglect of their duties in the home.[43]

The prison house of the home comprised both institutional homes and the private domestic space through which women's lives and 'duties' were constitutionally contained. Furthermore, this 'architecture of containment' is upheld by conceptual as well as material frames; limiting myths of femininity are part of the assemblage that confines women's expression and limits her freedom.

The experience of alienation and of feeling unaccommodated is augmented by women's exclusion from the fabric of Irish cultural life. This is articulated in a contemporary context by Mothers Artists Makers (MAM), a feminist movement created by mothers who are professional members of the creative industries. The group came together in 2016, inspired by the #WakingTheFeminists (#WTF) movement and by Tara Derrington's placard at the first #WTF meeting in November 2015, which asked, 'Where are the disappeared women of the arts? . . . At the school gates now.'[44] The experience of exclusion is thus an enduring one and Anna McMullan highlights the unhomely experience in Marina Carr's plays as one defined by the women's lack of self-expression and cultural representation: 'By

---

[42] James M. Smith, *Ireland's Magdalen Laundries and the Nation's Architecture of Containment* (Indiana: University of Notre Dame Press, 2007), p. 2. Initially, Magdalen was spelt without a second 'e' and this spelling continues to be used by many historians, however contemporary usage tends towards Magdalene.

[43] *Constitution of Ireland – Bunreacht Na hÉireann*, www.taoiseach.gov.ie/DOT/eng/Historical_Info rmation/The_Constitution/Constitution_of_Ireland_-_Bunreacht_na_h%C3%89ireann.html [Accessed 29 April 2010].

[44] Find MAM on Twitter at @MAMIreland.

14   Women and Embodied Mythmaking in Irish Theatre

unshackling the female figure from her traditional associations, Carr reveals her lack of place within the culture outside of the maternal function.'[45]

Drawing on Sigmund Freud's *unheimlich* and Homi Bhabha's characterization of the unhomely, McMullan maps the unhomely experience onto feminist philosopher Luce Irigaray's term *déréliction* which marks woman's displacement outside of culture and the symbolic. I employ McMullan's approach and consciously avoid defining a universal model of the unhomely experience by locating the plays discussed in their historical context. For this reason, historical background is integrated into each chapter rather than given as a summary in this introduction.[46] While following the logic of the above argument, we need to be aware that construing the home simply as a space of confinement for women may leave some feeling unaccommodated by feminism. Developing an understanding of when the home functions as an imprisoning patriarchal construct, while also acknowledging the value of gendered care work will be the fraught terrain that will be navigated in the lead-up to the proposed referendum to review the extant Article 41.[47]

The theatrical work discussed here exposes the perils and possibilities of mythmaking in performance; it reveals the unhomely experience, as well as opening up more accommodating spaces. In this introduction I want to embark on the process of exposing how the imposition of idealized myths of femininity, oftentimes in conjunction with the patriarchal framework of the home, results in violence and stagnation. This then leads us to consideration of how women's mythmaking might offer a revised conception of spaces and myths which accommodate female expression. Following discussion of these processes, we see how the attempt to negotiate new

---

[45] Anna McMullan, 'Unhomely Bodies and Dislocated Identities in the Drama of Frank McGuinness and Marina Carr', in *Indeterminate Bodies*, ed. Roger Cook, Naomi Segal and Lib Taylor (Basingstoke: Palgrave Macmillan, 2003), pp. 181–91 (pp. 187–88).

[46] With ground-breaking work by Margaret Ward, Margaret MacCurtain and Maria Luddy, the 1980s vitalized the field of women's history in Ireland. More recent publications include: *The Field Day Anthology Volumes IV and V*, ed. Angela Bourke et al. (Cork: Cork University Press, 2002); Rosemary Cullen Owens's *A Social History of Women in Ireland, 1870–1970* (Dublin: Gill & Macmillan, 2005); *The Irish Women's History Reader*, ed. Diane Urquhart and Alan Hayes (London and New York: Routledge, 2001); *Irish Feminisms: Past, Present and Future*, ed. Clara Fischer and Mary McAuliffe (Galway: Arlen House, 2015).

[47] Kitty Holland, 'Constitutional Protection for Women in the Home "Out of Date"', *Irish Times*, 23 August 2016. The referendum was originally expected to be held in October 2018 but is now set for May 2019, see www.thejournal.ie/referendums-in-2019-ireland-4350135-Jan2019/ [Accessed 14 March 2019].

Introduction: A Creative Female Corporeality

forms and reshape space underpins my proposal of a genealogy of women in Irish theatre as a newly conceived 'home' for their body of work.

The Violence of Mythmaking

Stasis and containment define violent mythmaking. Marina Carr's *On Raftery's Hill* (2000) unleashes a searing critique of the imprisoning framework of the patriarchal home as the cradle of the nation's mythmaking.[48] Within the context of Celtic Tiger Ireland, the play offers a critical take on nostalgic visions of the domestic space. Act One is set within the claustrophobic confines of the Raftery kitchen and closes with the climactic moment of the play: the brutal rape of the youngest daughter Sorrel by her father Red Raftery, the horror of which we are left to imagine as the lights black out before we see the act take place. Act Two plays out much the same action as the first act and the family remain trapped within a violent and repressive cycle. The lack of any change between the acts, save for Sorrel's worn clothes and subdued demeanour in Act Two of the premiere production, reinforces this bleak outlook.

The sense of entrapment and endless repetition is also created through the actions of Shalome, Red Raftery's mother, who provides comic relief, though this comedy soon bows under the oppressive weight of the play. Shalome's repeated efforts to leave the farm, 'I'm going back to Kinneygar and to Daddy',[49] reinforce the futility of the cyclical repetitions of the past as she never gets any further than the end of the lane. While being lead back upstairs by Dinah, Shalome remarks: 'All my life I've waited for my life to start, somehow it never has.'[50] Through her storytelling, Shalome is the main proponent of mythmaking and romantic expectation in the play but her creativity is frustrated and distorted. Both her belief in the myth of home as a place to escape to and her father as a fantasy figure are exposed as delusions; home is an elusive space of refuge. The play closes with Red Raftery's entrance with Shalome in Sorrel's muddied wedding dress, reinforcing the women's entrapment within tropes of femininity. The various 'brides' that populate the wedding scene in Act Two of Carr's earlier play *By the Bog of Cats . . .* (1996) highlight how myth and gendered identity are performative as both depend upon repetition to achieve the

---

[48] Marina Carr, *On Raftery's Hill*. Director: Garry Hynes. Cast: Mary Murray, Michael Tierney, Cara Kelly, Valerie Lilley, Tom Hickey, Kieran Ahern, Keith McErlean. Designer: Tony Walton. Lighting: Richard Pilbrow. Costume: Monica Frawley (Druid Theatre Company/Royal Court co-production: Town Hall Theatre, Galway, opened 9 May 2000).

[49] Marina Carr, *On Raftery's Hill* (London: Faber, 2000), p. 10.   [50] Carr, *On Raftery's Hill*, p. 14.

16   Women and Embodied Mythmaking in Irish Theatre

force that perpetuates its meanings: it is 'a regulated process of repetition that both conceals itself and enforces its rules'.[51] The performativity of the idealized and iconic image of the perfect bride is parodied by the variations on this ideal: the jilted wife, the jealous mother-in-law and the child as a bride of Christ. In the premiere production each of these 'brides' wore a veil,[52] underlining the limitations that the 'tyranny of familial metaphors' offer.[53]

Following Shalome's final entrance, Dinah asks Red if he caught anything and he replies: 'Only this auld bird. I nearly shoh her.'[54] The lack of physical and financial freedom, for the women in particular, is encapsulated by the metaphor of the hunted animal; only Shalome is not shot and she is unable to escape the house. Fiona Becket suggests that: 'The fact that there is no alternative to the familial except death is the irony that informs Carr's work.'[55] This irony is taken one step further in *On Raftery's Hill* where not even death is an available alternative to the oppressive insularity of the family.[56] Melissa Sihra has drawn comparisons between *On Raftery's Hill* and *Kathleen ni Houlihan* in terms of the setting, characters and themes. Sihra notes that Shalome's final entrance in the wedding dress 'invert[s] the actions of the Poor Old Woman in the earlier drama and refus[es] the myth of an idealised Mother Ireland.'[57] The rejuvenation and rebirth of Kathleen ni Houlihan into a beautiful young queen is denied, thus exposing the myth as a dead end while simultaneously denying any alternatives.

The lack of movement and claustrophobia created by limiting myths is heightened by the incestuous relationships in *On Raftery's Hill*. The eldest daughter Dinah has taken on the mantle of the mother of the household and this together with her collusion with Red grants her a relative position

---

[51] Judith Butler, *Gender Trouble: Feminism and the Subversion of Identity* (Abingdon: Routledge, 1990; repr. 2007), p. 198.

[52] See images on the website of Monica Frawley, set and costume designer for the premiere: www .monicafrawley.com/#/by-the-bog-of-cats/ [Accessed 17 November 2016].

[53] Fiona Becket, 'A Theatrical Matrilineage? Problems of the Familial in the Drama of Teresa Deevy and Marina Carr', in *Ireland in Proximity: History, Gender, Space*, ed. Scott Brewster, Virginia Crossman, Fiona Becket and David Alderson (London: Routledge, 1999), pp. 80–93 (p. 91).

[54] Carr, *On Raftery's Hill*, p. 59. The strong Midlands accent of *On Raftery's Hill* is a striking feature of Carr's Midlands plays which preceded it.

[55] Becket, 'A Theatrical Matrilineage?', pp. 91–2.

[56] In the first draft of the play, dated January 1995, Act Two opens with Sorrel dripping wet as she emerges from a pool beside the cowshed. The implication is that she has tried to drown herself, echoing the deaths of the eponymous women of *Portia Coughlan* and *The Mai*, although Sorrel is not successful in her attempt and remains trapped on Raftery's farm. T2/276, p. 47 (Druid Theatre Archive, Hardiman Library, NUI Galway).

[57] Sihra, 'The House of Woman', in *Women in Irish Drama*, p. 213.

Introduction: A Creative Female Corporeality 17

of power: we learn that this is maintained by Dinah's continuing sexual relations with her father. Dinah's union fulfils all the female familial roles, mother, wife and daughter, and therefore reinforces female dependency on Red as well as colluding with the patriarchal family model's conferral of power. Dinah's brother Ded describes her power in farming terms which reinforce the patriarchal economy: 'Ud's Dinah decides everythin round here anyway. Dinah's Daddy's cattle daler. You and me is only the cattle, Sorrel.'[58] The toxic masculinity which infects the world of the play results in the exclusion of men who fail to perpetuate violent patriarchal behaviour and Ded is consigned to a life outside the home in the cow shed.

The inward looking vision of the family is magnified and distended to parody the notion of the idyllic rural family. This dystopian vision of the pastoral is defined by corruption and sickness, and the stench of the decaying corpses of Red's farm animals is continually referenced by the characters. Tony Walton's set design for the premiere production depicted grungy walls, broken window panes and rubble falling away from the worn stone fireplace.[59] The extent to which the past quells engagement with the present reinforces how the family is stifled by conformity to gendered models and inherited ideologies. The theme of incest relates to all the families in the play and is explicitly linked to myth by their neighbour Isaac: 'Zeus and Hera, sure they were brother and sister and they goh married and had chaps and young wans and the chaps and young wans done the job wud the mother and father and one another'.[60] In this play, mythmaking, both Shalome's storytelling and the propagation of idealized myths of femininity, relentlessly perpetuates the oppressive claustrophobia.

The following chapters illustrate further instances where mythmaking denies movement and expression. In Mary Devenport O'Neill's ballet-poem *Bluebeard* (premiere 1933), the central character Ilina's enervated and unintentional movements reveal the restrictions placed on women's participation in the public sphere (see Chapter 5). The defiant haunting of the ghosts of Bluebeard's wives culminates in unleashing their revenge at the end of the play, only for their threatening energies to be dissipated. In contrast, the tableaux vivants performed by the Inghinidhe na hÉireann in 1901 (see Chapter 1) might appear to be defined by stalled movement, yet it is an immobility in tension with motion. Similarly, Olwen Fouéré's

---

[58] Carr, *On Raftery's Hill*, p. 37.
[59] Blueprints of the set for the premiere production. See T2/1164, T2/1165, T2/1169 (Druid Theatre Archive, Hardiman Library, NUI Galway).
[60] Carr, *On Raftery's Hill*, p. 43.

18   Women and Embodied Mythmaking in Irish Theatre

Sodome, My Love plays with moments of stillness to communicate Lot's wife's control of her authorship, whilst also signalling the constraints that have to be negotiated to effect change. Movement, or indeed the tension of pending movement, indicates the prospect of rewriting myth and shaping the future.

A 'Poetics of the Possible'

Richard Kearney distinguishes 'between a *mythologising* form of politics which interprets the present in terms of a unifying past (sacred tradition) and a *demythologising* form of politics which interprets the present in terms of a pluralising future (secular progress)'.[61] *On Raftery's Hill* brutally exposes the dangers of static mythmaking but, as in *Bluebeard*, there is no sense of a pluralizing future. Coupe highlights the three features of myth as 'paradigm, perfection and possibility',[62] and Richard Kearney and Paul Ricoeur offer two means of approaching this sense of 'possibility': Kearney's advocation of myth as a verb, and Ricoeur's suggestion that myth can offer 'a disclosure of unprecedented worlds, an opening onto other *possible* worlds which transcend the limits of our *actual* world'.[63] Myth has proved to be a vital source for the development of second-wave feminist thought: Hélène Cixous and Luce Irigaray deploy myth with critical rigour and poeticism to dismantle the foundations of Western thought and the perpetuation of patriarchal structures. I argue that the theatrical work discussed in this book utilizes the power of myth against itself, to not only deconstruct existing myths but to also create rich and expansive mythopoeias which accommodate women's expression.

Ricoeur acknowledges myth's ideological role but he also points to a possible liberatory function. He expresses his belief in the positive possibilities myth offers as he distinguishes between myth as deviant expression and as 'genuine' myth 'which can be reinterpreted in terms of *liberation*'.[64] Ricoeur's advocation of myth as a 'poetics of the possible'[65] incorporates the potential for creativity and imagination which Roland Barthes's theory of myth does not. Barthes addresses the claims of tradition and ideology on myth but Ricoeur's utopian view goes beyond this to address the creative possibilities of the future: 'The *mythos* of any

---

[61] Richard Kearney, *Myth and Motherland* (Derry: Field Day, 1984), p. 13.   [62] Coupe, *Myth*, p. 9.
[63] Paul Ricoeur, 'Myth as the Bearer of Possible Worlds', in *A Ricoeur Reader*, ed. Mario J. Valdés (Hemel Hempstead: Harvester Wheatsheaf, 1991), pp. 482–90 (p. 490).
[64] Ricoeur, 'Myth as the Bearer of Possible Worlds', p. 485.
[65] Kearney, 'Between Tradition and Utopia', p. 69.

Introduction: A Creative Female Corporeality 19

community is the bearer of something which exceeds its own frontiers; it is the bearer of other *possible* worlds.'[66] In Carr's Midlands Trilogy (*The Mai, Portia Coughlan,* and *By the Bog of Cats ...*) we see her creation of new mythopoeias and 'other *possible* worlds' which converge on the landscape as a space of female expression. In *By the Bog of Cats ...* Hester, like her mother and the mythic Catwoman, freely roams the bog and this is juxtaposed with Hester's sense of never having 'felt at home' in her house.[67] The bog accommodates shifting identities, the supernatural and the mythic realm, and the lighting in the Abbey Theatre's premiere production, designed by Nick Chelton, emphasized this mutable landscape.[68] In all three of the Midlands plays, the central character has a private mythology which connects the landscape with the lost other. This creates a tension in the female mythmaking of Carr's plays: it can reinforce a restrictive model of family and female genealogy but it also offers the women an alternative space of expression and attempts to house a female symbolic. Hester's private mythology intertwines fate and genealogy in a potentially stifling manner but the mythmaking in the play also opens up 'pluralising futures' through Hester's rewriting of both limiting models of femininity and her tragic ending, and through cultivating the possibilities of the bog.

Like Carr, the women theatre makers examined in this book critically engage with the process of mythmaking in order to utilize myth's 'dual potential of creation and critique: the disclosure of possible worlds which are suppressed in our present reality and whose very otherness provides us with alternatives to the established order'.[69] It is in the mythic realm of the plays that the women locate an alternative to realism as a 'conservative force that reproduces and reinforces dominant cultural relations'.[70] In contrast to the deadening (or possibly hysterical) realism which reflects the women's entrapment on Raftery's Hill and prevents exploration of 'other *possible* worlds', the women in Carr's Midlands plays use the poetics of mythmaking and storytelling to create a space through which to forge new models of female subjectivity. The focus of Chapter 2 is an exploration of how different theatrical forms might accommodate expression of the unhomely

---

[66] Ricoeur, 'Myth as the Bearer of Possible Worlds', p. 489.
[67] Marina Carr, *By the Bog of Cats ...,* in *Plays One* (London: Faber & Faber, 1999), p. 266.
[68] Marina Carr, *By the Bog of Cats ...* Director: Patrick Mason. Cast: Olwen Fouéré, Siobhan Cullen, Pauline Flanagan, Tom Hickey, Eamon Kelly, Pat Kinevane, Ronan Leahy, Pat Leavy, Fionnuala Murphy, Conor McDermottroe, Joan O'Hara, Kerrie O'Sullivan, Conan Sweeny. Lighting: Nick Chelton. Set and costume: Monica Frawley (Abbey Theatre, Dublin, opened 7 October 1998).
[69] Kearney, 'Between Tradition and Utopia', p. 65.
[70] Dolan, *The Feminist Spectator as Critic,* p. 84.

20   Women and Embodied Mythmaking in Irish Theatre

experience: the fractured realism of Paula Meehan's *Mrs Sweeney* attempts to engage with spaces beyond the boundaries of the realist stage while the Brechtian-influenced fluid performance style of Mary Elizabeth Burke-Kennedy's *Women in Arms* reshapes myth and the landscape through the body. In Chapters 1 and 5 we see how Eva Gore-Booth utilizes symbolism to engage with realms beyond the mimetic stage world to advocate non-binary and non-essential gendered and sexual identities. In contrast, Lady Gregory deploys naturalism to defend the eponymous Grania as a desiring subject in tension with her mythic frame (see Chapter 3). Through a range of theatrical forms, the plays deploy 'genuine' myth to reveal a disjunction between the confined onstage world that the female protagonists are forced to adapt to and an alternative world which enables their expression and agency and is suggested through performance.

The notion of 'genuine' mythmaking is thus fundamental to my argument and I uncover the theatrical strategies which open up myth and enable both interrogation and innovation; 'to understand myth, "fragile" as it is, as a disclosure rather than a dogma: as a narrative whose potential always evades the given order, with its illusion of truth'.[71] Ricoeur's use of the word 'genuine' to describe his liberatory and open-ended myth may suggest an original or authentic myth and thus an essentialist agenda. However, his deployment of the term is more ethical in its connotations as his utopian vision resists the limits imposed by myths which look to the past and congeal meaning (and, of particular relevance to this study, significations of femininity), and thus opens onto 'other *possible* worlds'. I make reference to Ricoeur's notion of 'genuine' mythmaking throughout but in order to avoid the essentialist connotations inferred by the term 'genuine', I refer to liberatory myth in process, which encompasses both creation and critique, as interrogative myth.

My use of the term interrogative myth also draws on Kearney's suggestion that myth function as a verb: as an ongoing process of retelling and, in the context of the work discussed in this book, reperformance. Myth attempts to suppress cultural context but it is also reinvigorated by it; old mythic worlds are retold to offer new worlds which are informed by, and reinterpreted in, the present. Thus, self-conscious awareness of myth's incompleteness, of it as an ongoing process, offers the possibility for critical intervention. Myth as a process which counters dominant and patriarchal ideologies is central to this book: unloosing models of femininity perpetuated through myth into an ongoing process of negotiation. Myth as verb

---

[71] Coupe, *Myth*, p. 196.

Introduction: A Creative Female Corporeality 21

can facilitate women's participation in the cultural fabric of society; not simply as the icons of myth, but as authors who rewrite these models. Kearney delineates between the Irish revivalists' mythmaking in the early twentieth century which, he argues, calcified into nationalist ideology, in contrast to James Joyce's mythmaking in *Ulysses*: 'Whereas myth was a noun for the Irish revivalists it was a verb for Joyce.'[72] My analysis of *riverrun* in the concluding chapter expands on the limits of Joyce's myth-making as verb: Fouéré's re-vision of the final section of *Finnegan's Wake* is rewritten by Anna Livia Plurabelle's body. Moreover, my analysis of the tableaux vivants performed by the Inghinidhe na hÉireann illustrates that myth was not a noun for these women: their mythmaking was very much engaged in 'pluralising futures' and the creation of an independent Irish state which incorporated gender equality. Yet, as detailed in Chapter 1, their mythmaking in process has been largely ignored by Irish theatre scholarship due to disregard of the ways in which it is animated by corporeal experience and female expression.

The Body as the Unhomely Archive

My exploration of embodied mythmaking addresses the resurfacing of obscured (theatrical) histories of female corporal experience, as well as the expression of a creative female corporeality. This approach raises two intertwined issues which are fundamental to my study: how to write the body and how to document the body. These questions give rise to the overarching question of this book, namely how to 'house' the body of women's work in Irish theatre. In *Performing Remains: Art and War in Times of Theatrical Reenactment*, Rebecca Schneider interrogates perfor-mance studies enthralment to concepts of vanishing, ephemerality and disappearance to ask, 'if we think of performance as the antithesis of preservation, do we limit ourselves to an understanding of performance predetermined by a cultural habituation to the patrilineal, West-identified (arguably white-cultural) logic of the archive?'[73] Schneider argues that 'the logic of the archive, [...] [does] in fact *demand that performance disappear*'[74] and thus the question is how do we address the ways in which performance remains? This book reveals the body as the unhomely presence in an archive of myths of femininity: tracing the residue and

---

[72] Richard Kearney, 'Editorial', in *The Crane Bag Book of Irish Studies (1977–1981)*, ed. Mark Patrick Hederman and Richard Kearney (Dublin: Blackwater Press, 1982), pp. 155–7 (p. 156).
[73] Schneider, *Performing Remains*, p. 97. [74] Schneider, *Performing Remains*, p. 100.

22   Women and Embodied Mythmaking in Irish Theatre

impact of these myths forms the connective tissue in a network of embodied mythmaking. The role of the body in the transmission of memory is central to my argument and it is the female writing body which facilitates the reappearance and reassertion of the archive's remains; fleshing out a rich and unmined vein of creativity and resistance in Irish theatre.

In *The Archive and the Repertoire*, Diana Taylor looks to the ways in which 'traditions are stored in the body' and communicated in the present.[75] Taylor proposes that counter to the archive, 'The repertoire on the other hand, enacts embodied memory: performances, gestures, orality, movement, dance, singing – in short, all those acts usually thought of as ephemeral, nonreproducible knowledge.'[76] Taylor's assertion of the validity of embodied memory resonates with my examination of embodied mythmaking. However, Schneider warns against the binary logic which opposes archive and performance 'as if writing were not an embodied act, nor an embodied encounter across time, and as if performance were not discursive (nor discourse performative or performatic)'.[77] Schneider goes on to outline how Taylor 'works to situate the repertoire *as another kind of archive*, rather than emphasizing the twin effort of situating the archive as *another kind of performance*'.[78] Schneider suggests that the archive is therefore

> *also* part of an embodied repertoire – a set of live practices of access, given to take place in a house (the literal archive) built for live encounter with privileged remains, remains that, ironically, *script* the encountering body as disappearing even as the return of the body is assumed by the very logic of preservation that assumes disappearance. That is, the split between archive and repertoire, a split that Taylor to some extent reiterates, is the archive's own division.[79]

Through the process of writing this book I am performing an archive; I am engaged in the act of retrieving and preserving performances in order to house their remains. Yet, as already discussed, within the fabric of Ireland's cultural and social life, women's experience is one marked by unhomeliness. Thus, by acknowledging 'the archive [as] a live performance space, and the performance space [as] an archive for the revenant',[80] the act of interrogative mythmaking examined in this book is one shaped by resurfacing and remains. However, rather than resting with claims for

---

[75] Diana Taylor, *The Archive and the Repertoire: Performing Cultural Memory in the Americas* (Durham and London: Duke University Press, 2003), p. 24.
[76] Taylor, *The Archive and the Repertoire*, p. 20.   [77] Schneider, *Performing Remains*, p. 107.
[78] Schneider, *Performing Remains*, p. 108.   [79] Schneider, *Performing Remains*, p. 108.
[80] Schneider, *Performing Remains*, p. 110.

Introduction: A Creative Female Corporeality   23

this work as an archive I engage with the historiography of Irish theatre studies to conceive of the work collected in this archive as a genealogy of women in Irish theatre. The genealogy offers an alternative approach to studying, anthologizing and teaching Irish theatre which offers the means to engage further with alternative histories to the male-dominated literary canon of Irish theatre.

A Genealogy of Women in Irish Theatre

Fiona Becket suggests that Carr's *The Mai* and *Portia Coughlan* 'disrupt the presumed solidarity of mother/daughter (daughter/mother) relationships that frequently underpin feminist family mythologies'.[81] In *By the Bog of Cats . . .* Hester's matrilineal relationships similarly question the benefits of this model of genealogy and Hester denies its perpetuation by killing her daughter. Mother/daughter relationships which result in physical violence recur through Carr's plays; they are evident in *Portia Coughlan* and *Ariel*, supporting Becket's argument that Carr's work 'challenge[s] the notion that a strong feminine identity rests on the familial, female kinship, model'.[82] Carr confronts the idealized mother/daughter relationship and exposes how female genealogies can function repressively, perpetuating a closed mythic system of a patriarchal familial which denies difference and change. However, Carr's mythmaking also opens up 'other *possible* worlds', thereby supporting Luce Irigaray's suggestion that when female relationships are refigured outside of the familial model which grants pre-eminence to the idealized mother, strong lines of female genealogy can offer opposition to patriarchal lineage:

> In our societies, the mother/daughter, daughter/mother relationship constitutes a highly explosive nucleus. Thinking it, and changing it, is equivalent to shaking the foundations of the patriarchal order.[83]

The structure of this book is intended to aid the process of rethinking a matrilineal tradition in Irish theatre.

In order to assert a coalition of women in Irish theatre united by their unhomely experience and mobilized through the collective action of embodied mythmaking, I employ Alison Stone's conception of a genealogy through which she explores the potential of Judith Butler's

---

[81] Becket, 'A Theatrical Matrilineage?' p. 89.   [82] Becket, 'A Theatrical Matrilineage?' p. 90.
[83] Luce Irigaray, 'Women-Mothers, the Silent Substratum of the Social Order', in *The Irigaray Reader*, ed. Margaret Whitford (Oxford: Basil Blackwell, 1991), pp. 47–52 (p. 50).

24 Women and Embodied Mythmaking in Irish Theatre

advocation of 'a *feminist genealogy* of the category of women'.[84] Stone outlines the bind that feminism found itself in from the 1980s onwards: namely that post-structural anti-essentialism seemed to undercut the possibility of women existing as a distinct social group. Following Friedrich Nietzsche's work on genealogy, Stone argues for a feminist genealogy wherein 'all cultural constructions of femininity re-interpret pre-existing constructions and thereby compose a history of overlapping chains of interpretation, within which all women are situated'.[85] The emphasis is on how women 'are assembled into a determinate social group through their location in this complex history', rather than sharing 'a common understanding or experience of femininity'.[86] It is therefore essential to address the different myths of femininity within their historical framework, as well as the experiences and histories which inform the embodied mythmaking of the women in this genealogy of Irish theatre. The experiences of Ascendency class women at the turn of the century, such as Eva Gore-Booth, differ in many ways from those of the contemporary writer, working-class Dubliner Paula Meehan. The women are not united by essential characteristics, nor indeed are the myths; instead we can address the ways in which their work intersects through their interrogative mythmaking: 'All women are thus located within chains of reinterpretation that bring them into complex filiations with one another.'[87] The women discussed in this book are mobilized around an action, embodied mythmaking, which draws attention to its socio-cultural situation. They explicitly engage in the process of breaking and creating links in the chains of reinterpretation of myths of femininity. Therefore, there are women in Irish theatre whose work I do not address but it is my hope that my proposal of the genealogy will open up the possibilities for future research that sheds new light on the (de)construction of the (Irish) theatrical canon.

The energy and dynamism which pulses through the body of mythmaking discussed in this book bears testament to women's enduring demand for change, though what that means, both in terms of how it is negotiated, what the desired outcome is, and what is achieved, depends on the context of the period from which the play emerges. The difficulty of effecting transformation and change, metamorphosis and revolution, underlies each of the chapters that follow as power structures have proved to be resilient,

---

[84] Quoted in Alison Stone, 'On the Genealogy of Women: A Defence of Anti-Essentialism', in *Third Wave Feminism: A Critical Exploration*, ed. Stacy Gillis, Gillian Howie and Rebecca Munford (Basingstoke: Palgrave Macmillan, 2004), p. 85.
[85] Stone, 'On the Genealogy of Women', p. 86.   [86] Stone, 'On the Genealogy of Women', p. 86.
[87] Stone, 'On the Genealogy of Women', p. 93.

Introduction: A Creative Female Corporeality 25

though not insurmountable. Women's progress towards equality in Ireland has met, and continues to meet, obstacles which have meant that not only has progress been inconsistently sustained, it has at times appeared to stall and threatened to disconnect a tradition of women in Irish theatre; for example, the conservatism of the decades of the Free State, the recessionary period of the 1980s, or late twentieth century postfeminism's 'undoing' of feminism in the Celtic Tiger Years.[88] Yet, the performances discussed in this book speak to one another across the decades through their embodied mythmaking and my weaving together of these vibrant and rebellious voices marks my contribution to the performance of a genealogy of women in Irish theatre.

In order to rewrite history we need to reframe it and Stone's genealogy as a coalition of difference offers an alternative to the male-dominated literary canon of Irish theatre. The chapters of this book are not organized chronologically and plays from different historical periods are placed alongside one another to offer an engagement which remains aware of their differing contexts, while concurrently drawing lines of connection. Women's theatrical critique and rewriting of limiting myths of femininity coheres and overlaps, yet also diverges over the myths and limits that pertain to their specific context. Furthermore, the question of how the individual might make a meaningful intervention in the face of myth's power (and the resilience of power structures) lies in myth's communal aspect and is harnessed by the concept of the genealogy as a coalition. Some of the plays discussed here have not been performed; others have been performed but have left sparse records, while others have received national and/or international attention. Through my identification of a genealogy of women in Irish theatre, we can acknowledge how all these voices make important contributions to the ongoing and communal work of embodied mythmaking.

---

[88] On the 'undoing' of feminism, see Angela McRobbie, *The Aftermath of Feminism: Gender, Culture and Social Change* (London: Sage, 2009).

CHAPTER I

Revolutionary Bodies: Mythmaking and Irish Feminisms

Maire Nic Shiubhlaigh, activist and actress, sets the scene: 'This was 1900 ... Dublin bristled with little national movements of every conceivable kind: cultural, artistic, literary, theatrical, political.'[1] This vibrancy offered women opportunities to engage in a range of activities which firmly asserted their presence and agency in public arenas and, furthermore, offered the possibility of exploring a range of feminisms. This chapter is concerned with the plays and tableaux vivants authored and performed by women at the turn of the twentieth century, which disrupt the perpetuation of limiting icons of femininity and expose the gap between myth and reality through the embodiment of these icons in performance. Irish myth was identified as a source for the creation of a national theatre, and indeed was the cultural bedrock for an independent nation, but it was also a source for women's activism and theatrical work: the claim of ownership over these myths set discourses of feminism, nationalism and modernism into dialogue and, at times, conflict.

The relationship between nationalism and feminism was complex and fluid. From 1912 onwards, some activist women choose to prioritize nationalism and support of the Home Rule Bill over their support for suffrage in the belief that freedom for the nation would result in equal citizenship for women. The years of the Home Rule Crisis, 1912–14, contributed to an increased militancy in politics and Dana Hearne suggests that by 1914, Irish feminists coalesced into three strands: 'a nationalist anti-imperialist tendency, which involved the struggle for an independent Irish State and the encouragement of armed civic virtue; a unionist pro-empire position; and a pacifist feminist tendency which challenged state power on the basis of its militarism and its exploitation and exclusion of women'.[2]

---

[1] Maire Nic Shiubhlaigh, *The Splendid Years* (Dublin: James Duffy, 1955), p. 3.
[2] Dana Hearne, '*The Irish Citizen*, 1914–1916: Nationalism, Feminism and Militarism', *The Canadian Journal of Irish Studies*, 18:1 (July 1992), 1–14 (p. 2).

Revolutionary Bodies

The performances discussed in this chapter reveal that both nationalist and pacifist strands are evident in women's theatre work at the start of the twentieth century and that within these strands women held complex positions which at times appeared contradictory. Through comparison of nationalist feminist performances: the tableaux vivants performed by the Inghinidhe na hÉireann in 1901; Maud Gonne's performance in *Kathleen ni Houlihan*[3] in 1902; and Gonne's play *Dawn* (published in 1904), with the pacifist feminism of Eva Gore-Booth's play *The Triumph of Maeve* (written in 1902 and published 1905), we can see how women's diverse approaches to mythmaking and theatrical form provide a revealing study in the challenges that feminist politics faced in Ireland in the early years of the twentieth century. In addition to acknowledging the breadth of theatrical forms and feminisms at play, examining mythmaking enables us to affirm that which unites a genealogy of women in Irish theatre. Intervening in, and exploiting, the contradictions and tensions which animated this period of political ferment allowed these women to utilize myth to facilitate their self-authorship and to assert the presence and creativity of female bodies; a revolutionary action which engaged with the rise of the woman-nation figure and countered disembodied icons of femininity.

The Mythmaking of the Inghinidhe na hÉireann

This chapter marks our point of entry into a genealogy of women in Irish theatre through the tableaux vivants performed at the turn of the twentieth century by the nationalist women's organization, the Inghinidhe na hÉireann (Daughters of Ireland). Analysis of these tableaux engenders a foundational discussion of the act of embodying mythic women, which underpins all the work that constitutes this genealogy. The tensions of the tableau form are used by the Inghinidhe to reflect women's embodied experience as both icon and icon maker, as well as their negotiation of nationalist and feminist politics. The establishment of the Inghinidhe na hÉireann in 1900 was a response to the exclusion of women from nationalist societies. Nic Shiubhlaigh, an Inghinidhe member, describes the importance of this 'politico-cultural society of young women founded by

---

[3] The spelling of Kathleen ni Houlihan is not standardized. It is spelt Kathleen ni Houlihan in the Abbey Theatre programme, 1902, and Gregory used Kathleen [see James Pethica, '"Our Kathleen": Yeats's Collaboration with Lady Gregory in the Writing of *Cathleen ni Houlihan*', *Yeats Annual No. 6* (Basingstoke: Macmillan Press, 1988), pp. 3–31]. Other publications to which I refer, including the edition of Yeats's selected plays, spell her name Cathleen ni Houlihan. For consistency I refer to the play as *Kathleen ni Houlihan*, unless it is spelt differently within a quote or book title.

28 Women and Embodied Mythmaking in Irish Theatre

Maud Gonne as an auxiliary of the old Celtic Literary Society . . . It was, probably, the only organization of its kind working in Dublin at that time which offered young women an opportunity of taking part in national work.'[4]

Nationalism was not the sole inspiration for the movement: parallel was 'the growth of a number of specifically women's political and pressure groups and what might be termed a political movement', notably Unionist women politicized in the wake of two Home Rule crises, as well as the growing suffrage movement.[5] Members of the Inghinidhe na hÉireann had to navigate a path which held on to their belief in women's suffrage, while asserting their political demands as nationalists. Senia Pašeta describes how 'most Irish nationalists remained stubbornly attached to a purely nationalist vernacular' and so the women worked to make them 'bi-lingual':[6] conversant with both nationalism and feminism.

The women initially came together in 1900 to organize a patriotic Children's Treat as an alternative to the events celebrating Queen Victoria's visit to Dublin: it was the success of this event that persuaded them, later that year, to set up a permanent group under the name of Inghinidhe na hÉireann. The Inghinidhe worked within existing nationalist tropes to both support and contest them: 'A nationalist pedagogy which conflated women's roles with their maternalism could prove unaccommodating to political activists such as the Inghinidhe who positioned themselves as daughters rather than mothers.'[7] Both educational work and the employment of myth underpinned the group's commitment to their aim of combating English influence. Ella Young describes how they taught Irish language and history to uneducated Dublin children: 'I have undertaken, under their auspices, to teach Irish history by a re-telling of the saga and hero-tales.'[8] The women were aware of the political potential of the children and this is also apparent at the Children's Treat where 'Miss Maud Gonne addressed the children before they dispersed homewards.'[9] Significantly, the Inghinidhe's educational work was, as Margaret Ward notes, 'undertaken in the role of political activist, and not as wife and

---

[4] Nic Shiubhlaigh, *The Splendid Years*, p. 2.

[5] Senia Pašeta, *Irish Nationalist Women, 1900–1918* (Cambridge: Cambridge University Press, 2013), p. 34.

[6] Pašeta, *Irish Nationalist Women*, p. 15.

[7] Antoinette Quinn, 'Cathleen ni Houlihan Writes Back: Maud Gonne and Irish Nationalist Theatre', in *Gender and Sexuality in Modern Ireland*, ed. Anthony Bradley and Maryann Gialanella Valiulis (Amherst: University of Massachusetts Press, 1997), pp. 39–59 (p. 41).

[8] Ella Young, *Flowering Dusk* (London: Longmans, Green & Co., 1945), pp. 70–1.

[9] 'Patriotic Children's Treat', *United Irishman*, 7 July 1900, p. 7.

mother'.[10] At times, they appeared to inhabit the roles expected of them in order to use them in service to their activism; a move which is reflected in their embodiment of myth.

Myth provided a foundation for the group: both as a means of promoting Irish culture, and in promoting women's political involvement and activism. The Inghinidhe adopted Brigit as their patron: a complex pre-Christian figure whose influence did not wane with the arrival of Christianity when she transitioned from a Mother Goddess into a saint. Mary Condren notes that elements of her Mother Goddess role were never completely eradicated and that despite becoming a virgin saint, 'Brigit would not give in to the norms of a patriarchal spirituality without a fight.'[11] The group did not wear a uniform and members adopted ancient Gaelic names: Maud Gonne was 'Maeve' and Constance Markievicz, who joined in 1908, became known as 'Macha'. Both these measures served to ensure anonymity. Many of the women did not want to be recognized as members of a nationalist organization since they worked in shops and businesses owned by pro-British bosses.[12] Inghinidhe member Helena Molony offers an additional reason: rejection of 'the "Seoneen" fashion of using "Miss" before their names'.[13] Adoption of these mythic names provided them with the possibility of locating a female genealogy outside the traditional realm of hearth and home. The group drew on women of the past as inspirational role models and at their monthly ceilidhs, which involved music, dancing and songs, 'a member of Inghinidhe would read out a paper on a Celtic heroine.'[14] Nationalist feminists drew on a pre-colonial heritage in which women were free of both colonial and patriarchal restrictions – a sentiment articulated in *The Irish Citizen*, the newspaper of the women's suffrage movement:

> A woman (unlike modern Eng'ish Law) [*sic*], was a person in the sight of our ancient Gaelic legislators; she could lead hosts of warriors to battle like Queen Maibh; she could command a fleet like Grace O'Malley in the days of Queen Elizabeth; in fact she was free to do whatever she was capable of achieving.[15]

---

[10] Margaret Ward, *Unmanageable Revolutionaries: Women and Irish Nationalism* (London: Pluto Press, 1989), p. 59.

[11] Mary Condren, *The Serpent and the Goddess: Women, Religion and Power in Celtic Ireland* (New York: HarperCollins, 1989), p. 75.

[12] Sinéad McCoole, *No Ordinary Women* (Dublin: O'Brien Press, 2004), p. 23.

[13] Pašeta, *Irish Nationalist Women*, pp. 39–40.   [14] Ward, *Unmanageable Revolutionaries*, p. 52.

[15] *The Irish Citizen*, 6 September 1913, p. 127.

30 Women and Embodied Mythmaking in Irish Theatre

In this article, the author references Celtic Ireland in order to refute that the suffrage movement is a foreign import and to connect the fates of nationalism and women's suffrage, arguing that both go 'hand in hand with the national reconstruction of Ireland'.[16] However, discourses of feminism and nationalism did not always align and this is most explicit in the trope of woman-as-nation, to which I will return in detail.

The Inghinidhe's activism was a vital intervention within a culture which circulated representations of woman as icon and further marginalized women's cultural participation through their relegation to the domestic sphere. Their mythmaking invigorated their theatrical endeavours and the Inghinidhe drew on a popular theatre form of the time to stage a series of tableaux vivants, 'a grand display of Gaelic historic and legendary scenes',[17] in April and August 1901. These 'living pictures' were performed in the Antient Concert Rooms and proved popular among nationalist audiences: the review in the *United Irishman*, 13 April 1901, describes 'a crowded house' at the first performance, that the 'hall was crammed in every part' on the second evening and that due to popular demand, a third evening of tableaux performances was added. A second series of shows were performed during Dublin Horse Show week, 26–31 August, and at the Saturday night performance, given for the benefit of the Rooney Memorial Fund, 'the house was thronged'.[18]

The simplicity of the form ensured that costs were kept low, and the tableaux shows proved to be a very profitable means of fundraising. The tableaux were accompanied by Irish music, song and dancing, as well as ceilidhs, and the programme for the August shows included three plays: Alice Milligan's *The Deliverance of Red Hugh O'Donnell* and *The Harp that Once*, and P.T. MacGinley's Irish language play *Eilís agus an Bhean Dhéirce*. A review of the show on 8 April 1901 describes a finale of tableaux in which a series of great Irish women were presented; the mythic and historical figures included Queen Maeve, Grania Mhaol, St Brigid, the Inghean Dubh, Sarah Curran (Red Hugh's mother) and Anne Devlin. This series culminated in the tableaux of the woman-as-nation figure, Ireland Fettered and then Ireland Free, which received rapturous applause.[19] The importance of the Inghinidhe na hÉireann's theatrical work did not go unnoticed at that time: in 1902, the *United Irishman* asserted, 'The stage of Ireland has been one of the most inimical influences

---

[16] *The Irish Citizen*, 6 September 1913, p. 127.
[17] Advertisement in the *United Irishman*, 6 April 1901.
[18] *United Irishman*, 7 September 1901, p. 4.
[19] 'The Gaelic Tableaux', *United Irishman*, 13 April 1901, pp. 4–5.

Revolutionary Bodies

against our national life, and until Inghinidhe na hÉireann two years ago, with the invaluable aid of the Messrs. Fay, begun the work, we had but a faint resemblance to a National Theatre.'[20] The staging of these tableaux positioned women at the heart of a project of claiming and rewriting myth: one inflected by nationalism *and* feminism.

In *Ireland's National Theaters: Political Performance and the Origins of the Irish Dramatic Movement*, Mary Trotter argues that histories of Ireland's dramatic movement have tended to omit 'the significant aesthetic, organizational, and political contributions women made both in the context of Irish theater and in the nationalist project of which that theater was a part'.[21] The fundamental role which the Inghinidhe na hÉireann played in harnessing the power of performance in service to the formation of a national theatre is noted by Cathy Leeney:

> Inghinidhe na hÉireann effectively invented performance as a site of political and ideological empowerment through tableaux vivants; their concerts and entertainments constitute one point of origin of the Irish theatre movement and its formative role in cultural nationalism.[22]

Elision of the movement's contribution to a history of modern Irish drama was underway from the very moment of its supposed inception. W.B. Yeats's and Lady Gregory's play *Kathleen ni Houlihan* is routinely taken as the starting point for many histories of modern Irish theatre: Robert Welch states: 'Modern Irish theatre begins here, with this performance of a play.'[23] Despite the Inghinidhe's role as producer, Yeats ignored their contribution in his speeches following the premiere performances, as Jennie Wyse Power told Alice Milligan: 'Mr Russel and Mr Yates [*sic*] each made speeches praising the Fays for having founded a National Theatre – and never once referred to the Society that had financed the whole affair.'[24] Overlooking the work of the Inghinidhe not only erases women from the story of a national theatre, it also serves to neglect the influence of popular and non-literary theatre forms which emphasize physical performance.

---

[20] *United Irishman*, 4 October 1902, p. 1.

[21] Mary Trotter, *Ireland's National Theaters: Political Performance and the Origins of the Irish Dramatic Movement* (New York: Syracuse University Press, 2001), p. 74.

[22] Cathy Leeney, 'Women and Irish Theatre Before 1960', in *The Oxford Handbook of Modern Irish Theatre*, ed. Nicholas Grene and Chris Morash (Oxford: Oxford University Press, 2016), pp. 269–85 (p. 271).

[23] Robert Welch, *The Abbey Theatre 1899–1999: Form and Pressure* (Oxford: Oxford University Press, 1999), p. 16.

[24] Letter from Jennie Wyse Power to Alice Milligan, dated 7 April [1902], p. 48, MS 5048, 'Letters to Alice Milligan', National Library of Ireland.

32 Women and Embodied Mythmaking in Irish Theatre

The role of the corporeal in the reproduction and modification of mythic narratives and myths of femininity was central to the tableaux vivants, or living pictures, which staged the tension of female embodied experience as both icon and icon maker. At first glance, the framing of the tableaux contains women within icons of femininity, and yet the apparent silence and immobility of the tableaux belies a resistance which we can explore by attending to the affective potential of the form.

Audience and Affect

The Inghinidhe's staging of tableaux vivants prominently placed politically engaged women in the public sphere, both through their organizational activities and through their onstage performances.[25] Traditionally, the history of the tableau form is not one marked by female agency. In Italy in the late eighteenth and early nineteenth centuries, Emma Lyon Hamilton performed poses of classical statuary in aristocratic drawing rooms and palaces. Hamilton had a degree of creative agency in her posing but as the form became mainstream entertainment the potential for female agency was lost. This is evident in performances of tableaux in Dublin before the turn of the twentieth-century Gaelic tableaux. The Queen's Royal Theatre hosted visiting performers who worked within a subgenre of *poses plastiques* which took advantage of Victorian censorship laws whereby the suggestion of nudity was permitted if the work emulated classical subjects. One such example is Madame Warton's tableaux of 'Lady Godiva' and 'Venus Rising from the Sea' in 1848 which it was felt warranted police inspection.[26] Nineteenth-century audiences were also familiar with the tableau form as it was employed in popular melodramas to close scenes; a climactic silence charged with emotion and a pause in response to a moment of realization. The Inghinidhe's tableaux similarly offered a pause which generated emotion and took advantage of audience familiarity with visual codes to engage with both feminist and nationalist politics.

The theatrical realization of the affective charge of the women's activism is noted by historian Margaret Ward: 'The Inghinidhe were unique: they brought a new dimension to nationalist life, imbuing the movement with

---

[25] Pašeta names the women who undertook the range of tasks that constituted the group's theatrical work as Alice Milligan, Sinead Flanagan, Anna Johnston, Maire Nic Shiubhlaigh, Helen Laird, Susan Mitchell and Ella Young (*Irish Nationalist Women*, p. 52).

[26] Kevin Rockett and Emer Rockett, *Magic Lantern, Panorama and Moving Picture Shows in Ireland, 1786–1909* (Dublin: Four Courts Press, 2011), p. 197.

Revolutionary Bodies

a theatrical element which stirred the imagination and aroused more emotion than a thousand meetings or earnest revolutions ever did.'[27] Affect is a felt intensity that circulates between us, our bodies and our environment, and thus can be a potent force in moving us to action. The review of the tableaux in the *United Irishman* suggested that:

> Such performances as those which have delighted Dublin this week will powerfully help all who believe that by inducing the Irish people to study their own history, learn their own language, cultivate their own art, music, and literature, support their own industries, and increase their own self-respect [sic] the way for the salvation of the nation can be cleared.[28]

However, reading the affective potential solely through a nationalist lens ignores the Inghinidhe's deployment of feminist affect in their activism. Paige Reynolds suggests that 'because women played such a crucial role in the genesis of national theatre, Irish audiences came to accept that women might express their political beliefs through dramatic display'.[29] Thus, the Inghinidhe's theatrical work 'rendered feminist political discourse more palatable than it might have been otherwise' and that: 'In these conservative nationalist contexts, Irish audiences deemed public women not simply permissible, but praiseworthy.'[30] The tableaux created a public space in which women could engage politically, but the appeal of the tableaux was not limited solely to nationalist politics; there is also an appeal to an audience who share a feminist desire for change.

The Inghinidhe were an energetic and highly organized movement who provided inspiration for an alternative model for nation-building. Their work generated a belief in the ability of women to effect change: in their capacity to negotiate freedom from restrictions and for self-determination, both as a colonized nation and as women. An article in the *United Irishman* praised their work and explicitly referenced their rewriting of myths of femininity:

> For you can't get over the fact that Eve did steal an apple for fun, and did admit she stole it, while Adam only gobbled it and lied . . . Woman rushes in where man fears to tread, and makes him look foolish and fall back on the apple story to save himself. But it is getting worn out now. I wish to Manannan every town in Ireland had its branch of Inghinidhe, and was practical, and if in course of time we in Ireland and the remnant of the earth

---

[27] Ward, *Unmanageable Revolutionaries*, p. 58. [28] 'The Gaelic Tableaux', p. 5.

[29] Paige Reynolds, *Modernism, Drama and the Audience for Irish Spectacle* (Cambridge: Cambridge University Press, 2007), p. 79.

[30] Reynolds, *Modernism, Drama and the Audience*, p. 79.

34 Women and Embodied Mythmaking in Irish Theatre

came to live under a gynocracy, I should not repine. I am weary living in a world with men with mouse-hearts and monkey-brains, and I want a change.[31]

Women could offer a more effective, and affective, model of nation-building. Key to the success of the Inghinidhe's theatrical work was their collaboration with northern nationalists Alice Milligan and Anna Johnston, whose numerous activities included the co-editorship of the nationalist magazine, *The Shan Van Vocht* (1896–99), as well as organizing tableaux shows. Both Maire Quinn and Maud Gonne wrote to Milligan requesting her assistance with the proposed series of tableaux; Quinn asked Milligan for 'any hints and suggestions you have as to the best way of working them out, also as to other tableaux, dresses required, scenery, grouping, music and songs appropriate etc.'.[32]

Milligan first worked with the tableau form in 1893 when she designed Irish scenes for the Chicago World Fair. Milligan and Johnston then adapted the form to nationalist ends when, in conjunction with the Gaelic League in Belfast in 1898, they staged tableaux 'performed in Irish communities by Irish people as part of a national movement to regenerate national theatre and national language'.[33] Milligan stated that the Belfast shows were staged 'with undoubted success'[34] and she went on to stage tableaux in Derry (1899) and Belfast (1900), and took shows across Ireland to schools and Gaelic League branches.[35] Whether on stage or in the audience of the Inghinidhe's tableaux shows, women who desired change and envisaged a more equal nation, must surely have been affected by the success of the shows, underpinned as it was by the creation of a network of politically active women.

The Tension of Immobility

The shows were performed by men and women from the Celtic Literary Society and the Inghinidhe, but as the tableau form emerged from a tradition of offering woman as spectacle, to draw on an Irish cultural

---

[31] *United Irishman*, 24 August 1901, p. 2.
[32] Letter from Maire T. Quinn, 30 December 1900, p. 34, MS 5048, 'Letters to Alice Milligan', National Library of Ireland.
[33] Catherine Morris, 'Alice Milligan: Republican Tableaux and the Revival', *Field Day Review*, 6 (2010), 132–65 (p. 141).
[34] Letter from Alice Milligan to *The Daily Express*, 21 January 1900. Reprinted in Robert Hogan and James Kilroy, *The Irish Literary Theatre, 1899–1901* (Dublin: The Dolmen Press, 1975), p. 53.
[35] Catherine Morris, *Alice Milligan and the Irish Cultural Revival* (Dublin: Four Courts Press, 2012), p. 262.

Revolutionary Bodies

tradition of representing woman-as-nation, I focus on the women performers and mythic figures to investigate whether the Inghinidhe were able to assert female authorship of the myths. Historically, the staging of tableaux has served to objectify woman as spectacle and this is most apparent in the erotic subgenre of *poses plastiques*. The silence of the performer, her suggestive attire in a flesh body stocking, as well as the use of spotlights and rotating pedestals, all positioned woman as the object of desire. The silence and immobility of the form is read as containing women. However, there is potential for the body to speak and to articulate women's embodied experiences.

Reading the tension that lies beneath the veneer of silence and immobility offers the possibility for shifting emphasis from the female body as bearer to maker of meaning. The tension between women's expression and restriction, as well as between nationalism and feminism, is encapsulated in the tension contained in the Inghinidhe tableaux between movement and stasis, verbal silence and the speaking body. Ultimately, this serves to reflect Irish women's embodied experience at the turn of the twentieth century, and the navigation of both possibilities and limits.

First, it must be noted that the Inghinidhe's tableaux shows were not staged in silence. Avid theatre-goer and diarist, Joseph Holloway, was critical of the 'melancholy eternal dirge-like airs'[36] sung by an accompanying chorus, and he was similarly unimpressed by the narrator, Mr Wyse Power, whose 'descriptive matter relative to the tableaux' was 'unintelligible'.[37] This would suggest that the narration (by a man), as well as the music, gave 'voice' to the women's stories. However, a comment in Holloway's diary suggests this may not have been the case:

> Miss T. Lawson gave a quite dramatic recital of 'Anne Devlin' and won great applause. I admire this young ladys [sic] Gaelic recitations even more than the English efforts. Somehow her pathos, dramatic fire and intensity sits more naturally on her when she tells of her woes in 'the old tongue'. This is a strange confession for me to make who understands not my own language, but Miss Lawson's eloquent recitals in Gaelic are so expressive as to be understood by all.[38]

Interestingly, Holloway did not feel excluded by the use of the Irish language, instead he suggested it could be 'understood by all', even

---

[36] Joseph Holloway, *A Dublin Playgoer's Impressions 1901*, Wednesday 10 April 1901, p. 100. Microfilm P8517, National Library of Ireland.

[37] Holloway, *A Dublin Playgoer's Impressions 1901*, Wednesday 10 April 1901, pp. 102–3. Microfilm P8517.

[38] Holloway, *A Dublin Playgoer's Impressions 1901*, Wednesday 10 April 1901, p. 102. Microfilm P8517.

36   Women and Embodied Mythmaking in Irish Theatre

someone like himself who did not speak Irish. The silence of the tableau form could serve to create an inclusive space, as Catherine Morris notes of Milligan's work in the form:

> Tableaux were vital in forging communities, for women in gaining space in the public life of the nation, for connecting people in difficult political contexts, for learners at different levels of Irish language training, for the inclusion of northern Protestants, like Alice Milligan herself, whose upbringing led them to believe that Irish was not their native language or their national culture.[39]

The inclusivity of the Inghinidhe tableau was engendered by the expressiveness of Miss Lawson's performance. The tableau's articulation was dependent on the affect created through voice, gesture and movement, and their successful handling by Miss Lawson demonstrates that the women were not necessarily silenced as icons, and that their bodies 'spoke'.

The affect of the tableau form depended on its immobility and the resultant tension between movement and stasis. This is evident in the review of one of Milligan's 1898 Gaelic tableaux: 'The champions displayed the most wonderful powers of standing still as statues in strained and difficult attitudes.'[40] The tension between movement and stasis was put to good effect in the Inghinidhe tableau of 'Ireland Fettered and Ireland Free'. Reviews note the gestures and expressive actions in the latter part of the tableau: 'Ireland Free, erect against the cross, her harp newstrung at her feet, her green robe flowing round';[41] 'Erin as a beautiful girl with broken chains falling from her and a drawn sword in her hand appeared.'[42] The movement of her robe and the falling chains suggest her physical freedom and by implication that of the nation.

Movement also counters the containing aspect of myth and threatens the emergence of embodied experience at the expense of the restriction of woman within the trope of nation. Furthermore, the discrepancy between myth and reality would have been apparent to audience members who may have recognized some of the women activists as they performed the myths. Emma Lyon Hamilton's mythic posing in the late eighteenth century was structured around the Pygmalion-like 'tension between motion and stasis, the illusion that

---

[39] Morris, *Alice Milligan and the Irish Cultural Revival*, p. 265.
[40] 'The Gaelic League Festival', *The Irish News and Belfast Morning News*, 8 May 1898. Reprinted in Robert Hogan and James Kilroy, *The Irish Literary Theatre, 1899–1901* (Dublin: The Dolmen Press, 1975), p. 57.
[41] 'The Gaelic Tableaux', p. 5.
[42] 'At the Children's Matinee', *United Irishman*, 7 September 1901, p. 3.

Revolutionary Bodies

she was frozen in motion, but at any moment, the statue might become a living woman again'.[43] This is a double-edged sword which pertains to the Inghinidhe's embodied mythmaking: on the one hand, the mythic figure is frozen within the tableau, and yet their bodies refuse to be contained within the myths. The still moment therefore offers the potential for critique in the tension between stasis and movement, and in the efforts, and failure, of the form and the myths to contain the disruptive presence of the women's bodies and realities. The Inghinidhe embraced myths endorsed by the nationalist cause in order to assert women's authorship as an activist expression firmly embedded in the public arena, yet their bodies strain against the myths and the restrictive framing of them within the tableau form, to carve out new and more complex representations of women.

The Tension Between Nationalism and Feminism

In *Modernism's Mythic Pose*, Carrie Preston traces a history of Delsartism, a movement which 'promoted the practices of solo posing and poetic recitation for health and personal development, as well as professional performance'.[44] Preston argues that mythic posing was central to modernism and suggests: 'Delsartism posed myth in ambivalent relation to modernity, as a *still* or pause that could function both as skeptical critique and nostalgic diversion.'[45] The idea of a still that functions both as sceptical critique and nostalgic diversion illustrates the bind that the Inghinidhe found themselves in as, through their own mythic posing, they drew on modernism and revivalism. The Inghinidhe was 'a profoundly modern organization, both in its views about women's roles and in the way it adopted contemporary methods and technologies when they proved useful'.[46] Their theatrical work was engaged with revivalist tropes in order to open up the possibilities for alternative futures free of both colonial and patriarchal oppression.

However, the choice of myths presented in the Inghinidhe's tableaux was partially informed by nationalist and feminist nostalgia for a pre-colonial time. Hanna Sheehy-Skeffington, founder of the Irish Women's Franchise League, argued that recognition of women's past glories and rights in Celtic Ireland was 'barren comfort for us Irishwomen' in 'the

---

[43] Carrie J. Preston, *Modernism's Mythic Pose: Gender, Genre, Solo Performance* (Oxford: Oxford University Press, 2011), p. 34.
[44] Preston, *Modernism's Mythic Pose*, p. 4.   [45] Preston, *Modernism's Mythic Pose*, p. 5.
[46] Pašeta, *Irish Nationalist Women*, p. 51.

Women and Embodied Mythmaking in Irish Theatre

abject present'.[47] However, this nostalgia could serve strategically to critique the present as it linked nationalist and feminist aims. The alignment of these aims was not an easy one, as outlined by Francis Sheehy-Skeffington:

> the combination of Nationalism with opposition to women's enfranchisement may seem excusable; but to those who understand the meaning of Nationalism, such a combination must appear hideously unnatural. The principles of self-government and self-reliance which vitalise the nationalist movement are identical with the basic principles of the women's suffrage movement.[48]

The issue of whether demands for women's suffrage implied recognition of the British Parliament was one which highlighted the difficulties involved in negotiating a nationalism that accommodated feminism. Belying the simplicity of the tableau form is the complex negotiation of revivalism, modernity and feminism; a negotiation which we can trace through the choice of myths in the tableaux.

During the performances in April and August, the choice of tableaux changed each evening but certain figures and stories recur, including the story of King Brian, the Children of Lir and certain Irish heroines: Maeve, Dark Rosaleen, St Brigid, Anne Devlin and the tableau of 'Ireland Fettered and Ireland Free'. The choice of female mythic figures reflects both nationalist and feminist concerns, and this is most explicitly illustrated in the first show on the afternoon of Monday 8 April 1901. This performance incorporated the story of the High King of Ireland, Brian Boru, and the events of the Battle of Clontarf (1014), when Irish troops successfully fought off the Viking invaders. Within this tableaux series, women take on easily recognized myths of femininity:

> The bejewelled lady who wandered through our island, protected only by her maiden smile ... symbolized for us the glory of Brian's rule. Then the raven's wings were heard flapping in the invitation of Gormlai (a notable and interesting woman in our history) to her compatriots the Danes, as we call them. The eve of the fateful battle, and warning of the banshee.[49]

The wandering lady's freedom is afforded by Brian's 'glorious' rule and thus the well-being of women is dependent on male authority. Furthermore, her virtuous body is conflated with the nation, whose

---

[47] Quoted in C.L. Innes, *Woman and Nation in Irish Literature and Society, 1880–1935* (Athens: University of Georgia Press, 1993), p. 139.
[48] Quoted in Pašeta, *Irish Nationalist Women*, p. 63. [49] 'The Gaelic Tableaux', p. 4.

Revolutionary Bodies 39

integrity is threatened by the invaders summoned by Gormlai who together with the banshee, heralds death. The virtuous maiden is presented in contrast to the destructive nature of the Morrígan: a battle-crow and goddess of war, referenced by the raven's wings, whose dominance in early Irish literature had been largely eradicated by the twentieth century. The inclusion of Gormlai in the tableau draws on the dynamism and energy of this figure; a woman who is central to Lady Gregory's *Kincora* (1905 and 1909), and, as Cathy Leeney argues with reference to the 1905 version, 'provides a theatrical opportunity to represent a dangerously unpredictable and ambivalent embodiment of a vilified female energy as it challenged the centralizing hegemonies of church and state'.[50] The mythic women included in the Inghinidhe tableau both support *and* undermine the figure of the woman-nation, thereby unsettling the virgin–whore dichotomy and woman's connection with both fertility and decay. Following Brian's story, another tableaux series called 'The Fairy Changeling' was staged in which a Fairy Queen steals a baby from an Irish cottage – another threatening other-worldly woman. This was succeeded by a ceilidh, a social gathering in an Irish cottage at which there was singing and dancing. The ceilidh presented 'real' women in traditional gendered roles: 'the old woman working the spinning-wheel and the young one rocking her baby'.[51]

The Inghinidhe's skilful navigation of traditional and subversive representations of women culminated in the final series of tableaux of Irish heroines which highlighted women's central role and agency:

> Maeve, greatest of Ireland's heroines, Grania Mhaol visiting Elizabeth and pulverising the virgin monarch, who strove to impress the splendid Irishwomen; St Brigid, the Inghean Dubh, Red Hugh's mother; Sarah Curran, and Anne Devlin, the betrothed and faithful servant of Emmet. Ireland Fettered and crouching over her unstrung harp at the base of the Celtic cross, and then Ireland Free, erect against the cross, her harp now strung at her feet, her green robe flowing round her, the cap of liberty on her head, and in her hand a shining sword. This tableau evoked a tremendous outburst of enthusiasm and shouts of 'Arís! Arís!' caused its repetition again and again.[52]

The women presented are warriors and rebels; a series of women united by their resistant actions. Their power is embodied in paused action: from Grania Mhaol's 'pulverising' treatment of Queen Elizabeth I, to Ireland's erect stance with a sword in her hand and Maeve in her chariot.

---

[50] Leeney, *Irish Women Playwrights, 1900–1939*, p. 40.   [51] 'The Gaelic Tableaux', p. 4.
[52] 'The Gaelic Tableaux', pp. 4–5.

40   Women and Embodied Mythmaking in Irish Theatre

Some of these women were included in Milligan's 1898 tableaux in Belfast (Maeve, Granuaile and Dark Rosaleen),[53] and were then reprised in the tableaux show staged by the Irish Women's Franchise League (IWFL) in 1914, which featured some of the Inghinidhe performers. The suffrage tableaux comprised some of the same 'great women', notably Maeve and Anne Devlin, while adding others such as Joan of Arc, Sappho and Florence Nightingale.[54] The IWFL were assisted by other women's organizations, including Cumann na mBan: the newly formed women's auxiliary of the Irish volunteers, which Hanna Sheehy-Skeffington described as having 'no function beyond that of a conduit pipe to pour a stream of gold into the coffers of the male organisation, and to be turned off automatically as soon as it has served this mean and subordinate purpose'.[55] With the rise of a nationalist militant strand, the differences between feminist groups were to become more distinct. These tensions are already evident in the Inghinidhe's tableaux in 1901 and the group's nationalist and feminist concerns collide in the iconic figure of woman-as-nation.

The figure of woman-as-nation was a highlight of the Inghinidhe's shows and was used to close most of the performances. The tableaux were staged during a period when this figure was modified to merge Mother Ireland and the Virgin Mother and offer a model of femininity defined by passivity and subservience.[56] Yet, the Inghinidhe's staging of 'Ireland Fettered and Ireland Free' intervenes in this mythmaking and draws on the *Shan Van Vocht* to position women as icon makers and to assert their role as activists. Rosalind Clark describes the rebelliousness of the nineteenth-century personification of Ireland, the *Shan Van Vocht* (The Poor Old Woman) who 'gives a vigorous new life to the poor Sovereignty who had been moaning and complaining helplessly for so long. The Shan Van Vocht personifies defiance and resistance'.[57] Indeed, in 1896 Milligan and Johnston established a newspaper titled *Shan Van Vocht* which offered a vibrant cultural community in which women's voices were central: 'The poor old woman was speaking out and speaking

---

[53] See *The Irish News and Belfast Morning News* review, reprinted in Robert Hogan and James Kilroy, *The Irish Literary Theatre, 1899–1901* (Dublin: The Dolmen Press, 1975), pp. 56–8.

[54] 'Irish Women's Franchise League: Daffodil Fete', *Irish Times*, 25 April 1914, p. 9.

[55] Quoted in Ann Matthews, *Renegades: Irish Republican Women 1900–1922* (Cork: Mercier Press, 2010), p. 100.

[56] Innes, *Woman and Nation*, p. 23.

[57] Rosalind Clark, *The Great Queens: Irish Goddesses from the Morrígan to Cathleen ni Houlihan* (Gerrard's Cross: Colin Smythe, 1991), p. 169.

Revolutionary Bodies 41

back against colonial occupation, cultural Anglicization, and the factional unionist and nationalist misogyny Irish women encountered'.[58]

The question of women's freedom and agency is open to a variety of interpretations in the final tableau of 'Ireland Free': whether the aforementioned tension between immobility and movement, suggested by her flowing robe and falling chains, indicated pending physical freedom or containment through iconization. Indeed, women in the audience may have seen her as a reflection of their newly negotiated freedoms and hopes for their further development. Drawing on the work of Luce Irigaray, Elin Diamond outlines a womb-theatre where essence, truth and origin are put into play: 'Irigaray transforms the mirror into a political weapon: "mimesis imposed" becomes mimicry unleashed.'[59] The performance of 'Ireland Free' potentially offers what Diamond describes as the doubleness of feminist mimesis, rooted on the one hand in the desire for stability and coherence, and on the other, an unravelling of unity, as the tableau presents not just the possibility of Ireland's freedom, but also women's.

Despite the potential in 1901 for unleashing the significations of the tableau, the possibility of seeing the nationalist and feminist movements as co-equal became increasingly untenable. The 1916 Proclamation of Independence guaranteed 'religious and civil liberty, equal rights and equal opportunities to all its citizens', as well as 'the establishment of a permanent National Government, representative of the whole people of Ireland and elected by the suffrages of all her men and women'.[60] Despite the granting of suffrage to property-owning women over 30 in 1918, which extended to all women over 21 in 1922, the promise of equal citizenship was quashed by the Free State through a series of retrograde laws and the 1937 Constitution. Subsequently, the tensions which animated the Inghinidhe's tableaux were defused and feminism had to adapt.[61] Women's politics were admitted no space in the Free State: the potential of women's revolutionary bodies was contained and their theatrical expression in the public arena was denied.

---

[58] Morris, *Alice Milligan and the Irish Cultural Revival*, p. 179.

[59] Elin Diamond, *Unmaking Mimesis* (New York and London: Routledge, 1997), p. xi.

[60] Proclamation of Independence, www.taoiseach.gov.ie/eng/Historical_Information/State_Comme morations/Proclamation_of_Independence.html [accessed 18 February 2017].

[61] The Irish Housewives' Association is a case in point as it operated within women's remit in the home. Acknowledging their contribution forges a link between the suffrage campaign of the early twentieth century and second-wave feminism of the 1970s. See Alan Hayes (ed.), *Hilda Tweedy and the Irish Housewives' Association: Links in the Chain* (Galway: Arlen House, 2012).

42 Women and Embodied Mythmaking in Irish Theatre

To 'Hold the Still Live'

The process of reanimating what appears to be silent has driven my analysis of the Inghinidhe's tableaux vivants: the desire to find what is living, despite the potential impulse of both tableaux and myth to freeze time and impose death. This is echoed in Rebecca Schneider's work on re-enactment as she describes the still as a 'site where liveness finds articulation'.[62] For Schneider, the ability to 'hold the still live'[63] is located in the process of re-enacting the tableau, of citing it, and thus speaking both to the past and to other possibilities. This speaks to a genealogy of women in Irish theatre as an alternative to a linear history, and thus one which 'undoes archive-driven determinations of what disappears and what remains'.[64] There is little archive-driven documentation surrounding the Inghinidhe's tableaux, save for a handful of reviews, but a genealogical approach to Irish theatre offers us a means of acknowledging and exploring the gaps and silences surrounding women's contributions through the discernment of links between their work. These connections are vital and exemplify Schneider's evocative description of the still as 'a call toward a future live moment when the image will be re-encountered, perhaps as an invitation to response'.[65] This genealogy of embodied mythmaking enables us to re-encounter the performances discussed in this book as they resonate with one another and invite our response.

The embodied image, and presence, of the still as a moment of tension echoes throughout the performances in this book. The presence of the Inghinidhe's tableaux can be traced in contemporary work such as Olwen Fouéré's *Sodome, My Love* which is addressed in detail in the concluding chapter. The Inghinidhe and Fouéré are both engaged in a project of engaging with and dismantling myths of femininity, and through their exploration of stasis and movement as a means of addressing the limits placed on female corporeal expression, they seek other possibilities. The Inginidhe's tableau of Maeve in her chariot continues to move through the gestic tableau of Maeve in Mary Elizabeth Burke-Kennedy's *Women in Arms*: ceremoniously astride her chariot which has been formed by the bodies of the other actors (see Chapter 2). These tableaux may be temporary but they provide a lasting challenge if we do not confine the possibilities that they generate to the individual work, instead looking across this

---

[62] Rebecca Schneider, *Performing Remains: Art and War in Times of Theatrical Reenactment* (London and New York: Routledge, 2011), p. 149.
[63] Schneider, *Performing Remains*, p. 149.   [64] Schneider, *Performing Remains*, p. 144.
[65] Schneider, *Performing Remains*, p. 141.

Revolutionary Bodies

genealogy of embodied mythmaking to identify the traces that have been left behind and the ways in which they reverberate through the present.

The Limits of Mother Ireland

The trope of woman-as-nation held theatrical interest for nationalist women activists as within the context of the early twentieth century there was scope for them to engage both their nationalism and feminism, thereby intervening in the mythmaking of the period. In a gestic hail, the Inghinidhe's 'Ireland Fettered and Ireland Free' tableau resonates with the woman-nation figure presented in *Kathleen ni Houlihan*, co-authored by W.B. Yeats and Lady Gregory. The Inghinidhe sponsored the premiere performance of *Kathleen ni Houlihan* (1902) in which Maud Gonne played the title role. The tension of the Inghinidhe's tableaux precedes Maud Gonne's *unheimlich* performance as the eponymous *Kathleen ni Houlihan* as both utilize affect to reveal the unhomely condition of women in Ireland, and the possibilities and difficulties entangled in aligning feminist and nationalist politics. Through analysis of *Kathleen ni Houlihan*, as well as Maud Gonne's play *Dawn* (1904) in which she authors her own version of the Mother Ireland icon, we can explore the extent to which employment of this figure might hold disruptive potential for women, and enable them to position themselves as authors rather than icons.

Kathleen ni Houlihan visually combines several aspects of perpetuated models of Irish womanhood: woman as representative of land and nation; the idealized mother who is centre of the home and nation; and a link between woman and the supernatural. The play is set in the cottage of the Gillane family on the eve of their son Michael's wedding. The wedding preparations are interrupted by the arrival of Kathleen, the Poor Old Woman, who is welcomed into the home. Kathleen sits by the fire and her responses to the family's questions reinforce her symbolic function as she references the four provinces of Ireland:

PETER: Was it much land they took from you?
OLD WOMAN: My four beautiful green fields.[66]

The marriage of the sovereignty figure is achieved through Michael's rejection of both material goods and his betrothed in favour of Kathleen, a fairy bride, and sacrifice for the nation. Marriage emphasizes the fertility

---

[66] W.B. Yeats, *Cathleen ni Houlihan*, in *Selected Plays*, ed. Richard Allen Cave (London: Penguin, 1997), pp. 19–28 (p. 23).

44 Women and Embodied Mythmaking in Irish Theatre

aspect of the sovereignty figure yet Kathleen ni Houlihan demands death and sacrifice of the men 'who died for love of me'.[67] The play simultaneously reinforces the importance of the hearth and home, while demanding the lives of the young men who live in them: 'he must give me himself, he must give me all'.[68] As Clark notes of Kathleen: 'She became interested in the sacrifice of her subjects, and not their prosperity [...] She is the poor old woman who appears when trouble is coming, and the battle-crow that feasts on the slain.'[69]

The ambivalent representation of 'woman' as both fertility and death, womb and tomb, is addressed in more detail in Chapter 4; suffice to say at this point that, within the world of the play, Kathleen's threatening qualities are not perceived as such. The reason for this is contained within her final offstage transformation from the Poor Old Woman to the beautiful maiden or *aisling*; 'a young girl, and she had the walk of a queen'.[70] Two sovereignty traditions are combined to represent the power of sacrifice to rejuvenate the nation – a process which ennobles and aestheticizes death. Moreover, Kathleen's function as fertility goddess is desexualized: 'With all the lovers that brought me their love I never set out the bed for any.'[71] Kathleen functions as representative of land and fertility, the growth of the nation, without retaining any sexual aspects of the sovereignty figure – a virgin queen to surpass the English monarch Queen Victoria.

The connection between 'woman' and nation underlines the passive feminine role as beautiful object to-be-looked-at and as stimulus to male action and martyrdom. The importance of blood sacrifice within nationalist mythology in the early twentieth century delineates Kathleen ni Houlihan as the idealized Mother Ireland and Virgin Mother who inspires the sacrifice of the male, thus rendering her without agency. Furthermore, the focus is on the mother–son relationship which supports the contract between nation and men, at the expense of all others. At the end of the play, Michael's fiancée Delia asks him, 'Why do you look at me like a stranger?'[72] in a moment which marks the ability of the woman-nation to make strange the reality, and the woman, Michael then chooses to reject.

Despite Delia's pleas, Michael is lured offstage by Kathleen ni Houlihan's voice and Delia is left silently crying in Bridget's arms. The potential to reveal the destructive consequences of this trope for 'real'

---

[67] Yeats, *Cathleen ni Houlihan*, p. 24. [68] Yeats, *Cathleen ni Houlihan*, p. 25.
[69] Clark, *The Great Queens*, p. 185. [70] Yeats, *Cathleen ni Houlihan*, p. 28.
[71] Yeats, *Cathleen ni Houlihan*, p. 25. [72] Yeats, *Cathleen ni Houlihan*, p. 27.

women is located in the gap between myth and reality, as reflected in the play's shifting emphasis from realism to symbolism. The manuscript of *Kathleen ni Houlihan*, held in the Berg Collection in the New York Public Library, reveals that although Yeats provided the genesis for the play, it was largely written by Lady Gregory. Gregory has written at the end of the first section of ten pages, 'All this mine alone', and 'This with WBY' at the start of the second section.[73] Gregory contributed the peasant dialogue and thus set the realist frame of the play, where Yeats's energies were focused on writing Kathleen's poetic speech and the end of the play. The primacy of symbolic woman, and the assertion of her voice and her needs over those of 'real' women, is thus not only evident in the content of the play, but also through assertions of the play's authorship as solely attributable to Yeats.

The play reinforced woman's role as icon through the repeated use of the image of Kathleen ni Houlihan, standing in the doorway to the cottage, on posters for early Abbey Players' productions: Kathleen is framed and contained as iconic symbol.[74] However, these images also highlight the influence of the tableaux vivants and throughout the play, there are stilled and framed moments which create a tension between the onstage and offstage worlds. The audience's first view of Kathleen is of her face framed by the window through which she looks at Michael as she slowly passes, and Michael is seen frozen by the pull of the offstage world as he stands in the doorway looking out prior to Kathleen's arrival. At the end of the play Kathleen pauses on the threshold before she departs, only to lure Michael after her with her singing, and Michael also pauses on the threshold before his final departure. The tableau form can be traced in the framed moment's potential for holding different discourses in tension. However, we might also read this tension through a feminist lens and thus offer the possibility to expose the gap between myth and reality; a tension which we can explore through the involvement of Maud Gonne: icon and activist.

Realism's Excess

Maud Gonne's portrayal of Kathleen cannot be divested of audience knowledge of her politics and activism. Her high-profile engagement in nationalist political activity contributed to the mythologizing of the play.

---

[73] James Pethica, '"Our Kathleen": Yeats's Collaboration with Lady Gregory in the Writing of *Cathleen ni Houlihan*', *Yeats Annual No. 6* (Basingstoke: Macmillan Press, 1988), pp. 3–31.

[74] Poster included in Commentaries and Notes to *Cathleen ni Houlihan*, in *Selected Plays*, p. 281.

46   Women and Embodied Mythmaking in Irish Theatre

Fellow actress Maire Nic Shiubhlaigh's recollections of Gonne's performance are illuminating in their conflation of Gonne, Kathleen and nation:

> Watching her, one could readily understand the reputation she enjoyed as the most beautiful woman in Ireland, the inspiration of the whole revolutionary movement. She was the most exquisitely-fashioned creature I have ever seen. Her beauty was *startling*. Yeats wrote *Kathleen ni Houlihan* specially for her, and there were few in the audience who did not see why. In her, the youth of the country saw all that was magnificent in Ireland. She was the very personification of the figure she portrayed on the stage.[75]

Gonne's work within the nationalist movement, as well as her elevation as Yeats's (and the nation's) muse, encouraged Gonne's alignment with the woman-nation figure. However, in contrast to Kathleen, her role as revolutionary activist was not one of passive inspiration but of action and leadership. As Antoinette Quinn suggests, Gonne's 'personal alliance of nationalism and the occult [...] rendered the woman-nation *unheimlich*, antithetical both to material values and to the home'.[76] The tension between the realist world of the peasant cottage and the symbolist framing of Kathleen as Ireland is heightened in Gonne's performance to reveal the discrepancy between symbolic woman and the lives of real women.

We can feel this *unheimlich* disruption at work in Gonne's famous entrance, as described by Nic Shiubhlaigh: 'Maud Gonne arrived late the first night and caused a minor sensation by sweeping through the auditorium in the ghostly robes of the Old Woman in *Kathleen ni Houlihan* ten minutes before we were due to begin.'[77] Gonne's entrance further exposed the gap between myth and reality, as did her performance of the Poor Old Woman. In addition to Nic Shiubhlaigh's description of Gonne as 'ghostly', Joseph Holloway notes, in his theatre diary, 'the weird uncanny conduct of the strange visitor' and that Gonne's performance 'was realised with creepy realism'.[78]

The way in which Gonne renders the realism of the icon *unheimlich* can be understood through Elin Diamond's reading of the potential for feminist critique to exploit realism's contradictions. In *Unmaking Mimesis*, Diamond explores the subversive potential of Elizabeth Robins's portrayal of Ibsen's Hedda Gabler which insists 'on the untranslatability of a woman's (body) language before the law – the law represented by the

[75] Nic Shiubhlaigh, *The Splendid Years*, p. 19.
[76] Quinn, 'Cathleen ni Houlihan Writes Back', p. 47.
[77] Quinn, 'Cathleen ni Houlihan Writes Back', p. 17.
[78] Joseph Holloway, *A Dublin Playgoer's Impressions 1902*, April 1902, p. 172. Microfilm P8518, National Library of Ireland.

dramatic fiction and the representational law of realism [...] figuration writes over mimesis producing a realism without truth: hysteria's realism.'[79] The audience at *Kathleen ni Houlihan* 'applauded each redhot patriotic sentiment'[80] but another, equally rebellious, sentiment haunts the play. Gonne's performance made present the unhomely experience of women represented as icons of the nation which perpetuate limiting myths of femininity, and enabled the resurfacing of a body that can be neither read nor contained. The affect of Gonne's entrance and her *unheimlich* performance lay in the unease generated by contradiction as she both reinforced existing myths and exceeded them, as the ghostly traces of the material realities and histories of the performer's body cannot be erased. Gonne's embodied mythmaking facilitates 'the icons return to haunt the icon makers':[81] a haunting which reverberates throughout the genealogy which this book offers.

Gonne's *Dawn*: Blending Realism and Allegory

The figure of Mother Ireland certainly seems to have haunted Gonne and in 1904 she authored her own incarnation in *Dawn*. The play was published in the *United Irishman* on 29 October 1904 but was never staged: Antoinette Quinn suggests that this may have been due to Gonne's preoccupation with her failing marriage.[82] However, we can still note the importance of Gonne's authorship as an assertion of women's voices in the cultural nationalist project. The extent to which the content and form of the play affirms women's presence is less straightforward. The influence of the Inghinidhe's theatrical work is explicit in *Dawn's* structuring around three tableaux: Sunset, Night, Dawn. Gonne's interpretation of the tableau form is also shaped by her experience of using magic lantern shows and slides, including ones 'of battering rams and eviction scenes',[83] to accompany her lectures on the injustices and suffering experienced at the hands of colonial oppressors.

The setting for the tableaux of Sunset, Night and Dawn does not change as the 'ruined, roofless cottage by the roadside on the edge of a bog' remains throughout.[84] Instead, it is the lighting that symbolizes the changing

---

[79] Diamond, *Unmaking Mimesis*, p. 37.
[80] Holloway, *A Dublin Playgoer's Impressions 1902*, April 1902, p. 172. Microfilm P8518.
[81] Boland, *Object Lessons*, p. 197. [82] See Quinn, 'Cathleen ni Houlihan Writes Back', p. 55.
[83] Margaret Ward, *Maud Gonne: Ireland's Joan of Arc* (London: Pandora, 1990), p. 45.
[84] Maud Gonne, *Dawn*, in *Lost Plays of the Irish Renaissance*, ed. Robert Hogan and James Kilroy (California: Proscenium Press, 1970), p. 73.

48   Women and Embodied Mythmaking in Irish Theatre

fortunes of the peasant community: the sun sets and the community descends into the darkness of night as they struggle to survive following their evictions by the Stranger, an English landlord, but the final hopeful tableau of Dawn accompanies the decision of the characters to fight back and reclaim their land. The use of lighting to symbolically evoke interior experience aligns Gonne's work with contemporary European theatre and her blend of symbolism and realism evokes the spirit of Ibsen. Gonne's tableaux are symbolic in their evocation of experience, but they also add a realist, almost photographic, backdrop which reinforces Gonne's unsentimental depiction of peasant poverty which is rooted in physical suffering, hunger and exhaustion.

The blend of realism and symbolism is much less of a contrast than in *Kathleen ni Houlihan*, where the disjunction between the iconic Kathleen and the real peasant women is evident. Instead, Gonne's blend of realism and allegory is encapsulated in the central character of Bride as both peasant *and* symbolic representative of Ireland. The tableau form, as employed by the Inghinidhe, held bodies in tension to reflect the relationship between nationalism and feminism, but Gonne's use of tableaux does not create a contradiction so where does Gonne locate women's potential for resistance against limiting myths?

The play focuses on enduring resistance to colonial oppression, and Bride is presented as a much less passive and helpless figure than Kathleen ni Houlihan. Bride's ability to withstand the anger of the Stranger suggests the strength of her defiant resistance: 'she never goes – far from her land; each day she wanders round the fields that was hers – it's that which angers the Stranger against her'.[85] Her defiance is given further expression through her lament for the dead which, together with Bride's song, was written by poet and fellow Inghinidhe member Ella Young. Angela Bourke argues that the Irish caoineadh, or keening tradition, can be read as feminist utterance, as 'it offers women a licence to speak loudly and without inhibition, and frequently to defend their own interests against those of men'.[86] Like Kathleen, Bride seeks to recruit loyalty when she promises the coming of a new dawn to those who remain faithful and she promotes resistance through militant action. The final tableau of dawn accompanies the decision of the other community members to fight back and reclaim

---

[85] Gonne, *Dawn*, p. 74.
[86] Angela Bourke, 'Lamenting the Dead', in *The Field Day Anthology of Irish Writing Volume IV: Women's Writing and Traditions*, ed. Angela Bourke, Siobhán Kilfeather, Maria Luddy, Margaret Mac Curtain, Gerardine Meaney, Máirín Ní Dhonnchadha, Mary O'Dowd and Clair Wills (Cork: Cork University Press, 2002), pp. 1365–7 (p. 1366).

Revolutionary Bodies

Ireland: 'Bride, you shall have your land again. We will fight for you and for the land. We will drive the Stranger out.'[87] Bride's defiant claim to her territory and her keening for the dead may make her strength and presence felt but ultimately at the end of *Dawn* it is men who go off to fight for her and for Ireland.

Gonne contributes to the conflation of Mother Ireland–Mother Church in the final moments of the play when one of the characters pledges, 'we will make Bride of the Sorrows Bride of the Victories'.[88] Perhaps, as in *Kathleen ni Houlihan*, we need to look to the other woman in the play, Bride's daughter Brideen, to locate resistance to the dominance of iconic woman. Brideen's faith is tested in the second tableau when the Stranger offers her work as a servant. Despite the fact that she is starving, Brideen refuses and the second section closes with her death. The only other way for the peasants to escape their immiseration is through emigration to America, although it is made clear that Bride sees this option as defeat. Bride's son Eoin has already gone to America and intends to send Bride and her daughter the passage money so that they can join him, but Brideen reveals: 'Mother will not go, and I will never leave her. If Eoin were to earn big money she would not go. It's not money she cares for, it's her land she wants. It is vengeance for her dead she wants.'[89] It is the onstage presence of Brideen's dead body throughout the final tableau that potentially exposes the gap between myth and reality. Her immobile body is a poignant reminder of the lack of opportunity afforded to women who serve symbolic 'woman', as well as the denial of their embodied experiences at the expense of the representation of symbolic and sacrificial female bodies.

In the years between *Kathleen ni Houlihan* and *Dawn*, J.M. Synge's one act play *In the Shadow of the Glen*, performed by the Irish Literary Theatre Society in 1903, courted controversy resulting in a walkout: 'a demonstration by the cast of the original *Kathleen ni Houlihan* and its sponsors against the displacement of the woman-nation's troubles and their replacement by the personal distress of Synge's Nora Burke'.[90] The focus on Irish peasant women's sexuality was not deemed an appropriate matter for a national theatre, and if we are to read *Dawn* as a response, Gonne's representation of Irish peasant women emphasizes sacrifice, loyalty and resistance in the name of the nation, not the individual. Antoinette Quinn highlights Gonne's own position at the time: a woman with two children from her relationship with Lucien Millevoye and experiencing marital

---

[87] Gonne, *Dawn*, p. 84. [88] Gonne, *Dawn*, p. 84. [89] Gonne, *Dawn*, pp. 75–6.
[90] Quinn, 'Cathleen ni Houlihan Writes Back', p. 48.

50   Women and Embodied Mythmaking in Irish Theatre

difficulties with John MacBride which would lead to divorce in 1905, and thus Quinn concludes: 'Maud Gonne's opposition to *In the Shadow of the Glen* would appear to have been political and strategic, not moral.'[91] The play is primarily nationalist propaganda but perhaps Gonne's emphasis on political resistance in *Dawn*, as well as the conflation of nation/church in the figure of Bride, was also intended to distract from her own personal affairs – a move which forecloses the representation of women's embodied experiences.

The play's publication in the *United Irishman* designated that the Inghinidhe na hÉireann held the performing rights, so how might a performance of the play with Gonne in the role of Bride have shaped reception? The blend of symbolism and realism in the play, both in Gonne's use of the tableau form and in the figure of Bride as icon and peasant, ensures there is no tension as with the Inghinidhe's tableaux or Gonne's performance of Kathleen ni Houlihan. The gap between myth and reality is smoothed over resulting in the neutralization of the potential for the disruption of Gonne's real life affairs if the play had been performed. However, the lack of any contradiction in the play removes any excess in the realism; this results in closing down a space in which feminist critique might locate itself, thus ensuring that the nationalist message dominates. This anticipated the sentiment which would gain increasing support among Irish women nationalist activists as the decade wore on, that nation came first and suffrage second, as articulated in Inghinidhe na hÉireann's newspaper, *Bean na hÉireann*: 'the rights of Irishwomen are in Ireland, and must be won in Ireland, not in England or any foreign country'.[92]

The use of the trope of Erin Free, the Poor Old Woman, Mother Ireland, Bride of the Victories, enabled women in Ireland at the turn of twentieth century to engage in political and cultural debates pertaining to the shape of an independent nation, and through their activism to assert their presence. Through differing theatrical strategies and with differing affect, the Inghinidhe's tableaux vivants, Gonne's performance in *Kathleen ni Houlihan* and Gonne's allegorical *Dawn*, all wrestled with woman as icon and attempted to seize control of authorship. The woman-nation figure may have intimated freedom but the liberation of a symbol does not translate into change in reality: Irish women needed to be liberated from the symbol of Mother Ireland. Women activists at the turn of the twentieth

---

[91] Quinn, 'Cathleen ni Houlihan Writes Back', p. 50.
[92] *Bean na hÉireann*, 1:3 (February 1909), p. 1.

Revolutionary Bodies 51

century defiantly and energetically worked to carve a place for women within nationalism, as is evidenced by their willingness to engage on nationalist terms through the trope of woman-as-nation, but nationalism was not willing to accommodate their voices in the newly formed Irish nation. Both politically and theatrically, Eva Gore-Booth's *The Only Triumph of Maeve* offered an alternative approach; yet, the play's publication history reveals traces of her own negotiation of pacifism, nationalism and feminism.

Gore-Booth's Maeve: Pacifism and Feminism

Eva Gore-Booth's (1870–1926) background was one of advantage and status: she hailed from an Ascendency class family who lived in the family seat at Lissadell House, County Sligo. Her commitment to radical politics was made abundantly clear by her decision to reject her privileged lifestyle when, in 1897, she chose to go and live with Esther Roper in the bustling industrial city of Manchester, England. Gore-Booth and Roper had met in Italy in 1896 while convalescing from illness and they were to remain partners for life. Roper was 'greatly respected as the mainstay of the women's suffrage movement in Manchester in the 1890s with her mission to unionise women industrial workers'.[93]

On her return from Italy, Gore-Booth – inspired by Roper's suffragism – worked with her sisters at a local level to secure votes for women at general elections to which end they formed the Sligo branch of the Irish Women's Suffrage and Local Government Association. Once she had moved to England, her commitment to social justice was pursued through her engagement in a range of suffragist and trade unionist activities. One aspect of her work for social reform involved the organization of a dramatic society for female factory workers in the poor working-class district of Ancoats.[94] Gore-Booth's pacifist stance was reflected in her tireless campaigning for a range of causes, including condemnation of the death penalty and support for conscientious objectors.

The Triumph of Maeve was written in 1902, the same year as *Kathleen ni Houlihan* premiered, and was first published in 1905, though never performed. The play is governed by women's voices and Maeve's strength is central: she is a decisive leader clearly in control of her court and troops.

---

[93] Gifford Lewis, *Eva Gore-Booth and Esther Roper: A Biography* (London: Pandora Press, 1988), p. 28.

[94] Sonja Tiernan, *Eva Gore-Booth: An Image of Such Politics* (Manchester: Manchester University Press, 2012), p. 54.

52   Women and Embodied Mythmaking in Irish Theatre

Maeve was a popular mythical figure and as a militant warrior she was venerated by nationalist feminists who included her in their tableaux, but Gore-Booth engages in a much more radical rewriting of Maeve through her exploration of the possibilities that pacifism and a female genealogy might offer for a profoundly different future. At the end of the play, 'Maeve casts away her kingdom and all her many possessions and ambitions ... she finds the way into faery land, the way to her own soul.'[95] This otherworld is defined by peace and sustained by female relationships and the play contrasts with *Kathleen ni Houlihan* in its disavowal of war over land and incitement to male heroics and sacrifice. Surprisingly, Gore-Booth re-published Acts Three–Five in 1916 in response to the events surrounding the Easter Rising: an armed insurrection to end British rule. The illustrations for the re-publication, titled *The Death of Fionavar*, were drawn by her sister Constance Markievicz while she was held in Mountjoy Prison for her role in the Rising. *The Death of Fionavar* is preceded by a poem, addressed to those involved in the Rising, which incorporates both praise and lament:

> Poets, Utopians, bravest of the brave,
> Pearse and MacDonagh, Plunkett, Connolly,
> [...]
> Would you had dreamed the gentler dream of Maeve ...
> Peace be with you, and love for evermore.[96]

Gore-Booth was very vocal in her opposition to the First World War and she did not support militancy in the suffrage movement, the cause of her rift with Christabel Pankhurst whom she had mentored;[97] yet, her response to nationalist militancy is less straightforward. She identifies with them as 'Utopians', sharing their passionate belief in freedom. Sonja Tiernan points out that Gore-Booth's article, 'Sinn Féin Rebellion', published in the autumn of 1916, 'does not denigrate the armed rebellion', which is surprising as the article was published in the pacifist *Socialist Review*. Tiernan goes on to quote from Gore-Booth's private notes in which she expresses that, 'You cannot have peace unless you fight the

---

[95] Eva Gore-Booth, 'An Interpretation', in *The Death of Fionavar* (London: E. MacDonald, 1916), pp. 11–15 (p. 15).

[96] Eva Gore-Booth, *The Death of Fionavar* (London: E. MacDonald, 1916), p. 9. In 2015, The Irish Research Council funded a reading of the play, organized by Dr Maureen O'Connor, School of English, and Dr Marie Kelly, Drama and Theatre Studies, University College Cork. The event was staged in Cork Gaol and can be viewed at www.rte.ie/centuryireland/index.php/articles/eva-gore-booth-and-constance-markievicz-and-the-death-of-fionavar [Accessed 2 January 2017].

[97] Tiernan, *An Image of Such Politics*, p. 95.

Revolutionary Bodies

militarists. You cannot have peace without war.'[98] The concession that war is sometimes a necessity is also expressed in Gore-Booth's League of Peace and Freedom Pamphlet, *Rhythms of Art:*

> Thus the 'Dark Rosaleen' is a far more beautiful poem than 'Rule Britannia', because the rhythm that finds vent in rebellion, imperfect as it must be, or else it could not find vent in violence, is still a more subtle and beautiful rhythm than the vibration that expresses itself in the ponderous pomposity and violence of Empire.[99]

It would appear that while Gore-Booth does not condone the use of force to conquer, both in *The Death of Fionavar* and the above pamphlet, she can accept that it may be necessary to use violence in rebellion against such forces. Just as the Inghinidhe had a complex relationship with nationalism, so too did Gore-Booth.

Visionary Otherworlds

Gore-Booth's apparently contradictory position reflects the complex and shifting relations between nationalism and feminism at the time. However, Gore-Booth's use of myth and theatrical form takes a very different approach to that of nationalist feminists in its assertion of the possibility of alternative worlds beyond the framework of the 'nation'. Her dramaturgy sees her pursuit of social justice and equality realized in otherworlds that refuse to be limited by structures of male power. This resonates with pre-First-World-War pacifist feminists in Ireland and elsewhere who 'branded war as the ultimate expression of male politics'.[100] Paradoxically, Gore-Booth's dramaturgy employs the supernatural to demystify and her suggested use of lighting and atmospheric effects unsettle the distinction between reality and the mythic. These effects pose challenges for staging the play: from the glowing spear which flies onstage to the earthquake tremors which accompany Maeve's vision of the new god. These challenges may be best met by focusing on the potential of the mythic and supernatural to expose and undermine the limits of a realist frame for female expression. Gore-Booth's evocation of the world of the imagination resonates with Yeats's exploration of the 'drama of the interior'[101] but her approach draws on a symbolist tradition to offer

---

[98] Tiernan, *An Image of Such Politics*, p. 96.
[99] Eva Gore-Booth, *Rhythms of Art*, League of Peace and Freedom Pamphlet No.12, D/4131/L/4, Lissadell Papers, Public Record Office of Northern Ireland.
[100] Hearne, '*The Irish Citizen*, 1914–1916', p. 2.
[101] See Katherine Worth, *The Irish Drama of Europe from Yeats to Beckett* (London: Athlone Press, 1978).

a powerful feminist critique through its destabilization of realism's mimesis. Cathy Leeney describes Gore-Booth's 'supra-mimetic stage world' which '(r)ather than mirroring reality . . . is the site for the projection of that which is beyond reality; her stage is an imaginative, not a mimetic space'.[102]

The potential of the diegetic space is further evoked through Gore-Booth's poetic language. In addition to writing seven plays, Gore-Booth published nine volumes of poetry and her skill as a poet is evident in her playwriting; particularly in the later acts of *The Triumph of Maeve*, where the rhythm, metre and symbolism of the songs are both affective and evocative. Tension has been a key feature of the theatrical forms already discussed in this chapter and Gore-Booth's play is no exception. Through both theatrical form and the use of space, *The Triumph of Maeve* suggests that the tension between inherited myths of Maeve, as well as contemporary versions of her as a nationalist feminist, and a radical rewriting of her as pacifist feminist and lesbian, can only be realized in a visionary otherworld beyond the realist frame.

The Triumph of Maeve is structured into five acts written in verse form and follows Maeve's journey from active engagement in battle to a life of spiritual contemplation. Act One introduces us to Maeve in her palace as both queen and warrior: '*She is dressed in a heavy golden robe with a gold crown on her head. She has a sword at her side, and is surrounded by a bodyguard of warrior women.*'[103] Maeve's redefinition of herself moves beyond the realms of the palace and battlefield, and this is reflected in the play's locations. The play is infused with the supernatural, incorporating faeries and druidesses, and Act Two is located at the hillside entrance to the magic cave of Cruhane. The play is set on the night of Samhain, when those who inhabit otherworlds are free to enter this one, as the door to the cave is opened. From the opening of the play, there is a portentous atmosphere and this is explicitly associated with the otherworld: Maeve remarks that she wishes her palace were not so near the Hill of the Sidhe. Fionavar's ominous visions add to the troubled ambience, and this is then compounded by Maeve's unexpected question: 'Fergus, dost thou remember Deirdre? / Deirdre of the Prophecies . . . '[104] The stage directions state that this question is met with silence save for the moaning wind. The unease of Act One is accompanied by the disruption of Maeve's initial presentation as warrior queen: she hears a song about Deirdre and responds: 'I am weary

---

[102] Leeney, *Irish Women Playwrights, 1900–1939*, p. 66.
[103] Eva Gore-Booth, *The Triumph of Maeve*, in *Poems of Eva Gore-Booth: Complete Edition* (London: Longmans & Co., 1929), p. 317.
[104] Gore-Booth, *The Triumph of Maeve*, p. 320.

Revolutionary Bodies

of war and the world's tears.'[105] The model of Maeve as triumphant battle queen, rejoicing in her victories as in the Inghinidhe's tableaux, is interrupted and the initiation of this myth's breakdown introduces discontinuities: 'Men tell of ancient wars and great deeds done / Yet I rejoice not, and my heart is cold.'[106]

In contrast to the rousing appeal to battle in both *Kathleen ni Houlihan* and *Dawn*, we see here a questioning of violence and military actions. Yet, the process of Maeve's redefinition is gradual: she is encouraged to 'conquer' the Hill of the Sidhe and she embraces the challenge, exhorting her troops to accompany her. Maeve's desire to enter the land of the Sidhe is patronized as 'but a faery tale, / A woman's dream'[107] by Fergus's conflation of woman with the otherworld, which he contrasts to the robust warrior-men of the North, the Red Branch. The exchange between Maeve and Fergus reveals the hierarchical gendered binaries which Maeve struggles against through her negotiation of power as a warrior queen. Fergus appals Maeve's troops of warrior women when he says:

> My star shall triumph, and though I serve thee now,
> Being a man, I shall rule in the end.
> Let it not grieve thee that I being a man
> Am greater, for no warrior soul could bend
> To a woman's rule since the world began.[108]

Maeve's strength of character emphasizes her agency and is initially linked to violence and military power but her measured response to Fergus surprises her troops and their leader Fleeas remarks that '[a] year ago thou wouldst have struck him down / With the sword ...'[109] Nonetheless, Maeve has only begun the process of change which results in rejection of violence and her calm response reveals a latent military rhetoric: 'Some day he will build the city of his dreams, / I go to conquer mine.'[110] The irony of this statement is that Maeve does not realize that their aims will indeed diverge but that the city of her dreams by the end of the play is a much more spiritual ideal than she can conceive of in Act One. In a symbolic gesture, Maeve's harpist Nera exchanges his instrument for a sword but Maeve warns him against casting his dreams aside: her discontent is expressed by her prophetic description of 'my heart now like a broken lyre'.[111] Act One closes with the troops' procession offstage,

---

[105] Gore-Booth, *The Triumph of Maeve*, p. 323.
[106] Gore-Booth, *The Triumph of Maeve*, p. 325.
[107] Gore-Booth, *The Triumph of Maeve*, p. 329.
[108] Gore-Booth, *The Triumph of Maeve*, p. 329.
[109] Gore-Booth, *The Triumph of Maeve*, p. 331.
[110] Gore-Booth, *The Triumph of Maeve*, p. 331.
[111] Gore-Booth, *The Triumph of Maeve*, p. 334.

56   Women and Embodied Mythmaking in Irish Theatre

accompanied by battle cries, and the pomp of this exit is contrasted with the quiet of the final moment of the act when Nera laments, 'Alas, I would I had my harp again.'[112]

The tensions between war and peace are thus captured in the performance of the final stages of the first act. Through the course of Act One, Maeve's thoughts and actions initiate a questioning of the motivations which propel the narrative of *Kathleen ni Houlihan* and advocate violence and battle over land; as Gore-Booth suggests: 'The meaning I got out of the story of Maeve is a symbol of the world-old struggle in the human mind between the forces of dominance and pity, of peace and war.'[113] Furthermore, Maeve is also in the process of questioning and remaking her own mythic frame.

The interior setting of *Kathleen ni Houlihan* witnesses the domestication of the supernatural but Act Two of *The Triumph of Maeve* opens up alternative spaces with its setting at the mouth of the cave of Cruhane. The staging of this act could permit the cave to dominate the space as the use of lighting gestures to the possibilities beyond: '*The ivory gates at the cave's mouth are wide open, and the cave is full of light.*'[114] The lure of a utopian offstage space whose presence is felt through the tension between the diegetic and mimetic spaces, and intimated through lighting, is a feature of Marina Carr's work (see Chapter 3's discussion of *The Mai* and Chapter 4 on *Ariel*). Both *Kathleen ni Houlihan* and *The Triumph of Maeve* visualize thresholds and offer a moment of pause defined by tension; a threshold which potentially frames and contains Kathleen, but for Maeve this liminal space offers the possibility of alternative means of expression and ways of living. The visual imagery of Nera's exchange of the harp for the sword is incorporated into his exhortation of Maeve to drink from the magic well in order to access the song of peace which is buried within her:

> Drink then, oh Queen, and dream of faery springs
> That fill the long grass with soft shining sounds
> Most musical, struck from the silver strings
> Of the world's harp, streams that flow underground
> Tunnelling the hard earth with a buried song.[115]

The metaphor of the buried song of peace recurs in Gore-Booth's *The Buried Life of Deirdre*, discussed in detail in Chapter 5, where nature becomes a reservoir of peace, experience and song. Maeve drinks from

---

[112] Gore-Booth, *The Triumph of Maeve*, p. 335.   [113] Gore-Booth, 'An Interpretation', p. 11.
[114] Gore-Booth, *The Triumph of Maeve*, p. 336.   [115] Gore-Booth, *The Triumph of Maeve*, p. 339.

Revolutionary Bodies 57

the springs and falls into a deep sleep where she is visited by a spirit who reveals herself as the mythic Deirdre. This scene has echoes of the *aisling* who, as the sovereignty figure, bemoans her partition from her king; however, the union in Gore-Booth's play is one of female solidarity where connections between the women of Irish myth are drawn. Gore-Booth also reshapes the myth of Deirdre as tragic victim as she is presented as possessing a strong and convincing voice. Deirdre is an active advocate of her beliefs as she tries to persuade Maeve, garbed in her battle dress, of her pacifist agenda: 'And a white shining peace is the soul's reward.'[116] Furthermore, Deirdre's tragic union in death with her lover Naisi is also undermined and rewritten as he longs for his comrades and a world structured by male power and bonds: 'I go to Naisi, he sits sullen-eyed / With folded wings and dreams still of the wars/ Of the world, and the Red Branch and his lost pride.'[117] Clark's description of the *aisling*'s 'longing for an impossible "Otherworldly" solution to Ireland's problems'[118] raises an important point in relation to Gore-Booth's alignment of women, peace and the supernatural, which risks imposing an essentialist identity. However, the longing evoked by Gore-Booth is not inefficacious: it evokes an alternative space of feminine eroticism and the possibility of inhabiting the world differently through the redefinition of gender.

A Female Genealogy

Gore-Booth's reworking of a mythic female genealogy which emphasizes the connection between women and peace, in contrast to men and war, is suggested through a redefinition outside of existing spaces. This is reinforced by Maeve's cry at the end of Act Two: 'Oh wilt thou not open the gate to me / Deirdre?'[119] In light of Gore-Booth's involvement with the suffragist movement, which advocated working partnerships and mentorships, the proposal of a fellowship between Maeve and Deirdre is unsurprising. Gore-Booth's lifelong partnership with Esther Roper offered an alternative paradigm of female relations, outside of patriarchal models. In the census return form for 1901, Roper and Gore-Booth 'drew a bracket around both of their names and under the heading "relation to head of house", they entered, "joint, both heads of the house"'.[120]

---

[116] Gore-Booth, *The Triumph of Maeve*, p. 341.   [117] Gore-Booth, *The Triumph of Maeve*, p. 343.
[118] Clark, *The Great Queens*, p. 156.   [119] Gore-Booth, *The Triumph of Maeve*, p. 351.
[120] Tiernan, *Eva Gore-Booth: An Image of Such Politics*, p. 71.

58   Women and Embodied Mythmaking in Irish Theatre

Gore-Booth was one of the editors of *Urania*, a journal established in 1916, which advocated 'complete refusal to recognise or tolerate the duality'[121] of socially constructed gender differences. Sonja Tiernan argues that: 'The editors of *Urania* were not frightened to embrace the idea of female partnerships; rather they present lesbian relationships as superior to heterosexuality.'[122] Gore-Booth and Roper's relationship was thus a challenge to the traditional family model and an alternative to marriage. *The Triumph of Maeve* stages an alternative landscape of feminine eroticism and Emma Donoghue notes Gore-Booth's preoccupation with Maeve which results in a 'feminist re-evaluation . . . that is motivated by erotic devotion'.[123] In the play, both Deirdre and Maeve reshape their inherited mythic narratives to propose a model of femininity based on fellowship, union and peace through active engagement with one another's beliefs. With reference to Gore-Booth's poetry, Donoghue points to the eschewal of the heterosexual love stories of mythology and highlights the central image: 'of one woman coming to rescue another from an urban prison, and leading her by the hand into a pastoral paradise'.[124]

There is an interesting echo of this imagery in a Suffrage tableau staged by the Irish Women's Franchise League in 1914: in 'The Suffrage Prisoner', Constance Markievicz is dressed in armour as Joan of Arc and comes to the rescue of the Irish suffrage prisoner, played by Kathleen Houston.[125] Both Markievicz's Joan of Arc and Gore-Booth's Maeve undermine fixed models of femininity and a narrative of masculine heroics. Furthermore, *The Triumph of Maeve* introduces discontinuities in the construction of Maeve as a 'masculine' woman, both as a warrior and in her refusal of heterosexual relations. Gore-Booth does not simply feminize the 'unfeminine' Maeve but her proposal of a feminine landscape opens up 'other *possible* worlds' which advocate non-binary and non-essential gendered and sexual identity.

---

[121] Mission Statement of *Urania* quoted in Sonja Tiernan, '"Engagements Dissolved": Eva Gore-Booth, *Urania* and the Radical Challenge to Marriage', in *Tribades, Tommies and Transgressives; Histories of Sexualities: Volume I*, ed. Mary McAuliffe and Sonja Tiernan (Newcastle: Cambridge Scholars, 2008), pp. 128–44 (pp. 130–1).

[122] Tiernan, 'Eva Gore-Booth, *Urania* and the Radical Challenge to Marriage', p. 135.

[123] Emma Donoghue, '"How Could I Fear and Hold Thee by the Hand?": The Poetry of Eva Gore-Booth', in *Sex, Nation and Dissent in Irish Writing*, ed. Eibhear Walshe (Cork: Cork University Press), pp. 16–42 (p. 29).

[124] Donoghue, 'How Could I Fear and Hold Thee by the Hand?', p. 18.

[125] See photo in *The Irish Citizen*, 9 May 1914, p. 401.

Revolutionary Bodies 59

A Vision of Non-resistance

Despite her dream-vision, at first Maeve does not fully embrace Deirdre's promotion of peace, instead she now has a new motivation for her battle: 'Deirdre must be avenged.'[126] Act Three sees her continue to act as a decisive military leader but the process of Maeve's change has begun and it is at this point that *The Death of Fionavar* begins. The location shifts to the '*[I]nterior of a tent, through which a little stream runs*'.[127] Once more, the fluid and unrestricted nature of the otherworld encroaches onstage with the stream and the curtained tent creates a provisional space where the divide between reality and the otherworld becomes even less distinct. This is terrain that Gore-Booth develops further in her later play, *The Buried Life of Deirdre*. In *Kathleen ni Houlihan*, the supernatural threat is neutralized, although Gonne's performance does reveal the potential to expose the gap between myth and reality, but in *The Triumph of Maeve* the tension between the two worlds grows, embodying the conflict between different and competing discourses.

The lighting is crucial to the interplay of the worlds: in Act Three Scene Two, the tent grows dark prior to a flash of lightening which reveals the faces of a host of spirits rushing through the tent. This is then followed by the entry of Ioldana's shining spear which flies into the tent and vanishes. Consternation and fear are evoked by the unidentified voices which are heard all around announcing a new god of pity. A darkening stage, lightening and earthquake tremors build to the climactic vision: '[t]hree crosses stand out for a moment against a lurid sky'.[128] Gore-Booth explains this vision: 'The birth of imagination, the new god of pity, is symbolised in the outside world by the crucifixion of Christ.'[129] In this dramatic moment several connections are made between light, Christ, peace and Fionavar, and are strengthened by Fionavar's prophetic pose, 'lying on the ground in a dead faint'.[130]

Gore-Booth's revisioning of Irish myth resonates with her theological work in *A Psychological and Poetic Approach to the Study of Christ in the Fourth Gospel* (1923), which also explores 'the critique of sacrifice, the ethic of non-violence, and even the Gaian hypothesis – the divine infusing nature'.[131] Fionavar's death on the battlefield in Act Four is

---

[126] Gore-Booth, *The Triumph of Maeve*, p. 355. [127] Gore-Booth, *The Triumph of Maeve*, p. 361.
[128] Gore-Booth, *The Triumph of Maeve*, p. 366. [129] Gore-Booth, 'An Interpretation', p. 11.
[130] Gore-Booth, *The Triumph of Maeve*, p. 366.
[131] Mary Condren, 'Notes on Eva Gore-Booth's *A Psychological and Poetic Approach to the Study of Christ in the Fourth Gospel*, in *The Field Day Anthology of Irish Writing Volume IV: Women's Writing and Traditions*, ed. Angela Bourke, Siobhán Kilfeather, Maria Luddy, Margaret Mac Curtain,

associated with Christ's sacrifice: it is reported that her heart 'broke / For pity of the dead lying on the grass / After the battle.'[132] Gore-Booth's play therefore shifts the focus from the mother–son relationship, which dominates blood sacrifice narratives such as *Kathleen ni Houlihan*, to a mother–daughter relationship in which women play an active role, rather than simply being the stimulus for the sacrifice. Furthermore, Maeve's love for Fionavar is emphasized whereas earlier versions presented Maeve bartering her daughter as a prize for warriors who would fight Cuchulain.[133]

Gore-Booth incorporates the Christian iconography of Calvary into Irish myth to reshape mythic associations. The trope of blood sacrifice was exploited by nationalists, particularly in the wake of the executions of participants in the 1916 Rising, so the play's re-publication as *The Death of Fionavar* potentially offers Fionavar as the Christ figure in a counter proposal of non-resistance which refutes the justification to fight, and to die, for the nation's rebirth, and reveals the cost in terms of innocent lives. The futility of battle is supported by Fionavar's final words in which she condemns not the soldiers who have died but Maeve, as Fionavar 'flung her arms out to the blue and cried, / "Is this the triumph of Maeve?" and shrieked and fell'.[134] Maeve is prompted into action which eschews conquering other territories but, unlike the anticolonial struggle, she no longer supports military ideals. Furthermore, in contrast to the figure of Kathleen ni Houlihan, she is not rejuvenated by death and sacrifice.

Following Fionavar's death, Maeve starts to comprehend Deirdre's pacifist message and the import of the vision of the crosses. She is therefore ready to embrace an alternative set of ideals and a new life, and the act closes with her appeal: 'Oh, wilt thou not open the gates to me, / Fionavar, Deirdre, the gates of Peace?'[135] This appeal once more evokes an alternative female genealogy associated with the otherworld. Fionavar functions as a symbol but she is a symbol that engages with pacifist and feminist discourses, on the whole eschewed by cultural nationalism.

Gerardine Meaney, Máirín Ní Dhonnchadha, Mary O'Dowd and Clair Wills (Cork: Cork University Press, 2002), pp. 659–63 (p. 659).

[132] Gore-Booth, *The Triumph of Maeve*, p. 377.

[133] See *Táin Bó Cúailnge: Recension I*, trans. by Cecile O'Rahilly (Dublin: Dublin Institute for Advanced Studies, 1976).

[134] Gore-Booth, *The Triumph of Maeve*, p. 378. [135] Gore-Booth, *The Triumph of Maeve*, p. 380.

Revolutionary Bodies 61

The 'Fighting Pacifist'

The 1916 re-publication as *The Death of Fionavar* offers a complex engagement with the tropes and narratives of the period. Constance's illustrations incorporated 'symbols of transformation, such as a repeated motif of larvae, caterpillars, butterflies and moths' which complemented Gore-Booth's pacifist values, but also offered 'a counternarrative of the Rising as a transformative defeat'.[136] Gore-Booth titled her 1916 collection of poems, 'Broken Glory': a conflicted sentiment which resonates with Maeve's description, following the death of Fionavar, of her 'grievous triumph'.[137] *The Death of Fionavar* is dedicated to 'To The Memory of the Dead. The Many who died for Freedom and the One who died for Peace.' The latter reference is to her friend Francis Sheehy-Skeffington, a pacifist who was shot by an illegal firing squad after the 1916 Rising despite having no involvement.

In her introduction to *The Death of Fionavar*, Gore-Booth describes how Maeve has yet to learn that 'the ambitious fighter is for ever an outcast from the country of the mind, which can only be entered by a pilgrim who has cast aside anger and power and worldly possessions'.[138] Gore-Booth does not deny the need to fight and make change, but she does suggest that the 'more ambitious fighter' is motivated by critical intellectual engagement and non-violence. This echoes Gore-Booth's characterization of Sheehy-Skeffington as a 'fighting pacifist':[139] she draws on William Blake to describe how, '(a)ll his life Skeffington had never "ceased from mental fight" against all forms of tyranny, oppression, and cruelty'.[140] Gore-Booth is able to praise both Sheehy-Skeffington and those who died fighting in the Rising through her belief in the will to fight for liberty from the forces of domination. Their shared belief in freedom enables her to find common ground with them despite her advocating non-resistance in the play.

Through the course of the play we see Maeve reject her ambitions to fight and conquer as she finally embraces the peaceful ideals represented by the otherworld. In contrast to her earlier behaviour, Maeve's interaction with her people in Act Five is characterized by justice and fairness, and her agency is no longer defined by participation in a male-dominated system

---

[136] Lauren Arrington, *Revolutionary Lives: Constance and Casimir Markievicz* (Princeton and Oxford: Princeton University Press, 2016), p. 152.

[137] Gore-Booth, *The Triumph of Maeve*, p. 378.   [138] Gore-Booth, 'An Interpretation', p. 12.

[139] 'Francis Sheehy-Skeffington', in *The Political Writings of Eva Gore-Booth*, ed. Sonja Tiernan (Manchester: Manchester University Press, 2015), p. 226.

[140] 'Holograph Account of a Visit to Dublin in the Aftermath of the Easter Rising', in *The Political Writings of Eva Gore-Booth*, p. 198.

62 Women and Embodied Mythmaking in Irish Theatre

which aligns violence and power. Yet, the ending of the play reveals the difficulties in reconciling her new stance within her court; Maeve's performance embodies the tension between war and peace as she struggles to redefine this binary in her newly negotiated role as a 'fighting pacifist'. In the final act a fight breaks out between two brothers over 'lean lands' and this is juxtaposed with Maeve's refusal of her role as either warrior queen or sovereignty figure. The stage directions reveal Maeve's despair and sense of now being at odds with the court as ambition for power, land and victory are no longer of importance to her: '*MAEVE is sitting on the throne with her head on her hands and her elbows on her knees.*'[141] This moment powerfully stages a discontinuity in the narrative of Maeve as powerful warrior queen. Maeve critiques the world which fails to accommodate her changed self through her embrace of an otherworld founded on feminine eroticism: this constitutes a rejection of her role as sovereignty, conferring fecundity on her people through union with the king, and thus of heterosexual relations.

The last scene of the play reveals a marked change in Maeve's appearance: both her costume and demeanour. Maeve takes off her crown and royal robes in a gesture which demonstrates her embrace of an alternative space and way of living. This is in contrast to Gregory's Grania who puts on her crown and robes at the end of the play to return to Finn's court (discussed in Chapter 3). Maeve dons a crown of primroses to represent her new life connected with nature and peace, and the imagery contrasts with the 'primroses all soaked in blood' on the battlefield.[142] Maeve once more reshapes her mythic narrative as the rejection of the 'rags of royalty',[143] which she wore in the opening act, disrupts the representation of her as triumphant battle queen. Furthermore, Maeve's authoritative departure suggests that she has already moved on to the otherworld: '*MAEVE goes slowly down the room like one in a dream – nobody dares to stop her.*'[144]

However, her convictions are given a disconcerting defence in the action of the final moments of the play and its abrupt ending. As Maeve leaves, Nera is stabbed and a warrior greedily rushes forward to grab Maeve's crown while another takes her sword. The stage directions indicate that '*the scene closes in confusion and wild disorder*'.[145] Maeve expresses her agency through the reshaping of her story and rejection of limiting definitions as a symbol of 'force and sovereignty' but this disrupts the closure of a neat ending in which order is restored. Her court is no longer the

[141] Gore-Booth, *The Triumph of Maeve*, p. 392. [142] Gore-Booth, *The Triumph of Maeve*, p. 377.
[143] Gore-Booth, *The Triumph of Maeve*, p. 393. [144] Gore-Booth, *The Triumph of Maeve*, p. 394.
[145] Gore-Booth, *The Triumph of Maeve*, p. 395.

Revolutionary Bodies

accommodating space it once was for the warrior queen and so she chooses to leave and withdraw her support of the male structures which once afforded her power.

The ending offers what Richard Kearney describes as 'a *demythologising* form of politics which interprets the present in terms of a pluralising future (secular progress)',[146] as Gore-Booth's radical reworking of myth enables her engagement with voices and politics which dissent from the dominant cultural nationalist agenda. Moreover, the world Maeve leaves behind is left in chaos thereby revealing its flaws. The link between utopian possibility and female genealogies is fundamental to Gore-Booth's, and indeed Marina Carr's, work. However, the loss of the first two acts from the 1916 play meant that the scene with Deirdre was omitted, and at first glance this may appear to reflect the increasing support among nationalist feminists at the time for the nation's independence to take precedence over suffrage issues. However, Gore-Booth's pacifism and radical suffragism are not silenced by nationalist concerns in *The Death of Fionavar*. The republication offered the opportunity to enact a female coalition founded on rebellion against forces of domination and subordination.

The New York Times Magazine review of *The Death of Fionavar* notes the irony of the collaborative nature of the publication, with the inclusion of Constance Markievicz's illustrations, which were drawn while she was in prison.[147] However, it is not an irony: it is a powerful statement of women's coalitional politics. This was not a new idea for suffragists or for pacifist feminists: Gore-Booth signed a letter together with 101 other British and Irish pacifist women which was addressed to their 'Sisters' in Germany and Austria during Christmas 1914.[148] At a time when the issue of whether to prioritize nationalism or suffrage threatened to create division between feminists in Ireland, the two sisters made concrete the possibility of a female coalition as an alternative path. They were united by their common belief in the need to fight for change, though they maintained their differences over the means with which to fight. Yeats's 1927 poem, 'In Memory of Eva Gore-Booth and Con Markievicz', alludes to Eva's dreams of 'Some vague Utopia',[149] but in both the content and theatrical form of *The Triumph of Maeve* and its collaborative publication as *The Death of*

---

[146] Kearney, *Myth and Motherland*, p. 13.
[147] 'Irish Rebel Illustrates Nonresistance Play', *The New York Times Magazine*, 10 September 1916, p. 2.
[148] Tiernan, *An Image of Such Politics*, p. 149.
[149] W.B. Yeats, *Collected Poems* (London: Vintage, 1990), p. 241.

64   Women and Embodied Mythmaking in Irish Theatre

Fionavar, Gore-Booth makes tangible an alternative future informed by dissenting voices.

Revolutionary Mythmaking

Gore-Booth's radical demand for alternative worlds beyond the framework of the nation was prescient; nationalist women were yet to fully realize the betrayal of their contribution to the project of shaping the nation. Yet, all the performances in this chapter make a vital intervention in the mythmaking of the period as they speak to the tension between unified and closed myths which perpetuate an idealized Irish femininity and women's embodied experiences. The articulation and felt presence of these experiences through their embodied mythmaking invigorates the women's defiant cultural and political engagement. The vibrancy and revolutionary potential that the early twentieth century offered was inimical to women's embodied mythmaking, but the tension which animated this work was 'resolved' by the Free State's obliteration of women's voices.

Despite this, during these years there are still some cracks in which feminist dissent and mythmaking can be located, as shown in the analysis in Chapter 5 of Mary Devenport O'Neill's ballet-poem *Bluebeard* (1933). The variety of theatrical strategies drawn on through the tableaux vivants, *Kathleen ni Houlihan*, *Dawn* and *The Triumph of Maeve* are united, to varying degrees, by their potential to expose women's dispossession by ideal myths of femininity and by their efforts to negotiate public and alternative spaces for female expression. Through the establishment of the Free State, the homely space of the nation proved unaccommodating for the expression of women's subjectivity; an experience that was to endure. Women's unhomely experience at the turn of the twenty-first century is the focus of Chapter 2 which further develops a feminist critique of theatrical form through examination of the restrictions placed on, as well as the potential for change enabled through, the relationship between bodies and space.

CHAPTER 2

Unhomely Bodies: Transforming Space

Chapter 1 explored how women's performing bodies might reshape myths through the disruptive articulation of their embodied experiences: a process which is underpinned by the employment of theatrical forms with the potential to hold conflicts in tension and offer feminist critique. This chapter develops this terrain by focusing on how the theatrical forms utilized in Paula Meehan's *Mrs Sweeney* (1997) and Mary Elizabeth Burke-Kennedy's *Women in Arms* (1984, 1988 and 2002) encapsulate the tension between the body and the space it inhabits, and how the process of their mutual reshaping negotiates the expression of marginalized experiences.

Mrs Sweeney explores the lives of a Dublin working-class community, bypassed by the Celtic Tiger, while *Women in Arms* retells the myths of the Ulster Cycle to acknowledge the pivotal, yet silenced, role of the women. Discussion of the framework of Ireland's 'architecture of containment' could be extended in a theatrical context to include realism as a patriarchal structure and '"prisonhouse of art" for women'.[1] Nonetheless, realism has been deployed, as Anna McMullan suggests, by women in Irish theatre 'to critique the constraints of the society they represent' and that 'Many go beyond realism in their staging of female dis-location.'[2] Both *Mrs Sweeney* and *Women in Arms* adopt very different theatrical forms to map the complex ways in which space and body intersect; yet both suggest that realism is inadequate to the task of expressing women's desires and look to alternative forms to carve out new spaces of expression.

The experience of dis-location for women in Ireland: of their fraught relationship with the unaccommodating territory of the home is a consequence of the configuration of space whereby the female body is rendered invisible. The tension between body and space offers a node

---

[1] Sue-Ellen Case, *Feminism and Theatre* (London: Macmillan, 1988), p. 124.
[2] Anna McMullan, 'Unhomely Stages: Women Taking (a) Place in Irish Theatre', in *Druids, Dudes and Beauty Queens*, ed. Dermot Bolger (Dublin: New Island, 2001), p. 74.

66   Women and Embodied Mythmaking in Irish Theatre

through which the unhomely experience emerges in these two plays through exploration of the home and the landscape. Bhabha's notion of the unhomely embodies the fusion of the personal and the political, and furthermore he points to feminism as an unhomely project which disturbs binaries: 'By making visible the forgetting of the "unhomely" moment in civil society, feminism specifies the patriarchal, gendered nature of civil society and disturbs the symmetry of private and public.'[3] Both feminism and the unhomely experience serve to question our understanding of home as a coherent, private and accommodating space. The communication of women's embodied experiences of space in *Mrs Sweeney* and *Women in Arms* renders the unhomely experience visible and demands the reconfiguration of space to intimate the possibility of inhabiting space differently, thereby facilitating female agency and expression.

In a review of *Mrs Sweeney*, Fintan O'Toole remarked that 'it is the wild myth of the Sweeney story and not the apparent social realism of O'Casey that is best able to get to the heart of lives on the edge of Irish society today'.[4] However, there is instability and conflict at the heart of O'Casey's realism, as Ronan McDonald suggests: 'It takes a production alert to the conflicts, tensions and contradictions in the plays to resist the reassuring "moral" messages which slide all too easily from plays performed in a cosy, naturalistic setting.'[5] In *Mrs Sweeney*, the unhomely experience highlights the social, economic and cultural structures which have disenfranchised women and the urban underclass, and denied them the opportunity to effect change in their own lives and on the wider social world. The 'cosy' realist stage is fractured by the individual's and community's experiences of alienation which disturb and reshape conceptions of the home. The play's unstable realism facilitates the resurfacing of repressed traumas in the public domain through myth, the carnivalesque and spaces beyond the boundaries of the realist stage. The mythic frame of *Women in Arms* charts the unhomely terrain of the landscape to contest the silencing of the female body by the trope of the woman-nation. Burke-Kennedy shifts the focus in the myths of the Ulster Cycle to the lived experiences and decisive role of the female characters: Nessa, Macha, Deirdre and Maeve. The play is invigorated by the adoption of a Brechtian-influenced fluid performance

---

[3] Homi K. Bhabha, *The Location of Culture* (London: Routledge, 1994), p. 11.
[4] Fintan O'Toole, *Critical Moments: Fintan O'Toole on Modern Irish Theatre*, ed. Julia Furey and Redmond O'Hanlon (Dublin: Carysfort Press, 2003), pp. 178–9.
[5] Ronan McDonald, 'Sean O'Casey's Dublin Trilogy: Disillusionment to Delusion', in *The Cambridge Companion to Twentieth-Century Irish Drama*, ed. Shaun Richards (Cambridge: Cambridge University Press, 2004), pp. 136–49 (p. 139).

Unhomely Bodies 67

style which exposes the construction and contingency of gender and myth to offer critique and transformation. My analysis of productions of both plays examines the layers of sculpting involved in the process of reshaping space and enables an exploration of how unhomely bodies might disturb and reconfigure their environment. Ultimately, this will assess the extent to which the plays offer 'the disclosure of possible worlds which are suppressed in our present reality and whose very otherness provides us with alternatives to the established order'.[6]

The Experience of Exile in *Mrs Sweeney*

Paula Meehan's reputation as a poet was firmly established when she turned her hand to playwriting in the 1990s. She wrote several plays for children with Team Educational Theatre Company (*Kirkle*, 1995 and *The Voyage*, 1997) but her first play for adults was *Mrs Sweeney*. The play premiered in a Rough Magic production in 1997 at Project @ The Mint in Dublin and was directed by Kathy McArdle.[7] The two-act play is set in a social housing complex in Dublin and focuses on the working-class community which includes Lil Sweeney and her husband Sweeney, both of whom are faced with a seemingly unending stream of adversities. We learn that their daughter Chrissie, who was addicted to heroin, died from an AIDS-related illness a year earlier, and the play opens with their flat being burgled for the fourth time that month. There is a strong sense that the community is barely holding things together and that they are unravelling under the pressure of these experiences.

Mrs Sweeney draws on Paula Meehan's own experiences of living in an inner-city flats complex in the 1980s, in one of the most economically marginalized areas of Dublin. The play is set in the early years of the Celtic Tiger period (roughly 1995–2007) but the benefits of the Tiger economy did not extend to all sections of society as Peadar Kirby outlines: 'these were the best of years for an elite of Irish society who were enriched immensely by the years of growth . . . in the case of other sectors of society, they either benefitted far less or were further marginalised'.[8] This is

---

[6] Richard Kearney, 'Between Tradition and Utopia: The Hermeneutical Problem of Myth', in *On Paul Ricoeur: Narrative and Interpretation*, ed. David Wood (London: Routledge, 2002), p. 65.

[7] Paula Meehan, *Mrs Sweeney*. Director: Kathy McArdle. Cast: Ger Ryan, Mick Nolan, Anto Nolan, Neilí Conroy, Gina Moxley, Tim Ruddy, Emmet Dowling, Barry White. Lighting: Paul Keogan. Designer: Barbara Bradshaw (Rough Magic Theatre Company: Project@ The Mint, opened 7 May 1997).

[8] Peadar Kirby, *Celtic Tiger in Collapse: Explaining the Weaknesses of the Irish Model* (Basingstoke: Palgrave Macmillan, 2010), p. 68.

68   Women and Embodied Mythmaking in Irish Theatre

certainly borne out in *Mrs Sweeney* where the community's disintegration and segregation is exacerbated. They have been physically and spatially sectioned off from society, and Lil describes how barbed wire separates the complex from the surrounding houses: 'The flats look like one of those concentration camp films in the moonlight. They'd gas us if they could.'[9] Who 'they' are, we are never told as the agents of their destruction remain anonymous which only further reinforces the community's alienation. The desire to both ignore and remove the community echoes Meehan's own experiences of isolation when the Dublin inner-city community she grew up in was relocated in the 1960s to Finglas, an area which was very remote from the city at the time. The experience of isolation is one which has endured and, though Dublin was in a phase of huge economic growth in the 1990s, *Mrs Sweeney* portrays the sense of isolation for the remaining inner-city communities who are under threat both as individuals and as a group from cultural and economic eradication, and this bleak outlook is compounded by the lack of any sense of the possibility of change for the characters.

Meehan wanted to capture the experience of internal exile, of both economic and social marginalization, and turned to the Irish myth of Suibhne (translated as Sweeney). Suibhne Geilt, as he appears in *Buile Suibhne*,[10] was a Celtic king who clashed with a priest called Ronan, who then cursed Suibhne and condemned him to exile wandering as a bird among the trees. In *Sweeney Astray*, Seamus Heaney offers a possible reading of the Suibhne myth with Sweeney as the figure of the displaced artist, arguing that 'it is possible to read the work as an aspect of the quarrel between free creative imagination and the constraints of religious, political and domestic obligation'.[11] Christianity is the dominant force that Suibhne rails against in the figure of Ronan, while for Meehan's Sweeney a secure sense of community is dismantled as all institutions, religious to trade unions, are portrayed as having let the community down. Sweeney's struggle to deal with experiences of loss and threat prompt his retreat

---

[9] Paula Meehan, *Mrs Sweeney*, in *Rough Magic: First Plays*, ed. Siobhan Bourke (Dublin: New Island, 1999), p. 432.

[10] See J.G. O'Keeffe's Introduction to his translation, *Buile Suibhne* (London: Irish Texts Society, 1913), which he based on a manuscript of 1671–74. O'Keeffe outlines the earliest references to Suibhne, who is mentioned in the ninth or tenth century Book of Aicill and also a poem of the eighth or ninth century in the St Paul manuscripts which was possibly written by St Moling. For further discussion of versions of the myth see Anne Clune, 'Mythologising Sweeney', *Irish University Review*, 26:1 (1996), 48–60.

[11] Seamus Heaney, 'Introduction', in *Sweeney Astray* (Derry: Field Day, 1983), p. viii.

Unhomely Bodies

into a bird-like existence and his transformation encapsulates the humour and the pathos of the play.

The experience of exile is also shared by the community of *Mrs Sweeney* who are exiled from an understanding of home by the constant invasions of their personal space. This is conveyed in the opening of the play which presents the ransacked Sweeney home – a situation that is compounded by the revelation that Sweeney's beloved pigeons have been killed in their coop. In contrast to the backdrop of the 1997 premiere, set against a period of obsession with property ownership as an expression of social status, home does not represent security and shelter in *Mrs Sweeney* but is a space under threat of invasion. Both Sweeney's and the community's desire for safety and the refuge of a homely space is evoked by Sweeney's nesting under the dining table.

'Home', as a stable centre of meaning, is absent and links the play to the notion of the unhomely; as Lib Taylor notes of the insecurity of the unhomely stage, it 'continually defer[s] and refract[s] any sense of "home"'.[12] Both Bhabha and Taylor focus on the unhomely as a threat to the unitary identity of home and nation through migration: 'the estranging sense of the relocation of the home and the world – the unhomeliness – that is the condition of extra-territorial and cross-cultural initiations'.[13] However, the displacement experienced by the inhabitants of working-class Dublin resonates with that of O'Casey's plays, described by Michael Pierse as 'an alienation of the centre': 'depicting the impoverished, anti-heroic Dublin poor at the epicentre of political tumult but simultaneously alienated by political power'.[14] In late twentieth-century Dublin, this alienation is due to the community's economic marginalization from the experience of the Celtic Tiger boom, as they are excluded from and denied a sense of home within the nation. The sense of internal exile felt by the community is movingly expressed in Lil's prayer at the end of Act One on behalf of the '[p]oor banished children of Eve' in 'this our exile'.[15]

In addition to Sweeney's and the community's unhomely experience, we need to consider the fraught relationship between women and home in Irish culture: the lack of accommodation and expression which the space

---

[12] Lib Taylor, 'The "Unhomely" Stage', *Studies in Theatre and Performance*, 26:3 (2006), 205–20 (p. 212).

[13] Bhabha, *The Location of Culture*, p. 9.

[14] Michael Pierse, *Writing Ireland's Working Class: Dublin after O'Casey* (Basingstoke: Palgrave Macmillan, 2011), p. 53.

[15] Meehan, *Mrs Sweeney*, p. 433.

70 Women and Embodied Mythmaking in Irish Theatre

affords Mrs Sweeney. Meehan's intention in writing the play, and rewriting the myth, was to focus on the character of his wife Lil. 'Mrs Sweeney', a poem from Meehan's 1994 collection of poetry: *Pillow Talk*, reveals Meehan's concern with shifting the emphasis of the myth to grant Lil Sweeney a central role and voice as she 'casts *her* song'[16] (own emphasis). The poem offers an interesting antidote to Yeats's 'Leda and the Swan', as images of birds, metamorphosis and sex are employed in a more positive light for the woman involved. Where Yeats's Leda is 'helpless' and 'terrified' as she is raped, Mrs Sweeney is in control of the erotic charge of the poem, as she 'casts her song on the water' and invites Sweeney to 'ravish' her.[17] The sexually charged moment sparks life into the participants and this links to the mating ritual we see performed in the play: a moment of communion for the Sweeneys, which offers a tender and spiritual encounter in contrast to the harsh world in which they live.

However, Meehan describes how 'Mrs Sweeney' initially inspired the play in quite a different way: 'Immediately I'd finished the poem the thought flashed – *get a grip woman, it wouldn't be songs cast on water at all, at all. Scraping the shite off the mantelpiece you'd be.*'[18] Meehan's response reveals the disparity between myth and reality through Lil Sweeney's experience of marginalization both as a member of a working-class community and as a woman left to clean up the shite, while Sweeney retreats into his life as a bird. The home is a place where patriarchal power is exerted as women are controlled and punished for failing to live up to the idealized myths of femininity: this violence is made palpable in *Mrs Sweeney* through Frano's experiences at the hands of her abusive husband. Thus, the home is a space in which myth and reality collide and an unstable realism has the potential to explore this tension, thereby exposing the unhomely consequences of the disparity for women.

In addition to addressing Sweeney's and the community's unhomely experience, it is imperative that we analyse Lil's experiences of the home: how her sense of confinement within the physical space and roles accorded to Irish women manifests itself in the play. I examine the differences between the unhomely experience as endured by the community, Sweeney, and Lil through assessment of the various theatrical strategies at work in *Mrs Sweeney* which enable the disruption of the unhomely to have a lasting impact by reshaping the space which contains their expression.

---

[16] Meehan, 'Author's Note' to *Mrs Sweeney*, p. 463.
[17] Meehan, 'Author's Note' to *Mrs Sweeney*, p. 463.
[18] Meehan, 'Author's Note' to *Mrs Sweeney*, p. 463.

Theatrical Form and Transformation

In addition to the inspiration drawn from the Sweeney myth, Meehan is clearly influenced theatrically by Sean O'Casey's staging of Dublin's working classes in his Dublin Trilogy (*The Shadow of a Gunman, Juno and the Paycock* and *The Plough and the Stars*). Lil's role as the heroic woman left to pick up the pieces echoes O'Casey's Juno, while Sweeney's bird-like posturing summons the swagger of the Paycock's performances. The banner of the socialist republican Irish Citizen Army provides the backdrop for the set of O'Casey's *The Plough and the Stars* and Lil Sweeney hangs the Starry Plough flag across her boarded-up window. Furthermore, O'Casey's Trilogy and *Mrs Sweeney* utilize an unstable realism to convey the alienation and fragmentation of the community: Ronan McDonald suggests that O'Casey's Trilogy avoids staging 'naturalist coherence and a neat opposition between domestic integrity and destructive political ideology'[19] to highlight 'confusion and disillusionment'.[20] Meehan is similarly attuned to the potential of this dissonance to reveal a relationship defined by tension between bodies and space. The hardships members of the community face, including drug addiction, HIV/AIDS, economic poverty, domestic abuse, burglary and vigilantism, all affect their experience of their bodies and relationships with others, as well as their relationship with the space they inhabit. The characters' embodied experience of unhomeliness is thus encapsulated in the tensions of the realist frame and the interrogation of the space of home, but the play also gestures towards other possible spaces of expression. To date, the play has only been staged professionally by Rough Magic in a production which was limited by the realist frame, but there is huge potential for alternative forms of staging which accommodate Lil's expression of her unhomely experience, as well as reconfiguring the physical spaces in order to suggest the possibility for change.

The extent to which the transformation of Sweeney's body is realized is instrumental in exploiting the 'confusion and disillusionment' of a broken realism which captures the unhomely experience. Unlike Freud's *unheimlich*, which is centred on the resurfacing of that which has been repressed in the unconscious, Bhabha's unhomely allows for a more phenomenal

---

[19] McDonald, 'Sean O'Casey's Dublin Trilogy', p. 139.
[20] McDonald, 'Sean O'Casey's Dublin Trilogy', p. 148.

72   Women and Embodied Mythmaking in Irish Theatre

interpretation. The unhomely disturbs the boundaries of what is private and public as it draws out the links between personal traumas and the broader social context. Sweeney's somatic experience expresses both personal and community-wide traumas and is physicalized through the process of becoming a bird. In the Rough Magic production, Sweeney's first transformation was conveyed corporeally, through gestures, movement and cooing noises.[21] Meehan has described how the actor Mick Nolan emphasized the pathos of Sweeney's incipient breakdown: he portrayed Sweeney with 'very bad knees, a beer belly and generally looked like a sad man'.[22]

Initially, his metamorphosis appears to be an immediate reaction to the killing of his much-loved pigeons; however, we learn from Lil that Sweeney did not deal with the death of his daughter Chrissie, 'King of the Avoiders would be more like. Head in the Sand Award',[23] and we realize that this trauma is resurfacing too. His personal traumas erupt into the public realm to expose their connection to the political as his unhomely experience critiques the failure of social and political structures to alleviate conditions for his community: namely lack of security and privacy as well as drug use and HIV/AIDS. His metamorphosis is both an escape from reality, into the mythic world of Suibhne, and a means of dealing with repressed trauma as his transformation corporealizes both his personal and his community's traumas and brings them into the public domain. Furthermore, Sweeney's vulnerable, bird-like body reveals the violent abjection of non-hegemonic masculinities as he fails to embody the Celtic Tiger myth of a 'working-class hard-body masculinity that created the properties on which fortunes were made'.[24] The unhomely is 'a site whose very indeterminacy fuels the production of alternative identities',[25] and this is reflected in Sweeney's metamorphoses: both his initial transformation into a pigeon and his later carnivalesque metamorphosis into a peacock.

Sweeney's first transformation sees him nesting and trying to find a home, whereas his second transformation, during the later carnivalesque scene, witnesses a sense of pride and acknowledgement of his personal

---

[21] *Mrs Sweeney*. Video recorded at Project @ The Mint, May 1997. The Rough Magic Theatre Company Archive is now held in Manuscripts & Archives, The Library of Trinity College Dublin.
[22] Correspondence with Paula Meehan, 12 January 2009.   [23] Meehan, *Mrs Sweeney*, p. 399.
[24] Brian Singleton, *Masculinities and the Contemporary Irish Theatre* (Basingstoke: Palgrave Macmillan, 2011), p. 191.
[25] McMullan, 'Unhomely Bodies and Dislocated Identities', p. 190.

Unhomely Bodies　73

traumas through the donning of a peacock costume: '*She produces from a black plastic sack a peacock costume made of feathers. This is for Sweeney who looks absolutely magnificent when they finally manage to coax him into it.*[26] The final moments of the play see all the characters toast Chrissie's shrine and this acknowledgement of their unhomely experience allows Lil to close the play with a final word of hope, 'magic'.

The presence of spiritual experience and transcendence in the ordinary informs both *Mrs Sweeney* and Meehan's poetry. In 'My Father Perceived as a Vision of St Francis', Meehan describes her father feeding the birds in the early morning light of their garden: 'and he was suddenly radiant,/ a perfect vision of St Francis.'[27] The power of transformation and magic in the commonplace are recognized as offering relief in the present through acknowledgement of the unhomely experience and therefore the past. Furthermore, these moments of transcendence located in the everyday celebrate the individual's and community's struggle to resist social and cultural marginalization; an issue to which I return through close analysis of the carnivalesque scenes of Act Two. The word 'magic' retells Chrissie's desire for flight and transformation during her final days, yet it is Sweeney who has come closest to achieving this by the end of the play. Sweeney transforms in the final moments when he wears his peacock wings and stands on the table placed centre stage. In the Rough Magic production, Mick Nolan put on cloth wings and used his arms to suggest Sweeney's wings, swooping and soaring through the air. The Rough Magic production did not exploit the instabilities and contradictions of realism in order to suggest the possibility of 'other *possible* worlds'. However, a more profoundly transformative effect was achieved in a workshop production of *Mrs Sweeney* in the Magic Theatre San Francisco in 1999 which cast a dancer in the role of Sweeney, who, instead of putting on a costume, 'used his body and "flew" about the place, up on tables and chairs and all over the set'.[28] The capacity of the dancer's body to articulate the possibilities of Sweeney's corporeal freedom intensified the suggestion of transformation and magic.

Sweeney's second metamorphosis celebrates the expression of both his personal and the community's traumas, as well as their tenacity and survival, but it also points to the inability to effect lasting change. Mária Kurdi proposes that Sweeney's transformation into a peacock 'replicates

---

[26] Meehan, *Mrs Sweeney*, p. 462.
[27] Paula Meehan, 'My Father Perceived as a Vision of St Francis', in *Three Irish Poets: An Anthology*, ed. Eavan Boland (Manchester: Carcanet, 2003), p. 13.
[28] Correspondence with Paula Meehan, 12 January 2009.

74 Women and Embodied Mythmaking in Irish Theatre

O'Casey's self-absorbed "paycock" strutting about, but unable to do anything fruitful'.[29] In addition to the nod to O'Casey, an Irish literary tradition is alluded to by references to Joyce and Beckett, the names of the doctor and the pub, which poignantly conjures the figure of the exiled Irish artist. Meehan points to the fact that the marginalized community of *Mrs Sweeney* is not given a voice within this tradition as the choice to leave is denied by economic and social limitations. Throughout the play Lil states that she wants to take Sweeney away and she repeatedly urges Mariah to leave: 'Go away. While you are still young and have the energy.'[30] However, after Mariah fails to get the job she applied for, running a women's project in the community, her response to Lil's encouragement is hopeless: 'It's the same everywhere.'[31] Meehan's references to an Irish literary and dramatic tradition, and Celtic myth, highlights the cultural exclusion of the economic underclasses, of the perpetuation of their 'alienation at the centre', yet it is in the carnivalesque moments of the play that we see the community members attempting to express themselves. The unhomely addresses how historical and personal traumas erupt in the present but it is through the carnivalesque that the play conveys the limits placed on the community's ability to effect change.

The Carnivalesque

Act Two sees a shift in the register of the play as the carnivalesque elements gradually intrude on the realist frame established in Act One and inflect the sense of possibility in Sweeney's second transformation. The carnivalesque reflects the indeterminacy of the unhomely experience: it challenges the stability of unitary notions of identity from within to enable the experience of alternative spaces and identities, though whether these alternatives can be maintained is questionable. Mikhail Bakhtin developed the term through discussion of the subversive elements of carnival in Rabelais' work; the carnivalesque expresses the 'temporary liberation from the prevailing truth and from the established order; it marked the suspension of all hierarchical rank, privileges, norms, and prohibitions'.[32] Thus, it is

---

[29] Mária Kurdi, 'Updating Male Texts, Humour and Theatricality: The Representation of Marginalised Irish Womanhood in Paula Meehan's *Mrs Sweeney*', *EPONA: E-journal of Ancient and Modern Celtic Studies*, 1:2 (2007), 1–9 (p. 7), www.epona-journal.hu/epona_languages/English/files/issue_0712/Kurdi_final.pdf [Accessed 15 August 2008].
[30] Meehan, *Mrs Sweeney*, p. 432. [31] Meehan, *Mrs Sweeney*, p. 453.
[32] Mikhail Bakhtin, *Rabelais and His World* (Massachusetts: Massachusetts Institute of Technology Press, 1968), p. 10.

Unhomely Bodies

a moment of threatening and anarchic potential. However, it functions within official ideology and thus can only be a temporary state of subversion, reflecting the constraints of the characters' economic and social situation in *Mrs Sweeney* through the reassertion of the status quo.

For Bakhtin, the carnivalesque was a utopian moment which 'was hostile to all that was immortalized and completed'[33] and 'demanded ever changing, playful, undefined forms'.[34] The grotesque body embodies this mobility and instability: 'it is always in process, it is always *becoming*, it is a mobile and hybrid creature, disproportionate, exorbitant, outgrowing all limits, obscenely decentred and off-balance'.[35] *Mrs Sweeney* offers two notable examples of grotesque bodies: Sweeney's body 'becoming' bird-like and the 'disproportionate' presence of the absent body of Chrissie who died from an AIDS-related illness. They serve as a carnivalesque disruption of the order of things as they are: a parody of the healthy, official body. There is a sense of fear of contagion from the grotesque body, 'outgrowing all limits', and this is underlined by Father Tom's fear of contagion from Sweeney as referenced by Lil's sardonic joke: 'You won't get AIDS or anything.'[36] Moreover, when Oweny takes Sweeney to Beckett's pub the other drinkers acknowledge and share his trauma by taking on animal personas in solidarity with Sweeney. Frano suggests that '[m]aybe what Sweeney has is infectious'.[37] This serves to underline the threat of the eruption of private traumas in public spaces; a threat which Father Tom is keen to repress and restrict. The unhomely body resurfaces in the public realm but ultimately neither of Sweeney's metamorphoses, as a pigeon and a peacock, is successfully accommodated within the stage world – a failure which is conveyed by the limits of the carnivalesque.

The dislocation of the onstage space of the home from the offstage space of the pub and the world beyond the flats creates a sense of claustrophobia for the audience which replicates the characters' sense of entrapment. This claustrophobia serves to heighten the audience's awareness of their position as the voyeuristic spectator who invades the privacy of the home. The spaces of retreat and freedom are diegetic, suggested but not seen on stage; however, a space of freedom is physicalized on stage in the final carnival scenes. The stage directions at the opening of Act Two describe the flat's '[*s*]*ense of entombment which will grow throughout this act*',[38] but the

---

[33] Bakhtin, *Rabelais and His World*, p. 10.   [34] Bakhtin, *Rabelais and His World*, p. 11.

[35] Peter Stallybrass and Allon White, *The Politics and Poetics of Transgression* (Ithaca: Cornell University Press, 1995), p. 9.

[36] Meehan, *Mrs Sweeney*, p. 444.   [37] Meehan, *Mrs Sweeney*, p. 456.

[38] Meehan, *Mrs Sweeney*, p. 434.

76 Women and Embodied Mythmaking in Irish Theatre

carnivalesque offers relief from the claustrophobia of both the realist frame and the material realities of the characters' lives. The transformation of the set, as the characters drape colourful bunting around, literally opens up the space available to them:

> *Where possible a pulley system so that when all is arranged a rope can be pulled and the whole thing can be hoisted like a ship getting ready to sail. It should be like the ceiling of the flat opens up to the sky.*[39]

Meehan suggests that the set provides an enabling space for the carnivalesque moment of symbolic transgression of social roles which define their bodily freedom and identity. The performance of the carnivalesque final scene of the play is vital in its creation of a space for the characters to express themselves within. However, can the carnivalesque offer possibilities for change through alternative spaces, subjectivities and corporealities, or is the ending of the play complicit with the dominant culture which licenses the carnivalesque moment?

Sweeney's transformation into a bird is the catalyst for the carnivalesque. The scenes in Beckett's pub, portrayed as being 'like the zoological gardens',[40] highlight the danger of, and desire for, an irreverent celebration of change. Following this description, Lil, Frano and Mariah embark on their own transformations and start to create an enabling space of expression: '*The three of them independent of each other stake a space on stage with their bits and pieces and begin transforming themselves into exotic birds.*'[41] Their individuality is emphasized by their separate spaces but the communal longing for change is expressed by their singing which leads them to believe in the power of the group: '*Repeat verse, they are all lost in it, harmonising. At end they've mesmerised themselves by their own voices.*'[42] This moment underlines what Robert Stam points to as 'carnival as loss of self, collective jouissance'.[43] The individual is transformed into the communal and the audience's encounter with the carnivalesque on stage implicates them in this experience. The power of the carnivalesque lies not just in transformation of individual bodies but in transformation of the communal body.

Lighting is a crucial element in the process of reconfiguring stage space. Meehan has suggested that, owing to budgetary constraints, the Rough Magic production did not achieve a sense of transformation through the

---

[39] Meehan, *Mrs Sweeney*, p. 452.   [40] Meehan, *Mrs Sweeney*, p. 456.
[41] Meehan, *Mrs Sweeney*, p. 457.   [42] Meehan, *Mrs Sweeney*, p. 457.
[43] Robert Stam, 'Mikhail Bakhtin and Left Cultural Critique', in *Postmodernism and its Discontents*, ed. E. Ann Kaplan (London: Verso, 1989), pp. 116–45 (p. 136).

Unhomely Bodies

set dressing, as described in the stage directions, but was instead realized through the lighting design.[44] The vertical concrete slabs, which defined the semi-circle area of the flat, imprisoned the characters during the early scenes of the play but in the final carnivalesque scenes they were lit from behind to open up the space. However, Paul Keogan's lighting design for the Rough Magic production did not simply generate a sense of expansion and inclusion; the harsh white/blue lighting gave the carnivalesque scenes a dislocated and surreal effect, as well as a heightened, expressionist feel as the dancing characters' exaggerated shadows loomed on the back walls. The lighting undermined the possibility of an experience of communion for the audience so that they too felt the displacement of the unhomely experience. Furthermore, there was a sense of confusion in the final scenes as the characters milled about while Sweeney remained removed from their celebrations, suggesting the failure of the moment as a statement of community. The scenes generated an affective experience of constraint which revealed the failure of the carnivalesque to provide community and sustained change. The reversal of the carnivalesque operates within existing structures to generate an unstable realism: an unhomely theatrical form which is a more accurate reflection of the 'reality' of the community of Maria Goretti Mansions. Furthermore, it is the exposure of the carnivalesque's limits that serves to facilitate the subversive articulation of the unhomely.

The complexity of the subversion unleashed during the carnival of the play can also be explored by examining the types of transformation that take place. The fact that the three women change into birds and Oweny is dressed as a woman exemplifies what Peter Stallybrass and Allon White point to as one of the carnivalesque's failings, what they term displaced abjection: 'the process whereby "low" social groups turn their figurative and actual power, *not* against those in authority, but against those who are even "lower" (women, Jews, animals, particularly cats and pigs)'.[45] Therefore, the emphasis of the carnivalesque moment of the play is not on the participants' anger at those in authority who fail to improve their disenfranchised position but rather on a moment of release and the celebration of their temporary freedom from their position within social hierarchies. Indeed, the suspension of all rules offers no comfort for a community desperately in need of structures that accommodate them and enable their meaningful participation within society – counter to their

---

[44] Correspondence with Paula Meehan, 12 January 2009.
[45] Stallybrass and White, *The Politics and Poetics of Transgression*, p. 53.

78 Women and Embodied Mythmaking in Irish Theatre

unhomely experience of an 'alienation of the centre'. The failure of the carnivalesque to evoke a lasting sense of community for the marginalized working-class population of Maria Goretti Mansions echoes their unhomely experience, whereby they are denied the means of cultural and political expression. The inability of the community to band together is thereby revealed to be the fault of social structures which fail to accommodate them and limit them culturally and economically.

Lil's Unhomely Experience

The carnivalesque scene is closely linked to Sweeney's transformation which results in exposing the failure of both to effect structural change. Yet, Meehan's impetus to rewrite the Sweeney myth was the desire to reveal the limits placed on Mrs Sweeney's life and to counter idealized myths with the realities of women's lives: of Lil being left '*scraping the shite off the mantelpiece*'.[46]

Home as the seat of patriarchal power is an even more unaccommodating space for Lil. Sweeney embraces myth and the home as a space of retreat and escapism; his bird-like nesting echoes his actions when his daughter was dying as he hid in the bedroom, rather than face the reality of her suffering and death.[47] In contrast, home is fundamentally a much more restrictive space for Lil, where she has no option but to take on the traditional responsibilities of women, as carer and homemaker. The home is also a threatening place where men assert their authority through violence, as depicted in the scene where Lil and Frano are hiding from Frano's violently abusive husband, in Lil's flat. Sweeney's unhomely experience is expressed through his becoming a bird, but how does Lil express her unhomely experience and containment within the home? Lil joins in the carnivalesque moment when she, like the other women, is dressed as a bird but the subversive nature of this moment is tempered by its impermanence. Moreover, the scene does not focus on Lil as an individual. In contrast to Sweeney's metamorphoses, the opportunities available to Lil are more limited and this is reflected by the fact that as a woman in the domestic space she is more fully bound by the realist frame. However, a key moment at the end of Act One holds the potential for staging Lil's desire for an alternative, more accommodating space, and thus for destabilizing the coherence of the realist stage. This was not explored in the Rough Magic premiere which left Lil trapped within a realist frame and

---

[46] Meehan, 'Author's Note' to *Mrs Sweeney*, p. 463.   [47] Meehan, *Mrs Sweeney*, p. 415.

Unhomely Bodies

gave fuller expression to Sweeney's unhomely experience, thereby closing down the possibility for Lil to reconfigure the space which limits her expression.

Lil is forced throughout the play to look beyond the world they inhabit for escape, whereas Sweeney retreats into it. This is poignantly suggested by the references throughout to the sky as a space of freedom and to the possibilities for magic and transcendence in the everyday; Chrissie delights in her final days in watching the birds swooping and flying over the flats, which she describes as 'magic'.[48] At the end of Act One, Lil reminisces about the space of her childhood home in Dublin's Georgian tenement buildings, when she describes how 'I was born in a ballroom'.[49] Underlining Lil's need to create space for herself in the crowded home, shared by a family of eight children, is her detailed recollection of the grandeur of the ceiling: 'Dripping with fruit and angels and these long trumpets and scrolls of paper with musical notes writ on them.'[50] Lil remembers how this opulence encouraged her to experience the space differently: 'I used dress up in me ma's old dance dress and spin round and round.'[51] This action simultaneously evokes corporeal freedom and the limiting inheritance of performative female roles defined within the family and home. Lil describes the effect of this abandon: 'Then I'd stop and the ceiling would go on spinning',[52] as the stability of the home is uprooted by her corporeal freedom. This moment has the potential to effect a transformation of the unhomely body and the unhomely stage space.

With reference to the drama of Frank McGuinness and Marina Carr, Anna McMullan points out that 'unhomely bodies are haunted sites where the repressed individual and communal past is played out, so that a revised relationship between past and present may be negotiated'.[53] Lil's unhomely memories are recreated and as they echo through her body they reveal the past in the present, as well as the ongoing need to renegotiate the relationship between body and space, both for Lil and her community. A production which is alert to the tensions between bodily experiences and patriarchal structures, and the onstage and offstage spaces, could exploit the potentially disruptive nature of this moment to highlight the dissonance between the confines of the realist stage and inherited gendered roles, and the experience of freedom in Lil's performance. The brief moments of transcendence in the play: Lil's childhood memory of dancing

---

[48] Meehan, *Mrs Sweeney*, p. 462. [49] Meehan, *Mrs Sweeney*, p. 432.
[50] Meehan, *Mrs Sweeney*, p. 432. [51] Meehan, *Mrs Sweeney*, p. 432.
[52] Meehan, *Mrs Sweeney*, p. 432.
[53] McMullan, 'Unhomely Bodies and Dislocated Identities', p. 182.

80 Women and Embodied Mythmaking in Irish Theatre

in a ballroom; Chrissie's enjoyment of pigeons in flight during her final days; the transformation of the stage set as '*the ceiling of the flat opens up to the sky*';[54] and Sweeney's desire for flight, all evoke spaces of corporeal freedom from the economic deprivations of Maria Goretti Mansions. However, the immense strain on Lil, who is responsible for helping her family survive hardship, means that she struggles to see a future and in the final scene she reveals her fortune-teller's prediction of 'a darkness' for herself.[55] Both Lil's and Sweeney's moments of individual corporeal freedom reveal the failure of words, and cultural, social and economic structures, to accommodate their unhomely bodies, but perhaps it is when bodies work together to reshape the space that contains them that there is the suggestion of more lasting change.

The 'Tender Gesture'

The temporary status of the carnivalesque reveals the constraints of realism on the unhomely body but the moments of 'tender gesture' which work on a more intimate and affective level, namely between Lil and Sweeney, may offer an alternative strategy for creating an accommodating space. Counter to the hardships that the Sweeneys and the community in the flats experience is Meehan's inspiration from the myth of Sweeney:

> There's a gesture in the old tale – the cook Muirghil would make a hollow with her heel in a cow pat and fill it with milk for the bird man to sip from. I witnessed that tender gesture again and again in contemporary guise many times when I lived there.[56]

The 'tender gesture' provides several key moments in the play where phenomenal experience and the performing body are more expressive of intersubjective relationships than the spoken word. Just as there are limits placed on Lil's expression, as captured in the ballroom scene, neither can Sweeney express himself in the world they inhabit, accentuated by his lack of speech and his cooing like a pigeon. In the Rough Magic production Meehan created a rhythmic sound score for Sweeney which underlined his attempts to communicate with Lil;[57] however, his alternative language is not understood. Sweeney is therefore rendered mute but the moments of 'tender gesture' offer self-expression through a corporeal language. These moments are set out in the stage directions but they provide key

[54] Meehan, *Mrs Sweeney*, p. 452.   [55] Meehan, *Mrs Sweeney*, p. 461.
[56] Meehan, 'Author's Note' to *Mrs Sweeney*, p. 464.
[57] Correspondence with Paula Meehan, 12 January 2009.

Unhomely Bodies

intersections where text and bodies echo and resonate through one another in a mutual process of construction. The first of these intercorporeal moments of 'tender gesture', where their relationship is expressed through the body rather than dialogue, occurs in Act One when Sweeney is clearly still upset by the death of his birds and we witness the initial stages of the physicalization of his trauma through his bird-like movements. In the Rough Magic production, Sweeney started to moan and Lil rushed over to him, sat on the arm of his chair and embraced him from behind. It was a very tender moment as she rocked him while making soothing noises. Once Sweeney had settled, Lil bathed his arms and face in an effort to comfort him in a maternal act which echoes Muirghil's 'tender gesture'. Lil sang while bathing Sweeney and the communion of this moment contrasted with the violence previously witnessed through the arrival of the dead birds' bodies and the beginnings of Sweeney's transformation. It is the first time we see the couple alone on stage but the intimacy is soon interrupted by the arrival of Oweny.

The emphasis in the play's text is on Lil's role as the stalwart who deals, emotionally and practically, with the hardships the couple face; interestingly, Ger Ryan, who played Mrs Sweeney in the Rough Magic production, went on to play Juno in an Abbey production of O'Casey's *Juno and the Paycock* later that year. However, the limiting inhibitions imposed upon Lil, of woman as mother and carer, are undercut by the fact that once Sweeney has undergone his transformation into a bird, it is Sweeney who, despite his silence, offers comfort to Lil. The start of Act Two sees Lil join in Sweeney's formal mating dance, '*laughing at first, then growing solemn and enrapt*'.[58] Ger Ryan underlined Lil's more carefree side in this scene, laughing and screaming uproariously as Sweeney chased her round the room before embracing her from behind and trying to 'mate' with her. The mating ritual is an extension of his desire to create a home and through the embrace of dance and movement the couple engage in a tender moment of communion. Sweeney refuses a hegemonic, 'dominance-oriented masculinity'[59] and his desire to nest positions him as the homemaker, reversing traditional gendered roles of Irish womanhood defined within the domestic realm and as reproducer of the nation. Sweeney tries to create a homely space of safety, encircling himself and Lil, but they are interrupted by the arrival of Frano and Mariah, and Sweeney retreats to his 'nest' under the table.

---

[58] Meehan, *Mrs Sweeney*, p. 435.
[59] Singleton, *Masculinities and the Contemporary Irish Theatre*, p. 12.

82   Women and Embodied Mythmaking in Irish Theatre

The 'tender gesture' which follows later in Act Two contrasts in tone with the mating ritual as a moment of enjoyment and release. The scene takes on a more serious and urgent tone as Lil is worried that Sweeney could be taken away – concerns raised by Father Tom's visit. Lil is seen sweeping up Sweeney's nest, trying to enforce more 'normal' behaviour, where at the start of Act Two she was happy to leave the nest and abandon her sweeping. Lil feels that she has to curb his behaviour and is forced into complicity with regulating norms concerning how one should live. In the Rough Magic production, Sweeney petulantly walked through the newspaper sweepings and Lil eventually lost her temper. Lil finally gave vent to all her frustrations and anger and started shouting and hitting the floor with the brush, before she slumped into the armchair, sobbing. Lil dealt with their hardships alone in the past but now that Sweeney has brought his own traumas to light, physicalized through his metamorphosed, soft bird-body which counterpoints a hard-body hegemonic masculinity, he is able to offer comfort to Lil. The tenderness of this moment was heightened in the Rough Magic production by Sweeney's slow walk towards Lil and initially tentative movements to place first one, then both arms (or wings) around her. The positioning of the two characters in this scene reversed the positions and roles of the first 'tender gesture' when Lil bathed Sweeney.

These intercorporeal moments see Lil and Sweeney not only sharing their traumas, which Sweeney failed to do in the past, but also reshaping space and roles to generate refuge and security. These very private moments between the couple see the creation of a homely space, albeit temporary, through the provisional use of their bodies and interconnectedness. Thus, the body offers a means of self-expression as Lil and Sweeney are able to communicate and commune through a corporeal language where words have failed to express their experiences. Each of the 'tender gestures' in the play is interrupted by the arrival of other characters into their home, with the exception of the final 'tender gesture' which was added in the Rough Magic production to the end of the carnivalesque scene. The closing moments of the production witnessed Lil's toast to Chrissie, while Sweeney stood on the table behind her before once more embracing her in his peacock wings. The other characters' isolation was underlined by the fact that they all stood separately around the table while the Sweeneys enjoyed another 'tender gesture', this time in communion with their daughter. The addition of this 'tender gesture' to the Rough Magic production suggested that the Sweeneys have now acknowledged their traumas to bring them together in a newly defined notion of family

Unhomely Bodies

and gendered roles, although with the sense that the wider community is still fragmented.

If realism reinforces patriarchal constructions of family and home, the 'tender gesture' proposes an alternative strategy to house the unhomely body and offer security and a sense of pride. Home is not offered as a stable centre of meaning but, like the carnivalesque, it is a concept which is inimical to immortality and completion. The notion of home as a unitary and fixed idea which asserts stability and closure is reconceived as adaptable space which can be created by bodies, even in unhomely spaces. The unhomely body serves as a haunting reminder of that which has been excluded, and forces a reassessment of identity and history. The grotesque bodies of the play, Sweeney's bird-like state and Chrissie's ghostly presence, reveal the experience of internal exile and lack of representation. Lil's dancing body, as she remembers the relative corporeal freedom of her childhood memory, facilitates the disruption of the realities of women's unhomely bodies: the expression of the tension between their embodied experiences of freedom and the limiting inheritance of idealized myths of femininity. However, her pessimistic prophecies following the carnivalesque moment of transformation undercut any possibilities for change. She prophesizes that: Frano will continue to be violently abused by her husband; Mariah will once more become addicted to heroin; Sweeney will end up in a psychiatric hospital, '[h]is lovely wings all crumpled in a straightjacket'; and that her own future is 'a darkness'.[60]

Lil's vision critiques the negative consequences of present ideological constraints on each of the characters as the community's fragmentation is blamed not on the individuals but on their alienation from Celtic Tiger Ireland's globalized experience and financial growth. Furthermore, the community's experience of precarity is one which has endured; it predates the boom by several decades and thus is much more deeply entrenched. The collapse of the community was suggested in the premiere production's closing scene where the characters were initially gathered round Lil, only to break away individually as their fortune was revealed and they were left occupying isolated spaces.

Mrs Sweeney closes with doom and fragmentation, but the process of acknowledging past traumas holds the promise of hope and community. The unstable realism of the play expresses these contradictions and acknowledges that both the carnivalesque and the 'tender gesture' are

---

[60] Meehan, *Mrs Sweeney*, p. 461.

84 Women and Embodied Mythmaking in Irish Theatre

constrained by the social and economic world in which the community live and cannot escape. However, the need to continue to engage in a process that puts pressure on the limits of space that suppresses unhomely experiences is an undercurrent that remains alive, despite the play's bleak outlook. Both Sweeney's transformation into a bird and Lil's memory of the freedom of dancing in a ballroom may be transient but they have a powerful affect on the audience and are testament to the enduring need to address the unhomely experience as a disruption of the past in the present, and thus as a means of healing and moving forward. Meehan's poem 'Home', from the same volume as 'Mrs Sweeney', echoes this sentiment:

> The wisewomen say you must live in your skin, call *it* home,
> no matter how battered or broken, misused by the world, you can
> heal.[61]

Within the unhomely environment of *Mrs Sweeney*, the 'tender gesture' employs corporeal vocabularies to rewrite the experience of home and explore new ways of inhabiting it. Moreover, Meehan's poem addresses the discrepancy between self-expression and the forms that society allows us to use for this expression. The accommodation of alternative means of communication within the dominant order is explored in *Mrs Sweeney* through the tensions of an unstable realism to evoke 'other *possible* worlds': worlds where the individual is in a mutual relationship with the surrounding space which enables, rather than contains:

> When the song that is in me is the song I hear from the world
> I'll be home.[62]

A more accommodating terrain in which the expression, or 'song', of the body and the environment are in communion to the point of being indistinct is realized more fully in Olwen Fouéré's *riverrun* (2013) which takes a much more radical approach to embodying the environment (see Chapter 6). In the next section of this chapter, I want to turn to Mary Elizabeth Burke-Kennedy's *Women in Arms* which explores the process of bodies, rather than structures, reshaping unhomely spaces through a very different theatrical form to *Mrs Sweeney*.

---

[61] Meehan, 'Home', in *Three Irish Poets: An Anthology*, p. 19.
[62] Meehan, 'Home', in *Three Irish Poets: An Anthology*, p. 18.

Unhomely Bodies 85

Women in Arms: The Landscape of Myth

Ireland's contemporary theatre sector has been instrumental in 'the development of the spectrum of theatre languages which have tended to be neglected in Ireland in the past'.[63] Furthermore, the independent theatre sector has proven to be more accommodating for women theatre makers: this continues to be the case as evidenced by the *Gender Counts Report: An Analysis of Gender in Irish Theatre, 2006–2015*, which highlights that representation of women is strongest at The Ark, Rough Magic Theatre Company and Dublin Theatre Festival, while women are least represented at the Gate and Abbey theatres.[64] Mary Elizabeth Burke-Kennedy founded Storytellers Theatre Company in 1986 and her play *Women in Arms* is rooted in the desire to broaden the landscape of performance conventions and to represent women. Burke-Kennedy wrote *Women in Arms* under commission to the Cork Theatre Company in 1984,[65] and following this earlier version, the play was produced for the Dublin Millennium Theatre Festival in 1988.[66] It was then developed and revived in 2002, opening in Dublin's Civic Theatre, Tallaght,[67] and published in the 2001 collection, *Seen and Heard: Six New Plays by Irish Women*, edited by Cathy Leeney.

In contrast to *Mrs Sweeney*, the theatrical form of *Women in Arms* offers a very different means of intimating the possibility of a provisional space which facilitates the articulation of unhomely experiences. Using Brechtian storytelling, the play generates fluid identities and interactions of bodies to offer a space of expression within a mythic framework, while simultaneously offering a critique of the ways in which power is exerted on, and negotiated through, bodies. *Women in Arms* is a witty and humorous

---

[63] McMullan, 'Reclaiming Performance: The Contemporary Irish Independent Theatre Sector', p. 38.

[64] *Gender Counts: An Analysis of Gender in Irish Theatre, 2006–2015*, Commissioned by #WakingTheFeminists. Funded by The Arts Council. Researched by Dr Brenda Donohue, Dr Ciara O'Dowd, Dr Tanya Dean, Ciara Murphy, Kathleen Cawley and Kate Harris, http://www.wakingthefeminists.org/research-report/ [Accessed 15 Jan 2018].

[65] *Women in Arms*. Written and directed: Mary Elizabeth Burke-Kennedy. Cast: Kate Hogan, Eamon Maguire, Kay Ray Malone, Melody McNamara, Dan Mullane, Bairbre ní Chaoime, Maurice Sheehan. Lighting: Patrick Murray (Cork Theatre Company: Ivernia Theatre, Cork, opened 31 July 1984).

[66] *Women in Arms*. Written and directed: Mary Elizabeth Burke-Kennedy. Cast: Kate Hogan, Kay Ray Malone, Melody McNamara, Bairbre ní Chaoime, Pat Nolan, Robert Byrne, Gerry McGrath. Design: Robert Armstrong. Lighting: Gerry Maher (Storytellers Theatre Company: John Player Theatre, Dublin, opened September 1988).

[67] *Women in Arms*. Written and directed: Mary Elizabeth Burke-Kennedy. Cast: Cathy Belton, Iseult Golden, Simone Kirby, Síle Nic Chonaonaigh, Ciaran McIntyre, Aidan Kelly, Simon O'Gorman. Set Design: Bláithín Sheerin. Costume Design: Catherine Fay. Lighting Design: Nick McCall (Storytellers Theatre Company and Cork Opera House: The Civic Theatre, Tallaght, Dublin, opened 9 April 2002). I attended the preview performance on 8 April.

86   Women and Embodied Mythmaking in Irish Theatre

retelling of the myths of the Ulster Cycle, which focuses on the female characters, Nessa, Macha, Deirdre and Maeve, and their pivotal role in the events of *The Táin*, as well as their attempts to reshape the spaces which contain their expression of agency.

Where the unaccommodating space of the domestic home is the setting for the unhomely experience in *Mrs Sweeney*, *Women in Arms* is concerned with unloosing the gendered coordinates which have been mapped onto a landscape that aligns the female body with the nation, fertility and nature. This unhomely landscape shapes the bodies and lives of all the characters as the actors 'are connected not just by chronology of plot, but by the texture of the landscape'.[68] Burke-Kennedy suggests that the 'play came out of the landscape':[69] a notion that is embodied by the fusion of the actors' bodies, both as people and 'extensions of the landscape'.[70] Richard Kearney maintains that the myth of the motherland of Ireland gained force from the eighteenth century: 'The more colonially oppressed the Irish became in historical reality the more spiritualized became the mythic ideal of the Motherland.'[71] Here we see the construction of binaries: myth/history, male/female, coloniser/colonized, oppositions that are put into play in *Women in Arms*. The unhomely experience which results from these hierarchical binaries is captured by Gore-Booth in her poem 'To Maeve' as the poet laments that Maeve's brave deeds are now retold as weakness and that her story is buried in the landscape:

> They have buried thy golden deeds under the cairn on the hill,
> [. . .]
> The sea lies dreaming about thee, even the mountains are dumb.[72]

The landscape becomes cloying and deadening when it merely perpetuates ideological interpretations of myths and denies the experiences of 'real' women. However, in Gore-Booth's plays the landscape opens up pluralizing futures through the provision of spaces which refuse to perpetuate binary identities (see Chapters 1 and 5), and *Women in Arms* similarly questions the notion of 'nature' and bodies as fixed and stable in their meanings. The women harness the fluidity of boundaries to negotiate space and expose the contingency of power. *Women in Arms* offers a corporeal reclamation of the Ulster cycle myths, enabling the women to take control

---

[68] 'Note to Performers', *Women in Arms*, in *Seen and Heard: Six New Plays by Irish Women*, ed. Cathy Leeney (Dublin: Carysfort Press, 2001), p. 4.
[69] 'Afterword', *Women in Arms*, in *Seen and Heard*, p. 47.
[70] *Women in Arms*, in *Seen and Heard*, p. 5.   [71] Kearney, *Myth and Motherland*, p. 20.
[72] Gore-Booth, 'To Maeve', in *Poems of Eva Gore-Booth*, p. 195.

of both their stories and bodies, and to disrupt perpetuated models of femininity which deny their embodied experiences. Like the Inghinidhe na hÉireann's tableaux vivants, the inevitability of the mythic frame is countered by the women's energy in performance and the refusal of stillness in the key *gestus* of their stories. However, the realization of 'other *possible* worlds' is tempered by the constraints of the women's present world, as well as, in the cases of Nessa and Maeve, their complicity with patriarchal structures; these constraints are vividly exposed by the Brechtian storytelling.

Brechtian Storytelling

Storytelling is fundamental to Storytellers Theatre Company's artistic policy: 'Exploring "stories" in terms of fable, fiction and falsehood', as well as '[t]he desire to revisit and revitalise classic, neglected or forgotten texts'.[73] In his book *On Stories*, Richard Kearney describes storytelling as a means of offering new perspectives on the world which can have a profound effect on the audience: 'So that when we return from the story-world to the real world, our sensibility is enriched and amplified in important aspects.'[74] Kearney highlights the ethical capacity of storytelling and thus its vital importance within society as 'narrative is an open-ended invitation to ethical and poetic responsiveness'.[75] *Women in Arms* requires the active participation of the audience who are made aware of the multi-perspectival view of storytelling in the Prologue. The published script (2001) opens with a multiplicity of voices competing to be heard as each actor tries to assert their version of the ensuing story:

MACHA: One time . . .
DEIRDRE: Once, there was . . .
CONCHOBAR: Now in those days . .
MAEVE: Upon a time . . .
FERGUS: Now there was once . . .
NESSA: Then there was the . . .
    They keep repeating their lines, letting their voices mingle. As the voices build to a gentle climax, Naoise cuts through them.
NAOISE: Now once.[76]

---

[73] www.storytellerstheatrecompany.com/artistic.html [Accessed 27 October 2008]. The company ceased operations in 2009 due to Arts Council funding cuts and the website is no longer available. However, the company's archive is open to public access at the Dublin City Library and Archive.
[74] Richard Kearney, *On Stories* (London: Routledge, 2002), p. 133.
[75] Kearney, *On Stories*, p. 156.   [76] *Women in Arms*, in *Seen and Heard*, p. 5.

88   Women and Embodied Mythmaking in Irish Theatre

This Prologue was omitted in the 2002 production; instead, the four women stepped forward from the male actors to confront traditional versions of the myths through their assertion that 'the women were not silenced'.[77] The Prologue underscores how myth is perpetuated by a 'Darwinism of words'[78] and makes the audience aware of their participation in this process of selection. The role of the audience is further emphasized in Nessa's story as she inquires: 'You mean the story isn't over yet? We're all part of it?'[79] The continual and unending process of creating and recreating myths is self-reflexively underlined. Burke-Kennedy was very conscious of the audience's role in the perpetuation of myth and this was articulated for her by the myth of the monastic scribes committing *The Táin* to paper. The audience, like the scribes who visited Fergus's grave, act as witnesses for the cast who, like Fergus, appear out of the landscape and tell the story.[80] They are both witnesses and interpreters who contrive in the creation and generation of the power of myth.

The physical performance style of Storytellers Theatre Company is characterized by minimal use of props and set, instead using the body to evoke these as well as multiple characters. *Curigh the Shape Shifter*, produced by The Focus Theatre for the 1980 Dublin Theatre Festival, offers an earlier example of the company's deployment of this style to retell mythical stories. In ancient, pre-Christian Ireland official storytellers, or *scealai*, were the focal means for the dissemination of myths.[81] Burke-Kennedy's intention was to return to the spontaneity and fluidity of the oral form of storytelling, as well as exposing the ideological nature of myth: in Early Christian Ireland, monastic scribes committed the myths to page and this inevitably shaped the stories to reflect their Christian values.[82] In *Women in*

---

[77] *Women in Arms*, in *Seen and Heard*, p. 5.

[78] Hans Blumenberg, *Work on Myth*, trans. by Robert M. Wallace (Massachusetts: The MIT Press, 1985), p. xx.

[79] *Women in Arms*, in *Seen and Heard*, p. 12.

[80] Personal Interview with Mary Elizabeth Burke-Kennedy, 25 July 2002: 'There is a story about how the Ulster Cycle and The Táin in particular was accessed. A certain number of monks went to the tomb of Fergus and put what was called an enforcement on it, in other words they fasted around the tomb for three days and three nights. At the end of the third day/night he appeared to them in the form of a great mist and over the succeeding days and nights told them the story of The Táin and they wrote it down. In this production the audience is acting as an enforcement on the cast, and the cast or characters come out of their burial mound and they tell the story.'

[81] Patricia Lysaght, 'Traditional Storytelling in Ireland in the Twentieth Century', in *Traditional Storytelling Today: An International Sourcebook*, ed. Margaret Read MacDonald (London: Fitzroy Dearborn, 1999), pp. 264–72 (p. 264).

[82] See Maire Herbert, 'Celtic Heroine? The Archaeology of the Deirdre Story', in *Gender in Irish Writing*, ed. David Cairns and Toni O'Brien Johnson (Milton Keynes: Open University Press, 1991), pp. 13–22.

Arms the body offers an alternative source for the dissemination of myths: one which enables the expression of stories and experiences that have been elided. However, this is not an essentialist body and it is through the use of Brechtian techniques that the play underlines the role of the body in representation.

Burke-Kennedy deliberately eschews realism, adopting a Brechtian approach to articulate the unheard voices of the women: 'I wanted to retell these stories from this perspective, and looked for a fresh theatrical idiom in which to present them, free from the shackles of naturalism, poetic drama, or pageant.'[83] Burke-Kennedy draws on the conventions of Brecht's epic theatre in order to expose the illusion of the body, myth and gender as natural and inherent. Brecht proposed the 'alienation effect' as a means of effecting defamiliarization and creating a critical distance whereby the audience 'adopt an attitude of inquiry and criticism'.[84] *Women in Arms* utilizes the Brechtian A-effect as the actors are both characters and narrators: they step out of character to narrate one another's, and their own, stories, as well as directly addressing the audience with reported speech. This prevents audience identification with the characters to encourage critique of the ways in which power is wielded. Dialogue and narration seamlessly merge in the play to reveal the mechanics of storytelling, thereby forcing the audience to question their own positions and objectivity, as well as acknowledging the presence of a multiplicity of versions and experiences. Furthermore, the landscape and nature are fluidly recreated through the actors' bodies to become entities in process and man-made structures are similarly deconstructed: the actors create the 'natural' world to evoke the contingency of 'the landscapes of the imagined past'.[85]

Brecht suggests that the audience's critical stance is achieved through the actor's investment in a 'definite gest of showing'[86] and Elin Diamond's seminal work on the potential for a 're-radicalization of [Brecht's] theory through feminism'[87] highlights the consequences of this showing: 'When gender is alienated or foregrounded, the spectator is able to see what s/he can't see: a sign system *as* a sign system.'[88] *Women in Arms* is concerned with exposing the structures which perpetuate myths of femininity and

---

[83] *Women in Arms*, in *Seen and Heard*, p. 47.

[84] Bertolt Brecht, *Brecht on Theatre: The Development of an Aesthetic*, ed. and trans. by John Willett (London: Methuen, 1978), p. 136.

[85] Cathy Leeney, Programme Note for *Women in Arms*, Civic Theatre Tallaght, Dublin. Directed by Mary Elizabeth Burke-Kennedy. Opened 9 April 2002.

[86] Brecht, *Brecht on Theatre*, p. 136.   [87] Diamond, *Unmaking Mimesis*, p. 45.

[88] Diamond, *Unmaking Mimesis*, p. 47.

90 Women and Embodied Mythmaking in Irish Theatre

silence women's embodied experiences, and thus offers what Diamond has described as a gestic feminist criticism which 'would "alienate" or foreground those moments in a playtext when social attitudes about gender and sexuality conceal or disrupt patriarchal ideology'.[89]

Gestus and Reshaping Space

The actors' roles as characters and narrators serves as a 'gest of showing' for the audience which both exposes how representation is controlled and enables the women to utilize the process of theatricality to stage their own stories. Furthermore, the construction of an accommodating space is central to all four women's creation of agency within the worlds they inhabit, and the mutual reshaping of body and space is captured in a key *gestus* in each of the women's stories. The first story in the play is that of Nessa, an inquisitive and intelligent young girl, initially called Essa, who visits the court of Fergus. Fergus's court has no time for intellectual pursuits and is more interested in drinking and fighting. Essa very much feels the outsider when she visits and this is underlined by her ignorance of the Story of the Pig-keepers, as well as her 'aloofness' from the other women. Her identity and her relationship with the space she occupies are corporeally evoked by the other actors' bodies. The opening of her story introduces her as Essa, 'meaning gentle or docile',[90] and the other actors form a cloister round her to suggest the secure and protected space which she inhabits. The fluid boundaries of body and space then shift to break up the cloister and create Fergus's court.

The set of the 2002 production was sparse with just a raised circle placed stage left and tilted towards the audience, which was used to suggest both interior spaces such as Fergus's court but also to frame iconic scenes. Essa is a solitary figure seated on the raised circle, while the other actors evoke Fergus's court by dancing in a circle on the other side of the stage. Fergus wants to impress Essa but he is also urged by one of his men to '(t)each her a proper lesson',[91] betraying the court's disregard for Essa's knowledge and the violent imposition of their education. Fergus does this through a sexually suggestive action, when he swallows a sword and '*gyrates ecstatically*'.[92] In the 2002 production, this was a more explicit violation as the inference was that Essa had been raped: she lay in the centre of the court with her legs flung wide by Fergus and surrounded by his men who were thumping the floor in encouragement. Essa is horrified and her stay at

---

[89] Diamond, *Unmaking Mimesis*, p. 54.   [90] *Women in Arms*, in *Seen and Heard*, p. 6.
[91] *Women in Arms*, in *Seen and Heard*, p. 8.   [92] *Women in Arms*, in *Seen and Heard*, p. 9.

Unhomely Bodies

the court is described as 'an interminable ordeal' and the actors once more '*form the cloister around her again, urgently trying to protect her*'.[93]

On her return home, Essa's naivety is further dispelled by her discovery that her home and her twelve loyal tutors have been burnt to the ground. Her experience of losing the secure space of home is corporeally evoked by the 'crumbling' of the actors who form her cloister so that she is instead surrounded by a circle of dead bodies, a burial mound. Nick McCall's lighting design for the 2002 production, utilized harsh white lighting to reveal the actors frozen into positions which expressed their pain but Essa compassionately eased them into a more comfortable position, laying her tutors to rest. She is distraught but motivated to seek revenge by the apparent powerlessness of her position: 'There was nothing she – a woman – could do in the circumstances. Especially if the king had been at the back of it. *(Screams)* Revenge! Revenge!'[94] The destruction of her home exposes her unhomely position within a society that limits her agency. Her resolve to seek revenge is motivated by the thought provoked at Fergus's court, that society will not allow her an active role as a woman. Her frustration and determination are expressed through her scream; a moment of phenomenal import which articulates how she is unable to adequately express herself within Fergus's court. However, during the following months, as she tries to lead and encourage her soldiers, she realizes that she has to work within the system which has so angered her. She does so by changing her identity to become unrelenting and strong: 'They changed her name to Nessa – the Tough One.'[95] This change in identity is reflected in her changed body and the reshaped space that she inhabits.

In Thomas Kinsella's translation of *The Táin*, Nessa is referred to in the opening of Conchobar's story of 'how he took the kingship of Ulster',[96] but only as his mother and therefore an element of plot-space. In contrast, Burke-Kennedy focuses on the story of a strong, resolute and wily woman. Nessa's ability to insert herself into the power structures of Fergus's world is made clear as she '*takes over Fergus's throne*'.[97] In the 2002 production, Nessa negotiates a position of power for herself on the terms of the patriarchal court: she uses her sexuality and offers to 'indulge' Fergus in exchange for her son Conchobar's rule as king of Ulster for one year.[98]

---

[93] *Women in Arms*, in *Seen and Heard*, p. 9.   [94] *Women in Arms*, in *Seen and Heard*, p. 10.

[95] *Women in Arms*, in *Seen and Heard*, p. 11.

[96] Thomas Kinsella, *The Táin* (Oxford: Oxford University Press, 1970), p. 3.

[97] *Women in Arms*, in *Seen and Heard*, p. 13.

[98] Unpublished script for 2002 production of *Women in Arms*, ITA/258/01/11, p. 19 (Storytellers Theatre Company Archive, Dublin City Library and Archive).

92   Women and Embodied Mythmaking in Irish Theatre

Thereafter, she stands behind all that Conchobar will do throughout the play, as indicated by her role as the puppeteer: '*NESSA stands on the throne with CONCHOBAR. He sits in front of her. She controls him from above as if he were a puppet.*'[99] Nessa shapes Conchobar's court in contrast to Fergus's court as she benefits the community with civilizing policies which include the building of three houses in Emain Macha: one to house 'civilized entertainment' rather than orgies, a second to house weapons and a third to drink in. She also '"invited" the women to take instruction'.[100]

Nessa has successfully created space for herself in a society which initially tried to exclude her, but this is at the expense of relinquishing elements of her identity. This is reflected in a *gestus* through which Nessa's remodelling of space reflects her experiences as she 'restored her cloister for herself and no-one would threaten it again'.[101] In the 2002 production the first cloister was presented as an embracing space with the other actors facing Essa in a semi-circle, whereas the second cloister was constructed by the other actors in a much more confrontational stance, facing the audience in a V-shape with Nessa at the apex. This changed space is reflective of Nessa's newly espoused individualism and pursuit of power, and is reinforced by her final line: 'Nor could she recall anything about herself at the time when she had been their Essa.'[102] Nessa's complicity with the patriarchal court is suggested by her presence throughout all the stories which follow: she stands at Conchobar's side during Macha's and Deirdre's ordeals. Her story exposes how bodies and space interact to create and deny positions of power, and that all bodies bear the traces of their embodied experience.

Just as Nessa emerges from her outsider status to become a controlling force in the court, in the next story we see Macha negotiate a place for herself. However, where Nessa enters into the public realm of power, Macha enters into the private world of the family to gain control in what is traditionally seen as the feminine realm of the hearth. The stage directions at the opening of Macha's story state that Macha surveys Cruinniuc's family and '*decides she wants them*'.[103] Her active decision puts her in a position of power and this, together with her entry as a mysterious 'shadow' which 'fell across them from his open doorway',[104] echoes Yeats's and Gregory's *Kathleen Ni Houlihan*. In the 2002 production, the sons traced Macha's shadow on the ground to suggest their engagement

---

[99] *Women in Arms*, in *Seen and Heard*, p. 14.   [100] *Women in Arms*, in *Seen and Heard*, p. 15.
[101] *Women in Arms*, in *Seen and Heard*, p. 15.   [102] *Women in Arms*, in *Seen and Heard*, p. 15.
[103] *Women in Arms*, in *Seen and Heard*, p. 16.   [104] *Women in Arms*, in *Seen and Heard*, p. 17.

Unhomely Bodies

with her as an icon, rather than as a woman. The construction of woman as mysterious and threatening is further emphasized by Macha's initial silence. Macha takes on the position of mother and wife in the household but her husband Cruinniuc betrays his promise not to talk about Macha to anyone. At a festival the men attend he boasts that she could run faster than the king's horses, so Macha is compelled to take part in a world of machismo and to race against the horses. She gives birth at the finish line after winning the race, and curses the men of Ulster – as Anna McMullan suggests: 'transforming the traditional suffering of women into a powerful weapon'.[105]

Macha's experiences are portrayed in a powerful phenomenal *gestus* when she silently screams as she gives birth and the import of this *gestus* was heightened in the 2002 production by the unforgiving white lighting employed at this key moment. In a tableau which echoes Brecht's *Mother Courage and Her Children*, the stage directions specify that Macha should not actually scream but the other actors cover their ears at the imagined sound, recoiling in horror as they too are forced to share her pain both in the immediate moment and in the future, due to the curse. It is an affective moment in which the audience can share Macha's unhomely experience of having to negotiate a position of power for herself within the constraints of a patriarchal family and world of bravado and machismo. In Thomas Kinsella's translation of *The Táin*, 'The Pangs of Ulster' emphasizes the impact of the episode on subsequent events in Ulster, rather than on Macha herself. In *Women in Arms*, Macha's experience is corporealized into a silent scream which also portrays the silencing of alternative female-centred versions of *The Táin*.

On returning home with Cruinniuc's family after the race, Macha is clearly seen in a position of power as head of the house: the sons '*creep up to her again – soberly*',[106] at the hearthplace in an attempt to ingratiate themselves with her. The extent to which Macha is able to use the power of the mother in the Irish household to her advantage depends on the closing scenes of her story. In the 2001 published script, in contrast to her muted expression at the start of the story and her silent scream, Macha ends the story by asserting her importance and voice within Ulster's history as she stridently steps forward and says, '[b]ut she left her curse behind her'.[107]

---

[105] Anna McMullan, 'Gender, Authorship and Performance in Contemporary Irish Women Playwrights', in *Theatre Stuff: Critical Essays in Contemporary Irish Theatre*, ed. Eamonn Jordan (Dublin: Carysfort Press, 2000), pp. 34–46 (p. 37).
[106] *Women in Arms*, in *Seen and Heard*, p. 21. [107] *Women in Arms*, in *Seen and Heard*, p. 21.

94   Women and Embodied Mythmaking in Irish Theatre

However, the 2002 production emphasized how her place within the family was stifling her:

MAEVE: She kept house for them and looked after them well. She never rebuked them.
CRUINNIUC: They never heard her word, good or bad. For she never spoke again.[108]

The final tableau of Macha, sitting in silence by the hearth with her sons gathered around her could be read as simply the smothering imposition of the role of mother. Yet, we can also see this moment as a rejection of the disembodied, idealized mother if we acknowledge how her embodied experiences reshape the space of the home to accommodate her role as a strong woman in control, whose suffering will reverberate into the future.

The third story in *Women in Arms*, that of Deirdre, was one of the most commonly told of the Ulster Cycle myths and has therefore been susceptible to the most reinvention. Several playwrights of the early twentieth century, including Yeats and Synge, turned to Deirdre who, as C.L. Innes notes, 'forms a contrast with the typical male hero favoured by Irish cultural nationalists [. . .] Deirdre is passive and sorrowing, Cuchulain is active and aggressive.'[109] Burke-Kennedy's version allows us to see Deirdre from an early age and to gain some insight into her character prior to the events concerning Conchobar and Naoise that follow. Cathbad the Druid had prophesied that Deirdre's threatening beauty 'would be the destruction of Ulster'.[110] In response to the prophecy, many demanded her death but Conchobar undertakes to care for her and she is raised in the woods, away from society. She is hidden away from the court and aligned with nature as a threatening and uncontrollable force. The fluid boundaries of the set, props and actors' bodies reveal the contingent nature of the construction of power through control of discourse and space: '*To the set have been added tall spindly tree shapes. These serve to create the wood, Deirdre's prison, spears of the warriors.*'[111] Conchobar attempts to control and contain her as he tries to keep her as an untainted and idealized virginal cipher:

CONCHOBAR: What kind of silly talk is this? Do you know you sound like a tawdry serving girl, fit for nothing but gossip and fornication. Why do you

---

[108] Unpublished script for 2002 production of *Women in Arms*, ITA/258/01/11, p. 29.
[109] Innes, *Woman and Nation in Irish Literature and Society*, p. 34.
[110] *Women in Arms*, in *Seen and Heard*, p. 22.   [111] *Women in Arms*, in *Seen and Heard*, p. 22.

Unhomely Bodies

think I've had you educated out here by yourself? So as to keep your head clear of such stupid vulgarity.[112]

His desire to educate and own her echoes Fergus's desire for Essa. The 2002 production isolated Deirdre from the other actors as she opened her story downstage and they turned to listen to her from the raised circle of the set. She was constantly watched and when the other actors took up the narration of her prophecy, Deirdre crouched with her face turned down. The production revealed Deidre under the gaze of Conchobar in a *gestus* which clearly depicted her idealization as she knelt down to admire the leaping salmon. However, Conchobar stood behind Deirdre who was front-lit so that the audience was implicated in Conchobar's gaze and forced to look at her as an idealized icon of beauty and male desire. The audience's awareness of the pleasure and discomfort of this gaze ensures that this moment 'connotes not "to-be-looked-at-ness" – the perfect fetish – but rather "looking-at-being-looked-at-ness" or even just "looking-ness"'.[113]

Despite Conchobar's efforts to deny Deirdre any engagement with society, she takes her story into her own hands and decides to leave the old fortress where she has been held. On her journey she hears the sound of approaching hoof-beats so she hides in some woods close to Conchobar's seat of Emain Macha, and it is at this moment that she meets Naoise and, as prophesized, they fall in love. Conchobar is, of course, furious when he realizes that Deirdre has rejected him for one of his men and, just as Deirdre spent her early life on the outskirts of society, she is exiled to Scotland with Naoise and his brothers. Later, Conchobar tricks them into coming home, claiming that all is forgiven and forgotten, and Naoise agrees as he misses the court and feels 'the need to compete; the need to fight'.[114] In contrast, Deirdre is suspicious and her foreboding is realized when Naoise is killed on their return. Once more Deirdre's body is contained and controlled within the space which Conchobar has designated for her as he decides that she will spend alternate six-month periods with himself and Eoin, who stabbed Naoise: 'that will bring colour back to your cheeks'.[115] Another of Conchobar's suggestive remarks proves to be the last straw for Deirdre. They are travelling on a chariot to a fair and he remarks to Deirdre, standing between himself and Eoin: 'There you are now, my darling, a ewe between two rams.'[116] Deirdre decides to take

---

[112] *Women in Arms*, in *Seen and Heard*, p. 24.   [113] Diamond, *Unmaking Mimesis*, p. 52.
[114] *Women in Arms*, in *Seen and Heard*, p. 30.   [115] *Women in Arms*, in *Seen and Heard*, p. 32.
[116] *Women in Arms*, in *Seen and Heard*, p. 32.

96   Women and Embodied Mythmaking in Irish Theatre

control in the only available way: she kills herself by leaping out of the chariot and dashing her head against a rock. Her impotence is conveyed by this act and the 2002 production emphasized the 'unheroic' nature of her end through the understated performance of this key moment.

The early versions of the tale by monastic scribes imply that it is Deirdre's fault that the court is torn into disarray, as Maire Herbert points out: 'Like Eve, Deirdre had transgressed against the male authority, the king. She, too, lured a man to transgression along with her. Society could be seen to suffer turmoil and tribulation as a result.'[117] However, in *Women in Arms* Deirdre is not 'the temptress, the cause of man's downfall'[118] but, instead, is an innocent girl who through supernatural forces out of her control 'enchants' Naoise: 'The prophecy about her had come true but she was innocent.'[119] Burke-Kennedy's play exposes dishonour and Conchobar's deception as the root of the problem, with Fergus remarking: 'There is nothing worth keeping in a kingdom based on betrayal.'[120] The patriarchal order which Conchobar represents is shown to be rotten, upsetting the equilibrium between the natural and social worlds, which represented a system of complementarity between male and female in early Irish ideology.[121] This gendered alignment of female with nature, and male with culture and the social, is distorted by Conchobar to become a hierarchical binary. Through recovery of an alternative version of Deirdre's myth, *Women in Arms* rephysicalizes her story to convey her embodied experience of objectification, imprisonment and exile. Eva Gore-Booth's re-vision of Deirdre's story, *The Buried Life of Deirdre*, shares Burke-Kennedy's concern with exposing the power structures which enable these experiences and similarly undermines hierarchical binaries in the process (see Chapter 5).

The final of the four female protagonists is Maeve, a very strong-willed and proud warrior-queen who holds her own in male-dominated spheres of material and military strength. Her story sets the stage for *The Táin* as it accounts for the cattle raid's origins. The opening of the story depicts Maeve and her husband Ailill talking in bed. The 2002 production showed their contentment as they lay embracing one another until Ailill remarked to her that she has 'improved' since he married him. The other actors who formed the bedhead all turned and gasped at this remark, highlighting Maeve's anger, as she 'was who she was and always had been'.[122] Lying in

---

[117] Herbert, p. 22.   [118] Herbert, p. 21.   [119] *Women in Arms*, in *Seen and Heard*, p. 28.
[120] *Women in Arms*, in *Seen and Heard*, p. 32.   [121] Herbert, p. 18.
[122] *Women in Arms*, in *Seen and Heard*, p. 34.

Unhomely Bodies

bed, the couple were bathed in warm red lighting which was then replaced by starker white lighting as they embarked on a contest to prove who owns the most. Maeve, unlike the other female protagonists, has immense material possessions and property, and therefore holds a high position in a society which values these concerns. Ailill appears to win the contest as it is discovered that Finnbennach, the largest bull in the region, left Maeve's herd to join Ailill's as 'it wouldn't follow a woman'.[123] Maeve shows qualities of strength and leadership which merit her position as queen, so the fact that the deciding 'item' sides with Ailill reveals the 'loyalties' of the patriarchal system. Her pride is unrelenting and she is most upset by the thought that 'she was no more than a kept woman',[124] so when she hears of a bigger bull in Ulster, the Dun Bó Cúailinge, she determines to borrow it to breed an even larger bull. Her fierce belief in equality in the relationship between man and woman motivates her: 'He was the only man who really understood her. The only man who she really loved. And so it was more imperative than ever that she prove herself equal to him.'[125] However, her resolution is fired by a desire to prove herself within existing structures.

A woman in early Ireland could be a warrior and thus the myth and play justly reveal that a woman is as capable of encouraging and participating in '[f]ighting for the sake of killing'.[126] This is quite in contrast to the passive representations of woman in the nineteenth and early twentieth century. Innes argues in *Woman and Nation* that cultural nationalists' partiality for Deirdre over Maeve the warrior-queen could be explained by

> the discourse of colonialism and anti-colonialist nationalism [which] helps to produce an extreme division between what are seen as male qualities of militarism, and female qualities of passivity and submission.[127]

Of course, the tableaux vivants of the early twentieth century are testament to the appeal which Maeve held for nationalist women engaged in myth-making and the process of redefining gendered roles of militarism through their activism. In *Women in Arms*, Maeve is shown astride her chariot in a *gestus* of military power which breaks down gendered models of behaviour perpetuated by versions of the myths among early twentieth-century cultural nationalists. This was a powerful moment in the 2002 production when the other actors created the chariot around her and rhythmically rocked forwards to create a sense of relentless determination and action. In

---

[123] *Women in Arms*, in *Seen and Heard*, p. 36.   [124] *Women in Arms*, in *Seen and Heard*, p. 37.
[125] *Women in Arms*, in *Seen and Heard*, p. 39.   [126] *Women in Arms*, in *Seen and Heard*, p. 44.
[127] Innes, *Woman and Nation in Irish Literature and Society*, p. 34.

98   Women and Embodied Mythmaking in Irish Theatre

this moment, the tension between movement and stasis captures the failure to contain women's bodies in mythic icons, echoing the affect of the Inghinidhe's tableaux vivants. Furthermore, Maeve's *gestus* in the 2002 production serves as a moment of critique through its framing of contemporary feminist understandings of female agency: of the nature of Maeve's power and the implications of her assertion of it for equality between the sexes and among women.

Postfeminism and the Illusion of Empowerment

Women in Arms was first produced in 1988, following an earlier commission in 1984, and the play was subsequently developed and revived in 2002. These versions emerge from very different contexts: 1980s Ireland was characterized by mass unemployment and emigration, while Ireland was riding the wave of the Celtic Tiger boom at the turn of the twenty-first century. Presaged by the visit of Pope John Paul II in 1979, the recessionary 1980s was an era of conservativism in response to the gains of the feminist movement in the 1970s. The Pro-Life Amendment Campaign (PLAC) was established by a range of Catholic groups which sought to block progress on abortion rights by enshrining the illegality of abortion in the Constitution. In the 1983 referendum 66.9 per cent of voters voted in favour of inserting the anti-abortion clause, the Eighth Amendment. A referendum in 1986 saw 63 per cent of voters reject a proposal to remove the constitutional ban on divorce. As a result, when writing in 1984, Burke-Kennedy 'was more conscious of the political act implicit in foregrounding the women' but did not feel that it needed to be carried so consciously in the 2002 production.[128] Burke-Kennedy's comments illustrate the shifting landscape of feminism as shaped by neoliberal politics: of the postfeminist narrative of Celtic Tiger Ireland that claimed to herald opportunity and achievement for women through the accumulation of wealth, thus deeming feminism as no longer necessary. However, on closer inspection, we can see how *Women in Arms* questions Celtic Tiger Ireland's spin on feminist gains and the construction of female agency and empowerment within the context.

Burke-Kennedy has suggested that Maeve's pursuit of equality based on material gain does not necessarily offer a positive alternative to traditional models of femininity:

---

[128] Personal interview with Mary Elizabeth Burke-Kennedy, 25 July 2002.

Unhomely Bodies

The battle starts and it turns very black and nasty and it ends with their love over, Maeve's lost everything for the sake of this imagined equality. I was surprised that I haven't had more of a combative response from some feminists because that story is critical of the whole idea of the false pursuit of equality.[129]

This 'false pursuit of equality' resonates with the context of the Celtic Tiger years, where women's freedom and choice are understood as symbolically agential within the parameters of consumer culture, rather than as politicized actions. Angela McRobbie describes the displacement and substitution of feminism by late capitalism as an 'abandonment of feminism . . . [which] is amply rewarded with the promise of freedom and independence, most apparent through wage-earning capacity, which also functions symbolically, as a mark of respectability, citizenship and entitlement'.[130] Some women did indeed benefit from the Celtic Tiger, as Pat O'Connor notes of 'the widespread misperception of the gender of what has become known as the Celtic Tiger, in a situation where male employment has been virtually static and female employment has increased dramatically'.[131] Just as Maeve offered militant nationalist feminists at the start of the twentieth century a 'masculine' woman who engaged with men, partially, on their terms, Maeve the Celtic Tigress is willing to embrace the freedom promised by neoliberalism to secure her legibility: a freedom achieved at the expense of, to use McRobbie's term, the 'undoing' of feminism. Earlier in the play, Nessa is seen as willing to relinquish elements of her identity, and indeed a feminism which advocates equality among women, in order to attain the illusion of power. Her collusion with Conchobar was vividly illustrated in the 2002 production by her steadfast presence at his side throughout Macha's and Deirdre's stories. In contrast to Gore-Booth's Maeve, in *Women in Arms* Maeve supports the patriarchal system by exchanging her daughter for advancement in battle.

In his study of occupational change in Ireland during 1991–2002, Proinnsias Breathnach notes that the increase in female employment since the 1990s illustrates the inegalitarian impact of Irish economic growth, 'of an increasing professionalization and polarization of the Irish workforce, with the growth of female employment playing a key role in

---

[129] Personal interview with Mary Elizabeth Burke-Kennedy, 25 July 2002.
[130] Angela McRobbie, *The Aftermath of Feminism: Gender, Culture and Social Change* (London: Sage, 2009), p. 2.
[131] Pat O'Connor, *Emerging Voices: Women in Contemporary Irish Society* (Dublin: Institute of Public Administration, 1998), p. 256.

Women and Embodied Mythmaking in Irish Theatre

driving both these processes'.[132] The polarization of women sees Maeve as Celtic Tigress thrive at the expense of other women, whose marginalization is further embedded. In *The Aftermath of Feminism*, McRobbie references Caryl Churchill's play *Top Girls* which, though set in a different era and location – Thatcher's England in the 1980s, shares with *Women in Arms* a fierce critique of right-wing, individualist postfeminism. As managing director at the Top Girls employment agency, Marlene's perception of her equality negates her need to engage with the inequalities that prevent other women, such as her sister Joyce, from escaping the gendered limitations placed on their ability to secure opportunity and change their lives.

Within Celtic Tiger Ireland, Maeve may offer an economically empowered alternative to the myth of Irish femininity as defined by passivity and domesticity, but as McRobbie notes, 'the loss of feminism . . . creates new forms of female confinement'.[133] The consequences for women of buying the myth of empowerment, as shaped by a postfeminist and neoliberal individualist discourse, is exposed in the anti-climactic *gestus* which concluded Maeve's battles in the 2002 production. Earlier in Maeve's story, the bull Finnbennach was created by all the other actors' bodies, to suggest the immensity of his size: the largest actor formed the horns with his arms, three others made up the body and one actor stood at the back with her leg swinging to suggest the bull's swinging tail. It was an animated and lively image, quite in contrast to the anti-climax when Maeve and her troops find the Dun Bó Cúailinge, created solely by the largest actor. All the other actors formed individual bulls, dejectedly putting up their arms to suggest horns; a motionless and disappointing tableau compared to Finnbennach. Maeve's failure to achieve material parity and a 'false equality' is corporeally evoked as are the consequences of her ruthless ambition which results in bloody battle. The 2002 production concluded Maeve's story with an image of desolation as each actor fell to the ground after they delivered the final lines of her story, changing from a bull into a slain body. Maeve's territorial and acquisitive battle reveals her engagement with an individualist and materialist discourse, the very rules which Conchobar was undone by, and she fails in her pursuit of a 'false equality' on these terms. Maeve thus provides a contrast to Deirdre who shuns jealousy and possessiveness and is not willing to engage in the rules of Conchobar's world where

---

[132] Proinnsias Breathnach, 'Occupational Change and Social Polarisation in Ireland: Further evidence', *Irish Journal of Sociology*, 16:1 (2007), 22–42 (p. 40).

[133] McRobbie, p. 122.

Unhomely Bodies

ownership is paramount: 'That meant nothing to her. Owning it. Older people were always on about ownership. Just be.'[134]

At the end of Maeve's story in *Women in Arms*, she has come full circle and is seen back in her marital bed with Ailill; the myth of a postfeminist equality has resulted in the reassertion of the structures of the patriarchal home. In contrast, Gore-Booth's Maeve entertains no such compromise and refuses to engage with the court on their terms, instead she embraces a space outside of these confines.

Process and Becoming

The process of claiming space and agency are thoroughly intertwined in the women's stories and the Brechtian exposure of this enables both critique and the exploration of alternatives. These women resist exclusion, and explore alternatives, by manipulating fluid boundaries. The play stages the process of theatricality to enable the women to reclaim their representation and take control of the staging of their stories. Nessa's cloisters are invaded but she rebuilds a space for herself, while Macha reshapes her realm of hearth and home. The performing body renegotiates space to accommodate the women's reshaped identities; yet all the women have to compromise to create an enabling space within the existing order. Nessa and Macha are seen in newly defined spaces which accommodate them at the end of their stories, though their agency is qualified by its negotiation within patriarchal structures. Maeve would appear to offer the most radical challenge to traditional models of femininity, but in the 2002 production this was presented as a willingness to exchange feminist equality for individual empowerment and at the end of her story she was back in the space of her marital bed. Deirdre attempts to create space for herself in the exiled realms of the woods and Scotland but ultimately removes herself through death in a refusal to compromise.

Gore-Booth's Deirdre and Maeve radically reconfigure space but they choose to do this outside patriarchal limits, instead of working within what is available to them. What is radical about Burke-Kennedy's women is their insistence on the presence of their embodied experiences and how this reshapes existing myths of femininity and the spaces which contain them. A feminist gestic criticism exposes the constraints that limit the women, yet there is also an exhilarating sense of the potential for change and we should not underestimate the power of the performance of Nessa's, Macha's,

---

[134] *Women in Arms*, in *Seen and Heard*, p. 23.

Deirdre's and Maeve's embodied experiences to destabilize the imposition of fixed icons. The fluid physical performance style of *Women in Arms* makes clear that 'what appears in the *gestus* can only be provisional, indeterminate, nonauthoritative',[135] thereby opening up 'other *possible* worlds'. Diamond describes the Brechtian 'not ... but' as 'the theatrical and theoretical analogue to "differences within"'.[136] Burke-Kennedy's women reveal other possible ways of inhabiting and reshaping the stage space and theatrical frame which contains their story. Furthermore, the 'pleasure and significance of contradiction – and of contradictions that, at any given moment are emerging but unseeable',[137] stimulate the spectator's experience of *Women in Arms* as a multiplicity of voices. This opens up a space for the audience member's participation in the creation of 'other *possible* worlds' through the ongoing process of interrogative and embodied mythmaking.

Women in Arms is fundamentally concerned with the violence of myth, particularly for women, when it operates as a closed system of signification. The 1984 production was set in a butcher's shop and the violent undertones resonated with the conflict in Northern Ireland, but Burke-Kennedy removed this frame in the 1988 production in order to focus on the women and the emergence of their stories from the landscape. Violence and destruction underpin the story of the pig-keepers, which is referenced throughout the play. Initially the pig-keepers were friends but they listened to rumours that each was taking advantage of the other and their suspicions escalate into bloody battle which climaxes in their taking on the form of bulls who 'ripped each other to pieces'.[138]

The ending of their story is withheld until the Epilogue, which might suggest that its revelation asserts closure and the sense of a stable master narrative but the performance of the Epilogue undermines the authority of the text. The play's final embodied image of deadlock provides a powerful contrast with the fluidity of the actors' movement as they transform into different roles and the animation of a key *gestus* such as Maeve's chariot. In the published text the Epilogue presents all the actors as bulls whose horns lock in battle, while in the 2002 production the actors narrated the events that led to the battle but did not move. Both ways of staging the Epilogue therefore suggest that it is only by animating the myths with a self-awareness of cultural context that alternative worlds and interrogative myth can be evoked and the destructive nature of static symbols denied.

---

[135] Diamond, *Unmaking Mimesis*, p. 54. [136] Diamond, *Unmaking Mimesis*, p. 49.
[137] Diamond, *Unmaking Mimesis*, p. 49. [138] *Women in Arms*, in *Seen and Heard*, p. 46.

Unhomely Bodies

The actors' bodies, which have undermined any sense of stable identity and iconography, impress upon the audience that storytelling is contingent and expose myth's cultural context. Furthermore, the form of the play fosters the sense that both bodies and alternative worlds are in process and do not have to be prescriptively envisioned. Where past versions of *The Táin* dephysicalized the women as icons and repressed their corporeal experience, *Women in Arms* asserts the creative potential of the performing body and female corporeality to animate the women's stories. The energy of resistance together with the suggestion of transformation and change invigorates both *Mrs Sweeney* and *Women in Arms*, and it is to the potential of metamorphosis, of both myth and the body in process, that the next chapter turns.

CHAPTER 3

Metamorphic 'Bodies That Matter': Process and Resistance

Chapter 2 explored the relationship between theatrical form and space through unhomely bodies that reshape the environments that hinder their expression. The capacity to generate new forms is pursued further in this chapter through attention to the process of corporeal change: how the metamorphic body might refute and escape its unhomeliness. Metamorphosis can be a survival strategy and it can be a bold statement of resistance; it can expose the limits of existing structures and it can evoke a female morphology which demands expression through an alternative cultural imaginary. Ovid's *Metamorphoses* presents a variety of transformations, including violent and peaceful, liberating and incarcerating changes. These metamorphoses are sometimes punishments inflicted by the gods, when Arachne is changed into a spider by Minerva, and sometimes offer escape, when Daphne transforms into a tree to avoid being raped by her pursuer. Shape-shifting is a familiar trope in Irish mythology: the children of Lir who are turned into swans by their wicked stepmother; the selkie who sheds her seal-skin to transform from a seal to a human only to long to return to the freedom of the sea. Shape-shifting does not guarantee liberation but these protean bodies can draw attention to, and undermine, the relationship between form and the limitations it imposes.

This chapter looks at two plays, Lady Gregory's *Grania* (written 1910 and published 1912) and Marina Carr's *The Mai* (premiered in 1994), in which the central women live in exile, yet attempt to negotiate expression of their embodied subjectivity. Metamorphosis offers both myth and the body as sites of creative potential which trouble myths of femininity and enable exploration of the creation of identity through cultural signification and corporeal performance.

Metamorphosis is the ideal trope through which to explore Simone de Beauvoir's assertion that woman is 'not a completed reality, but rather a becoming',[1] as well as examining which bodies are permitted to emerge as

---

[1] de Beauvoir, *The Second Sex*, p. 66.

Metamorphic 'Bodies That Matter'

subjects within cultural signification. The idea of metamorphosis speaks to feminist theories of gendered identity as both fluid and culturally constructed. Luce Irigaray articulates woman's lack of accommodation within existing patriarchal structures through evocation of a fluid morphology which supports a female imaginary; she asks: 'How can I speak to you, who remain in flux that never congeals or solidifies?'[2] For Irigaray, the fluidity of the feminine is generative and opposes the limits imposed by the symbolic: 'Rather than being settled, stabilized, immobilized. Separated.'[3] Margaret Whitford's non-essentialist reading of Irigaray's female imaginary proposes 'something which does not yet exist, which still has to be created'.[4] The emphasis on process is reiterated by Butler's approach: 'To understand "women" as a permanent site of contest, or as feminist site of antagonistic struggle, is to presume that there can be no closure on the category, and that, for politically significant reasons, there ought never to be.'[5] For both Irigaray and Butler, process and resistance to static forms is a political imperative.

Examination of the struggle involved in the metamorphoses in *Grania* and *The Mai* affords the opportunity to examine the historical constitution of models of femininity since 'regulatory schemas are not timeless structures, but historically revisable criteria of intelligibility which produce and vanquish bodies that matter'.[6] Elizabeth Grosz's description of the 'lived body' highlights the body situated within its material and historical context:

> The body is neither brute nor passive but is interwoven with and constitutive of systems of meaning, signification, and representation. On one hand it is a signifying and signified body; on the other, it is an object of systems of social coercion, legal inscription, and sexual and economic exchange.[7]

Exploring the body as process requires acknowledgment of both the multiple possibilities of embodiment, and the precarity and risk of erasure that attends its expression: 'It cannot be simply taken for granted as an accomplished fact, for it must be continually renewed.'[8] Both *Grania* and *The Mai* expose the material effects of the dominant structures of power on

---

[2] Luce Irigaray, 'When Our Lips Speak Together', trans. by Carolyn Burke, *Signs*, 6:1 (Autumn 1980), 69–79 (p. 76).

[3] Irigaray, 'When Our Lips Speak Together', p. 77.

[4] Margaret Whitford, *Luce Irigaray: Philosophy in the Feminine* (London and New York: Routledge, 1991), p. 89.

[5] Judith Butler, *Bodies That Matter: On the Discursive Limits of Sex* (London: Routledge, 1993), p. 221.

[6] Butler, *Bodies That Matter*, p. 14.   [7] Grosz, *Volatile Bodies*, p. 18.

[8] Grosz, *Volatile Bodies*, pp. 43–4.

106   Women and Embodied Mythmaking in Irish Theatre

the material body, as well as the efforts towards, and possibilities for, renewal; both playwrights convey the experiences of the lived and desiring female body to invigorate their mythmaking.

Fundamental to my discussion of metamorphosis is an assessment of the difficulty of effecting transformation within a landscape of deep-rooted ideas and inflexible structures. In *Gender Trouble*, Butler's theory of performativity highlights the embodiment of the effects of power, yet also suggests the body's mutability through 'subversive repetition' which allows for the 'immanent possibility of contesting' the constitution of identity.[9] In her subsequent work, *Bodies That Matter*, Butler clarifies that performativity is not to be confused with performance and free will granted to the subject, instead it is a 'reiterative and citational practice by which discourse produces the effects it names'.[10] *Bodies That Matter* places greater emphasis on the difficulty of stimulating change through discussion of bodies that are not permitted to emerge as subjects within cultural signification. This question is central to my analysis of two plays which emerge from very different periods at either end of the twentieth century. While I draw on Irigaray's advocation of a creative female corporeality which evokes a female imaginary, I also look to Butler's definition of the construction of both the material body and gender through the process of materialization as the 'acquisition of being through the citing of power'.[11] Butler's attention is focused on those bodies which fail to signify or matter, and are delegitimated and abjected at the boundaries of the dominant social order; banished to 'those "unliveable" and "uninhabitable" zones'.[12] The cultural production of abjection results in the deeming of certain bodies and lives as unliveable, but Butler argues that they remain a disruptive force: 'It is not as if the unthinkable, the unliveable, the unintelligible has no discursive life; it *does* have one. It just lives within discourse as the radically uninterrogated and as the shadowy contentless figure for something that is not yet made real.'[13] What happens when this figure is made real and interrogated? How might the bodies in *Grania* and *The Mai* emerge from these unliveable zones to assert themselves as metamorphic bodies that matter? Can inhabiting a creative female corporeality support the process of taking control of the shaping of one's own life in order for the 'not yet' to be 'made real'?

---

[9] Butler, *Gender Trouble*, p. 201.   [10] Butler, *Bodies That Matter*, p. 2.
[11] Butler, *Bodies That Matter*, p. 15.   [12] Butler, *Bodies That Matter*, p. 3.
[13] Irene Costera Meijer and Baukje Prins, 'How Bodies Come to Matter: An Interview with Judith Butler', *Signs*, 23:2 (1998), 275–86 (p. 281).

Transitional Places

In *Fantastic Metamorphoses, Other Worlds*, Marina Warner suggests that 'it is characteristic of metamorphic writing to appear in transitional places'[14] and this is certainly borne out in the exploration of the material realities of women's lives in both *Grania* and *The Mai*. Lady Gregory wrote *Grania* in 1910, an era which saw Irish women play a vital role in many political and cultural movements, including the cultural revival, emerging nationalist organizations, and the women's suffrage movement which was gaining momentum. Gregory's own position was complex as she had to reconcile her status as a member of the Anglo-Irish gentry (she was the youngest daughter of the Persse family and married Sir William Henry Gregory) with her role as a leading force of the Irish cultural nationalist movement.

The space opened up by shifting and competing discourses enable Grania, and indeed Gregory herself, to negotiate a complex position which incorporates apparently contradictory positions. In *Grania*, Gregory draws on the Irish myths of the Fianna cycle, focusing on the tripartite relationship between Grania, Finn – whom she is to marry – and Diarmuid, whom Grania has fallen in love with. Diarmuid is Finn's most loyal and trusted comrade and thus the play charts the power struggle between the three: the battle to assert either patriarchal bonds or a freer definition of sexuality and gender.

The play was published in 1912 but it was never performed at the Abbey, nor has it received a professional production in Ireland to date. In her biography of Gregory, Mary Lou Kohfeldt suggests that the play was not staged as 'Augusta told more about herself in *Grania* than she wanted known': the relationship between Grania and Diarmuid echoed Gregory's affair with Wilfrid Scawen Blunt.[15] However, as Richard Allen Cave argues, Gregory had offered the title role to Sara Allgood and intended that the play should go into rehearsal.[16] Cave points to the modernity of the play with its focus on passion and sexual longing, and that as it was authored by a woman, a production in 1912 would surely have been greeted with outrage akin to that received by Synge's *The Playboy of the Western World*. Cathy Leeney places discussion of the play within the context of the

---

[14] Marina Warner, *Fantastic Metamorphoses, Other Worlds* (Oxford: Oxford University Press, 2002), pp. 17–18.

[15] Mary Lou Kohfeldt, *Lady Gregory: The Woman Behind the Irish Renaissance* (London: Deutsch, 1985), p. 216.

[16] Richard Allen Cave, 'The Dangers and Difficulties of Dramatising the Lives of Deirdre and Grania', in *Perspectives of Irish Drama and Theatre*, ed. Jacqueline Genet and Richard Allen Cave (Gerrard's Cross: Colin Smythe, 1991), pp. 1–16 (p. 11).

emerging figure of the New Woman from the late nineteenth century and notes that Yeats dissuaded Gregory from seeking an Abbey production: 'It seems he recognised Grania as part of the contemporary theatrical canon of powerful women's roles in now classic realist plays which had shocked audiences in performances featuring exceptional actresses across Europe and North America.'[17] Grania embodies the clash of feminism with nationalism and patriarchy but, through her exploration of her embodiment and metamorphosis, Grania finds a way to insert herself into a world of male desire and violence as epitomized by Finn and Diarmuid's relationship.

In Act One, Grania is set up as a sovereignty figure whose marriage to Finn is claimed to be for the good of Ireland but Finn's attitude towards her changes when he discovers Grania and Diarmuid's feelings for one another. The lovers are exiled to woods on the outskirts of society and Diarmuid promises Finn that he and Grania will remain celibate, thus reasserting their homoerotic bonds. Act Two is set in the woods which are constructed as an abject space in relation to the court and it is here that we witness the expression of Grania's sexuality. However, Grania wants to be able to celebrate their relationship within the structures of society and return to Finn's court at Almhuin. In the final act of the play, news of Diarmuid's injury in battle initially sets Grania and Finn up in a power struggle to claim their relationship with Diarmuid as the dominant one. Finn asserts the homoerotic bonds of male love and violence, while Grania realizes that she will need to adopt the role of queen once again in order to insert herself between Finn and Diarmuid, engaging with the structures of society to disturb the male system of relationships. She therefore undertakes to reshape her destiny and decides to 'battle it out to the end'[18] with Finn. Grania's choice of metaphor reveals her aim to unsettle the alliance of violence, power and signification with men as she attempts to negotiate a place for herself in Finn's court. Just as Gregory negotiated a role in Irish cultural politics which utilized her Ascendancy confidence, at the end of the play Grania embraces her queenly role and her departure offstage silences the mocking laughter of the Fianna. Grania's final exit as metamorphosis sees her manipulate her role as queen and an icon of nation circulated among men, to become an agent with control of her own signification. The extent to which Grania's metamorphosis registers as a radical act is a question I return to through comparative analysis of both plays.

---

[17] Leeney, *Irish Women Playwrights, 1900–1939*, p. 44.   [18] Gregory, *Grania*, p. 214.

Metamorphic 'Bodies That Matter'

Where *Grania* emerges from the competing discourses of the early decades of the twentieth century, the transitional period from which The Mai's metamorphosis materializes is the latter end of the century. *The Mai* (premiere 1994)[19] is a memory play narrated in the present by Millie, now a 30-year-old woman, who charts her own transition into adulthood as she looks back to events that occurred when she was 16 years old. Millie is haunted by her mother The Mai's decision to drown herself and the reach of history further structures the play through the inclusion of four generations of women from Millie's family: Grandma Fraochlán is 100 years old, her daughters are in their 70s, and The Mai and her sisters are in their 30s. Across these generations, and thus the twentieth century, Irish female corporeality has been the site for the construction of an idealized femininity which supports nostalgic tropes of Irish cultural identity, rather than an experience of embodied subjectivity. In 'Homelysexuality and the "Beauty" Pageant', Fintan Walsh outlines the performative construction of Irish women's sexuality through pageants such as the *Rose of Tralee*, *Calor Housewife of the Year* and *Miss Ireland* which, Walsh argues, produce a 'homelysexuality': 'a domesticated, marketable, and commercially profitable sexual accent, paradoxically devoid of eroticism, but integral to the brand concept "Irishness"'.[20] *The Mai* engages with the legacy of these concerns over the control of woman's body and expression of sexuality by national patriarchal discourse. Indeed, The Mai was born in 1939: two years after the Irish Constitution was enshrined in law and four years before Éamon de Valera's speech which famously evoked 'comely maidens dancing at the crossroads'.[21]

The action of *The Mai*, as staged through Millie's memories, is set in 1979 and thus at the end of a decade which achieved great change for the lives of Irish women. The establishment of the First Commission on the Status of Women in 1970 and the formation of the Council of the Status of

---

[19] Marina Carr, *The Mai*. Director: Brian Brady. Cast: Olwen Fouéré, Derbhle Crotty, Owen Roe, Michele Forbes, Maire Hastings, Stella McCusker, Bríd Ní Neachtain, Joan O'Hara. Music: Michael O'Suilleabhain. Lighting: Aedin Cosgrove. Set and costume: Kathy Strachan (Peacock Theatre Dublin, opened 5 October 1994).

[20] Fintan Walsh, 'Homelysexuality and the "Beauty" Pageant', in *Crossroads: Performance Studies and Irish Culture*, ed. Sara Brady and Fintan Walsh (Basingstoke: Palgrave Macmillan, 2009), pp. 196–209 (p. 197).

[21] Quoted in *Crossroads: Performance Studies and Irish Culture*, ed. Sara Brady and Fintan Walsh, p. 1. It should be noted that debate surrounds the exact wording of de Valera's speech. The version that persists in popular memory is that of the 'comely maidens dancing at the crossroads', whereas a recording of the speech reveals that he spoke of 'happy maidens' and did not mention dancing or crossroads, www.rte.ie/archives/exhibitions/eamon-de-valera/719124-address-by-mr-de-valera/ [Accessed 4 October 2017].

Women in 1972 pressed the demands of women on a range of issues, particularly in the areas of discrimination, equal pay and women in employment. Following the Council's 1973 Report, the 'marriage bar', under which women had to leave their jobs in the civil service when they got married, was lifted. A more radical and outspoken approach to advancing these demands emerged with The Irish Women's Liberation Movement (IWLM), which was established in 1970. Their manifesto, *Chains or Change*, called for: 'one family one house, removal of the marriage bar, equal pay, equal access to education, legal rights and availability of contraception'.[22]

In 1971 members of the IWLM travelled to Belfast by train in order to buy contraceptives in protest against the ban of their sale in the Republic. The 'contraceptive train' forced discussion of family planning, as did the landmark case concerning Mary McGee – a mother of four with a history of toxaemia in pregnancy which could have potentially fatal complications – who had the contraceptives she had ordered from England on medical advice seized by customs. McGee's legal challenge was upheld in 1973 when the Supreme Court ruled that married couples had a constitutional right to make private decisions on family planning. The ruling did not mean that contraceptives could be sold but it forced the government to confront, and legislate for, family planning. The Health and Family Planning Act of 1979 gave married couples access to contraception with a doctor's prescription.[23] Charles Haughey, then Taoiseach, described the Act as 'an Irish solution to an Irish problem'; a turn of phrase which has come to mean an unsatisfactory compromise which sidesteps the fundamental issue. Ireland's accession to the European Economic Community in 1973 was crucial for those lobbying for women's rights and seeking change in Irish law. European directives resulted in legislation on equal pay in 1974 and the Employment Equality Act of 1977.

Despite the gains of the 1970s, the intervening years between the action of *The Mai* in 1979 and Millie's narration in the 1990s, was one largely defined by conservative backlash during the economic recession of the 1980s. Following a referendum in 1983, the insertion of the Eighth Amendment into the Constitution of Ireland explicitly protected 'the right to life of the unborn'. This effectively placed a ban on abortion

---

[22] Linda Connolly, *The Irish Women's Movement: From Revolution to Devolution* (Basingstoke: Palgrave Macmillan, 2002), p. 118.

[23] Diarmaid Ferriter, *Occasions of Sin: Sex and Society in Modern Ireland* (London: Profile, 2009), p. 423.

Metamorphic 'Bodies That Matter'

which was repealed on 25 May 2013. In 1984, a 15-year-old girl named Ann Lovett died alongside her stillborn baby in a field in front of a grotto dedicated to the Virgin Mary in Granard, County Longford. The brutal consequences of the disparity between idealized myths of femininity and women's lived realities could not be starker. The election of Mary Robinson as President in 1990 pointed to a decade of more positive, though qualified, change for women. *The Mai* premiered in 1994, a period when the issue of abortion had come to the fore once more following the X Case in 1992 when a 14-year-old suicidal pregnant rape victim was initially denied the right to travel to England to obtain an abortion. Referenda on three constitutional amendments were held in 1992: voters rejected the threat of suicide as grounds on which to allow abortion but ratified amendments which would allow women free access to information and freedom to travel to another state for an abortion. Moreover, referenda on divorce led to continued debate over the construction of woman's role as mother and wife: a 1986 referendum upheld the prohibition of divorce but this was then removed in 1995.

Millie's narration of events from the present moment is Janus-faced: as the next generation she gestures to the future, but her potential to do things differently is impeded by the hold and structures of the past. Millie's position on the cusp between past and future indicates the difficulty of making change; a position which is echoed by the impact of the Celtic Tiger on women in Ireland. In 1994, the country was entering a period of huge economic growth which would generate further change, albeit for some women. Women's role in Irish society changed enormously over the course of the twentieth century: 40 per cent of married women were in the workforce by the end of the century, compared to just 5 per cent in 1966.[24] Nonetheless, Pat O'Connor highlights the discrepancy between the changes in Irish women's material lives and the obdurate nature of the institutions of Irish society, institutions which perpetuate limiting tropes of 'woman':

> Some 'places' (e.g. families) have changed; married women have increasingly participated in others (e.g. in paid employment); and the world of education and training seems to be available to young women regardless of gender. Yet in many ways the institutional realities of the church, the state and the economic system have changed very little.[25]

---

[24] Diarmaid Ferriter, *The Transformation of Ireland 1900–2000* (London: Profile, 2005), p. 666.
[25] O'Connor, *Emerging Voices*, p. 246.

112 Women and Embodied Mythmaking in Irish Theatre

The Mai is the head teacher of a local school and owns her own home on Owl Lake but she still does not feel accommodated within the spaces available to her. Although O'Connor does not employ the term postfeminist, her observations clearly reflect on a postfeminist landscape to address the illusion, or over-estimation, of power as generated by the changes in Irish women's lives in the last quarter of the twentieth century:

> Ironically, perhaps, the ability of women to change the parameters of their own private lives has generated in some an optimism which fails to recognise the implicit male bias in these systems and under-estimates the strength and flexibility of the processes and practices involved in the maintenance of patriarchy. This optimism is legitimated by ideas about meritocracy and equality which are fostered within what purport to be gender neutral structures.[26]

The Mai gives the audience pause to consider the changes *and* continuities in the lives of women in Ireland across the twentieth century.

Certainly, much of the action in the *The Mai* is shaped by continuities which support the maintenance of, and women's dependence on, patriarchal structures. The play opens with the return of Mai's[27] husband Robert, for whom Mai has been waiting several years, and the tableau of a woman waiting at the window recurs through the play, from Mai's onstage action to her sister Julie's accusation that their mother Grandma Fraochlán neglected them for her husband: 'I brought myself up and all the others. You were at the window pinin' for the nine-fingered fisherman!'[28] Even when Robert and the nine-fingered fisherman are gone, their presence looms large and the waiting women themselves are absented from full engagement in their lives. All the women in *The Mai* are enthralled by romantic expectations and the desire for 'life to be huge and heroic and pure as in the days of yore',[29] but Western myths of romance expose the disjunction between the world of narratives and the women's material lives: Robert ultimately does not live up to the ideal of Mai's 'dark-haired prince'[30] and continually disappoints her. Grandma Fraochlán describes the repeated cycles of history: 'we can't help repeatin', Robert, we repeat and we repeat, the orchestration may be different but the tune is always the same'.[31] The generations of women presented on stage in *The Mai* expose the repeated acts of gender which they are compelled to perform. The 1994

---

[26] O'Connor, *Emerging Voices*, pp. 250–1.
[27] In order to reinforce The Mai's mythic status, she is referred to throughout the play as The Mai as well as just Mai.
[28] *The Mai*, p. 141.   [29] *The Mai*, p. 163.   [30] *The Mai*, p. 162.   [31] *The Mai*, p. 123.

Metamorphic 'Bodies That Matter'

premiere production of *The Mai* revealed Millie literally reperforming Grandma Fraochlán when she stood behind and copied her movements as Grandma Fraochlán retold and relived dancing with her husband at the Cleggan Fair.

Act One closes with the endpoint of the play, the image of The Mai lying dead in Robert's arms, and we expect her narrative to be silenced. However, she subverts linear chronology and expectation by being resurrected in Act Two in the first of her metamorphoses. Act Two is set one year on and further charts the disintegration of their marriage as The Mai confronts Robert about the affair he has been having, as well as his treatment of her: 'You think I can put up with anything, well I can't.'[32] The Mai's refusal to put up with any more is enacted by her decision to drown herself in Owl Lake, an action that is suggested acoustically in the final moments of the play: '*Sounds of geese and swans taking flight, sounds of water. Silence.*'[33]

The intimation of suicide and the thematic intertwinement of woman, death and water is central to an Abbey play from the early decades of the twentieth century: *The Woman* by Margaret O'Leary which premiered on 10 September 1929. Throughout the play, Ellen Dunn, the eponymous Woman, longingly talks of the dark waters of Poulgorm where her grandmother drowned. Ultimately, Ellen is punished for the expression of her sexual desires, namely her relationship with the recently widowed Maurice whom she wishes to elope with, and the play closes with the suggestion that Ellen exits to drown herself in Poulgorm. Lisa Fitzpatrick has examined how O'Leary changed the ending of the play at Yeats's insistence that 'the heroine must die and we must know she dies; all that has been built up is scattered and degraded, if she does not come to the understanding that she seeks something life, or her life, can never give'.[34]

However, as Fitzpatrick argues, the action or script does not confirm this death and O'Leary chooses to refuse the revelation of a female corpse. *The Mai* goes beyond ambiguity to refuse the ending as an act of defeat, through the presentation of this moment as The Mai's second metamorphosis: an action which refuses her abject status. We can interpret The Mai's decision to commit suicide as a reclamation of control over her body. Moreover, The Mai's suicide and metamorphoses transgress the prescribed limits of the female body's signification to inhabit a creative female

---

[32] *The Mai*, p. 178. [33] *The Mai*, p. 186.

[34] Quoted in Lisa Fitzpatrick, 'Taking Their Own Road: The Female Protagonists in Three Irish Plays by Women', in *Women in Irish Drama: A Century of Authorship and Representation*, ed. Melissa Sihra (Basingstoke: Palgrave Macmillan, 2007), pp. 69–86 (p. 75).

Women and Embodied Mythmaking in Irish Theatre

corporeality. Her metamorphic body cannot be contained in the existing structures of the stage world and demands an alternative space of expression; the extent to which this is realized in production is bound up with dramaturgical decisions concerning exploration of the non-mimetic, mythic elements of Carr's work.

Unliveable Bodies

In order to analyse the metamorphoses of both Grania and The Mai as acts of creative resignification, I want to first explore their initial state of abjection. Employing Butler's framework in *Bodies That Matter*, abject bodies are those that are excluded from cultural signification and therefore fail to matter. In *Powers of Horror*, Julia Kristeva attends to the abject as a haunting presence on the borders of the symbolic order which remains within the order to circumscribe its limits. Kristeva addresses the exclusion of the abject as the unclean or improper which we 'permanently thrust aside in order to live'.[35] Drawing on Kristeva, Butler speaks to abject bodies which operate on the borders and at the limits of signification, and therefore constitute the subject:

> The forming of a subject requires an identification with the normative phantasm of 'sex' and this identification takes place through a repudiation which produces a domain of abjection, a repudiation without which the subject cannot emerge.[36]

The abject is excluded from signification and deemed unliveable, thereby confronting 'those boundaries of bodily life where abjected or delegitimated bodies fail to count as "bodies"'.[37] The limits of cultural intelligibility are historically constituted and so too are the bodies which are excluded and deemed non-viable. Butler's use of the term 'abject' has a material and political focus in the historical specificity of the unliveable body. Butler addresses queer identities, as well as other non-viable bodies, giving broad scope to the question: 'For whom is outness a historically available and affordable option?'[38] This ensures that the abject is not a universalizing term but one which is regulated by the changing cultural forms which exclude certain bodies and deny them access to political status and ontology. This denial is, as Butler notes, at times violent as it depends upon erasure and selectivity.

---

[35] Julia Kristeva, *Powers of Horror* (New York: Columbia University Press, 1982), p. 3.
[36] Butler, *Bodies That Matter*, p. 3.   [37] Butler, *Bodies That Matter*, p. 15.
[38] Butler, *Bodies That Matter*, p. 227.

The Mai opens with the long awaited return of Mai's husband Robert. Their initial exchange highlights The Mai's objectification as muse rather than creator. Robert defines the boundaries of The Mai's body as he shapes her as his cello:

ROBERT: Well – well – well.
He taps her shoulder, hip bone, ankle, on each of the 'Wells'.
THE MAI: Just look at you.
ROBERT: You are as beautiful as ever.
THE MAI: Am I?
Now he plays the cello bow across her breasts. The Mai laughs.[39]

Robert enables her signification through the imposition of the iconography of the cello; she is the conduit and instrument of his creativity and thus her corporeal expression is erased. The Mai's body is permitted to signify within the limits that Robert designates and initially she complies. The Mai's waiting echoes the Greek myth where the defiant Electra waits for the return of her brother and is also 'a reversal of the Odysseus legend viewed from the perspective of Penelope'.[40] Furthermore, this is suggestive of passivity as Mai waits for her heroic prince to generate the action; the references to the Cinderella story ironically point to Robert's failings as the heroic prince. The Mai adopts the roles available to her through inherited myths and narratives of romance but these do not offer a life she deems liveable; having built her house at Owl Lake to accommodate herself and her children, she says: 'It's the kind of house you build when you've nowhere left to go.'[41] Anna McMullan highlights the sense of exile and 'unhomeliness' that Carr's women experience within patriarchy:

> Luce Irigaray uses the term *déréliction* to describe a kind of exile experienced by women, who have not been adequately represented or 'housed' within culture except through the maternal function, and can find no place within the dominant currencies of symbolic exchange.[42]

The Mai fails to locate her sense of self within the cultural imaginary but The Mai's tolerance of this space as home suggests her initial acceptance of ways of living sanctioned by a patriarchal society.

Just as The Mai is objectified in the opening of the play, Gregory's Grania is introduced as Finn's prospective bride, having been passed from

---

[39] *The Mai*, p. 108.
[40] Clare Wallace, 'Tragedy and Abjection in Three Plays by Marina Carr', *Irish University Review*, 31:2 (2001), 431–49 (p. 438).
[41] *The Mai*, p. 158.   [42] McMullan, 'Marina Carr's Unhomely Women', p. 16.

116   Women and Embodied Mythmaking in Irish Theatre

her father's to her husband's care. In spite of this, Grania warns Finn of her autonomy when she states: 'My father was for the King of Foreign, but I said I would take my own road.'[43] Gregory's play *Grania* differs from her retelling of the myth in *Gods and Fighting Men*: the introduction of the King of Foreign incorporates the possibility of appealing to nationalist sentiments. However, this interpretation is undercut by Gregory's exploration of, and emphasis on, Grania's agency:

> I think I turned to Grania because so many have written about sad, lovely Deirdre, who when overtaken by sorrow made no good battle at the last. Grania had more power of will, and for good or evil twice took the shaping of her life into her own hands.[44]

Grania introduces a tension between inherited narratives and their reperformance; furthermore, Cathy Leeney highlights the uneasy tension 'between the nationalist interrogation of culture on one hand, and the proto-feminist interrogation of gender on the other'.[45] The love triangle between Grania, Finn and Diarmuid manifests this struggle. When Finn recognizes Diarmuid and Grania's love for one another, Diarmuid tries to protect Grania but she is determined to take her destiny 'into her own hands': 'It is not his fault! It is mine! It is on me the blame is entirely! It is best for me to go out a shamed woman. But I will not go knocking at my father's door!'[46] The assertion of her agency results in Diarmuid's oath of divided loyalty between her and Finn. Indeed, the first act closes with Finn's physical collapse indicating his weakened status.

Expression of Grania's agency and desire is made possible by her acceptance to leave Finn's court and live on the borders of society in the woods. She has been exiled to where 'bodies fail to matter' as woman's sexuality and desire have no place in the structures of Finn's patriarchal realm. Her body exposes the boundaries of bodily life within Finn's order. It is while she is in the woods that Grania is able to satisfy her sexual desires, and after consummating her relationship with Diarmuid, we see her trying out the laws of the patriarchal world that objectify her, informing him that: 'You are entirely my own.'[47] Tellingly, the consummation of their relationship only occurs when Diarmuid becomes jealous of the King of Foreign's attempt to seduce Grania. The dominant narratives of nationalism and patriarchy are reasserted as Diarmuid reads Grania's body as Ireland, in

---

[43] Gregory, *Grania*, p. 181.   [44] Gregory, *Grania*, p. 362.
[45] Cathy Leeney, 'The New Woman in a New Ireland? Grania After Naturalism', *Irish University Review*, 34:1 (2004), 157–70 (p. 160).
[46] Gregory, *Grania*, p. 189.   [47] Gregory, *Grania*, p. 194.

Metamorphic 'Bodies That Matter'

need of protection from invasion by England. Diarmuid tries to affirm the patriarchal laws of ownership of both land and woman through possession of Grania but her assertion of her body and its desires attempts to reclaim her subjectivity. Grania realizes that her agency is limited by her abjected status in the woods and wants to leave in order to express her desires in the public realm of the court where bodies matter: 'I would wish my happiness to be seen, and not to be hidden under the branches and twigs of trees.'[48] Unlike Diarmuid, Grania refuses to accept exile and instead wants to seize what is rightfully hers, her role as a sexually empowered woman within society: 'I have not had the full of my life yet, for it is scared and hiding I have spent the best of my years that are past.'[49]

Diarmuid's suggestion that they live in the otherworld of Tír na nÓg reinforces Grania's concern that she is being stifled: 'We are the same here as if settled in the clay.'[50] She wants recognition and corporeal expression within the social realm, not just the private. Through the symbolic act of crumbling the round loaf which signifies the unity of Diarmuid's oath to Finn, Grania defiantly reveals that the King of Foreign's kiss has roused her sexual desires. This gesture conveys her wish for her body to signify in the symbolic as well as the exiled realm of the woods. She refuses to allow herself to be fixed as mythic icon or a symbol of Ireland and sovereignty, as 'no more than a memory and a name'.[51]

Articulating the Abject

Both myth and gender work within pre-existing structures so how does metamorphosis trouble inherited significations? In *The Mai* Millie introduces the potential for metamorphosis to articulate women's *déréliction* through the myth of Coillte, who was abandoned by her lover and dissolves into a lake – a story which foreshadows The Mai's death:

> One night, seizing a long awaited opportunity, the dark witch pushed Coillte into her lake of tears. When spring came round again Bláth was released from the dark witch's spell and he went in search of Coillte, only to be told that she had dissolved.[52]

This echoes the myth of Byblis in Ovid's *Metamorphoses* which portrays a girl who, after the loss of her lover, 'melted away in her weeping and

[48] Gregory, *Grania*, p. 195.   [49] Gregory, *Grania*, p. 195.   [50] Gregory, *Grania*, p. 195.
[51] Gregory, *Grania*, p. 196.
[52] Marina Carr, *The Mai*, in *Plays I* (London: Faber & Faber, 1999), p. 147.

118   Women and Embodied Mythmaking in Irish Theatre

changed to a mountain spring'.[53] In Act One The Mai's only narration of her identity comes in the form of a dark dream where Robert is stabbed and The Mai walks towards a dark cavern of futility; 'away in the distance I see a black cavern and I know it leads to nowhere and I start walking that way because I know I'll find you there.'[54] This dream illustrates her sense of the inevitability of her fate as defined by Robert. However, through examination of the trope of metamorphosis we can address the potential for Mai to control her own expression and to assert her creativity and embodied experiences: both through her first metamorphosis which sees her return onstage in Act Two, after we have seen her dead body, and the second more mythically redolent metamorphosis suggested in the closing moments. The women of Carr's Midlands trilogy have been accused of 'disappointingly, throw[ing] in the towel by committing suicide'.[55] However, I address the potential for creativity in the performance of these transformative acts, as well as examining the limits placed on The Mai's agency.

Butler highlights the importance of the failure to identify, and comply, with gendered norms: 'Indeed, it may be precisely through practices which underscore disidentification with those regulatory norms by which sexual difference is materialized that both feminist and queer politics is mobilized.'[56] So how does metamorphosis in *Grania* and *The Mai* serve to expose disidentification and to what extent can it offer a creative female corporeality? Butler suggests that the body and sex are materialized through citation, or reperformance, of regulatory norms. This process stabilizes and fixes gendered identity and sexed bodies, and thus attempts to naturalize them 'as *a process of materialization that stabilizes over time to produce the effect of boundary, fixity, and surface we call matter.*'[57] However, the need for reiteration reveals that 'materialization is never quite complete, that bodies never quite comply with the norms by which their materialization is impelled'.[58] The instability of these rematerializations can be exploited to unsettle the perpetuation of naturalized gendered bodies and identities:

> If subversion is possible, it will be a subversion from within the terms of the law, through the possibilities that emerge when the law turns against itself and spawns unexpected permutations of itself. The culturally constructed

---

[53] Ovid, *Metamorphoses*, trans. by David Raeburn (London: Penguin, 2004), p. 372.
[54] *The Mai*, p. 126.   [55] Wallace, 'Tragedy and Abjection in Three Plays by Marina Carr', p. 435.
[56] Butler, *Bodies That Matter*, p. 4.   [57] Butler, *Bodies That Matter*, p. 9.
[58] Butler, *Bodies That Matter*, p. 2.

Metamorphic 'Bodies That Matter' 119

body will then be liberated, neither to its 'natural' past, nor to its original pleasures, but to an open future of cultural possibilities.[59]

Can metamorphosis generate 'unexpected permutations' that bring abject bodies to bear disruptively on the process of the creation of female identity and thus open up a 'future of cultural possibilities' which both disrupt and refuse to be bound by the limits of liveable bodies?

In Act One of *The Mai*, Mai is made to matter through Robert's imposition of iconography; however, this is disrupted at the end of the act when The Mai's corpse is brought onstage. Kristeva defines the ultimate abject which 'disturbs identity, system, order'[60] as the corpse: 'a border that has encroached upon everything'.[61] As Maria Doyle suggests, with reference to both *Portia Coughlan* and *The Mai*, cleanliness and catharsis are denied by the appearance of the dead body midway through the play.[62] Arguably, the best known of female metamorphoses in Irish theatre is that of Kathleen ni Houlihan in Gregory's and Yeats's play. Indeed, her metamorphosis repressively materializes and fixes her as the ideal woman-nation symbol, though this was deemed a liberating transformation by nationalist rhetoric. Her metamorphosis occurs offstage and her potential for threatening fixed boundaries of identity is thus rendered less troubling. The appearance of The Mai's dead and abject body midway in the play is disruptive, both of the chronology of the play and of the idealized female body. The Mai's dead body at the end of Act One unsettles the iconography of the tragic dead female body as silenced victim to reveal a potential for creative resignification (I return to this issue in my discussion of sacrificial and dying bodies in Chapter 4). The Mai's dead body risks reinforcing her powerlessness and silence as an objectified individual. However, through its rematerializations, her body challenges constructions of passive female corporeality and creatively disrupts the conventions of embodiment which control her, specifically Robert's dream of The Mai: 'I dreamt you were dead and my cello case was your coffin.'[63] In the 1995 National Theatre touring production, these lines were delivered while Robert stood behind The Mai – who was seated – and played his bow across her breasts.[64]

---

[59] Butler, *Bodies That Matter*, p. 127.   [60] Kristeva, *Powers of Horror*, p. 4.

[61] Kristeva, *Powers of Horror*, p. 3.

[62] Maria Doyle, 'Dead Center: Tragedy and the Reanimated Body in Marina Carr's *The Mai* and *Portia Coughlan*', *Modern Drama*, 49:1 (2006), 41–59 (p. 49).

[63] *The Mai*, p. 125.

[64] Marina Carr, *The Mai*. Director: Brian Brady. Cast: Olwen Fouéré, Catherine Mack, Robert O'Mahony, Maire Hastings, Stella McCusker, Bríd Ní Neachtain, Joan O'Hara, Joan Sheehy.

120   Women and Embodied Mythmaking in Irish Theatre

In *Myth and Motherland*, Richard Kearney outlines the central trope of martyrdom and the pietà to the mythology of the 1916 Rising:

> Posters appeared on the streets of Dublin showing the martyred Pearse reclining *pieta*-like on the bosom of a seraphic celestial woman brandishing a tricolour: a mixture of Mother Ireland, the Virgin Mother of Christ and the Angel of the Resurrection.[65]

The 1995 touring production of *The Mai* reversed the iconography of the gendered roles of Christianity and Irish cultural nationalism, of the male who is sacrificed to enable Kathleen ni Houlihan and the nation to be reborn, with the framed image of Robert with The Mai's body in his arms at the end of Act One.[66] Similarly, in the Peacock Theatre's 2007 production of Carr's *Woman and Scarecrow* (discussed in detail in Chapter 4), director Selina Cartmell chose to conclude with a pietà tableau, where death is not an act of finality but part of a creative process. Susan Cannon Harris argues that within a twentieth-century Irish context women are not eligible for the role of sacrificial victim as the materiality of the dead female body makes her resistant to idealization, functioning instead as the 'female counterpart – the mother/wife/lover who accepts the sacrifice and whose body can then fulfill the more "natural" role of transforming that death into a rebirth'.[67] However, the female corpse of the pietà is not a victim but an unsettling resignification whose materiality frustrates idealization and refuses the role of the Virgin Mary – a corpse that brings the abject to bear on idealized models of femininity. The return of The Mai in Act Two serves to question control over women's bodies through an unsettling mimicry of the Christ-like male body's ability to be born again and of Kathleen ni Houlihan's rejuvenation. This first metamorphosis is an 'unexpected permutation' that enables The Mai's abject, yet resurrected, body to trouble the definition of 'bodies that matter'.

Music: Michael O'Suilleabhain. Lighting: Aedin Cosgrove. Set and costume: Kathy Strachan. (Abbey Theatre Production: Abbey Centre, Ballyshannon, opened 24 April, 1995. Tour concluded by returning to the Peacock Theatre, Dublin).

[65] Kearney, *Myth and Motherland*, p. 19.

[66] Though Robert carried The Mai in his arms and stood framed by the window in the 1994 premiere production, the position of their bodies did not reference the pietà image as clearly. Instead, Robert held Mai much lower on his body and she had her arms around his neck rather than lying back across his arms.

[67] Susan Cannon Harris, *Gender and Irish Drama* (Bloomington: Indiana University Press, 2002), p. 4.

Metamorphic 'Bodies That Matter' 121

Grania's Metamorphosis

The reappearance of The Mai's body illustrates Butler's suggestion that the abject can be 'a critical resource in the struggle to rearticulate the very terms of symbolic legitimacy and intelligibility'.[68] Similarly, Grania's decision to return to Almhuin enables her desiring body to unsettle the limits of Finn's court. Grania questions the norms available to her as wife and lover: 'And why should I always be a widow that went so long a maid?'[69] Following her exclusion, Grania re-positions herself, telling Finn: 'I will have my turn . . . It is I will be between him and yourself, and will keep him outside of that lodging for ever!'[70] Her decision to disruptively insert her body serves to destabilize positions within existing power structures. Grania's physical actions support her seizing of narrative control and thus her journey, as Leeney describes it, 'from containment within a narrative, to control of that narrative is the journey of woman from image to active subject'.[71] The extent of Grania's control and defiance can be further explored through interpretation of her final exit as an extension of her metamorphosis from abjection to agential subjectivity. However, it is crucial that we address both the control and compromise that is bound up in Grania's final exit and her efforts to make 'good battle at the last'.[72]

Grania understands that her body functions as an effect, and possible disruption, of power and turns this to her advantage, reiterating the role of queen at the end of the play by putting on her royal signifiers, crown and dress, to destabilize the heterosexual patriarchal hegemony which Diarmuid and Finn exclude her from:

> Give me now the crown, til I go out before them, as you offered it often enough. (*She puts it on her head.*) I am going, I am going out now, to show myself before them all, and my hand linked in your own. It is well I brought my golden dress.[73]

Grania rejected this role in Act One, yet the iconography of Grania the queen is self-consciously reinterpreted in Act Three to gain control of her own narrative and corporeal identity. Grania's reperformance exposes the disjunction between her body and the conventions which make it matter so that, though she is compelled to operate within a set of norms, she is able to expose the mechanics of the system: 'Just as bodily surfaces are enacted *as* the natural, so these surfaces can become the site of a dissonant and

---

[68] Butler, *Bodies That Matter*, p. 3. [69] Gregory, *Grania*, p. 213. [70] Gregory, *Grania*, p. 212.
[71] Leeney, *Irish Women Playwrights, 1900–1939*, p. 45. [72] Gregory, *Grania*, p. 362.
[73] Gregory, *Grania*, p. 213.

122 Women and Embodied Mythmaking in Irish Theatre

denaturalized performance that reveals the performative status of the natural itself.'[74] Following her decision to return to Almhuin with Finn, Grania undermines the myth of fickle woman: 'It is women are said to change, and they do not, but it is men that change and turn as often as the wheel of the moon.'[75] Grania cites this gendered myth through her decision to return to court but she also undermines it with reference to Diarmuid's refusal to pay any attention to Grania at his death, instead turning to Finn. Furthermore, as Christopher Murray points out, this line is a reiteration and refutation of the reason given in Gregory's *Gods and Fighting Men* for Grania's departure with Finn: 'because the mind of a woman changes like the water of a running stream'.[76] Grania's reciting of the role of queen highlights the tension between regulatory norms and Grania's expression of desire and agency. Grania appropriates the trappings of power within Finn's order, thus reaffirming it while creating a destabilizing role for herself within these limits.

Grania's re-positioning of herself disrupts the construction of gendered identities in Finn's court; it is an 'unexpected permutation' which allows her to unsettle social norms. Grania can bring her experiences of exile and sexual awakening to bear on a new performance of woman and queen in control of her own signification. Throughout the play, mocking laughter functions as a chorus which becomes 'specifically threatening to Grania as a corrective or punishment for the violation of the community mores'.[77] However, the play closes with the silencing of this ideologically repressive unit as Grania has engineered its disruption, suppressing its power of discourse, albeit temporarily, with her entrance into its world: '*She opens the door herself. Finn puts his arm about her. There is another great peal of laughter, but it stops suddenly as she goes out.*'[78] Her exit defiantly silences the norms which erase bodies through abjection and thereby refuses the definition of viable bodies as permitted by Finn's court. Her metamorphosis brings about change as she effects a corporeal disruption of these social norms but there are limits to Grania's renegotiated position. This is signalled by Finn's presence at Grania's side when she exits, with a protective and possessive arm around her. Grania appears to submit to Finn's authority whilst assimilating its trappings to negotiate a position for herself.

---

[74] Butler, *Bodies That Matter*, p. 200.   [75] Gregory, *Grania*, p. 213.
[76] Quoted in Christopher Murray, *Twentieth-Century Irish Drama: Mirror up to Nation* (New York: Syracuse University Press, 2000), p. 59.
[77] Maureen Waters, 'Lady Gregory's *Grania*: A Feminist Voice', *Irish University Review*, 25:1 (1995), 11–24 (p. 19).
[78] Gregory, *Grania*, p. 214.

Metamorphic 'Bodies That Matter'

Grania's donning of the golden robe and crown and subsequent entrance into the court provides a notable contrast with the last scene of Gore-Booth's *The Triumph of Maeve*. Maeve rejects her status, casting aside her crown and royal robes, before departing from the court for the otherworld. Maeve refuses to participate further within the court, a system in which she had power as a queen and warrior. Her departure expresses her agency and signals her rejection of the court, though this results in her future exclusion where Grania remains within the patriarchal court.

In his exploration of 'woman' as fantasy object in Gregory's historical tragedies, Paul Murphy highlights how 'the moment of desublimation occurs when the heroine exercises agency in terms of desiring another lover or choosing a different political allegiance'.[79] This is evident when Grania chooses Diarmuid over Finn and again when she admits the arousal of her desires by the King of Foreign. The play's ending has the potential to negotiate a subversive and desublimated role for Grania within the patriarchal world of Finn's court. Murphy suggests that: 'Grania's status as object cause of desire is immediately reinstated when she performs the role of Queen and wife to Finn [...] she self-consciously utilizes her status as fantasy object to save herself from the deplorable state which befell Gormleith and Dervorgilla'.[80] I would further argue that Grania is no longer simply a sublime object as she refigures the role of queen to incorporate her experiences as a desiring subject. Grania's metamorphosis and self-conscious reperformance sees her employ the normative as a subversive strategy which enables her excluded abject body to bear disruptively on social norms. However, the result of Grania's renegotiation of agency through her final reperformance of queen is not addressed in Gregory's play which closes with Grania's exit: we do not see how Grania will wield any of the negotiated power she has claimed for herself. Her silencing of the Fianna and performative contestation of Finn's authority risks giving the illusion of power without actualizing it. However, there is the suggestion of a different order as Grania's reperformance enacts new possibilities: it reveals the potential of performatively destabilizing existing structures of power to enact a role for Grania as a desiring subject within Finn's court.

---

[79] Paul Murphy, 'Woman as Fantasy Object in Lady Gregory's Historical Tragedies', in *Women in Irish Drama: A Century of Authorship and Representation*, ed. Melissa Sihra (Basingstoke: Palgrave Macmillan, 2007), pp. 28–41 (p. 38).

[80] Murphy, 'Woman as Fantasy Object', pp. 38–9.

124   Women and Embodied Mythmaking in Irish Theatre

Gregory's historical and mythical dramas were foundational to the development of a national theatre, as were the theatrical contributions of another neglected woman playwright: Alice Milligan. Chapter 1 documented Milligan's involvement in the tableaux vivants performed by the Inghinidhe na hÉireann in 1901. In addition, Milligan wrote plays which drew on mythic sources, including *The Last Feast of the Fianna* (1900): the first part of a trilogy based on the Fenian legends, which features Grania in her old age.[81] Milligan's one act play opened the second season of the Irish Literary Theatre in 1900 and presented Grania as a haughty and scornful woman.[82] Oisín bemoans that, 'Since Grania came to bide here with her angry looks and bitter words ... my life has known no peace.'[83] Milligan described her motivation in writing the play: 'I simply wrote it on thinking out this problem. How did Oisín endure to live in the house with Grania after all that happened?'[84] From the perspective of the feminist spectator it is of more interest to ponder how Grania endured her life in Fionn's court after all that had happened. From the outset Fionn diminishes Grania's authority when he disparagingly comments that 'it is by the cunning wiles of love a woman alone can triumph'.[85] Grania has no authority in Fionn's political order: 'Woman, you have not yet learned that you are far from Rath Grania, and from that foolish Diarmuid O'Duibhne, who let you rule his house. You are now in the house of Fionn.'[86] Grania clearly has not created a place for herself in this realm of warriors and is quite literally displaced by the supernatural idealized woman, Niamh of the Sidhe, who is invited by Fionn to sit in Grania's throne.

Imelda Foley reads Milligan's play as a critique of 'the bard and warrior as dreamer and irresponsible escapist [. . .] The analogy of dreaming poet and Yeatsian spiritualist is clearly and consistently emphasised.'[87] Grania is the only character who is critical of Oisín, bemoaning his detachment from reality:

> It is not fitting, oh bard of Fionn, that you should darken the feast with your
> sorrow, that you should constantly deplore the dead and take no heed to

---

[81] The other two plays, *Oisín in Tír na nÓg* and *Oisín and Padraig* were never performed but they were published in *The Daily Express* in 1899.

[82] Performed 19 February 1900 by the Irish Literary Theatre at the Gaiety Theatre, Dublin. Published in the *Daily Express*, 23 and 30 September 1899.

[83] Alice Milligan, *The Last Feast of the Fianna: A Dramatic Legend* (Chicago: De Paul University Press, 1967), p. 54.

[84] Alice Milligan, 'The Last Feast of the Fianna', *Beltaine*, No. 2 (February 1900), 18–21.

[85] Milligan, *The Last Feast of the Fianna*, p. 49.   [86] Milligan, *The Last Feast of the Fianna*, p. 51.

[87] Imelda Foley, *The Girls in the Big Picture: Gender in Contemporary Ulster Theatre* (Belfast: The Blackstaff Press, 2003), p. 18.

Metamorphic 'Bodies That Matter'

please the living [. . .] Take your harp from the wall and tune it and sing for the joy of Fionn, your father.[88]

On the one hand, Grania appears to be promoting Fionn (and his court) who Oisín ultimately betrays through his decision to leave the Fianna with Niamh for the land of eternal youth, Tir-nan-Oig.[89] Furthermore, Grania's description of Niamh's threatening and alluring femininity perpetuates myths of feminine beauty and decay (discussed in more detail in Chapter 4): 'She would be revealed black as night, a hideous, uncomely hag, with yellow teeth and with claws, with gaunt bones and with wrinkles'.[90] However, in juxtaposition with this collusion are Grania's actions in the final moments of the play. Her final words to Oisín upon his departure with Niamh are an attempt to assert the authority of her opinion: 'Though you are going for evermore, Grania alone does not weep. Oisín's words are sweet to all, bitter alone to her.'[91] Her proud stance contrasts with the broken, weeping men around her. Grania in both Milligan's and Gregory's plays is an isolated figure struggling to pose resistance through her presence to the authority circulated between men. Seeing this moment as a challenge exposes Grania's exclusion and supports 'Milligan's sophisticated irony and veiled parody of male heroism'.[92]

In her biography of Milligan, Catherine Morris draws attention to contemporary responses to *The Last Feast of the Fianna* which suggested that 'the play owed more to the *tableau vivant* tradition of theatrical spectacle than to realist dramaturgy'.[93] If, as I argued in Chapter 1, the affect of the tableau form depended on its immobility and the resultant tension between movement and stasis, we might see Grania's final tableau as 'a call toward a future live moment when the image will be re-encountered, perhaps as an invitation to response'.[94] Gregory accepts the invitation and her Grania offers a more successful contestation of authority; Cathy Leeney notes that, 'Gregory develops and transforms Milligan's use of laughter at Grania's expense in *The Last Feast of the Fianna*'.[95] Where Milligan's Grania is laughed at, 'OISÍN: I cannot but laugh, though my heart is heavy, to hear Grania preach modesty',[96] and silenced by the end of

---

[88] Milligan, *The Last Feast of the Fianna*, p. 48.
[89] Spelling of Tir-nan-Oig as in published script: Milligan, *The Last Feast of the Fianna*.
[90] Milligan, *The Last Feast of the Fianna*, p. 52.   [91] Milligan, *The Last Feast of the Fianna*, p. 55.
[92] Foley, *The Girls in the Big Picture*, p. 18.
[93] Morris, 'Alice Milligan: Republican Tableaux and the Revival', p. 244.
[94] Schneider, *Performing Remains*, p. 141.
[95] Leeney, *Irish Women Playwrights, 1900–1939*, p. 212.
[96] Milligan, *The Last Feast of the Fianna*, p. 52.

126   Women and Embodied Mythmaking in Irish Theatre

the play, Gregory's Grania silences the Fianna's laughter. Milligan's Grania is left isolated and immobile on stage and this contrasts with the corporeal transformation of Gregory's Grania whose metamorphosis and final exit enact a symbolic contestation of her mythic iconography and can thus gesture towards the possibility of accommodating her desires within newly negotiated limits.

The Mai's Ovidian Metamorphosis

Grania's final exit as metamorphosis attempts to negotiate expression of her embodied subjectivity but her refusal to be excluded leaves the structure of the court and Finn's authority intact. More radical is The Mai's second Ovidian metamorphosis which goes beyond operating within legitimate cultural forms to embrace her abject status and exclusion to 'those "unliveable" and "uninhabitable" zones':[97] a space beyond the stage and outside the house. Millie's final speech and narration of The Mai's life is replete with images of claustrophobia and drowning: she describes Owl Lake as 'a caul around my chest' and she highlights the repeated image of 'The Mai at the window again'[98] to underline a sense of entrapment. However, The Mai's actions in the final moments of the play attempt to articulate the abject and thus evade the fate of tragedy: a fate where woman is silenced and, as a passive victim, cannot control her signification. Butler asks: 'How is it that certain kinds of subjects lay claim to ontology, how is it that they *count* or *qualify* as real?'[99] The Mai's second metamorphosis is an uncompromising and transformative assertion of a creative feminine corporeality that lays claim to ontology through evocation of alternative spaces and means of expression.

The Mai's reclamation of her corporeal expression is pre-empted earlier in Act Two. This act opened, in both the Peacock's 1994 premiere and 1995 touring production, with The Mai lying on her back with the cello on top of her but as the act progresses she refutes the imposition of iconography on her body and regains her creativity. Through her resurrected and metamorphosed body of Act Two, The Mai plays her own body as a cello:

> She taps the bow along her toes, stops, pulls a string from it, looks at Robert, looks away, resumes playing herself: knees, thighs, stomach. Then she stops to snap a string as it suits her. She plays her breasts and makes notes on her throat with her other hand. Eyes closed, playing herself.[100]

---

[97] Butler, *Bodies That Matter*, p. 3.   [98] *The Mai*, p. 184.
[99] Costera Meijer and Prins, 'How Bodies Come to Matter', p. 280.   [100] *The Mai*, p. 156.

Metamorphic 'Bodies That Matter'

The action which contextualizes this moment is another of Robert and The Mai's blazing rows and in the premiere production, the moment of The Mai 'playing herself' was more aggressive than sensual as she confronted Robert. Following this scene, the premiere production added a more private and personally intimate moment, which draws on the mood of the earlier stage direction of The Mai playing herself with her eyes closed. The Mai moved to the shadows at the rear of the stage and once more played her body as a cello while Millie watched. The Mai's resurrected body asserts its creativity and capacity for the generation and control of meaning, counter to the imposition of limiting iconography that erases women's material experiences.

Butler suggests that the term abjection, like 'queer', should be used strategically and 'never fully owned, but always and only redeployed, twisted, queered from a prior usage and in the direction of urgent and expanding political purposes'.[101] The dramaturgical choices made in production are therefore a vital intervention in the process of articulating but not reinstalling the abject. Agency is located in the negotiation between freedom and constraint and this conflict is staged at the end of *The Mai* when Mai's final lines are juxtaposed with the energy and transformative power of her second metamorphosis. Whether this conflict is used to enable the abject body to expose the limits of signification, and thus 'in the direction of urgent and expanding political purposes', depends on the staging of the play. Her final words could signal a hopeless resignation in the face of a life without Robert:

THE MAI: People think I've no pride, no dignity, to stay in a situation like this, but I can't think of one reason for going on without him.
MILLIE: Mom, you've never tried.
THE MAI: I don't want to.[102]

These lines are in conflict with her body's movement away from the window, where she has stood waiting for Robert. She moves towards a place outside the stage space; a realm evoked by sounds and music, suggestive of alternatives where improper bodies might be permitted to matter. The 1994 Peacock production of *The Mai* was scored by cello music composed by Michael O'Suilleabhain which drew attention to The Mai's creative silence: she no longer plays the cello, while Robert does. Instead of the *sounds of water* suggested in the stage directions, the cello music accompanied The Mai's departure so that the intimation of her final

---

[101] Butler, *Bodies That Matter*, p. 228.   [102] *The Mai*, pp. 185–6.

128   Women and Embodied Mythmaking in Irish Theatre

dissolution into the lake was lost. It could be argued that this music indicated her regained control of her subjectivity and creativity, however, there was no sense of the music's connection to Mai as in the moment when she played her own body as a cello. The 1995 touring production of *The Mai* emphasized her negotiation of agency more clearly as The Mai's ghostly figure walked offstage then across the window where she paused to look back defiantly. The Mai's movement is underlined; she is no longer trapped behind the window looking out but is now able to look back in. Her bold stance confronts the audience's signification of her as a victim, while this framed image reminds them that her freedom is not unmitigated.

In contrast, the McCarter Theatre's 1996 production, directed by Emily Mann,[103] reasserted a narrative of tragic destiny and dependency on Robert. A review of the production commented on the composer Baikida Carroll's 'haunting sound effect to echo Millie's tale of the cry a swan releases when lamenting its fallen mate' and the reviewer goes on to describe how this 'underscores the ghostly image of Robert carrying the drowned body of Mai with which [Emily] Mann ends each act'.[104] The repeated image of Robert holding The Mai's body reiterates Act One, rather than offering movement, change and metamorphosis. Moreover, the employment of the keening swansong referred to in Millie's narration further highlighted The Mai's relationship with Robert and the inevitability of her tragic fate.

The Mai's suicide is problematic as regards agency, with a tradition of women in theatre for whom transgression results in suicide and punishment by death, as per Yeats's revised ending of Margaret O'Leary's *The Woman* (1929). With reference to Greek and Shakespearean theatre, Hélène Cixous argues that theatre perpetuates the violence directed against women by denying her expression: 'It is always necessary for a woman to die in order for the play to begin. Only when she has disappeared can the curtain go up; she is relegated to repression, to the grave, the asylum, oblivion and silence.'[105] The notion of a living death runs through Carr's play, from The Mai's continual return to the window and sense of

---

[103] Marina Carr, *The Mai*. Director: Emily Mann. Cast: Katherine Borowitz, Myra Carter, Miriam Healy-Louie, Barbara Lester, James Morrison, Colleen Quinn, Kali Rocha, Isa Thomas. Composer: Baikida Carroll. Lighting: Peter Kaczorowski. Set: Thomas Lynch. Costume: Candice Donnelly (McCarter Theatre, Princeton, New Jersey, opened 4 November 1996).

[104] David Callaghan, 'Performance Review: The Mai', *Theatre Journal*, 49:3 (1997), 373–5 (p. 373).

[105] Hélène Cixous, 'Aller à la Mer', in *Twentieth Century Theatre: A Sourcebook*, ed. Richard Drain (London: Routledge, 1995), pp. 133–5 (p. 133).

Metamorphic 'Bodies That Matter'

imprisonment in her home, 'I'm trapped!'[106] to Millie's description of Owl Lake as 'that dead silent world'.[107] My reading of The Mai's suicide engages with death as an enabling process through creative metamorphosis, rather than a punitive inevitability. The potentially creative performance of The Mai's metamorphosis highlights the failure of available myths of femininity to accommodate her experiences. Her suicide contrasts freedom and constraint as she simultaneously expresses herself and reveals the futility of attempting to realize herself as a desiring subject within existing spaces. Melissa Sihra contends that in Carr's work:

> Death on stage does not indicate finality but *movement*; it is a poetic drive to excavate what it means to live. The plays cannot offer transformative possibility if they are reduced to the literal, where death is regarded in terms of plot rather than poetics.[108]

Carr's later play *Woman and Scarecrow* explores the process of dying as a reflection of the way one has lived and in Chapter 4 I further pursue the feminine death as the unsettling and 'creative resurrection of the represented woman'.[109] If we apply this to The Mai's death we see agency in the act of her creative and imaginative metamorphosis, the suggestion that she has the potential to live her life 'huge and heroic',[110] but through an alternative heroism of female mythmaking.

In *Metamorphoses* Ovid suggests that the spirit is relocated in different bodies: 'Our souls however are free from death. They simply depart / from their former homes and continue their lives in new habitations.'[111] Sihra describes 'the process of woman "rehousing" herself through the act of creation and storytelling'[112] in Carr's work and this is illustrated through The Mai's metamorphosis which transforms the lake into a space of expression. The process of metamorphosis enables this rehousing by putting pressure on available representations of 'woman' in the cultural imaginary and by evoking alternatives through the provisional and metamorphic body: a creative female corporeality and the attendant evocation of a female imaginary. Wallace suggests that 'although the dramas seem to open the traumatic unstable space of subjectivity, they always achieve

---

[106] *The Mai*, p. 162. [107] *The Mai*, p. 184.
[108] Melissa Sihra, 'Renegotiating Landscapes of the Female: Voices, Topographies and Corporealities of Alterity in Marina Carr's *Portia Coughlan*', *Australasian Drama Studies*, 43 (October 2003), 16–31 (p. 28).
[109] Elisabeth Bronfen, *Over Her Dead Body: Death, Femininity and the Aesthetic* (Manchester: Manchester University Press, 1992), p. 401.
[110] *The Mai*, p. 163. [111] Ovid, *Metamorphoses*, p. 601.
[112] Sihra, 'The House of Woman', p. 207.

130 Women and Embodied Mythmaking in Irish Theatre

a "destined" closure'.[113] In contrast, I would argue that, in performance, metamorphic bodies can engage with the 'traumatic unstable space of subjectivity' to disrupt destiny and expose the power structures which construct death as an inevitability for women in tragedy. With reference to both Carr's *By the Bog of Cats* . . . (1998) and Teresa Deevy's *Katie Roche* (1938), Cathy Leeney highlights how 'the energy of human presence in performance celebrates the potential for transformation, and even where the story ends tragically and transformation is denied and delayed, the energizing voltage of performance remains'.[114] Hester's suicide at the close of *By the Bog of Cats* . . . leaves us with a haunting sense of her energy rather than defeat and The Mai's death has the potential to engage with a creative female corporeality that refuses silence. Both The Mai and Grania rewrite their mythic destinies to 'rehouse' themselves and avoid closure in their final metamorphoses.

'Radical Rearticulation' Through a Negative Utopia

Grania's and The Mai's 'disidentification with those regulatory norms by which sexual difference is materialized'[115] is performed through their metamorphoses but to what extent do they generate 'an enabling disruption, the occasion for a radical rearticulation of the symbolic horizon in which bodies come to matter at all'?[116] Grania's desiring body demands expression in the realm of Finn's court and she engages with the dominant order to work within 'the *limits* of agency and its most *enabling conditions*'.[117] Her reperformed version of queen functions disruptively *within* the patriarchal framework. The contradictory nature of her self-determination resonates with Michelene Wandor's description of bourgeois feminism as an individualist self-advancement which elides class, and yet, importantly, provides a model for woman as 'a responsible agent determining her own life and development'.[118] Indeed, this description resonates with Gregory's own position as a leading cultural nationalist figure.

---

[113] Clare Wallace, *Suspect Cultures: Narrative, Identity and Citation in 1990s New Drama* (Prague: Litteraria Pragensia, 2006), p. 270.
[114] Cathy Leeney, 'Ireland's "Exiled" Women Playwrights: Teresa Deevy and Marina Carr', in *The Cambridge Companion to Twentieth-Century Irish Drama*, ed. Shaun Richards (Cambridge: Cambridge University Press, 2004), pp. 150–63 (p. 150).
[115] Butler, *Bodies That Matter*, p. 4.   [116] Butler, *Bodies That Matter*, p. 23.
[117] Butler, *Bodies That Matter*, p. 228.
[118] Michelene Wandor, *Carry On, Understudies: Theatre and Sexual Politics* (London and New York: Routledge, 1986), p. 135.

Metamorphic 'Bodies That Matter'

More radical is The Mai's rejection of existing frameworks: the evocation of a creative feminine morphology necessitates rehousing in a female symbolic. Yet, there is no suggestion that The Mai has any future political agency; rather, agency is located in the process of metamorphosis and the institution of identity 'as a site of permanent political contest'.[119] The suggestion is that change is cumulative and this is signalled through Mai's daughter, Millie. The tableau of The Mai at the window can be viewed as a pause that gestures towards the future through acknowledgement of Millie's inheritance: for Millie to carry forward the movement and change generated by The Mai. Millie is not stalled, looking out of the window like Mai, and though she is haunted by her past, as the narrator she displays both self-awareness and the critical distance to suggest she will learn from the past. The sense of inevitability and of stasis is tempered by the potential for both The Mai and Millie to effect change, within the limits of their differing contexts.

In performance, metamorphosis can highlight Grania and The Mai's transformative energy in order to undermine their representation as victims. Warner notes that in Ovid's text, metamorphosis 'often breaks out in moments of crisis, as expressions of intense passion'.[120] Both Grania and The Mai are desiring women and it is the denial of expression of their passion within the limits of the worlds they inhabit which results in crisis. They seek new forms which can articulate their desires and agency, and they explore this through the process of metamorphosis. Moreover, as expressions of intense passion, these metamorphic forms facilitate the abject's signification to trouble fixed categories of proper and improper bodies, particularly idealized and desexualized representations of Irish 'woman'. Olwen Fouéré, who played The Mai in the premiere production, has spoken about the 'female rage'[121] in Carr's work and in performance The Mai's metamorphosis has the potential to mirror her emotional intensity. Similarly, Grania's transformation engages with a desiring female corporeality which can disrupt the transfer of authority between men. My interpretation locates the possibility of defying the inevitability of Grania's and The Mai's mythic destinies in the corporeal resistance of their departures. Their metamorphoses question interpretations of both plays'

---

[119] Butler, *Bodies That Matter*, pp. 221–2.

[120] Warner, *Fantastic Metamorphoses, Other Worlds*, p. 16.

[121] Olwen Fouéré, 'Journeys in Performance: On Playing in *The Mai* and *By the Bog of Cats . . .*', in *The Theatre of Marina Carr: 'Before Rules Was Made'*, ed. Cathy Leeney and Anna McMullan (Dublin: Carysfort Press, 2003), pp. 160–71 (p. 165).

132   Women and Embodied Mythmaking in Irish Theatre

endings as an act of despair and submission to abjection, instead offering performative confrontations with cultural representations of viable bodies.

In both plays it is not the bodies that need to be made liveable through conformity but the world around them which needs to change to accommodate these metamorphic and improper bodies. That said, we need to acknowledge the intransigence of the structures which organize those worlds. Ricoeur's utopian advocation of 'genuine' myth, which suggests 'other *possible* worlds which transcend the limits of our *actual* world',[122] risks disengagement from social conditions and effacement of the deep-rooted nature of symbolic structures. The concept of utopia is of most value when it is something to be worked towards and not necessarily attained as 'to discharge it would be to reify it'.[123] Neither The Mai's nor Grania's metamorphoses present 'other *possible* worlds', instead they suggest the need for them through their critique of their present world and its limits. Both plays end with an offstage contestation of male authority which results in silence: Grania's silencing of the Fianna's laughter, and The Mai's suicide: '*Sounds of geese and swans taking flight, sounds of water. Silence.*'[124]

The tension of that silence can be explored through Sue-Ellen Case's proposal of the negative utopia as 'the contradiction between the evident possibility of fulfilment and the just as evident impossibility'.[125] This contradiction is embodied by The Mai and Grania through the tension between their expression and desires, and the regulatory norms which restrict them; the conflict between their agency as suggested in performance and the mythic narratives which they narrate themselves through. Myth suggests 'other *possible* worlds' but the limits of the worlds Grania and The Mai live in reveal utopic change as an impossibility. Case's analysis of Sarah Kane's *4.48 Psychosis* as a negative utopia is applicable to the desire for change contained in *Grania* and *The Mai*: 'The longing for change inscribed in the play, seeking semiotic and social liberation through the reception of its performance is its negative utopia.'[126] It is the circulation of the affective desire for change in tension with the accompanying sense of impossibility that implicates the audience in that moment of

---

[122] Ricoeur, 'Myth as the Bearer of Possible Worlds', p. 490.

[123] Sue-Ellen Case, 'The Screens of Time: Feminist Memories and Hopes', in *Feminist Futures? Theatre, Performance, Theory*, ed. Elaine Aston and Geraldine Harris (Basingstoke: Palgrave Macmillan, 2006), pp. 105–17 (p. 113).

[124] *The Mai*, p. 186.

[125] Theodor Adorno, quoted by Sue-Ellen Case in 'The Screens of Time: Feminist Memories and Hopes', p. 111.

[126] Case, 'The Screens of Time: Feminist Memories and Hopes', p. 111.

silence: we *feel* the potential of change and transformation, rather than *seeing* it realized. Case appraises limiting representations of utopia and advocates the power of rebellion and underground movements which refuse containment, 'never really to actualize, be recognized, punished or tamed'.[127] The effect of the negative utopia on Kearney's assertion that '[o]ur exposure to new possibilities of being refigures our everyday being-in-the-world',[128] is the placing of responsibility for change and reconsideration of improper bodies on both Millie and on the audience. The affect of the negative utopia is potentially 'a radical rearticulation of the symbolic horizon in which bodies come to matter at all'.[129]

The conflict between the desire for change and its impossibility is replicated in the form of both plays which exploits the conflict between realist and mythic frames. Cathy Leeney argues that Gregory draws on naturalism, 'foregrounding emotion and psychology over mythic narrative',[130] and can therefore be placed within a European tradition of playwrights, such as Ibsen and Strindberg, who employ a naturalist frame to enable exploration of gender politics. The naturalist frame places the emphasis in Grania's final departure on her status as desiring subject, while the mythic frame engages with narratives in currency during the cultural revival. Thus, it is the 'clash between the mythic and the psychological'[131] that highlights Grania's negotiation of her position as both desiring subject and idealized mythic 'woman'. Carr similarly juxtaposes mythic and mimetic frameworks to expose the limits of cultural representations and theatrical forms to adequately articulate women's subjectivity.

However, Carr places an emphasis on the potential for creating new mythopoeias generated by women which might go some way to achieving this. The tension in both plays between naturalism/realism and myth enables us to view the metamorphic body as a 'site of intense inquiry, not in the hope of recovering an authentic female body unburdened of patriarchal assumptions, but in the full acknowledgement of the multiple and fluid possibilities of differential embodiment'.[132] Metamorphosis enables conception of the female imaginary not as biologically essentialist but as 'a social process, involving intervention in the symbolic' and thus

---

[127] Case, 'The Screens of Time: Feminist Memories and Hopes', p. 116.
[128] Kearney, *On Stories*, pp. 132–3.   [129] Butler, *Bodies That Matter*, p. 23.
[130] Leeney, 'The New Woman in a New Ireland? Grania After Naturalism', p. 159.
[131] Leeney, 'The New Woman in a New Ireland? Grania After Naturalism', p. 163.
[132] Margrit Shildrick with Janet Price, 'Openings on the Body: A Critical Introduction', in *Feminist Theory and the Body: A Reader*, ed. Janet Price and Margrit Shildrick (Edinburgh: Edinburgh University Press, 1999), pp. 1–14 (p. 12).

'the attempt to create a space in which women, in all their multiplicity, can *become*, i.e. accede to subjectivity'.[133] The vital importance of supporting becoming by enabling the body in process to invigorate mythmaking is further developed in Chapter 4, where I explore how the expression of women's material experiences undermines the stabilization and idealization of the beautiful female corpse. The struggle for articulation of the abject is pursued as the body continues to be the site of perpetual contest which offers alternatives to the limits of viable bodies and idealized myths of femininity.

[133] Whitford, *Luce Irigaray: Philosophy in the Feminine*, p. 90.

CHAPTER 4

Staging Female Death: Sacrificial and Dying Bodies

The dead female body is the 'perfect' trope onto which to impose an idealized femininity: silent, passive and with the capacity to be manipulated so as to please a patriarchal order. The process of attaining this perfection requires the repression of her body's material experiences and the denial of her expression in order to accomplish this feminine ideal – an unviable reality in which women are doomed to fail. Female death also functions punitively: the fate for women in tragedy is often death as a means of recuperating order and reasserting existing patriarchal structures. In Chapter 3 I cited Yeats's requirement that death be the endpoint of Margaret O'Leary's play, *The Woman* (1929). Many myths perpetuate models of femininity that align virtuous femininity, fertility and death: Creon punishes and silences Antigone by walling her up in a cave, a fate she accepts, 'So to my grave, / My bridal-bower.'[1] In *The Second Sex*, Simone de Beauvoir considers the culturally constructed connection between femininity and death, and the resultant womb–tomb dichotomy:

> Here the alliance between Woman and Death is confirmed; the great harvestress is the inverse aspect of the fecundity that makes the grain thrive. But she appears, too, as the dreadful bride whose skeleton is revealed under her sweet mendacious flesh.[2]

The womb–tomb association emphasizes woman's immanence and marks her ambivalence as signifier of fertility, while simultaneously evoking lack and decay: Antigone is potentially a 'dreadful bride', as is Kathleen Ni Houlihan. In order to examine the possibilities for resisting the enforcement of silence on women's bodies and their experiences by tropes of death and femininity, this chapter explores staging the ritual of sacrifice in Marina Carr's *Ariel* (2002) and Edna O'Brien's *Iphigenia* (2003), and probes the performance of the 'good death' in Carr's *Woman and Scarecrow* (2006).

---

[1] Sophocles, *The Theban Plays*, trans. by E.F. Watling (Harmondsworth: Penguin, 1974), ll. 890–891, p. 150.
[2] de Beauvoir, *The Second Sex*, p. 197.

136   Women and Embodied Mythmaking in Irish Theatre

In *Over Her Dead Body*, Elisabeth Bronfen highlights how 'Freud has termed "death" and "femininity" as the two most consistent enigmas and tropes in Western culture.'[3] The threat of death and femininity converges on the dead female body which is stabilized and symbolized through limiting myths of femininity which augment women's sense of a lack of accommodation within the cultural imaginary. The beauty of the female corpse 'marks the purification and distance from two moments of insecurity – female sexuality and decay'[4] and thus the good, or beautiful, feminine sacrifice and death is the result of the patriarchal drive to contain woman through the imposition of passivity and silence, and, concurrently, to maintain the status quo. Within an Irish context, this is supported by the legacy of postcolonial anxieties which have perpetuated idealized femininities that emphasize purity. This process of dematerialization and desexualization is illustrated by Bronfen's description of how

> representations of death may seek strategies to stabilize the body, which entails removing it from the feminine and transforming it into a monument, an enduring stone. Stable object, stable meanings: the surviving subject appropriates death's power in his monuments to the dead.[5]

These shrines to the erasure of women's corporeal experiences still have currency and offer recognizable cultural forms; my discussion of *Ariel*, *Iphigenia* and *Woman and Scarecrow* addresses the potency of these myths within Celtic Tiger Ireland, and within the context of postfeminist and neoliberal frameworks.

These plays premiered in the first decade of the twenty-first century – a period in which women in Ireland were increasingly engaged economically in the public realm. Peadar Kirby notes that the rate of women's employment 'was 35% as recently as the mid-1980s, it had increased to 44% by the late 1990s and to over 58% by 2006, well above the EU average'.[6] However, in contrast to these material changes, in 2002, the same year that *Ariel* premiered and the year before the premiere of *Iphigenia*, a referendum which proposed removing the threat of suicide as grounds for legal abortion in Ireland was only narrowly defeated.[7] Despite the Celtic Tiger resulting in increased financial autonomy for

---

[3] Bronfen, *Over Her Dead Body*, p. 11.   [4] Bronfen, *Over Her Dead Body*, p. 11.
[5] Elisabeth Bronfen and Sarah Webster Goodwin (eds), *Death and Representation* (Baltimore and London: The John Hopkins Press, 1993), p. 14.
[6] Kirby, *Celtic Tiger in Collapse*, p. 65.
[7] 49.58 per cent voted Yes and 50.42 per cent voted No. Voter turnout was 42.89 per cent, http://electionsireland.org/results/referendum/refresult.cfm?ref=200225R [Accessed 21 April 2010].

some women, Irish women's bodies continued to be the site over which questions of national identity and motherhood were contested. This reveals the legacy of the trope of woman as nation, but Carr's work also, as Patrick Lonergan points out, addresses issues related to globalization: 'the tendency within our culture to commodify the unspeaking female body'.[8]

Globalization is a double-edged sword: it has had a positive effect and granted financial independence to the many women who joined the workforce during the Celtic Tiger years but these financial forces are often underpinned by the commodification of women's bodies, as well as inequality regarding the impact of economic growth.[9] Allied with the legacies of postcolonialism, capitalist forces mute the female body as a commodity onto which cultural and moral values, as well as market value, can be projected. Further add to this mix an individualist postfeminist discourse which purports that women have achieved equality because *some* women have improved their economic power. According to neoliberal logic, this achievement enables women to negotiate their worth and agency, thereby creating an illusion of empowerment which is underpinned by inequality; I pursue the issue of postfeminist agency through discussion of women's violent revenge in these plays.

So how might representations of the sacrificial and dying female body intervene in these postfeminist and neoliberal discourses to reclaim self-authorship of the women's lives and deaths? How might the beautiful feminine corpse be reappropriated to destabilize woman's petrification as a monument to death and silence onstage? Bronfen suggests that '(d)eath and femininity both involve the uncanny return of the repressed, the excess beyond the text'[10] and the focus of this chapter is on how the three plays render the uncanny and unhomely visible and disruptive in performance. Freud's uncanny is marked by repetition, as 'something repressed which recurs'[11] and staging cultural representations of woman and death can potentially mobilize the troubling resurfacing of the uncanny: the eruption of unhomely pasts which unravel idealized myths of femininity. The re-

---

[8] Patrick Lonergan, *Theatre and Globalization: Irish Drama in the Celtic Tiger Era* (Basingstoke: Palgrave Macmillan, 2009), p. 174.

[9] Kirby highlights Ireland's low rate of participation in the workforce among women with young children (due to high childcare costs), and that the risk for poverty remained high during the 1990s and 2000s for all women, but especially for lone parents (most of them women) and older women (*Celtic Tiger in Collapse*, p. 65).

[10] Bronfen, *Over Her Dead Body*, p. xii.

[11] Sigmund Freud, 'The "Uncanny"', in *Art and Literature: Vol. 14* (Harmondsworth: Penguin, 1990), pp. 335–76 (p. 363).

138   Women and Embodied Mythmaking in Irish Theatre

presentation of tropes of death and femininity may enable the manipulation of instabilities and excesses of representation so that 'the regained order encompasses a shift'.[12] This echoes Judith Butler's suggestion that rematerialization can undermine fixed significations as bodies never fully comply with the norms which materialize them, and therein lies the possibility for resistance. However, there is always the risk that drawing on these tropes will also serve to reinforce them. Bronfen's proposition to preserve 'the uncanniness of the interstice of femininity and death'[13] may therefore offer a creative and disruptive strategy that undermines hierarchical binaries which align death and woman.

First, I want to explore the extent to which Ariel and Iphigenia in Carr's and O'Brien's plays disrupt the sacrificial process and defy the silence of women's fate in tragedy through exploration of death as a 'creative moment'.[14] In the second section of this chapter I examine how Carr takes this unsettling potential a step further to offer the creativity of death through 'self-sculpting'[15] in *Woman and Scarecrow*. Representing the process of death onstage figures a threshold which explores the body in the process of representation, as the audience witness Woman's reshaping of her dying body. This can potentially refuse the fixed moment of idealization. In Chapter 3 I advocated interpretation of The Mai's metamorphosis as a creative death which offers resistance through a state of becoming, and this paves the way for death to be restaged as a journey of creative potential in *Woman and Scarecrow*. The 'good death' is re-signified as an uncanny threshold and creative space through which Woman can articulate her experiences of a 'living death', as well as taking authorship of her dying body.

Sacrifice's Violent Appropriation

Bronfen notes of the sacrificed woman:

> Over her dead body, cultural norms are reconfirmed or secured, whether because the sacrifice of the virtuous, innocent woman serves a social critique and transformation or because a sacrifice of the dangerous woman reestablishes an order that was momentarily suspended due to her presence.[16]

---

[12] Bronfen, *Over Her Dead Body*, p. xii.   [13] Bronfen, *Over Her Dead Body*, p. 434.

[14] Marina Carr, Programme Note for *Iphigenia at Aulis*, Abbey Theatre Dublin. Directed by Katie Mitchell. Opened 28 March 2001.

[15] Fiona Macintosh, Programme Note for *Woman and Scarecrow*, Peacock Theatre Dublin. Directed by Selina Cartmell. Opened 10 October 2007.

[16] Bronfen, *Over Her Dead Body*, p. 181.

Staging Female Death 139

The virgin–whore dichotomy is perpetuated through the sacrificial ritual. Furthermore, the victim's body and its signification are appropriated, all in the name of the greater good. Terry Eagleton describes sacrifice as 'relinquishing one's own desires in the service of a master's'.[17] Sacrifice silences, symbolizes and objectifies. The individual and their corporeality are repressed as the sacrificed victim is reborn as a representation. In the case of Iphigenia, her sacrificed body is appropriated as a metonymic substitute for the nation. Bronfen develops Kristeva's suggestion that the violence of sacrifice is paralleled by the imposition of the symbolic order and its regulations:

> At the corpse of the sacrificed victim, the violence of the semiotic chora is confined to a single place, receives a signifier, a fixed position, and by virtue of this representation, it can be detained and admitted into the symbolic, social order.[18]

The sacrificial process serves to contain the threat of unknowable femininity and death by fixing representations of the victim within the symbolic order. Yet there are key moments in *Ariel* and *Iphigenia* which, to varying degrees, inhabit 'the uncanniness of the interstice of femininity and death' to undermine the regulation and regeneration of sacrifice.

Euripides's *Iphigenia at Aulis* is centred on Agamemnon's sacrifice of his daughter Iphigenia in exchange for a wind that will allow his troops to sail to Troy and win victory for their nation. O'Brien's *Iphigenia* premiered at the Crucible Theatre in Sheffield, England in 2003, directed by Anna Mackmin, amid a context of debate over the legitimacy of military action.[19] The production opened in the weeks leading up to the second Iraq War, of which British Prime Minister Tony Blair was a central advocate, and was set against a backdrop of worldwide anti-war protests. In his review for *The Guardian*, Michael Billington praised the 'force and

---

[17] Terry Eagleton, *Sweet Violence: The Idea of the Tragic* (Oxford: Blackwell Publishing, 2003), pp. 274–5.

[18] Bronfen, *Over Her Dead Body*, p. 195.

[19] Euripides, *Iphigenia*. Adapted by Edna O'Brien. Director: Anna Mackmin. Cast: Joanna Bacon, John Marquez, Jack Carr, Lloyd Owen, Charlotte Randle, Lisa Dillon, Susan Brown, Dominic Charles-Rouse, Ben Price, Kristin Atherton, Olivia Bliss, Veejay Kaur, Francesca Larkin, Charlotte Mills, Kitty Randle, Stacey Sampson, Rachael Sylvester, Andrew Hawley, Martin Ware. Set Design: Hayden Griffin. Lighting: Oliver Fenwick. Sound: Huw Williams. Choreography: Scarlett Mackmin. Music: Benn Ellin and Terry Davies (Crucible Theatre, Sheffield, UK, opened 11 February 2003).

O'Brien was keen for the Abbey to produce her play but the published diaries of the Artistic Director at the time, Ben Barnes, reveal that after Katie Mitchell's *Iphigenia* and Carr's *Ariel* he felt 'we are all "iphigenied" out'. Entry dated 13 July 2004, in Ben Barnes, *Plays and Controversies: Abbey Theatre Diaries 2000–2005* (Dublin: Carysfort Press, 2008), p. 274.

140   Women and Embodied Mythmaking in Irish Theatre

clarity' of O'Brien's adaptation: 'what impresses is the swift narrative drive of this 75-minute version and the vigour and irony of O'Brien's language'.[20]

The narrative thrust of O'Brien's play remains much the same as the original, save for some additional characters (a Witch and Iphigenia's Nurse who function as narrators, a Chorus of Young Girls, and the Sixth Girl of the Chorus who has an affair with Agamemnon), and a crucial shift in emphasis in the ending to prophesize Clytemnestra's bloody revenge on Agamemnon. This results in a greater emphasis on the voices and experiences of women and children, but does not afford them an increased capacity to intervene in events. The scenes which chart Agamemnon's changes of mind and final decision to sacrifice Iphigenia emphasize the exchange of women between male figures of authority: it is the conversation between Menelaus and Agamemnon that decides Iphigenia's fate. This scene is followed by Clytemnestra's arrival and her exclusion from questions of war and death, despite the fact that they impinge on her. Her powerlessness is underscored by her acquiescent response to her husband: 'I am used to doing what you say ... in everything.'[21] Iphigenia also submits to Agamemnon's authority: despite initially pleading for her life, she willingly complies with his orders and accepts her sacrifice.

Yet, in contrast to these examples of the women's submissive actions, the final scene of *Iphigenia* presents Clytemnestra drenched by bloody rain. The Young Girls *'rise vivified'* to deliver the final prophetic lines in which they foretell how Clytemnestra will exact revenge for her daughter's murder by killing Agamemnon. Edith Hall notes of O'Brien's adaptation that:

> What seems to be troublesome to the contemporary world is the idea that *both* Iphigenia and Clytemnestra suffer passively, without assuming moral agency or putting up any appreciable resistance. By extracting the murder of Agamemnon from Aeschylus, and fusing it with the Euripidean version, Clytemnestra is rescued from victimhood, and transformed into a responsive moral subject and autonomous agent.[22]

However, this is not a straightforward assertion of agency. Rosalind Gill alerts us to the difficulties of drawing on terms such as agency, autonomy and choice for feminist ends in neoliberal and postfeminist times:

---

[20] Michael Billington, 'Review of *Iphigenia*', *The Guardian*, 12 February 2003.
[21] Edna O'Brien, *Iphigenia*, in *Triptych and Iphigenia* (New York: Grove Press, 2003), p. 89.
[22] Edith Hall, 'Iphigenia and Her Mother at Aulis: A Study in the Revival of a Euripidean Classic', in *Rebel Women: Staging Ancient Greek Drama Today*, ed. John Dillon and S.E. Wilmer (London: Methuen, 2005), pp. 3–33 (p. 19).

Staging Female Death

Yet one of the problems with this focus on autonomous choices is that it remains complicit with, rather than critical of, postfeminist and neoliberal discourses that see individuals as entrepreneurial actors who are rational, calculating and self-regulating.[23]

Initially, I address women's exclusion from power through consideration of the process of appropriating the sacrificed female body, and I then develop this discussion by turning to the ways that women in O'Brien and Carr's plays question the 'empowerment' of the postfeminist subject. How might the violence of the sacrificial process intervene, not only within the context of political rhetoric, 'spin' and the justification of military action, but also within a discourse of postfeminism?

O'Brien subtitles her play a 'loose adaptation', while Carr's play is a more radical reworking. Carr's *Ariel* premiered in the Abbey Theatre in 2002, directed by Conall Morrison.[24] The play has a contemporary Irish setting but, as in her previous plays, Carr explicitly refers to Greek theatre and myth, and the first act is loosely based on Euripides's *Iphigenia at Aulis*. Ariel's father, Fermoy, has 'drames [*sic* dreams] of a conqueror', invoking 'Alexander the Greah, Napoleon and Caesar',[25] and sacrifices his daughter for political power. The constituents which drove Ireland's economic growth shifted in the early 2000s, following the bursting of the dotcom bubble in the USA, to an unsustainable property price and construction boom.[26] *Ariel* explicitly critiques the excesses and greed of the property-obsessed Celtic Tiger years with 'the money pouring in from cement and gravel',[27] by pointing to imminent self-inflicted destruction.

As in *Iphigenia at Aulis*, the father's sacrifice of his daughter highlights ruthless greed and ambition, as well as the use of political rhetoric to manipulate the situation and justify his actions. Act Two is set on the tenth anniversary of Ariel's death and opens with Fermoy, now Taoiseach (Ireland's Prime Minister), being interviewed by a journalist. Ariel's sister Elaine assists him in his careful spin-doctoring, thus clearly drawing alliances between family members: those who advocate the necessity of Ariel's death in order to gain power and those who condemn the sacrifice as murder. This division

---

[23] Gill, 'Culture and Subjectivity in Neoliberal and Postfeminist Times', p. 436.

[24] Marina Carr, *Ariel*. Director: Conall Morrison. Cast: Des Cave, Ingrid Craigie, Siobhan Cullen, Mark Lambert, Barry McGovern, Elske Rahill, Dylan Tighe, Eileen Walsh. Lighting: Rupert Murray. Costume: Joan O'Clery. Set Design: Frank Conway (Abbey Theatre, Dublin, opened 1 October 2002).

[25] Marina Carr, *Ariel* (Oldcastle, Co. Meath: The Gallery Press, 2002), p. 14. Like Carr's Midlands Trilogy, *Ariel* is marked by a strong Midlands phoneticized dialect.

[26] See Kirby, *Celtic Tiger in Collapse*.   [27] Carr, *Ariel*, p. 32.

142   Women and Embodied Mythmaking in Irish Theatre

is underpinned by the characters' control of language as Fermoy's political rhetoric places him centre stage while Ariel's sacrifice results in the silence and appropriation of her body. Carr's later play *The Cordelia Dream* (2008)[28] centres on an acrimonious father–daughter relationship and references sacrifice when the father suggests that Cordelia in *King Lear* wanted to be hung as '(h)er death was necessary for her father's salvation.'[29] This is followed by the father's revelation to his daughter that, 'All I know is for me to flourish you must be quiet.'[30] Both father and daughter are composers but the expression of his creativity depends upon the silencing of hers; a situation which echoes that of Robert and The Mai.

Fermoy's tyrannical lust for power finds expression in his advocation of Napoleon's vision of the world: 'He talked abouh hees battlefields like they were women. Which a tha battlefields was more beauhiful than the other. That's the stuff we nade to learn.'[31] The violent appropriation of land and women underpins Fermoy's political ambitions, ultimately expressed through Ariel's sacrifice. Elaine is acutely aware of this as evidenced by her advice to Fermoy following his interview: 'Ariel's your trump card. Play ud [...] Don't be afraid to give em Ariel.'[32] Elaine understands the appeal of Fermoy's portrayal to voters as a bereaved parent and this further appropriates Ariel as a symbol which confers power on Fermoy. Fermoy's sacrifice of Ariel attempts to secure social norms of virtuous femininity, as well as attempting to fulfil his political vision of transformation of the nation; a dream which rests on an unforgiving Old Testament God and advocates the self-made man.

Ariel was originally titled *Destiny*[33] and throughout we see Fermoy manipulate fictions of fate and tragic destiny; he mystifies his desire for power and his sacrifice of Ariel to justify his actions. Fermoy creates visions and fictions which support his belief in fate and the gods, namely his dream of a yellow courtyard where God lends Ariel to him:

> I had a drame, a drame so beauhiful I wanted to stay in ud till the end of time. I'm in a yella cuurtyard wud God and we're chewing the fah and then

---

[28] Marina Carr, *The Cordelia Dream*. Director: Selina Cartmell. Cast: David Hargreaves, Michelle Gomez. Designer: Giles Cadle. Lighting: Matthew Richardson. Music: Conor Linehan. Sound: Fergus O'Hare (Royal Shakespeare Company: Wilton's Music Hall, London, opened 11 December 2008).

[29] Marina Carr, *The Cordelia Dream* (Oldcastle: The Gallery Press, 2008), p. 19.

[30] Carr, *The Cordelia Dream*, p. 20.   [31] Carr, *Ariel*, p. 42.   [32] Carr, *Ariel*, p. 45.

[33] 'Marina Carr in Conversation with Melissa Sihra', in *Theatre Talk: Voices of Irish Theatre Practitioners*, ed. Lilian Chambers, Ger Fitzgibbon and Eamonn Jordan (Dublin: Carysfort Press, 2001), pp. 55–63 (p. 55).

Staging Female Death 143

this girl appears by hees side. And I says who owns her? And God says she's his. And I say give us the loan of her, will ya?[34]

Fermoy's haunting by his daughter draws on Shakespeare's Ariel from *The Tempest* who can only be seen by Prospero, the magician to whom he is in service, and on the ghostly voice of Ariel from Isaiah 29 whose voice is heard from deep in the earth. These cultural associations are further reinforced by Fermoy's creation of Ariel as an ethereal and angelic being: he points to the fact that she was born with wings, though Frances undermines this by stating that they were simply growths.[35] He idealizes her as the virtuous and 'beauhiful dead' and he attempts to justify his actions by affirming her destiny, as an angel belonging to God. Her symbolization as the pure and virginal sacrificial victim passed between those in positions of authority confers power on Fermoy through association with God and supports a male system of authority.

Fermoy narrates Ariel's fate through the yellow courtyard dream which attempts to impose his vision and a fixed narrative of destiny. There is one reference to Ariel's sense of destiny and fate when she recounts a haunting dream where the phrase '[g]irl in a graveyard' is repeated as a lullaby. At the level of narrative this would appear to perpetuate the constriction of fate, as well as tropes of death and femininity, but the dream also evokes creativity and self-authoring in death. In 2001, the year before the premiere of *Ariel*, Carr wrote the programme note for the Abbey's production of *Iphigenia at Aulis* directed by Katie Mitchell. In the note, Carr draws attention to the creativity of death:

> But the unrighteous passion of it all, the ghoulish love of blood and Death, axe on bone. Isn't there something beautiful about that? Something defining? Death is the creative moment, it appears.[36]

Perhaps death as a 'creative moment' which supports the regeneration of the sacrificial process and the authority of the dominant order can be refigured into a resistant space which has the potential to rewrite the sacrificial narrative, thus disrupting woman's signification as silent and passive victim, and the manipulation of Ariel's sacrifice as a political 'trump card'.

---

[34] Carr, *Ariel*, p. 57.   [35] Carr, *Ariel*, p. 57.
[36] Carr, Programme Note for *Iphigenia at Aulis*. Directed by Katie Mitchell. Opened 29 March 2001.

144 Women and Embodied Mythmaking in Irish Theatre

Disrupting the Sacrificial Ritual

Euripides' plot is shaped by Iphigenia's plea for her life, followed by her speech accepting her sacrifice, so I begin by addressing the extent to which Carr and O'Brien deviate from this narrative arc. In *Ariel* there is no plea followed by acceptance but Ariel's exit at the end of Act One does allude to Iphigenia's sacrifice, with her words, 'I'll puh ouh the ligh so.'[37] As Fiona Macintosh notes, 'a farewell to the sunlight in Greek tragedy heralds almost every character's departure from this life'[38] and thus Iphigenia's final words, 'Farewell, welcome light!',[39] support the interpretation of her embrace of her sacrifice. However, the staging of *Ariel* has the potential to counter this narrative: Ariel's words may indicate her acceptance of her sacrifice and vindicate Fermoy's fate for her but Rupert Murray's lighting design for the Abbey production shifted the meaning in performance. Ariel departed into the light shining through the door stage right, a space and light which would evoke her presence throughout the play. Iphigenia leaves the light, while Ariel walks into a lit space of creativity and death. The light remains after Ariel has left the audience's view, accusingly shining on to Fermoy in a tableau which is echoed in Act Two. The light simultaneously incriminates Fermoy and creates an uncontainable offstage space of expression for Ariel.

In contrast, O'Brien's *Iphigenia* retains the plea and acceptance speech as Iphigenia proclaims: 'I will die. Let me save Hellas [...] I will do it gloriously.'[40] O'Brien is acutely aware of the symbolization of the female body: in *Mother Ireland* she writes how 'Ireland has always been a woman, a womb, a cave, a cow, a Rosaleen, a sow, a bride, a harlot, and of course, the gaunt Hag of Beare.'[41] Despite this, O'Brien adheres to Euripides more closely and does not interrogate the containment of the sacrificial process and the substitution of woman as land and nation. In her introduction to the play, O'Brien outlines her deviation from the report of Iphigenia's sacrifice. There is uncertainty as to whether Euripides wrote the section at the end of the play which describes the substitution of Iphigenia's body with that of a deer and O'Brien suggests that: 'It seems unthinkable that an artist of Euripides's unflinching integrity, with a depth and mercilessness of

---

[37] Carr, *Ariel*, p. 37.

[38] Fiona Macintosh, *Dying Acts: Death in Ancient Greek and Modern Irish Tragic Drama* (Cork: Cork University Press, 1994), p. 98.

[39] Euripides, *Iphigenia at Aulis*, in *The Bacchae and Other Plays*, trans. by John Davie (London: Penguin, 2005), l. 1507, p. 220.

[40] O'Brien, *Iphigenia*, p. 106.

[41] Edna O'Brien, *Mother Ireland* (London: Weidenfeld & Nicolson, 1976), p. 11.

Staging Female Death

sensibility, would soften his powerful story for public palliation.'[42] O'Brien's Iphigenia, dressed in her bridal veil, is carried off to be sacrificed and this maintains the trope of death and virtuous femininity, thereby neutralizing her potential as a 'dreadful bride'. The Sixth Girl's report of the offstage sacrifice evokes the violence of the deed, yet also fetishizes the beautiful victim: 'The blood from her gashed throat matted the curls of her hair.'[43] O'Brien accuses the author of the last section of Euripides's play of offering a palliative ending, yet she endorses the symbolization of Iphigenia as rebirth and beauty masking decay and violence: the Witch prophesizes early in the play that: 'She comes to nourish with the drops of flowing blood the altar of the divine goddess from her own throat, her lovely body's throat.'[44] The Iphigenia story has the potential to disrupt the Irish blood sacrifice narrative as the sacrificial victim in this instance is female. However, O'Brien suggests that:

> Iphigenia is for the chop but at the moment when her little universe is shattered, when she realises that she is being betrayed by both God and man, she pitches herself into an exalted mental realm, the realm of the martyr-mystic who is prepared to die but not to kill for her country.[45]

The presentation of Iphigenia as a 'martyr-mystic' and a beautiful corpse mystifies and idealizes her; furthermore, her death leads to regeneration of the nation and the dominant political order.

In O'Brien's play the language used to describe Iphigenia draws on Catholicism and evokes the Virgin Mary: Iphigenia is 'ripe for beatitude'[46] and 'Blessed above all the maidens'.[47] Iphigenia is chosen as the sacrificial victim because she is pure and virginal, and O'Brien underscores her innocent state through her initial presentation as a child playing with her sisters, and also through her coming of age: she '*lets out a cry – her menstrual blood has started to flow*'.[48] Iphigenia is employed as a symbol in opposition with Helen of Troy and they mark the two extremes of femininity: 'the margins or extremes of the norm – the extremely good, pure and helpless, or the extremely dangerous, chaotic and seductive'.[49] The women are placed in opposition by Artemis' comments that Iphigenia is a 'child without blemish', who can 'undo these wrongs'; wrongs bought about by Helen, '[t]he blame for all these troubles'.[50] Iphigenia's sacrifice is justified by the actions of dangerous and seductive Helen, and Iphigenia therefore

---

[42] O'Brien, *Iphigenia*, p. 63.   [43] O'Brien, *Iphigenia*, p. 108.   [44] O'Brien, *Iphigenia*, p. 69.
[45] O'Brien, *Iphigenia*, p. 62.   [46] O'Brien, *Iphigenia*, p. 101.   [47] O'Brien, *Iphigenia*, p. 103.
[48] O'Brien, *Iphigenia*, p. 77.   [49] Bronfen, *Over Her Dead Body*, p. 181.
[50] O'Brien, *Iphigenia*, p. 103.

146   Women and Embodied Mythmaking in Irish Theatre

atones for the sins of woman. The other woman who is key to O'Brien's play is of course Iphigenia's mother Clytemnestra, who is Helen's sister, and I return to her (in the section 'The Agency of Revenge') in conjunction with discussion of women's violent actions and agency, but first I want to pursue the discussion of Iphigenia's sacrificial body through analysis of Ariel's.

The Integrity of Ariel's Sacrificial Corpse

In contrast to O'Brien's representation of the sacrificial body, Carr's *Ariel* undermines the integrity of the corpse to evoke the 'uncanniness of the interstice of femininity and death'. This serves to disrupt the sacrificial process and expose Fermoy's political rhetoric. Ariel is sacrificed following the close of Act One but in Act Two she subversively accesses the stage space after her death and, unlike Iphigenia, has a voice. Fermoy's world, characterized by political spin, confines Ariel to a space of silence and death but she brings this abject space into play, participating in, and disrupting, the narrative. In Act Two Fermoy receives a ghostly phone call from Ariel just as he is about to leave for her anniversary Mass. Prior to her death, Ariel does not plead for her life as she is not aware of the sacrifice her father intends to make. However, her phone call functions as a delayed plea: 'Come and get me, will ya? [...] Please, just brin me home.'[51] Ariel's ghostly return disrupts the naturalist frame of the play and the linear narrative of Greek tragedy, a strategy also deployed in *Portia Coughlan* and *The Mai*. The uncanny return of Ariel's presence marks her absence. Her sacrifice removes her body from the world which Fermoy wants to control but she refuses to be contained and her voice emanates from the otherworld; the stage directions state, *'let Ariel's voice come from everywhere.'*[52] The boundaries between this world and the otherworld, life and death, realist and mythic, are dissolved to create unease.

The impossibility of Ariel's request to be 'brought home', except as a corpse, exposes the myth of home as a refuge and safe haven. During the phone call we learn that Ariel is in Cuura Lake, a space in which she is no more at home than in the Fitzgerald household, and she tells her father: 'There's a huge pike after me.'[53] Cuura Lake is an abject, border realm which defines the limits of home and language. The lake is redolent of the layers of repressed memory which Ariel's uncanny phone call enables to resurface and invade the space from which she has been excluded. The

[51] Carr, *Ariel*, p. 56.   [52] Carr, *Ariel*, p. 55.   [53] Carr, *Ariel*, p. 56.

programme for the Abbey's production of *Ariel* included a quote from Isaiah 29 which evokes the fallen archangel Ariel through the vocal: 'Your voice shall come from the ground like the voice of a ghost.'[54] Ariel's phone call articulates the misery of her experience and exposes the violence of the sacrificial process; moreover, Ariel's ghostly phone call serves as a remonstrance to her father from her watery grave. In the Abbey production this scene echoed the end of Act One as a bright light shone onstage through the door stage right to simultaneously accuse Fermoy of his crime and evoke death as a disruptive, 'creative moment' and expressive space for Ariel.

Ariel's childish sobbing at the end of the phone call in the Abbey production embodied her refusal to be contained and silenced as a fixed symbol of purity and innocence whose sacrifice would lead to the generation of Fermoy's political vision. This was a powerful and affective moment in performance, perhaps more so than the actual dialogue, as her vulnerable weeping echoed round the auditorium. Ariel's disembodied voice emerged to disrupt the stability of the sacrificed victim, where 'the violence of the semiotic chora is confined to a single place.'[55] However, the onstage appearance in Act Three of Ariel's corpse in a coffin initially appeared to reunite her body with its voice or owner, thus undoing its threatening potential.

In *The Acoustic Mirror*, Kaja Silverman suggests that the potentially troubling nature of the voice-off in Hollywood cinema is recuperated by the voice's reunion with its body: the voice-off 'exceeds the limits of the frame, but not the limits of the diegesis; its "owner" occupies a potentially recoverable space [...] it generally contributes to the unity of the classic cinematic text by carving out a space beyond the frame of one shot for the next to recover.'[56] The reunion of Ariel's disembodied voice with its owner, her corpse, should support the unity of the sacrificed corpse; however, just as evocation of the semiotic chora offers a strategy of resistance to the sacrificial process, so too does Ariel's decayed corporeality.

Edith Hall argues that both *Ariel* and *Iphigenia* fail to engage with blood sacrifice in an Irish context as they do not address Iphigenia's sacrifice for the nation.[57] However, I would argue that rather than being disengaged

---

[54] Mark Patrick Hederman, 'Musings on Ariel', in Programme for Abbey Theatre Production of *Ariel*. Directed by Conall Morrison. Opened 2 October 2002.
[55] Bronfen, *Over Her Dead Body*, p. 195.
[56] Kaja Silverman, *The Acoustic Mirror: The Female Voice in Psychoanalysis and Cinema* (Bloomington: University of Indiana Press, 1988), p. 48.
[57] Hall, 'Iphigenia and her Mother at Aulis', p. 20.

148   Women and Embodied Mythmaking in Irish Theatre

from the trope of blood sacrifice in Ireland, *Ariel* refuses it. Ariel's coffin is brought onstage and, like the phone call, marks her uncanny threat from beyond the silence of death. In contrast to woman's immanence, Ariel's decayed body marks her as material and therefore, as Susan Cannon Harris argues of the female martyr, ineligible for the sacrificial role.[58] The regenerative potential of the sacrificial process is denied by Ariel's disruption of the female corpse as idealized symbol of nation which, in turn, undermines affirmation of Fermoy's authority and his political vision. Both the phone call and Ariel's corpse present Ariel's body as fragmented; she is described as being 'wizened to a nuh',[59] and together with the open coffin, this generates an unease in the audience as to whether her decayed body will be revealed. The audience's discomfort is toyed with in the moment when we see Elaine lift Ariel's skull out of the coffin in a scene reminiscent of Hamlet's discovery of Yorick's skull.[60] The sacrificial process attempts to prescribe which bodies matter within the dominant order through imposition of a symbol onto the sacrificed body. However, Ariel's shrivelled body signals Fermoy's failure to turn her into an idealized symbol of the regeneration of his political vision; Ariel's abject corpse is a decayed and fragmentary body which reveals the limits of signification and the limits of Fermoy's ability to perpetuate the political rhetoric of his order.

We never discover whether she voluntarily takes part in the sacrifice like Iphigenia, nor is her death or body allowed to be reported and fixed. The lack of a whole corpse, and the threat of her fragmented one, serves to underline the silence surrounding her sacrifice which frustrates the audience's efforts to piece together the narrative. The final moments of the Abbey premiere further disturbed attempts to contain her corpse's threatening material presence within a coffin. The curtains closed to leave Ariel's coffin visible onstage, a presence which remains when the play ends and the other characters disappear. The inability to repress the uncanny return of Ariel's corpse serves to refuse the containment of the feminine death and question the limits of both the play and of signification within Fermoy's political order.

Violent Landscapes

The past refuses to be repressed in Carr's work and consistently prevents narrative closure as other lives and worlds move across fluid time and space

---

[58] Harris, *Gender and Irish Drama*, p. 3.   [59] Carr, *Ariel*, p. 70.
[60] William Shakespeare, *Hamlet*, Act V, Scene 1.

Staging Female Death

boundaries. Ghosts and corpses populate many of Carr's plays as they return to seek vengeance and bring past crimes to light: the ways in which haunted bodies evoke cultural memory in *Portia Coughlan* is central to Chapter 5. In addition to ghostly bodies and corpses, the use of space is central to the troubling return of the past in *Ariel*. The 2001 Abbey production of *Iphigenia at Aulis*, directed by Katie Mitchell, offered a visually powerful representation of Iphigenia's sacrifice when a strong wind, accompanied by white light, blasted through the door stage right. Iphigenia's sacrifice is offstage and reported to the audience but this moment intimated the moment of her death; a presence which is not contained in the sacrificed and symbolized body. The premiere of *Ariel* utilized the relationship between mimetic and diegetic space in order to evoke a creative space for Ariel. The diegetic space, which suggests the presence of Ariel and death, overlaps the mimetic space to evoke both Ariel's absence and Fermoy's guilt. Similarly, the inability to confine Cuura Lake offstage underscores the lake's refusal to conceal a violent past: we learn that Fermoy was present when his mother was drowned by his father and the recovery of Ariel's body from the lake is accompanied by the recovery of Fermoy's mother's body. The resurfacing of Ariel's disembodied voice, and both Ariel's and her grandmother's corpses, serves to interrupt the transactions of female bodies between male figures of power.

The lake is an unhomely space which enables the expression of that which has been repressed and facilitates Ariel's dislocation of the boundaries of the world she has been excluded from. In the Abbey production the lake was largely suggested as an offstage space evoked by light through the doorway stage right and thus linked to Ariel and the otherworld. However, the liminal space of the scene change between Acts Two and Three was used to convey the lake's seepage onstage, partly through the blue lighting on the back wall. The set change was suggestive of divers searching the lake as the stage hands wore head lights, spotlights swung around the stage and pulleys dropped down. The sense of an echoing, watery and haunting space was also evoked through an affective soundscape: the reverberations of Frances's unsettling wails were accompanied by haunting piano music. Cuura Lake enables the articulation of private traumas in the public realm and thus insists that all have to take responsibility for these past crimes; both those who violently meted them out and those who are complicit in their role as silent witness. In Carr's work the landscape offers alternative spaces which refuse the very values which many of the men, from Xavier Cassidy in *By the Bog of Cats* ... to Fermoy Fitzgerald, embody: power coupled with land-ownership. The refusal of containment and embrace of

150   Women and Embodied Mythmaking in Irish Theatre

process by both bodies and landscape is likewise central to Mary Elizabeth Burke-Kennedy's *Women in Arms* and Olwen Fouéré's *riverrun* (see Chapters 2 and 6), which refute the domination of woman and land through the creative exploration, and redefinition, of this relationship.

The Agency of Revenge

The uncontainable nature of both Ariel's body and Cuura Lake disrupts the appropriation of the sacrificed body, and exposes the power at play in the sacrificial process. I now turn to discussion of women's attempts to exert power in *Ariel* and *Iphigenia*. The complicity of women and the illusion of agency are intertwined in both plays through the act of revenge as implemented by Ariel's sister Elaine and their mother Frances, as well as O'Brien's Clytemnestra. The ending of O'Brien's play witnesses the assertion of Clytemnestra's voice and attempted negotiation of agency as she adopts Agamemnon's violent methods and enacts revenge – this counters the earlier scene when Iphigenia is taken away to be sacrificed and we see Clytemnestra gagged by Agamemnon's soldiers. In an early draft of the play, O'Brien has crossed out the following description of Clytemnestra in the final moments: 'CLYTEMNESTRA stands drenched in blood, smiling ecstatically – a warrior queen.'[61] This is much how the ending was staged, as Edith Hall's review of the production reveals:

> It turned out to be a prophetic rendering of Clytemnestra's incomparable soliloquy from an earlier Greek tragedy, Aeschylus' *Agamemnon*, when the avenged mother exults in the drops of bloody rain with which she has been spattered while murdering her husband. Standing in twin pools of light and blood, O'Brien's Clytemnestra reassures the audience that the dastardly Agamemnon will be punished.[62]

The bloody rain imagery is taken from Clytemnestra's lines in *Agamemnon*:

> he drenched me in the dark red showering gore,
> and I rejoiced in it, rejoiced no less
> than all the plants rejoice in Zeus-given
> rainfalls at the birthtime of the buds.[63]

---

[61] Dated 10 November 2002. OB/526, p. 62. Edna O'Brien Papers, University College Dublin Library Special Collections.

[62] Edith Hall, 'Barbarism with Beatitude', *Times Literary Supplement*, 21 February 2003.

[63] Aeschylus, *Agamemnon,* in *The Oresteia*, trans. by Alan Shapiro and Peter Burian (Oxford: Oxford University Press, 2003), ll. 1584–87, p. 93.

Staging Female Death 151

O'Brien's ending echoes this imagery both visually, with the revitalizing bloody rain falling onstage, and narratively, in Clytemnestra's final lines:

> Sweeter to me your words
> Than Heaven's raindrops
> When the cornland buds.[64]

O'Brien notes in the stage directions of the final scene that the Chorus of Young Girls '*rise vivified*' after the bloody rain falls.[65] This moment is in stark contrast to their exit following the scene where Iphigenia learns of her impending marriage to Achilles and her menses start: '*The Girls lie on the floor on their bellies and one starts a pre-wedding hymn, the others join in and slowly with balletic precision they make their way on their bellies along the stage and off.*'[66] The blood that invigorates them in the final scene is that of Agamemnon, and thus the blood of revenge rather than sacrifice, which could potentially mock the transformative effect of blood sacrifice. However, both sacrifice and revenge leave patriarchal structures intact and thus support the violent imposition of silence on women. Through sacrifice, Iphigenia's virtuous femininity secures victory for Agamemnon and through revenge, Clytemnestra is construed as transgressive and mad, resulting in her death as punishment by her son Orestes.

Iphigenia does not interrogate the monumentalizing process of sacrifice which substitutes an idealized symbol for woman, nor does it disabuse us of the postfeminist illusion of Clytemnestra's agency enacted through her revenge. Death and femininity are offered as stable representations which can be controlled and which, by implication, reaffirm the authority of Agamemnon's male-dominated social order. O'Brien's adaptation strives to afford both Iphigenia and Clytemnestra greater expression but the cycles of sacrifice and revenge are unbroken, thus denying the women full access to agency and expression.

In *Ariel*, it is initially suggested that Frances is complicit with Fermoy's actions as intimated by her silent presence at the side of the stage during Fermoy's interview. However, Act Two closes with Frances's murder of her husband in response to her discovery that he killed Ariel; actions which also recall Clytemnestra in Aeschylus' *Agamemnon*. The opening of Act Two of the Abbey production of *Ariel* had visual echoes of *Agamemnon* as the stage was bathed in red light, suggestive of the bloody rain and the increasingly violent actions of Acts Two and Three. René Girard suggests that sacrifice, as a regulation of violence, 'prevents the spread of violence by keeping

---

[64] O'Brien, *Iphigenia*, p. 110. [65] O'Brien, *Iphigenia*, p. 109. [66] O'Brien, *Iphigenia*, p. 78.

152   Women and Embodied Mythmaking in Irish Theatre

vengeance in check'.[67] The focus in both *Ariel* and O'Brien's *Iphigenia* on Frances's and Clytemnestra's violent revenge defies that 'sacrifice is primarily an act of violence without risk of vengeance'.[68] Frances and Clytemnestra take violent retribution into their own hands to undermine the regulation of sacrifice as beneficial and purifying violence. However, Clytemnestra's retribution attempts to offer reassurance and narrative closure in O'Brien's *Iphigenia*, whereas it is not the endpoint of Carr's play. Instead, it is Elaine who enacts the final violent action.

Elaine's alliance with her father is a demonstration of her hatred for her mother; a hatred which is given full expression in Act Three when, echoing Sophocles' *Electra*, Elaine murders Frances in revenge for Fermoy's death. In *The Oresteia*, Orestes kills his mother Clytemnestra as punishment for her transgressions and thus reinstates patriarchal structures; as Luce Irigaray suggests: 'The murder of the mother results, then, in the non-punishment of the son, the burial of the madness of women – and the burial of women in madness.'[69] However, in *Ariel*, Elaine's murder of her mother suggests that regulation of the social order through violence is not simply available to the male characters, thereby offering the suggestion of agency. Yet, Elaine represents 'the active, freely choosing, self-reinventing subject of postfeminism',[70] whose supposed empowerment supports patriarchy. She endorses Fermoy's power-hungry worldview and his rhetoric of fate, and her mother Frances comments that Elaine has 'spint too long round the min'.[71] Elaine draws on Fermoy's rhetoric when she distinguishes between her father's sacrifice of Ariel and her mother's murder of Fermoy:

> I can tell the difference between a crime of eternihy and a low, blood-spahhered, knife-frenzied revenge [. . .] Whah my father done to Ariel had the grandeur a God in ud. Pure sacrifice. Ferocious, aye. Buh pure. Whah you done to him was a puckered, vengeful, self-servin thing wud noh a whiff of the immortal in ud.[72]

Elaine's accusation is illustrated by Girard's discussion of what happens when the distinction between purifying and impure violence breaks down:

---

[67] René Girard, *Violence and the Sacred* (London: The Athlone Press, 1995), p. 18.
[68] Girard, *Violence and the Sacred*, p. 13.
[69] Luce Irigaray, 'The Bodily Encounter with the Mother', in *The Irigaray Reader*, ed. Margaret Whitford (Oxford: Basil Blackwell, 1991), pp. 34–46 (p. 37).
[70] Gill, 'Culture and Subjectivity in Neoliberal and Postfeminist Times', p. 443.
[71] Carr, *Ariel*, p. 64.   [72] Carr, *Ariel*, p. 64.

Staging Female Death

> The *sacrificial crisis*, that is, the disappearance of the sacrificial rites, coincides with the disappearance of the difference between impure violence and purifying violence. When this difference has been effaced, purification is no longer possible and impure, contagious, reciprocal violence spreads through the community.[73]

The failure to obtain and contain a sacrificial body, of Ariel's absent corpse, signals this breakdown, but the distinctions between 'impure violence and purifying violence' are further weakened by the violence brought onstage by Frances and Elaine, and Clytemnestra's revenge in O'Brien's play. Women can take part in 'purifying violence' only if it supports patriarchal structures as Elaine's murder of her mother illustrates. Nevertheless, despite Elaine's defence of Fermoy's sacrifice, there is no one to speak up on her behalf, illustrating that ultimately 'purifying violence' is always exercised by patriarchal forces. Like O'Brien's Clytemnestra, Elaine acts under the false belief in a postfeminist empowerment achieved through the adoption of vengeful violence which ultimately supports patriarchal structures.

Interestingly, both Carr and O'Brien return to the figure of the grieving and vengeful mother through the story of the tragic Trojan queen, Hecuba. In Carr's *Hecuba* (2015), the queen's efforts to control the telling of her story is underscored by the reported speech which structures the play as the characters narrate the events.[74] This has a distancing effect which is amplified in the scene where one of her remaining daughters, Polyxena, is sacrificed by Agamemnon on the altar of Achilles: it is described in more detail than is enacted. The action is sparse in this scene but the RSC production created a visual counterpoint to the immaculate Polyxena when her sister Cassandra dipped her hands into a bowl of blood, smearing it all over herself. This is not the only exposure of the messy reality of the sacrifice. It is a 'botched ritual'[75] as Polyxena is not killed with one clean cut across her throat. Agamemnon cuts her throat again and when this fails one of the priests steps forward and plunges a knife under her ribs.

As in *Ariel*, the political potential of the sacrifice is undermined by Polyxena's uncooperative body. Hecuba's initial response to the sacrifice is

---

[73] Girard, *Violence and the Sacred*, p. 49.

[74] Marina Carr, *Hecuba*. Director: Erica Whyman. Cast: David Ajao, Nadia Albina, Derbhle Crotty, Ray Fearon, Edmund Kingsley, Amy Mcallister, Chu Omambala, Lara Stubbs, Marcus Acquari/ Nilay Sah/Luca Saraceni, Sebastian Luc Gibb/Christopher Kingdom/Daniel Vicente Thomas/ Yiannis Vogiaridis. Designer: Soutra Gilmour. Lighting: Charles Balfour. Composer: Isobel Waller-Bridge. Sound: Andrew Franks (Royal Shakespeare Company: Swan Theatre, Stratford-upon-Avon, opened 17 September 2015).

[75] Marina Carr, *Hecuba*, in *Plays 3* (London: Faber & Faber, 2015), p. 245.

154   Women and Embodied Mythmaking in Irish Theatre

juxtaposed with Clytemnestra's: she is enervated, 'speechless', and with 'no hint of the fabled queen now'.[76] In Euripides' *Hecuba* she wreaks violent revenge on Polymestor – who was meant to be safeguarding her murdered son Polydorus – by murdering his sons. In contrast, Carr's Hecuba does not engage in violence and thereby rewrites the myths that were set 'in stone to bolster their [the Greek state] sense of themselves and validate their savage conquests'.[77]

In the same period in which she wrote *Iphigenia*, Edna O'Brien was also developing a script which incorporates the story of Hecuba: *Trojan Women/Greek Men*, which has not been staged to date.[78] The contrast with Carr's *Hecuba* echoes the difference of approach between *Ariel* and O'Brien's *Iphigenia*. The first draft of *Trojan Women/Greek Men* reveals Polyxena's acceptance of her sacrifice: she '*grows strangely calm*' before stating that she is 'willing to die'.[79] She is taken away to be sacrificed offstage and Hecuba responds by '*hurl(ing) herself again and again against a rock*'.[80] O'Brien adheres more closely to Euripides than Carr and both Polyxena and Hecuba succumb to the narrative of fate and silence; the play closes with Hecuba being led off in chains as Odysseus' slave and the final projected image is that of the 'pendulum of fate' swinging.[81] The presentation of Hecuba in the close of Carr's play is more equivocal: there is a sense of pride as she has rewritten her myth, but the description of her standing motionless by the death pyre of her last child, waiting quietly for her own death, could be read as acquiescent. This uncertainty is embedded in the form of the play: the struggle for narration through the use of reported speech is amplified by the distance created by descriptive, rather than physical, action. Yet, Hecuba's quiet and immovable waiting in the final moments of the play refuses a tragic climax and the emotional restraint is in contrast to Euripides' *Hecuba* and to the ending of *Woman and Scarecrow*. Carr's plays consistently present women who utilize death as an unstable threshold to deny catharsis and undermine narratives which advance the inevitability of women's fate as punishment through death and silence.

---

[76] Carr, *Hecuba*, p. 247.   [77] Carr, 'Introduction', in *Plays 3*, p. x.

[78] Drafts and notes for the script are held in the Edna O'Brien Papers, UCD Library Special Collections. The first draft, OB/522, is dated June 2002, and Ben Barnes's diary entry for 1 February 2004 reveals that she approached the Abbey about staging the play. Barnes states that her play needs to be more 'hard-hitting' and he is critical of her 'well-intentioned but dangerous tropes': *Plays and Controversies: Abbey Theatre Diaries 2000–2005*, p. 325.

[79] OB/522, p. 15. Edna O'Brien Papers, University College Dublin Library Special Collections.

[80] OB/522, p. 16. Edna O'Brien Papers, University College Dublin Library Special Collections.

[81] OB/522, p. 43. Edna O'Brien Papers, University College Dublin Library Special Collections.

Staging Female Death

Failure and Silence

Ariel's somewhat apocalyptic vision serves as a cautionary tale of greed for power, money and land, yet, as Leeney points out, at the end of the play we are left facing a world barren of ethics or morals:

> The audience is left with nothing to cling to: no hero or heroine, no sense of right against wrong; only a future formed by bitter recrimination, loss, jealousy and dumb revenge. The extraordinary rhetorical power of the language up to this endgame is silenced. Elaine says nothing. There is nothing left to say.[82]

Fermoy's repressive mythmaking and evocation of fate attempts to fix Ariel's body as a regenerative image of his political order, but her refusal to be silenced reveals the empty promise of his vision. Fintan O'Toole notes in his review of *Ariel* that 'the three pillars of the old Ireland – Church, State and Family – are in an advanced state of decay'.[83] Despite growing signs of economic collapse, the prolonged excesses of the Celtic Tiger diminished public belief in political judgement. This sense of disintegration was highlighted by Frank Conway's set design for the Abbey production: 'He made the floor of the stage a botched map of the world, one corner of which jutted perilously into the auditorium and fell away like a cliff collapsing into the ocean.'[84] The reference to environmental issues signalled 'the betrayal by older generations in their failure to husband the resources of the natural world for those coming after'.[85] Moreover, that sense of betrayal by the generation which reaped the benefits of the Celtic Tiger without regard for the economic consequences, was prescient in 2002. However, the decision to end the Abbey production with Elaine curling up on the floor in front of her mother's body and wrapping Frances's arms around her, read as an awkward attempt to mitigate the bleakness of the play's vision and reassert matrilineal bonds.

Edith Hall suggests that *Iphigenia at Aulis* is a play 'which will always speak loudest to an audience themselves characterised by intense, secularised moral *aporia*'.[86] O'Brien's *Iphigenia* was performed against a backdrop of international instability and backlash against military action

---

[82] Cathy Leeney, 'Marina Carr: Violence and Destruction: Language, Space and Landscape', in *A Companion to Modern British and Irish Drama 1880–2005*, ed. Mary Luckhurst (Oxford: Blackwell Publishing, 2006), pp. 509–18 (p 513).

[83] Fintan O'Toole, '*Ariel*: Review', in *Critical Moments: Fintan O'Toole on Modern Irish Theatre*, (Dublin: Carysfort Press, 2003), pp. 188–91 (p. 188).

[84] Leeney, 'Marina Carr: Violence and Destruction', p. 514.

[85] Leeney, 'Marina Carr: Violence and Destruction', p. 512.

[86] Hall, 'Iphigenia and her Mother at Aulis', p. 29.

in the second Iraq War. *Iphigenia at Aulis* is fundamentally about the rhetoric of political language and Edith Hall suggests that this may explain the resurgence of interest in the play during the early years of the twenty-first century: 'it is in the power and dangers of spin-doctoring that lies the vivid contemporary immediacy of Euripides' play'.[87] However, *Ariel* goes further in its presentation of a world that is not simply fragile; instead, the audience is left with an overwhelming sense of irredeemable despair. O'Toole applauds Carr's courage in 'trying to find public myths for a society that no longer knows what anything means'.[88] More explicitly, Carr's courage lies in her efforts to reclaim myth's potential and to enable women's voices and experiences to shape these myths.

Hall argues that the performances of both O'Brien's and Carr's versions of the Iphigenia story were 'surprisingly conservative in the[ir] naturalism'.[89] I would agree that *Iphigenia* makes fewer imaginative departures from the original in narrative and performance. However, Hall fails to address the potential moments of resistance in performance of *Ariel* which are characterized by a conflict between the mythic and realist frames. *Ariel* was not as well received as her earlier plays and Harvey O'Brien points to the attempt 'to blend the narrative spaces of naturalistic drama with monumental villainy of the Greek tragedy' as not wholly successful, commenting that 'some of the audiences had given over to inappropriate laughter, suggesting that true balance between elements has not been achieved'.[90] Of course, inappropriate laughter might also signal audience discomfort as a result of their recognition of untold histories and experiences, and the defamiliarization of the recognizable setting. The uncomfortable juxtaposition of myth and realism in Carr's work offers points of resistance to the original versions as well as indicating the way to a new self-conscious mythopoeia interrogated in performance.

The sacrificial process may attempt to cement the power of Agamemnon's and Fermoy's order but the sacrificed body has the capacity to resist this process and disrupt the stabilization of meaning. Ariel's phone call and the decaying corpse mark the uncanny return of that which the sacrificial process has sought to repress and symbolize. Thus, where Iphigenia is easily substituted as a symbol of nation, Ariel refuses to support the hierarchy of Fermoy's political world. Uncanny evocation of 'the interstice of femininity and death' undermines the sacrificial process and

---

[87] Hall, 'Iphigenia and her Mother at Aulis', p. 25.   [88] O'Toole, '*Ariel*: Review', p. 190.

[89] Hall, 'Iphigenia and her Mother at Aulis', p. 12.

[90] Harvey O'Brien, 'Review of *Ariel*', 10 October 2002, https://culturevulture.net/theater/ariel-marina-carr/ [Accessed 17 June 2017].

Staging Female Death

troubles the frame of representation within the stage space. *Ariel* elucidates the emptiness of the prevailing order to expose the regulation of violence and control of the signification of bodies, even in death. Death as a 'creative moment' in Carr's work offers a space of resistance which can promote the failure of the sacrificial process as symbolization and silence.

Reperforming the 'Good Death' in *Woman and Scarecrow*

Ariel offers death as a 'creative moment' by enabling the presence of death, which has been contained offstage, to disrupt the stage space and sacrificial narrative, but in *Woman and Scarecrow* the 'creative moment' of dying is placed centre stage. *Woman and Scarecrow* marks a development from the suicides of Carr's earlier Midlands Trilogy to present a more sustained vision of self-authoring within the uncanny space of death and femininity. The dying protagonist, Woman, remarks of Ophelia: 'She had a good death.'[91] The 'good death' is beautiful, idealized and devoid of threatening decay, as painted by John Everett Millais in his saintly depiction of *Ophelia* (1851–52).

This section explores how introducing the dying female onstage in Carr's *Woman and Scarecrow* retains the ambivalent threat of the womb–tomb association as a strategy for disrupting the 'good death'. The alliance of death and woman in Carr's play is utilized to reveal Woman's self-authoring of both her death and dying body. *Woman and Scarecrow* develops the strategies discussed in *Ariel* which figure death and femininity as an unsettling and creative terrain, and deny catharsis. In order to explore how this uncanny realm manifests, I refer to two productions of the play: the 2006 premiere production at London's Royal Court, directed by Ramin Gray with Fiona Shaw as Woman and Bríd Brennan as Scarecrow, and the 2007 Peacock Theatre production in Dublin, directed by Selina Cartmell with Olwen Fouéré as Woman and Barbara Brennan as Scarecrow.[92]

Woman and Scarecrow charts the final bedbound hours of a character named Woman; a journey which is both moving and humorous. Woman

---

[91] Marina Carr, *Woman and Scarecrow* (Oldcastle, County Meath: The Gallery Press, 2006), p. 17.
[92] World Premiere. Marina Carr, *Woman and Scarecrow*. Director: Ramin Grey. Cast: Fiona Shaw, Bríd Brennan, Peter Gowen, Stella McCusker Design: Lizzie Clachan. Sound: Emma Laxton (The Royal Court Theatre, London, opened 21 June 2006).
    Irish Premiere. Directed by Selina Cartmell. Cast: Olwen Fouéré, Barbara Brennan, Bríd Ní Neachtain, Simon O'Gorman. Set and costume design: Conor Murphy. Lighting: Paul Keogan. Sound: Denis Clohessy (Peacock Theatre, Dublin, opened 10 October 2007).

158   Women and Embodied Mythmaking in Irish Theatre

is accompanied by her alter ego Scarecrow, who evokes the figures of the banshee and Morrígan,[93] and she is visited by just two other characters in the course of the play, her husband and Auntie Ah. The gothic presence of death is made felt by 'The Thing in the Wardrobe', whom we hear demonically laughing and battling with Scarecrow as Death tries to claim Woman. Carr has described *Woman and Scarecrow* as 'a death bed aria'[94] thus drawing inspiration from the lyrical big speech convention of Greek drama. In *Dying Acts*, Fiona Macintosh suggests that Greek drama is more interested in the process of dying than the point of death and this is also true of Carr's play. Macintosh goes on to highlight that the public nature of death in Ireland differs from modern conceptions of 'hidden' death, and she draws parallels between death rituals in Ireland, particularly rural Ireland, and ancient Greece: both engage with death as a process and perceive 'no rigid separation between the world of the living and the world of the dead'.[95] Carr is therefore successful in merging both Greek dramatic representations of death and Irish mythology. Macintosh outlines four stages in the dying process in Greek drama, of which *Woman and Scarecrow* fulfils two. The play chronicles the 'tussles with the arduous process of dying'[96] and this is given physical expression through the offstage frays between Scarecrow and 'The Thing in the Wardrobe'. The second stage that Macintosh identifies shows the dying person 'endowed with eloquence and insight, which secure victory, albeit temporarily, in the face of imminent defeat'.[97] The notion of imminent defeat is linked to the cathartic experience; an experience which Jeanie Forte suggests gives 'the illusion of change without changing anything'.[98] Is there potential for change through staging 'the arc of a life and the completion of that life'[99] in order to question the satisfaction of the 'imminent defeat' of the 'good death'?

---

[93] Rosalind Clark describes the Morrígan as a powerful war goddess whose 'dangerous and destructive nature is further emphasised by her identification with Badb [. . .] The word *badb* is a generic term signifying supernatural women, sometimes in the form of crows, who hover over the battlefield, foretelling the slaughter and later feeding on the slain.' Clark goes on to highlight the connection between the Morrígan and the banshee, a spectre who warns of death: 'Both are female spirits who prophecy death and destruction and terrify people with their fearsome howls.' *The Great Queens: Irish Goddesses from the Morrígan to Cathleen ní Houlihan*, p. 24.

[94] RTE Radio 'Playwrights in Profile' series. Interview with Marina Carr, 23 September 2007.

[95] Macintosh, *Dying Acts*, p. 31.   [96] Macintosh, *Dying Acts*, p. 58.

[97] Macintosh, *Dying Acts*, p. 58.

[98] Jeanie Forte, 'Realism, Narrative, and the Feminist Playwright – A Problem of Reception', in *Feminist Theatre and Theory*, ed. Helene Keyssar (Basingstoke and London: Macmillan, 1996), pp. 19–34 (p. 22).

[99] 'Marina Carr in Conversation with Melissa Sihra', p. 56.

Staging Female Death 159

Homi Bhabha's unhomely, as a rupturing expression of personal traumas of the past in the present and in the public realm, offers a strategy of reading the possibility of both inhabiting and disrupting tropes of femininity and death in *Woman and Scarecrow*. Through exploitation of the uncanny and unhomely, the resurfacing of that which has been repressed exposes the instabilities and excesses of representation. Bronfen warns that, 'the crucial point is that femininity, which in its linkage with death marks uncanny difference within, has not been translated into canny Otherness'.[100] Ambivalence needs to be retained, rather than recuperated, in order to unloose significations of woman and death, and enable the 'uncanny return of the repressed'[101] to be made visible and disruptive in performance. Woman's life is one of neglected potential and disappointment: she describes it as a 'half-existence',[102] while Scarecrow points to Woman's realization that '[t]he world has not yielded all you had hoped of it'.[103] It is this sense of insignificance that leads to Woman's 'female rage'[104] which is expressed through Scarecrow initially, yet culminates in their unified voices which articulate their disappointment with life and anger towards Woman's husband: 'I go to my grave bewildered by your cruelty. I go angry, I go unforgiving.'[105]

Woman and Scarecrow articulates and stages the unhomely experience of women's dislocation from limiting myths of femininity which repress the material realities of their lives. It is the resurfacing of these lived realities that negotiates more accommodating myths which express Woman as a desiring subject, and puts pressure on cultural representations of death and femininity. I want to explore the articulation of lived realities, first via Woman's reclamation of her story through her self-sculpting, before moving on to address the disruptive assertion of the materiality of the female body. I then pursue the uncanny through examination of the character of Scarecrow as a threshold of femininity and death.

Rewriting a Living Death

Through analysis of the staging of Woman's death in the final scene we can explore the ways in which her performance reconfigures the supposed endpoint of her life. Dying enables the articulation of Woman's suffering and a life of passion, as the following lines reveal:

---

[100] Bronfen, *Over Her Dead Body*, p. 395.   [101] Bronfen, *Over Her Dead Body*, p. xii.
[102] Carr, *Woman and Scarecrow*, p. 46.   [103] Carr, *Woman and Scarecrow*, p. 18.
[104] Fouéré, 'Journeys in Performance', p. 169.   [105] Carr, *Woman and Scarecrow*, p. 56.

160   Women and Embodied Mythmaking in Irish Theatre

WOMAN: And do you know what passion means?
SCARECROW: It comes from the Latin, *pati*, to suffer.
WOMAN: Well, I said to myself, if that's the definition of passion then I have
    known passion. Yes, I have lived passionately, unbeknownst to myself. Here
    it lay on my doorstep and I all the time looking out for it.[106]

Woman's life has been typified by disappointment and lack of fulfilment
but her passionate death grants her an opportunity to imbue her life with
the epic status she desires. Woman gains eloquence and insight but this
does not lead to her 'imminent defeat' as death is transformative in Carr's
work. It is the destabilizing return of the unhomely which characterizes
Woman's reperformance of death and highlights her transformation and
subversion of the 'good death'. Woman's dying serves as an uncanny
reminder of her suffering and her 'tussles' with a living death, as she says:
'How we die says it all about how we have lived.'[107] Indeed, the uncanny is
embodied in the idea of Woman as a living corpse and she describes how,
'I'm being buried alive. I am my own ghost.'[108] This sense of 'being buried
alive' echoes sentiments expressed by many of the women in Carr's previous plays, including The Mai, Sorrel in *On Raftery's Hill* and Portia
Coughlan. Woman's life has been characterized by repression of her
desires; a life lived, in her words, as '[e]xile from the best of ourselves'.[109]
Woman's sense of displacement and unhomeliness is captured by her claim
that 'I have never felt at home here.'[110] However, the play creates an
accommodating space in which she can reshape and rewrite her body
and life. The uncanny performance of dying enables the resurfacing of
Woman's passions and suffering, the best of herself, as 'something which
ought to have remained hidden . . . has come to light'.[111]

The tension between materiality and representation involved in the
attempt to reproduce the experience of death is conveyed in *Ariel* through
Ariel's haunting voice and corpse which refuse her containment as sacrificial symbol. Ariel's ghostly presence reveals the process of both death and
representation as unstable and open to creative resignification. Woman's
self-conscious reshaping of both her life and dying body highlights the
possibilities inherent in the process of reperformance. Scarecrow's desire to
'try and articulate it right'[112] is brought to fruition at the end of the play
when Scarecrow dips her quill into Woman's veins to write her life in her
blood. The performance of Woman's death has the potential to express her

---

[106] Carr, *Woman and Scarecrow*, p. 68.   [107] Carr, *Woman and Scarecrow*, p. 45.
[108] Carr, *Woman and Scarecrow*, p. 40.   [109] Carr, *Woman and Scarecrow*, p. 60.
[110] Carr, *Woman and Scarecrow*, p. 67.   [111] Freud, 'The "Uncanny"', p. 364.
[112] Carr, *Woman and Scarecrow*, p. 40.

Staging Female Death 161

anger with her unfulfilled life, as well as rearticulating it. The necessity of 'articulating it right' is also suggestive of the constraints placed on her expression by myths of femininity. Writing in Woman's blood highlights the construction and performance of Woman's body; a process whereby cultural codes and myths are inscribed on her body, yet these inscriptions are simultaneously rewritten and reperformed through her body. In the 2007 Peacock production, Woman's semi-naked state in the final scene (her nightdress was removed in the previous scene) highlighted her desire to rid herself of all the cultural significations and roles that have been imposed upon, and stifled, her. This dramaturgical decision also honed in on the connection between the sculptural image of the final scene and Michelangelo's pietà: the Virgin Mother with the semi-naked body of Christ lying across her lap. Paul Keogan's beautiful chiaroscuro lighting design heightened the sculptural quality of this scene.

There are several issues at stake in this scene: both in terms of the potential for viewing the naked female body as untainted material for re-fashioning myths of femininity, and in understanding the process of self-sculpting as agential. Rather than suggesting that the naked body is 'pure' or 'authentic' and devoid of cultural associations, the scene 'reveal[ed] the performative status of the natural itself'.[113] Woman's sculpted body exposed the artifice of constructions of gender and the feminine 'good death'. Woman's claim that 'I am slowly carving myself into a Greek statue',[114] sees her 'invoke the category' of tropes of femininity and death, both 'provisionally to institute an identity and at the same time to open the category as a site of permanent political contest'.[115] Opening up categories to 'permanent political contest' is not a straightforward assertion of free-dom or agency as the ability to institute an identity is always under pressure by the relentless creation of other, potentially limiting, identities. The contradictions involved in invoking myths of femininity are highlighted by Woman's request for a mirror in Act One:

> To watch myself die. I want to see how I am. I always look in mirrors to find out what's happening to me. [. . .] My dear! I have transformed myself into the ideal. Look at me! I am graveyard *chic*, angular, lupine, dangerous.[116]

Her self-aware shaping of her dying body highlights early twenty-first-century society's permutations of a living death through representations of ideals of feminine beauty which fetishize impossibly thin female bodies

---

[113] Butler, *Bodies That Matter*, p. 200.   [114] Butler, *Bodies That Matter*, p. 200.
[115] Butler, *Bodies That Matter*, pp. 221–2.   [116] Carr, *Woman and Scarecrow*, p. 21.

162 Women and Embodied Mythmaking in Irish Theatre

to propagate a deadly 'graveyard *chic*'. The 'choice' to aspire to this skeletal ideal offers an illusion of agency through one's self-sculpting; a 'choice' which shifts responsibility to the individual and obscures the power and inescapability of neoliberal and postfeminist discourses. However, Woman's self-sculpting is not that of 'the active, freely choosing, self-reinventing subject of postfeminism'.[117] Woman invokes the myth she is reshaping, the image of the self-sacrificing mother, and plays with notions of death and femininity; but paradoxically her assertion of control over the expression of her unhomely 'half-existence' is achieved through death. This bind is compounded by her final rewriting of her life: her expression is at the expense of her very life as she draws on her blood as the ink. Her self-fashioning is a stringent critique of the 'choices' available to women for narrating their lives outside of perpetuated ideals of femininity. Furthermore, by drawing on the 'natural' internalized materials of her body – her blood as ink – Woman's performance exposes the complex relationship between culture and subjectivity, whereby 'socially constructed ideals of beauty or sexiness are internalized and made our own, that is, really, truly, deeply our own, felt not as external impositions but as authentically ours'.[118] Women internalize these discourses, own them and maintain them through a self-discipline which is repackaged as 'choice' but Woman's self-sculpting reveals the material effects of these 'choices' through her perverse inhabitation of a creative and deathly femininity.

Feminine Beauty as 'a Mask for Decay'

Woman and Scarecrow inhabits the threshold between life and death both to explore constructions of the beautiful death as a reassuring trope, and to reveal the difficulties involved in rewriting a powerful and enduring cultural body of myths. Unlike much Greek drama, Carr brings the dying process onstage and emphasizes its materiality to undermine the idealized and stabilized image of Woman as a beautiful corpse. Referring to Edgar Allan Poe's essay on death and femininity, *The Philosophy of Composition*,[119] Elisabeth Bronfen argues that the anxiety which surrounds death is translated into desire in the beautiful female corpse: 'We invest in images of wholeness, purity and the immaculate owing to our fear of

[117] Gill, 'Culture and Subjectivity in Neoliberal and Postfeminist Times', p. 443.
[118] Gill, 'Culture and Subjectivity in Neoliberal and Postfeminist Times', p. 436.
[119] Edgar Allan Poe, 'the death of a beautiful woman is, unquestionably, the most poetical topic in the world'. Quoted in Bronfen, *Over Her Dead Body*, p. 59.

Staging Female Death 163

dissolution and decay.'[120] Woman references Ophelia's 'good death',[121] an aestheticized and idealized death free of decay. We also see this process of dematerialization and aestheticization at work in Kathleen Ni Houlihan's beautiful offstage transformation from an old woman into a young queen, alleviating any anxiety we may experience at the prospect of Michael's sacrifice for his country or indeed of her deathly body.

In *Woman and Scarecrow*, the decay in the dying process is highlighted by Woman's difficulty in breathing, swallowing and living, and underlines her uncanny state on the threshold between life and death, evoking fertility and decay. The unsettling deterioration of the corporeal resists fixing the beautiful corpse and exposes the ambivalent myth of femininity: 'the beauty of Woman [...] conceived as a mask for decay'.[122] The play emphasises the decay of the body and Woman's description of her 'skeletal queenality'[123] embraces the threatening figure of the 'dreadful bride'. The Peacock production played with the horror of this figure in an addition to Woman's final scene with Him: he removes her nightdress and their final moments together are in sexual union. In her more recent *Phaedra Backwards*,[124] Carr explores what society construes as the 'monstrous' expression of an older woman's desires. The outcome of this expression is physicalized in the character of the Minotaur, borne of Phaedra's mother and a bull, while Phaedra's lust for her stepson Hippolytus results in a gruesome punishment as she is savagely attacked onstage by ghosts who bite off lumps of her flesh.

Woman admits to Scarecrow that she is 'drowning in duty'[125] and the notion of sacrifice is introduced by Scarecrow telling Woman: 'You martyred yourself to a mediocrity',[126] meaning her husband. Woman's Husband also references her martyrdom in response to her revelation that she has had affairs, when he accuses her of deception and attempts to contain her actions within constrictive myths of femininity: 'All the time acting the weeping virgin, the bleeding martyr, the woman abandoned'.[127] Of course, while the messy actions of weeping and bleeding define the female body, they cannot be materialized as this would undermine idealized representations of virtuous femininity. Harris argues that within an Irish theatrical context female sacrificial blood is interpreted as threatening

---

[120] Bronfen, *Over Her Dead Body*, p. 62. [121] Carr, *Woman and Scarecrow*, p. 17.
[122] Bronfen, *Over Her Dead Body*, p. 67. [123] Carr, *Woman and Scarecrow*, p. 22.
[124] Marina Carr, *Phaedra Backwards*, in *Plays 3* (London: Faber & Faber, 2015). Premiere directed by Emily Mann (The McCarter Theatre, Princeton, New Jersey, opened 18 October 2011).
[125] Carr, *Woman and Scarecrow*, p. 27. [126] Carr, *Woman and Scarecrow*, p. 28.
[127] Carr, *Woman and Scarecrow*, p. 39.

164   Women and Embodied Mythmaking in Irish Theatre

and 'dirty' unlike their male counterparts' purifying blood. Furthermore, Harris highlights Irish dramatists' removal of sacrificial death from the stage space: 'Sacrificial drama worked for nationalists only when it did *not* allow the victims to "bleed and die" onstage.'[128] However, Woman rewrites her life and death in her own blood, centre stage, and in the final minutes of the Peacock production blood ran down Woman's chest from the wound in her neck. Woman's corporeal rewriting, or 'self-sculpting', paradoxically grants Woman expression of her life while bringing her closer to death, thus reworking the myth of the renewal of blood sacrifice. Like The Mai, Woman is a parody of the Christ figure's ability to be reborn.

In the Peacock production's final pietà tableau, both Woman and Scarecrow play with their expected roles as the Christ figure and Virgin Mother. Taking her cue from Marina Warner, Bronfen suggests that the lack of a decaying body for the Virgin Mary reasserts her purity and eternal nature; 'the myth of the Virgin Mary serves as a repository for fantasies about the preservation of body wholeness and integrity'.[129] In Act Two Woman describes Caravaggio's painting *Death of the Virgin* highlighting Mary's 'putrid greeny black' feet.[130] Woman stresses that Mary's immanence resists the fiction of her miracle and she is made ordinary: 'the miracle is over. Yes it is. She's going down into the clay. Not up to the blue beyond.'[131] Of course, in the pietà tableau it is Scarecrow who is the Virgin Mother with Woman draped across her lap. The Virgin's role in the pietà is to receive Christ's sacrifice and transform it into rebirth on behalf of all sinners.[132] However, Scarecrow is a creative resignification and grotesque parody of the Virgin as she assists Woman's transformation through an expressive and paradoxically revitalizing death.

Scarecrow as a 'Harbinger of Death'

While Woman resists the virgin–whore dichotomy, Scarecrow figures 'the myth of Medusa [. . .] a third variation on the conjunction woman-death-womb-tomb.'[133] The mythic significations of Scarecrow reinforce her monstrous, uncanny and morbid state. A scarecrow is quite simply an empty set of clothes so feminizing a scarecrow offers an enigmatic space onto which the threat of woman and death can be inscribed and contained,

---

[128] Harris, *Gender and Irish Drama*, p. 9.   [129] Bronfen, *Over Her Dead Body*, p. 68.

[130] Carr, *Woman and Scarecrow*, p. 43.   [131] Carr, *Woman and Scarecrow*, p. 42.

[132] Marina Warner, *Alone of All Her Sex: The Myth and Cult of the Virgin Mary* (London: Quartet, 1978), p. 223.

[133] Bronfen, *Over Her Dead Body*, p. 69.

Staging Female Death

but Carr harnesses Scarecrow's threat as an uncanny double, a figure without a fleshy body which reminds us of both the absence and excess of representations of death.[134] Just as Lady Gregory's *Kincora* (1905) and the tableaux vivants performed by the Inghinidhe na hÉireann drew on the dynamism and dangerous female energy of the crow-like Morrígan, so too does Carr. The Morrígan choreographs Cuchulain's death, where Scarecrow assists with the reperformance of Woman's life. Like Kathleen Ni Houlihan and the banshee, Scarecrow is vampiric and warns of imminent death, and in Act Two Scarecrow emerges from the wardrobe dressed as a crow to personify Death.

Carr's earlier plays represent death as a diegetic space, figured in the landscape in *The Mai*, *Portia Coughlan* and *Ariel*. In *Woman and Scarecrow* we are made aware of Death's menacing presence by the offstage grumblings and animalistic noises which emanate from the wardrobe. However, Death increasingly encroaches on the stage space with the crow's wing and 'clawed foot',[135] appearing at the end of Act One and through Scarecrow's personification in Act Two. The expressive realm of death is creatively refigured in Scarecrow, offering a contrast to Woman's cloying marriage and half-life. In terms of staging, Scarecrow's freedom is corporeally expressed through her movement, in counterpoint to the bedbound Woman. As an uncanny representation of Woman's repressed desires, Scarecrow enables Woman's disappointments to resurface and aids her to give corporeal and vocal expression to her unfulfilled life; Scarecrow serves to underline Woman's life as a performance that can be reshaped, though within the limits of death.

The Royal Court and Peacock productions placed different emphases on Scarecrow's mythic associations and this creates the potential for reading different aspects of Woman and Scarecrow's relationship as uncanny. The Peacock production conveyed a heightened mythic tone with Conor Murphy's set evoking a non-realist dreamscape: the snow-covered bedroom tilted towards the audience from the upstage right corner and was surrounded by transparent walls painted with swirling white clouds, behind which snow fell at different points during the performance. At times this created a nightmareish world with the animalistic growls and blasts of noise from the wardrobe but Denis Clohessy's sound design also

---

[134] Scarecrow was clearly identifiable as female in both the Royal Court and Peacock productions, which enables the audience to easily construe her as Woman's alter ego. However, a non-binary Scarecrow could have a very interesting effect on the play and perhaps reinforce the creative space of death in Carr's work.

[135] Carr, *Woman and Scarecrow*, p. 40.

166   Women and Embodied Mythmaking in Irish Theatre

drew on fairytale with slow piano music fused with twinkling bells. Scarecrow (Barbara Brennan) was dressed in a large black cloak and sunglasses, with her face caked in white make-up. This presented Scarecrow as a corpse-like and otherworldly figure, further underlining Death as a creative and mythic realm.

In contrast, the Royal Court production kept a tighter rein on the plethora of images and cultural references generated by Carr's script. The bedroom was smaller and more minimal in presentation with just the bed and wardrobe against plain, dark walls. Bríd Brennan was cast as Scarecrow to present her as a younger version of Woman and thus an uncanny double of Woman's possible life: she was described in the *Times* review as 'a sharp-tongued female in silky nightdress and heels'.[136] The Royal Court production's Scarecrow therefore suggested Woman as she might have been, had she fulfilled her desires and potential.

In Act Two of the Peacock's production Scarecrow emerged as Death dressed in a white nightdress and with long hair, echoing the visual appearance of Woman as well as traditional representations of the banshee: to use Freud's phrase, Scarecrow is an 'uncanny harbinger of death'.[137] Marina Warner suggests that, in the *danse macabre*, Death is usually dressed in the costume of the deceased, 'a grotesque exaggeration of the victim's usual activities'.[138] In the Peacock production, Scarecrow's appearance when she emerges from the wardrobe in Act Two exaggerates Woman's deathly appearance. In contrast, the Royal Court production's Scarecrow emerged from the wardrobe wearing a crow's head, thus shifting the character's presentation to a heightened realist and mythic frame. Despite the production's setting in a sparse, yet not wholly naturalist bedroom,[139] some critics found this shift too marked; the *Independent* review described it as 'strained'.[140] Warner examines the *danse macabre* within the development of a secularized individual identity, quoting Paul Binski:

> The image represents a future state – what the subject will become – and so contributes to the subject's sense of self. In this case the thing that is

---

[136] Sam Marlowe, 'Reviews: First Night', *The Times*, 23 June 2006, p. 22.

[137] Freud, 'The "Uncanny"', p. 357.

[138] Marina Warner, *No Go the Bogeyman: Scaring, Lulling and Making Mock* (London: Vintage, 2000), p. 106.

[139] See website of set designer Lizzie Clachan: www.lizzieclachan.co.uk/WomanandScarecrow47.html [Accessed 21 August 2017].

[140] Kate Bassett, 'Anyone Got a Stain-Remover?', *Independent*, 25 June 2006.

Staging Female Death   167

constructed [. . .] is the notion of the sinner [. . .] by means of its defamiliarization, it offers the capacity for self-examination.[141]

This moment of defamiliarization is facilitated in the Royal Court production by Scarecrow's entrance as a crow, a mythic representation of Death
which presents what Woman will become. Furthermore, within a mythic
realm characterized by the reperformance of contingent mythic significations, the emphasis is shifted from judgement to Woman's future of
possibility and transformation.

Myth, Memory and Closure

Both the strategies adopted by the Peacock and Royal Court productions,
of a heightened or more minimal approach to the evocation of a mythic
framework, can offer insight into the reception and performance of myth
as either a reassuring or distancing effect. The Royal Court's sparser setting
meant that the entrance of the mythic in the form of Scarecrow as Death
forced the audience to further question the play's realism and thus the
mythic served as an uncanny alienation effect. This shift highlighted
Woman's inability to express herself within a realist frame, requiring
alternative means of expression which are performed by Scarecrow as
uncanny and mythic double. The Peacock production created
a heightened and mythic realm from the opening of the play to grant
Woman's death a sense of the epic but it veered towards visual overload at
times. The evocation of a dream-like world risked disengaging with the
social context of the play. Woman's final speech was delivered front centre
stage against a backdrop of clouds on the transparent screen which divided
Woman from the space that contained her bed. The emotional intensity of
Olwen Fouéré's delivery of Woman's final speech reinforced the inherited
narrative of the Greek deathbed speech where death is the highlight,
running the risk of evading engagement with Woman's unhomely experience. The staging of this final scene as uninterrogated catharsis is in danger
of creating 'the illusion of change without changing anything'.[142]

The uncanny and unhomely status of Woman needs to be retained in
order to avoid containing her expression. Carr's suggestion that '[d]eath is
the creative moment'[143] depends upon disruption of the world which has
contained and disappointed her female characters. The Peacock

---

[141] Warner, *No Go the Bogeyman*, p. 106.
[142] Forte, 'Realism, Narrative, and the Feminist Playwright', p. 22.
[143] Carr, Programme Note for *Iphigenia at Aulis*.

168 Women and Embodied Mythmaking in Irish Theatre

production did evoke a mythic realm of possible creativity for Woman but the over-emphasis on the mythic may have disabled the potential of myth to serve as an alienation effect. Mythic representations cannot be destabilized and resignified without first inhabiting them; but situating the play in an entirely mythic realm runs the risk of presenting the mythic as uninterrogated spectacle and reassuring nostalgia, thus undermining the audience's critical distance. Still, the production did create a space of expression for Woman, offering the mythic as a provisional and accommodating realm which disrupts the naturalization of inherited representations of woman and death.

Maintaining the uncanny threat of tropes of death and femininity is vital to disrupt their perpetuation, yet the presentation of memory-making in *Woman and Scarecrow* also runs the risk of closing down engagement with Woman's unhomely experiences. Clare Wallace describes how, in Carr's work, destiny 'reveal[s] a lack which is amended through simulation – illusion, fantasy, false memory, story'.[144] Woman's lack, the loss of her mother and her inability to produce a reliable memory of her, was remedied in the Peacock production's staging of Woman's memories. However, does this present memory simply as a reassuring, homely fiction? The Peacock production opened with Woman's memories projected onto a screen: we watch old camcorder footage of a young girl wearing a red coat who walks away from the camera as the screen is raised to reveal Woman standing on her bed and surrounded by falling snow. All Woman's descriptions of her memories were accompanied by the same fairytale music which was played during the opening screened memories and helped create another space of memory which renders Woman's past present. Through representations of memory we try to fix the past but this process needs to be exposed in order to uncover an unhomely past, rather than a nostalgic one. Woman is trying to recreate and return to the homely space of her childhood and thus the presentation of memory needs to question its reliability and expose its performativity. Scarecrow undercuts Woman's memories of herself as a child visiting her mother:

WOMAN: And I was wearing my new red coat and my new red hat.
SCARECROW: (*Shakes* Woman) You were not.
[. . .]
WOMAN: Leave me the details.
SCARECROW: I'll leave you the details that are true.[145]

---

[144] Wallace, *Suspect Cultures*, p. 270.   [145] Carr, *Woman and Scarecrow*, p. 47.

Staging Female Death 169

Furthermore, in the Peacock production Scarecrow provided an uncanny reperformance of Auntie Ah's memory of Woman's dead mother, as she enacted the description of 'her walking across the sand'.[146] This served to destabilize the constancy of the memory, as well as evoking its presence and 'reality' for Woman. The staging of both memory and fate has the potential to reveal the instabilities inherent in these fictions. However, the production did not foreground the duplicity of these fictions and therefore served to reinforce Woman's nostalgia and offer narrative closure. The use of film and music perpetuated, rather than interrogated, Woman's memories.

In tragic theatre, death is the highlight of a life of suffering but in *Woman and Scarecrow* tragedy is reconfigured so that death offers a reclamation and articulation of Woman's unhomely experiences. Woman refuses to be 'just another of those invisible women past their prime'[147] and demands in her final speech that 'we must mark those moments, those passionate moments, however small'.[148] Death is rewritten so that it no longer signifies a fate of silence but becomes an expressive threshold and 'creative moment'. The instability and creativity of the process of death prevents the imposition of fixed representations of the beautiful female corpse and evades narrative closure on Woman's 'half-existence', instead opening up the possibility of articulating her repressed and passionate potential. Both the process of representation as a recuperation of the threat of death and woman, and the illusory satisfaction of the cathartic journey, are dislocated by Woman's exposure of her unfulfilled life and reperformance of her body. The emphasis on Woman's corporeality exposes the impossibility of guaranteeing a 'true' representation of death, as well as revealing the cultural construction of bodies and the internalization of mythic significations. In Carr's play feminine death becomes the unsettling and 'creative resurrection of the represented woman':[149] death is a paradoxical process of becoming. The 'good death' is no longer simply the fulfilment of a tragic life but is materialized and reperformed to reveal the idealization of its representation and to resist the closure of tragedy. Death is not a punitive inevitability, nor is it 'silent on all the ordinary unbearable tragedies';[150] instead it offers Woman the opportunity to resignify both her life and dying body, to unsettle and reperform the 'good death'.

---

[146] Carr, *Woman and Scarecrow*, p. 48.   [147] Carr, *Woman and Scarecrow*, p. 43.
[148] Carr, *Woman and Scarecrow*, p. 68.   [149] Bronfen, *Over Her Dead Body*, p. 401.
[150] Carr, *Woman and Scarecrow*, p. 20.

The Limits of Death

Both *Ariel* and *Woman and Scarecrow* demonstrate how a mythic frame can be utilized as an uncanny alienation effect which shatters the illusion of realist theatre and the naturalized outcome of tragedy for women. The productions of *Woman and Scarecrow* discussed pursue different approaches to create another world of Woman's creation, the Royal Court's pared-down aesthetic in contrast to the Peacock's amplified mythic resonance, yet both served to question the ability of realism to represent both Woman's subjectivity and refiguration of the 'good death'. Similarly, in *Ariel* the non-realist elements question the inevitability of the sacrificial narrative. Ariel haunts and disrupts the heightened realist frame as her phone call and corpse mobilize the potential of the realm of death to unsettle Fermoy's carefully controlled political order. The inevitable outcome for the sacrificed body, of silence and appropriation by the dominant order, is thus undermined. Furthermore, the abject space of Cuura Lake enables the unhomely to erupt into the public realm as the crimes of the Fitzgerald family resurface. However, where the mythic and the other-world disrupt Fermoy's vision from offstage, the mythic space of *Woman and Scarecrow* is brought centre stage to facilitate expression of Woman's unhomely 'half-existence', while simultaneously staging the passionate rewriting of her life through the performance of her death.

Death is rewritten in Carr's plays as an expressive space where identities in process can be articulated. In Carr's earlier Midlands Trilogy, suicide is a creative act of rewriting the self but one which is ultimately surrounded by silence and, as argued in Chapter 3 on metamorphosis, articulates a negative utopia. In an act which pre-empts the self-authoring of *Woman and Scarecrow*, The Mai attempts to exert artistic control and reshape expression of her life onstage through use of her body as a cello. Yet it is in her final offstage metamorphosis that The Mai creatively refigures her body and identity which serves to underline the inadequacy of the stage space and thus the limits of the world she lives in to figure and articulate these changes. The failure of the 'creative moment' of death in the Midlands plays figures the women's crisis of representation within the symbolic. The connection between suppression of the creativity of death and lack of female accommodation is developed further in the two plays that followed: *On Raftery's Hill* and *Ariel*. *On Raftery's Hill* stages the failure to escape the claustrophobic cycles of repetition, even through death, and this lack of movement denies the creativity of death. *Ariel* sees a movement from this repetitive stasis as even though death is imposed on Ariel, some

Staging Female Death

resistance to this repressive process is negotiated as the offstage realm of death disrupts the onstage space. Where *The Mai* and *Ariel* inhabit the offstage spaces to put pressure on representation within the onstage space, *Woman and Scarecrow* brings 'the uncanniness of the interstice of femininity and death'[151] centre stage to creatively refigure myths of femininity, both through the reperformance of Woman's life in death and the resurfacing of her repressed desires through Scarecrow. However, it is imperative that the material effects of these myths are presented so that Woman's self-sculpting is not presented as unconstrained. The complex ways in which we internalize ideals of femininity are not easily challenged and this is made clear by Woman's paradoxical use of death as a creative realm.

Performances of *Woman and Scarecrow* will always run the risk of reinforcing the representation of death and femininity as a fixed signification, just as the ritual aspect of the 'death bed aria' relies upon the emotional arc of tragedy. The productions of the plays discussed in this chapter succeed in the moments when they inhabit and unfix tropes of death and femininity to expose their constructed nature and stall their reproduction. O'Brien's *Iphigenia* does not question the naturalization of the myth of femininity and death, and Iphigenia's sacrifice enables the violent reproduction of the sacrificed female as silent icon. In contrast, Carr's plays navigate the space between reinforcement and critique of these myths. By retaining the unsettling, uncanny interstice of death and femininity the impulse towards redemption and rebirth inherent in narratives of sacrifice and threnody can be refigured by the dead woman. Myth is not simply reassuring or nostalgic; instead it functions interrogatively when the uncanny and unhomely erupt into the public realm to reveal the instability of constructions of woman and death as a space of unrepresentable silence. The following chapter further pursues these ideas through examination of the haunted body's refusal to allow death to impose silence, as well as its rejection of a restrictive linear chronology which denies the histories of women's embodied experiences.

---

[151] Bronfen, *Over Her Dead Body*, p.434.

CHAPTER 5

Haunted Bodies and Violent Pasts

The myth of the beautiful dead woman is central to the traditional folk-tale in which Bluebeard murders his wives and then preserves their corpses in a locked room. The tale is the source for Mary Devenport O'Neill's ballet-poem *Bluebeard* which premiered at the Abbey Theatre on 25 July 1933, and its key features resonate powerfully with the conservatism of 1930s Ireland. The period was notable for the severe curtailment of women's ability to participate in public life and the attendant drive to contain their bodies: the 1937 Constitution enshrined woman's role as a mother and defined her place through 'her life within the home'.[1] In the folk-tale women are punished through death and their desires are contained in Bluebeard's locked room, while his are fulfilled. When Bluebeard's most recent wife is to be left alone in his castle, he hands her a set of keys and issues her with strict instructions not to go into a forbidden room. However, her curiosity gets the better of her and she is horrified to discover a bloody chamber filled with the corpses of Bluebeard's previous wives. When Bluebeard returns to the castle he declares that he will punish her by killing her and placing her in the room with the dead wives.

In the original Brothers Grimm tale, her brothers rescue her and she escapes her fate, though there have been many adaptations of the tale.[2] What is striking about O'Neill's play is her decision to bring the ghosts of the murdered wives on stage and thus the haunted body enables the resurfacing of violent histories.

In this chapter I address the ways through which performance can highlight the body as a site of memory, history and forgetting. Memory relies on citation and repetition, and its reperformance in the present

---

[1] *Constitution of Ireland – Bunreacht Na hÉireann* www.taoiseach.gov.ie/DOT/eng/Historical_Infor mation/The_Constitution/Constitution_of_Ireland_-_Bunreacht_na_h%C3%89ireann.html [Accessed 1 March 2018].

[2] *The Complete First Edition. The Original Folk and Fairy Tales of the Brothers Grimm*, trans. and ed. Jack Zipes (Oxford: Princeton University Press, 2014), pp. 202–4.

Haunted Bodies and Violent Pasts

serves to transmit and reinvent the past. Key to a feminist project of reclaiming unrepresented female experiences, and envisioning a different future through dialogue with this past, is the process of reassessing dominant narratives of history and cultural memory. The reappearance of spectres of the past on stage can potentially prompt an excavation of the forgotten layers of embodied history and cultural memory. The three plays which are the focus of this chapter: O'Neill's *Bluebeard*, together with Eva Gore-Booth's *The Buried Life of Deirdre* and Marina Carr's *Portia Coughlan*, all offer ghostly performances which stage the unsettling effects of the past as it resurfaces in the present. The plays address both individual memory and the cultural memory of female experience as defined by limiting myths of an idealized and domesticated passive Irish femininity. The haunted body thus offers the means to examine the processes of memory and history as layers of somatic memories which are exposed and reperformed.

Joseph Roach's work in *Cities of the Dead* examines the cultural activity of the circum-Atlantic region as embodied through performance and is illuminating in its focus on the ways in which history and memory are enacted on, and remembered through, the body, thereby shifting the emphasis from discursively documented history. In this chapter I draw on Roach's key concepts of surrogation and genealogies of performance with reference to the haunted bodies in these three plays. Roach's genealogy of performance highlights repeated or reperformed behaviour as memory living through the body: 'Performance genealogies draw on the idea of expressive movements of mnemonic reserves.'[3] The haunted bodies in these three plays offer a genealogy of performance that exposes the body as the site which bears the consequences of the disavowal of violent pasts. The attempt to fix and then erase narratives of the past is undermined by the notion of return, which is key to uncovering the mechanics of myth, memory and history at work in these performances. Bhabha's unhomely will also inform this chapter through my discussion of subversive and uncanny performances of the past which question cultural memory. Through the performing body, both Roach and Bhabha engage with the resurfacing of that which has been repressed and forgotten, and this offers the means to address the potentially destabilizing and uncanny effects of performing elided pasts.

---

[3] Joseph Roach, *Cities of the Dead: Circum-Atlantic Performance* (New York: Columbia University Press, 1996), p. 26.

174   Women and Embodied Mythmaking in Irish Theatre

Critical engagement with the past through haunted bodies seeks to interrogate inherited versions with a view towards reshaping the future; Roach highlights Jonathan Arac's description of a critical genealogy which 'aims to excavate the past that is necessary to account for how we got here and the past that is useful for conceiving alternatives to our present condition'.[4] My discussion looks to the ways in which performance can enable critical engagement with the eruption of repressed pasts and thereby avoid nostalgic engagement which serves only to offer self-affirmation through recourse to myth and memory. Are the haunted bodies trapped in a purgatorial space of congealed history and memory, or can they evoke alternative futures? The structure of this chapter deliberately undercuts a straightforward redemptive or progressive narrative thrust as I do not look at the plays in chronological order: first, I analyse O'Neill's ballet-poem *Bluebeard* (premiered in 1933), then Carr's *Portia Coughlan* (1996), before finally turning to Gore-Booth's *The Buried Life of Deirdre* (written between 1908 and 1912 and illustrated in 1916–17, although not published until 1930).[5] Through the figure of the haunted body I want to offer a more complex picture of the shifting opportunities available to, as well as the limits placed on, women in Ireland across the twentieth and twenty-first centuries.

Bluebeard and Ireland's 'Architecture of Containment'

O'Neill's *Bluebeard* emerges from the decades of the Irish Free State (established in 1922) during which women's role in society was narrowly defined and restricted. Legislation denied women access to the public sphere and concurrently contained and idealized them within the domestic arena: in 1925 the right of women to sit all civil service examinations was curtailed; following the 1927 Juries Bill, women were only allowed to sit on juries if they specifically applied; and in 1932, compulsory retirement was imposed on all female teachers once they married and was later extended to the entire civil service.

In *Ireland's Magdalen Laundries and the Nation's Architecture of Containment*, James M. Smith outlines the consequences of the Carrigan Report (1931), which presented evidence of rising illegitimacy rates and sexual crimes: 'Such findings contradicted the prevailing language of

---

[4] Roach, *Cities of the Dead*, p. 25.
[5] The dates which document the development of Gore-Booth's play are quoted on p. 34 of *Poems of Eva Gore-Booth: Complete Edition* (London: Longmans, Green & Co., 1929) and in a 'Note' to *The Buried Life of Deirdre* (London: Longmans, Green & Co., 1930), p. xii.

Haunted Bodies and Violent Pasts

national identity formation, which emphasized Catholicism, moral purity, and rural ideals.'[6] Smith suggests that the way in which the Report and subsequent Criminal Law Amendment Act (1935) deployed official discourse, 'disembodied sexual practice by obscuring social realities, especially illegitimacy, in discursive abstractions. And they concealed sexual crime, especially rape, infanticide, and abuse, while simultaneously sexualizing the women and children unfortunate enough to fall victim to society's moral proscriptions'.[7] These 'problem' women and children were dealt with by Ireland's 'architecture of containment' which encompassed the domestic space and institutional homes. The horrifying lengths that Church and State were willing to go to in order to punish women and their 'illegitimate' children have only recently been coming to light. The work of Catherine Corless on the Bons Secours Mother and Baby Home in Tuam, Co. Galway (1925–61) came to national attention in 2014 when the discovery of a mass grave in a septic tank containing the bodies of as many as 796 babies and children made front page, and subsequently international, headlines.[8] The process of excavating this violent past is ongoing and The Mother and Baby Homes Commission of Investigation, established in 2015, is due to deliver its final report in February 2020.[9]

In O'Neill's play Bluebeard's bloody chamber is the ultimate 'architecture of containment' as the threat of female sexuality and decay is contained within his beautifully preserved corpses: 'Six mummy women in six long glass boxes.'[10] O'Neill describes how in *Bluebeard* she 'tried to express the conflict between beauty and life – life destroying without respite the beauty it has created'.[11] She goes on to explain that Bluebeard 'rates beauty above life' and we discover that his desire to arrest decay is made possible by 'old Jasper's drug, / A drug that kills all change and all decay, / It fixes beauty for ten thousand years'.[12] A feminist reading of the play enables us

---

[6] James M. Smith, *Ireland's Magdalen Laundries and the Nation's Architecture of Containment* (Indiana: University of Notre Dame Press, 2007), p. 6.

[7] Smith, *Ireland's Magdalen Laundries*, p. 2.

[8] Alison O'Reilly, 'A Mass Grave of 800 Babies', *The Mail on Sunday*, 25 May 2014.

[9] Initially the final report was due to be completed by February 2019 but the Government agreed to the Commission's request to extend the deadline to February 2020: www.mbhcoi.ie/MBH.nsf/page/Latest%20News-en [Accessed 28 March 2019].

[10] Mary Devenport O'Neill, *Bluebeard*, p. 7, MS. 21,440, Abbey Theatre Papers, National Library of Ireland. This is Ria Mooney's annotated script, dated June 1933, from the premiere production in which she played Sister Ann.

[11] Mary Devenport O'Neill, *Bluebeard*, in *Prometheus and Other Poems* (London: Jonathan Cape, 1929). The published poem is available online: http://marydevenportoneill.org/bluebeard-2/ [Accessed 1 July 2017].

[12] *Bluebeard*, MS. 21,440, pp. 4–5.

176   Women and Embodied Mythmaking in Irish Theatre

to posit this conflict as the gap between idealized myths of femininity and women's material realities.

Mary Devenport O'Neill was a poet and playwright who was actively involved in literary life in Dublin: 'Married to the writer Joseph O'Neill and settled in Dublin, she was a friend of W.B. Yeats and a member of George Russell's literary circle before forming her own salon.'[13] The salon is a space which fuses the public and private spheres, and enables women within certain, albeit more economically privileged, sections of society to negotiate cultural capital. Lucy Collins suggests that women poets of this period were 'adapting new modes to express their own particular creative issues',[14] and so too were women in theatre. The development of O'Neill's ballet-poems is an important, and neglected, part of the history of Ireland's experimental and dance theatre which was engaged with European modernist influences.[15] Furthermore, *Bluebeard* draws on symbolism, expressionism and the experimental form of the ballet-poem to expose Ireland's 'architecture of containment'.

Bluebeard was published in 1929 in O'Neill's collection *Prometheus and Other Poems*. She submitted the play to the Abbey and Lady Gregory advised her to send it to Yeats who 'requested the author to revise the play so that it could be produced in dance form without sacrificing the poetry'.[16] Yeats's *Four Plays for Dancers* had been published in 1921 (*At the Hawk's Well, The Only Jealousy of Emer, The Dreaming of the Bones* and *Calvary*) and demonstrate his interest in exploring the integration of movement and poetry. Yeats advanced his aspirations further through the establishment of the Abbey School of Ballet (1927–33) with choreographer and dancer Ninette de Valois. He had heard about de Valois's work at the avant-garde Festival Theatre, Cambridge, which included the choreography for his play *On Baile's Strand*, and invited her to set up a school of ballet at the Abbey Theatre. De Valois's autobiography makes clear Yeats's intention that not only would she perform his *Plays for Dancers* but that engaging with dance would broaden the scope of theatre in Ireland beyond the dominant realist mode:

> he would have a small school of ballet at the Abbey and I would send over a teacher. I would visit Dublin every three months and produce his Plays for Dancers and perform in them myself; thus, he said, the poetic drama of

[13] Lucy Collins, *Poetry by Women in Ireland: A Critical Anthology 1870–1970* (Liverpool: Liverpool University Press, 2012), p. 200.
[14] Collins, *Poetry by Women in Ireland*, p. 200.
[15] See Ian R. Walsh, *Experimental Irish Theatre: After W.B. Yeats* (Basingstoke: Palgrave Macmillan, 2012).
[16] 'An Irishman's Diary', *Irish Times*, 14 October 1943, p. 3.

Ireland would live again and take its rightful place in the nation's own theatre, and the oblivion imposed on it by the popularity of peasant drama would become a thing of the past.[17]

The Abbey Theatre School of Ballet's last programme opened on 25 July 1933 and ran for six performances; on the bill were Yeats's *At the Hawk's Well*, which was followed by Lady Gregory's *Hyacinth Halvey*, and the evening concluded with two new ballet plays, O'Neill's *Bluebeard* and Arthur Duff's *The Drinking Horn*. *Bluebeard* was directed by Arthur Shields and de Valois choreographed the movement as well as dancing the part of Ilina, Bluebeard's wife. Victor Wynburne performed as Bluebeard, while Ria Mooney and Joseph O'Neill were the narrators: Ilina's Sister Ann, and Cyril, Bluebeard's servant. The original music was composed by J.F. Larchet who was the conductor of the popular Abbey orchestra.

Although there are no detailed reviews which document the movement in *Bluebeard*, we do know what experiences and influences de Valois drew on in her work. In *A History of Irish Ballet from 1927 to 1963*, Victoria O'Brien describes how:

> The experience of dancing in innovative works by Michel Fokine, or with the choreographers themselves, notably Leonide Massine, Bronislava Nijinska and George Balanchine, impacted greatly on her choreography and teaching. These iconoclastic choreographers interlocked a blend of modern and classical movement: Fokine's romanticism, Nijinksa's blocks of movement (which look simple but belie a complicated structure), Balanchine's neoclassicism and Massine's development of character dance in ballet all influenced her style and approach.[18]

De Valois was foundational to the development of ballet in Ireland and her legacy is evident in the performance history of *Bluebeard* which was produced through the 1930s and 1940s. The first revival of *Bluebeard* was performed in 1938 by the Payne School of Ballet. The School's Director Sara Payne (also known as Sara Patrick) had been trained as a dancer by de Valois at the London Academy of Choreographic Art and had moved to Dublin to run the Abbey School of Ballet under de Valois's supervision from 1928 to 1931. She then moved back to England where she worked as a choreographer at the Festival Theatre in Cambridge and also taught at Sadler's Wells, before returning to Dublin to set up her own School in 1936.[19]

---

[17] Ninette de Valois, *Come Dance with Me* (London: Hamish Hamilton, 1959), p. 85.
[18] Victoria O'Brien, *A History of Irish Ballet from 1927 to 1963* (Bern: Peter Lang, 2011), p. 13.
[19] Kathrine Sorley Walker, 'The Festival and the Abbey: Ninette de Valois' Early Choreography, 1925–34, Part One', *Dance Chronicle*, 7:4 (1984–5), 379–412, see pp. 389 and 395.

178   Women and Embodied Mythmaking in Irish Theatre

Payne choreographed O'Neill's ballet-poem in a 1938 performance, where she played Sister Ann, while Joseph O'Neill reprised his role as Bluebeard's servant Cyril. Thelma Murphy, a student of the Abbey School, danced Ilina's part.[20] However, O'Neill was unhappy with this production as 'the three strands, verse, music and dancing' were 'uncoordinated'.[21] O'Neill's work is further connected with a desire to expand Ireland's theatrical and dance forms through its association with Austin Clarke's Lyric Theatre Players who, like the popular movement in Britain of the same period, produced verse-plays.[22] *Bluebeard* was 'performed as a straight play' in 1943 by the Dublin Verse Speaking Society who, under the direction of Clarke, presented the published verse-play.[23] Clarke's Lyric Theatre Players produced the ballet-poem of *Bluebeard* in 1948[24] and also premiered O'Neill's dance play *Cain* in 1945.[25]

At this point, it is useful to delineate the differences between the play published in O'Neill's poetry collection and the script for the performed ballet-poem. In the published play, there are four speaking parts: Ilina, Bluebeard, Sister Ann and Cyril. In the ballet-poem, all of Ilina's and Bluebeard's lines are given to Sister Ann and Cyril (and therefore revised as third-person narration), and Ilina and Bluebeard express themselves solely through gesture, dance and movement.[26] Yeats adapted his play *The Only Jealousy of Emer* to allow for the fact that de Valois refused to speak on stage and so it is possible that de Valois's reluctance to speak on stage may have shaped the revised version of *Bluebeard* as a ballet-poem.[27] Though Sister Ann and Cyril function as narrators, their movement is integral to the ballet-poem. Throughout the ballet they are seated facing one another on

[20] Performed on 19 June 1938, Father Mathew Hall, Dublin. Cast: Thelma Murphy, Joseph C. Dalton, Joseph O'Neill, Sara Payne. 'Payne School of Dance: Pleasing Programme in Father Mathew Hall', *Irish Times*, 20 June 1938, p. 2.

[21] Letter to Austin Clarke, 18 August 1944, http://marydevenportoneill.org/1944–2/ [Accessed 10 August 2017].

[22] Walsh, *Experimental Irish Theatre*, p. 35.

[23] 'An Irishman's Diary', *Irish Times*, 14 October 1943, p. 3.

[24] Performed on 14 and 21 November 1948. Cast: Maureen Cusack and George Green as Sister Ann and Cyril. 'Lyric Theatre Company', *Irish Times*, 6 November 1948, p. 6.

[25] 'The Lyric Theatre', *Irish Times*, 4 June 1945, p. 3.

[26] Although O'Neill states in a letter to Austin Clarke that Bluebeard did not dance: 'A man ballet dancer requires a very large stage. His leaps and springs and elevations cover a large space. For that reason Ninette de Valois would not let Bluebeard dance on the Abbey stage, though she, herself, as Ilina danced right through the play.' 9 August 1944 http://marydevenportoneill.org/1944–2/ [Accessed 10 August 2017].

[27] Walker, 'The Festival and the Abbey: Ninette de Valois' Early Choreography', p. 408.

Haunted Bodies and Violent Pasts

either side of the front of the stage, '*changing their positions slightly from time to time, but all their positions should be dance positions and their movements when changing from one position to another should be dance movements taken to the beat of the music*'.[28] The textual mise-en-scène of *Bluebeard* places the vocal poetry to the fore and, as noted by one reviewer, 'The poem is used as a commentary on the ballet.'[29] In *Collaborations: Ninette de Valois and William Butler Yeats*, Richard Allen Cave suggests that the emphasis on the authority of the poet as expressed through the detail and tenor of the script's directions for the dancers 'is not suggestive of possibilities but adamant in its authority, since the poet has devised the choreography in her mind's eye and left the choreographer scant room for manoeuvre'.[30]

Cave contrasts O'Neill's approach with the freedom that a Yeatsian dance text, specifically *At the Hawk's Well*, gives the choreographer and dancer. Yeats's efforts to intertwine poetry and dance left an important legacy to Irish theatre, as argued by Aoife McGrath: 'At a time in Irish history when the postcolonial need for racial, sexual and religious purity of identity was creating strict definitions of permissible bodies, Yeats' dance plays were a wonderful site of exciting experimentation and resistance to the status quo.'[31] It is my contention that exploring the haunted body in *Bluebeard* enables us to uncover equally resistant possibilities in O'Neill's ballet-poem, which articulate women's experiences during the years of the Free State.

On the whole, the premiere of *Bluebeard* was well received: one review described it as the 'piece de resistance [*sic*]'[32] of the evening's programme, while another claimed it was 'the more ambitious' of the two original ballets performed. However, Cave's argument that the movement in the ballet-poem was not allowed to reach its full potential is echoed in some of the reviews. The *Irish Independent* reviewer suggests that the dance was a backdrop to the poetry: 'There are so many periods of inactivity that the dance, as such, recedes into the background, and we find ourselves fascinated by the distinctive art of Joseph O'Neill in his admirable vocal declamation; the expressive narrative of Ria Mooney, as Sister Ann; or the enchanting beauty of the concealed vocal quartet.'[33] A review of the

---

[28] *Bluebeard*, MS. 21,440, p. 1.   [29] 'Ballets at the Abbey', *Dublin Evening Mail*, 26 July 1933, p. 4.
[30] Richard Allen Cave, *Collaborations: Ninette de Valois and William Butler Yeats* (Alton: Dance Books, 2011), p. 90.
[31] Aoife McGrath, *Dance Theatre in Ireland: Revolutionary Moves* (Basingstoke: Palgrave Macmillan, 2013), p. 51.
[32] 'Mixed Bill at the Abbey Theatre', *The Irish Press*, 26 July 1933.
[33] 'Beautiful Ballets', *Irish Independent*, 26 July 1933, p. 11.

180   Women and Embodied Mythmaking in Irish Theatre

1948 production by Austin Clarke's Lyric Theatre Company also reflects an uneasy cohesion between narration and movement: 'the movement of the figures has a dangerous resemblance to a certain toy-like device for fore-telling the weather'.[34] However, might the movement tell us something about the context of the work, rather than just conveying O'Neill's 'anxiety' to 'keep too tight a rein on proceedings'?[35] O'Neill was one of a handful of women, including Teresa Deevy and Margaret O'Leary, whose work was staged at the Abbey in the 1930s. The period was characterized by a cultural mistrust of the body, especially the female body and its expressive capacity; a fear and threat which is contained by the limits placed on women during the period. These playwrights had to find ways of negotiating these constraints, as Cathy Leeney notes:

> From the vantage point of the twenty-first century, one looks back to Irish women in theatre in the 1920s and 1930s with sympathy and admiration for their determined survival, and for their ingenious use of theatrical codes and devices to write dramas that could accommodate complex levels of meaning.[36]

Acknowledging the necessity for women to write drama that worked in code enables us to unlock the capacity of both the haunted body and of the movement in *Bluebeard* to convey women's experiences during the years of the Free State. In order to explore the potential for disrupting the containment of women's expression, I focus on Ilina's role in the ballet-poem as silent dancer, as well as the ghosts of the dead wives as embodiments of women's unhomely experiences, but first I address the role of Bluebeard in order to open up the potential for disruption of the male frame of authority.

Bluebeard's Melancholy

In his first entrance, O'Neill's Bluebeard is presented as a brooding, rather than sexually predatory, figure: '*The music starts again. It is slow, expectant, slightly ominous. Presently BLUEBEARD comes in. The music becomes meditative.*'[37] We soon discover the reason for his troubled disposition as the Chorus of voices, the murdered wives, are heard offstage and he recoils

---

[34] 'Lyric Theatre Programme at the Abbey', *Irish Independent*, 17 November 1948, p. 3.
[35] Cave, *Collaborations*, p. 89.
[36] Cathy Leeney, 'Interchapter 1: 1900–1939', in Sihra, *Women in Irish Drama*, pp. 23–7 (p. 23).
[37] *Bluebeard*, MS. 21,440, p. 4.

Haunted Bodies and Violent Pasts 181

in horror. This scene of haunting and Bluebeard's horrified response is repeated three times, with the ghosts making their entrance onstage on the third occasion. Bluebeard's thoughts are narrated by his servant Cyril who reveals how he wrestles with his decision to release the ghosts from the locked room, eventually deciding that: 'His eyes alone can pay them their life's worth.'[38] Bluebeard's melancholic state is defined by his decision to dwell on and repeat the past, resulting in the stagnation of his mind and the castle environs as he chooses to pursue his urge to contain the women as his private possession through beauty and death.

One possible reading of the play would be to focus on the ghosts as figments of Bluebeard's imagination, who torment him and thereby express his remorse. The ghostly voices trouble Bluebeard in that they figure his guilt, but he persists in reasserting his justification for his murderous actions, thereby returning to his depressed state, yearning for more. Alice Rayner suggests:

> If words are successful in naming the ghost, there is no ghost. If the experience of the uncanny does not precede the argument about its undoing of ontology or repetitions of history, it is only an idealization.[39]

Figuring the ghosts of the murdered wives as Bluebeard's psychic creations reasserts his possessive desire as it is realized through their idealization; this fails to disrupt the repetitions of history and the fate of the women. The evocative rhythms of the language in O'Neill's work evidences the influence of European symbolism; indeed, a review of the 1948 Lyric Theatre production commented on the 'introspective Pirandello-like figure' of Bluebeard.[40] Christopher Murray's description of Yeats's dance plays could be extended to O'Neill's brooding Bluebeard: '[t]he main point about [the dance plays] is that they are dream plays, which places their action at one remove from the audience [. . .] in some space beyond the real.'[41] However, rather than simply looking to the symbolism of *Bluebeard* as evocative of a dream-like world of Bluebeard's creation, we need to address the nightmare experienced by Ilina and the ghosts: an experience which was firmly embedded in the reality of 1930s Ireland for women.

---

[38] *Bluebeard*, MS. 21,440, p. 13.
[39] Alice Rayner, *Ghosts: Death's Double and the Phenomena of Theatre* (Minneapolis: University of Minnesota Press, 2006), p. xxiii.
[40] *The Evening Herald*, 20 November 1948, p. 5.
[41] Murray, *Twentieth-Century Irish Drama*, p. 26.

182 Women and Embodied Mythmaking in Irish Theatre

Ilina's Deathly Performance

Ninette de Valois's interpretation of the role of Ilina in the 1933 premiere received glowing reviews: one remarked that she 'gave a glorious performance, suggesting wonderfully well the varied emotions of that interesting creature',[42] while another noted her 'highly artistic and picturesque' presentation.[43] The reviews give us little in the way of details of de Valois's interpretation but the script certainly offers the potential for a feminist critique of the role. Such a reading expands on the limits placed on de Valois's interpretation, as outlined by Cave's argument which blames O'Neill's assertion of her authority as the writer, but might also be viewed as a reflection of the limits placed on female expression in the period.

Ilina's movements are contained from her first appearance: she performs a minuet and as Sister Ann narrates her entry she *'comes in walking with small creep steps, turning to look over each shoulder in turn. She moves to rhythm – the same rhythm that the others speak to.'*[44] Ria Mooney's annotations on the script notes where she has to 'Stop' after several of the lines and presumably Ilina looks over her shoulder in these moments. Yet the tension of the opening moments of the play are not echoed by Ilina's stock gesture, which we first see enacted following her creeping entrance: *'Ilina lifts her hands above her head and lowers them letting her fingers hang.'*[45] Ilina's movements following this gesture are also far from dynamic: when she first discovers the door to Bluebeard's locked chamber, she merely stands in front of it with her back to the audience. During Cyril's description of how 'That room is full of lovely precious things', she *'sinks to the floor, her dress is spread round her, she leans forward chin in her hand and slowly, to the rhythm of Cyril's speech, she moves gently from one attitude of rapt attention to another'.*[46] Cave suggests that the tone of the directions throughout 'is not suggestive of possibilities but adamant in its authority'.[47] However, I would suggest that rather than this being a denial of the 'artistic freedom'[48] of the dancer, the performance of Ilina can tell us much about the period's mistrust of the female body and the resultant suppression of its expression.

Following Cyril's disclosure of the riches of the locked room, Ilina *'rises slowly and begins to dance the scent dance'.*[49] However, the scent dance is not a moment of expression in contrast to the preceding restrictive movements:

---

[42] 'Ballets at the Abbey', *Dublin Evening Mail*, 26 July 1933, p. 4.
[43] 'Beautiful Ballets', *Irish Independent*, 26 July 1933, p. 11.   [44] *Bluebeard*, MS. 21,440, p. 2.
[45] *Bluebeard*, MS. 21,440, p. 2.   [46] *Bluebeard*, MS. 21,440, p. 3.   [47] Cave, *Collaborations*, p. 90.
[48] Cave, *Collaborations*, p. 91.   [49] *Bluebeard*, MS. 21,440, p. 4.

Haunted Bodies and Violent Pasts

she is dancing in response to Cyril's description of his experience of being 'overpowered' by the scent of the room when he was allowed to enter blindfolded. Cyril's verse details how: 'I was so happy that I could lie down, / I could have died there', as well as his desire to 'try to get the feeling back again'.[50] Ilina's dance reinforces the conflation of female sexuality and death. We are told that the smell that emanates from the room clings to everything that it comes into contact with and there is a clear sense of the oppressive nature of the room's secrets. The uncontainable and deadly desires that escape the room suggest the ghosts' threatening presence, yet the oppressive weight of the suppression of these desires is conveyed through Ilina's body. There is a jarring tension between the male-dominated narrative thrust (and Ilina's dancing in response) and Ilina's moments of immobility and uncontrolled movement. Ilina's next scene also depicts her as subject to other forces, rather than in control of her own narration. She is literally blown onto the stage:

> Here ILINA dances a few steps, running sideways on her toes leaning at a slight angle, her arms flowing out slightly from her sides – to represent the rain blown sideways by a gust. Then, standing quite straight, her arms hanging at her sides, ILINA continues dancing while CYRIL speaks the next line.[51]

Her adoption of a pose whereby her arms hang limply at her sides becomes a repeated gesture, echoing her earlier movement: letting her hands drop down and hang at her sides. This gesture indicates the stifling of bodily intention and her defeated ability to express herself, and this is compounded by the movements which follow as she 'turns and moves aimlessly to the music till she comes in front of the door of the secret room'.[52] It is in the stage directions that we can uncover a counternarrative which suggests Ilina's lack of agency through her unintentional movement. Ilina's limp movements and aimlessness present her as the living dead; a fate which foreshadows the dead women of the chamber and resonates with the eponymous Portia Coughlan in Marina Carr's play. Her body articulates a countermemory which reveals 'the disparities between history as it is discursively transmitted and memory as it is publicly enacted by the bodies that bear its consequences'.[53]

Ilina's discovery of the key leads to a moment of delight expressed through movement when she, prompted by Sister Ann, is tempted to unlock the riches of the room: 'ILINA holds the key above her head, and

---

[50] Bluebeard, MS. 21,440, p. 4.   [51] Bluebeard, MS. 21,440, p. 6.
[52] Bluebeard, MS. 21,440, p. 6.   [53] Roach, Cities of the Dead, p. 26.

184   Women and Embodied Mythmaking in Irish Theatre

dances, spinning round and round.'[54] A sense of both decision and abandon are captured and this contrasts with her previously 'undead' appearance. However, Ilina's spinning is immediately followed by Sister Ann's line: 'Old woods, old walls, old silence go on, defy them all.'[55] Mooney has written 'Slower' next to this line on the script and in this moment the weight of the past and Ilina's fate close in. Ilina's defiance will inevitably lead to punishment and the claustrophobia evoked by Sister Ann's line prefigures the revelation of Bluebeard's violent containment of his wives in glass coffins. Ilina unlocks the room and enters, but the music becomes discordant and she comes back out, *'crouching as if hurt'.*[56] In her discussion of the representation of women in nineteenth-century tableaux vivants, Mary Chapman outlines how Bluebeard's wife's response to the discovery of the murdered wives merges her with the dead wives: 'Bluebeard's most recent wife's assumption of the gaze results in her being rendered silent and immobile, both literally when she is paralyzed by fear and metaphorically when her story is dramatized in the *tableau vivant*.'[57] However, O'Neill's Ilina is not paralysed, instead her body is violently marked by her discovery of the brutality contained in the locked room. Both the vulnerability of Ilina's body, and her fear of the fate which awaits her, are exposed as she locks the room and *'creeps slowly out, crouching down as if hurt'.*[58]

In her final scene, we see Ilina buckle under the weight of this knowledge and impending punishment. When Ilina appears for the last time Sister Ann advises her that she should rest and we see her *'totter'.*[59] The immense weight of what she is forced to bear, as well as her fragility, are compounded by her final exit: '*ILINA, as if things had become unbearable, rushes out to the right, and music stops.*'[60] Her exit reinforces her passivity as she does not take part in the final confrontation with Bluebeard. First, Ilina's brothers fight him and then Bluebeard dies after the ghosts of the wives close in on him. Ilina is therefore sidelined from the struggle and plays no part in shaping her fate. Her movement throughout expresses a lack of motivation and energy which potentially reflects women's sense of helplessness in the face of the conservatism of 1930s Ireland. Richard Kearney suggests that a 'memoried self . . . recognizes the limits of remembering

---

[54] *Bluebeard*, MS. 21,440, p. 7.   [55] *Bluebeard*, MS. 21,440, p. 7.

[56] *Bluebeard*, MS. 21,440, p. 7.

[57] Mary Chapman, '"Living Pictures": Women and *Tableaux Vivants* in Nineteenth-Century American Fiction and Culture', *Wide Angle*, 18:3 (July 1996), 22–52 (p. 36).

[58] *Bluebeard*, MS. 21,440, p. 8.   [59] *Bluebeard*, MS. 21,440, p. 10.

[60] *Bluebeard*, MS. 21,440, p. 12.

Haunted Bodies and Violent Pasts

while resisting the fetishism of the immemorial';[61] and crucially, we have to ask of the ghostly bodies in O'Neill's, Carr's and Gore-Booth's plays: do they fetishize the past or acknowledge its limits? The memoried self acknowledges the layers of the past as they are embodied in present performances and thus addresses those pasts which have been forgotten and erased from individual and cultural memory, as well as those which have been perpetuated and become timeless. Ilina operates as a memoried self and her ghostly performance resists the fetishization of the past through exposure of the violent imposition of silence on women's experiences and expression. Yet, it is to the ghosts of the murdered wives that we must turn to encounter resistance to the violent, patriarchal forces which overwhelm and break Ilina.

The 'Weird Charm' of the Ghosts

We do not see the ghosts until the final moments of the play, although we hear the Chorus of their voices offstage during Bluebeard's scenes. This raises the possibility that they are his incarnation and contained in his head but their onstage invasion at the end of the play has the potential to refute this notion. Cyril ominously warns that the dead are not so easily contained or forgotten: 'Yet death is all around us, / We are deaf, we are blind.'[62] The verses sung by the Chorus of wives are repetitive and reiterate ideas of stillness and muffled sound, as well as tropes of woman and death through the juxtaposition of beauty and decay:

> The worms that writhe and creep
> About the dead
> Are not such ill,
> As this beauty we must keep
> Who are so still.
> Stiller than the dead.[63]

As in Carr's *Ariel*, the offstage voices put pressure on the limits of the onstage world and signal the women's refusal to be silenced through death. Cathy Leeney describes how Gore-Booth's 'heroines speak to create a diegetic world that overwhelms the mimetic stage'.[64] O'Neill also refuses the limits of realist conventions and creates another reality through language: one which accommodates the unacknowledged experiences of

---

[61] Richard Kearney, *Strangers, Gods and Monsters* (London: Routledge, 2003), p. 188.
[62] *Bluebeard*, MS. 21,440, p. 12.   [63] *Bluebeard*, MS. 21,440, p. 5.
[64] Leeney, *Irish Women Playwrights, 1900–1939*, p. 16.

186   Women and Embodied Mythmaking in Irish Theatre

women. O'Neill's ghosts articulate the refusal of women in 1930s Ireland to be violently contained 'offstage' and for their bodies to be denied visibility, agency and expression.

The appearance of the Chorus of murdered wives as dusk gathers at the end of the play draws on tropes of the beautiful female corpse, as well as revealing the dwindling power that Bluebeard holds over them:

> *The door of the secret room opens slowly and, one after another, six beautiful women come out. They glide rather than walk; they are otherwise motionless. They wear brilliant dresses and jewels; their hands hang by their sides; their hair is spread on their shoulders and hangs in plaits. Slow, solemn music plays – very soft and low as in a dream; BLUEBEARD, moving to the music, puts out his hands as if to press them back.*[65]

Their demeanour initially echoes Ilina's gestures with their motionlessness and their arms hanging by their sides. However, the final moments of the play, which are danced and not narrated, are defined by a building tension. There are two scores playing simultaneously, one for the sword fight between Bluebeard and Ilina's brothers, and another for the ghosts: *'the slow, solemn music continues to play very softly, and dreamily, and the six beautiful women move to it; quick, sharp, excitable music is played at the same time for the sword dance'*.[66] While ostensibly it is Ilina's brothers who strike and kill Bluebeard, O'Neill affords the ghosts power over him in the closing sequence. The brothers rush offstage and the slow, solemn march of the ghosts relentlessly progresses and they close in on Bluebeard:

> *They begin to move round BLUEBEARD in a wide circle. BLUEBEARD keeps turning his eyes to look at them. Slowly with an almost imperceptible movement beginning with the first and passing from one to another, their heads turn towards him. In the same way their bodies begin to lean towards him. Their necks stretch towards him. The circle they make round him grows smaller. Their expression grows tense. Their eyes grow tense. Their eyes grow eager. BLUBEARD still turns his eyes to look at them, but feebly. He dies.*[67]

Cyril's song, preceding the fight scene, is punctuated throughout by the word 'eyes' and places great emphasis on the possessive and controlling nature of the male gaze. The wives' subjugation by Bluebeard's proprietorial gaze is made explicit: 'Eyes on them night and day / Making their beauty moment by moment.'[68] Yet in the final dance the ghosts 'master' the gaze and their tense eyes subject Bluebeard to their hunger for his death. They

---

[65] *Bluebeard*, MS. 21,440, p. 13.   [66] *Bluebeard*, MS. 21,440, p. 14.
[67] *Bluebeard*, MS. 21,440, p. 14.   [68] *Bluebeard*, MS. 21,440, p. 13.

Haunted Bodies and Violent Pasts

paralyse him with their gaze and their movements work in union to contain him. The petrifying female gaze calls to mind the monstrous Medusa who Marina Warner describes as embodying an 'ambivalent potency, fatal and procreative at once'.[69]

Depending on the staging of this final dance, there is a risk that it might reinforce a vampiric and threatening female sexuality, as well as providing a sensational spectacle. Indeed, one review of the premiere production suggests that 'the final dance, when the locked room releases its lovely ghosts was a thing of rare beauty'.[70] However, another review notes the potential of the dance and ghosts to unsettle: 'the final dance of the six ghosts provided a fitting climax of *weird* charm' (my emphasis).[71] In 1926 at the Festival Theatre, Cambridge, de Valois choreographed the Chorus of matriarchal Furies who seek justice for Clytemnestra's murder by her son Orestes in the third part of Aeschylus's *Oresteia* trilogy. Norman Marshall's reflection on the performance is instructive: 'What Ninette de Valois achieved reduced one's memories of all other Greek choruses one had ever seen to a series of pretty posturings by comparison.'[72] Indeed, in *Collaborations* Cave includes a photograph from the production which illustrates the production's expressionist aesthetic and 'the chorus's elongated bodylines and stabbing gestures'.[73] Teresa Deevy, a contemporary of O'Neill's whose work was staged at the Abbey, deployed expressionist techniques within her realist plays to evoke the inner life of her female characters against a stifling world of conformity. Emphasizing the loveliness of Bluebeard's wives and the beauty of their dance neutralizes their 'ambivalent potency' and 'weird charm'; instead, we can draw on the potential suggested by de Valois's body of work to locate a feminist critique and enable the unhomely, haunted bodies to speak of their violent pasts.

The ghosts' final dance, following Bluebeard's death, is defined by a juxtaposition between tension and dissipation, which reverberates with Ilina's movements. The ghosts relax and appear to be about to return to their gliding when, abruptly, the music changes:

> It becomes wild and free and then as if a string connecting them snaps they separate: like pieces of crumpled paper caught in a gust they scatter, each with

---

[69] Marina Warner, *Monuments and Maidens: The Allegory of the Female Form* (London: Vintage, 1996), p. 113.

[70] 'Mixed Bill at the Abbey Theatre', *The Irish Press*, 26 July 1933.

[71] 'Ballets at the Abbey', *Dublin Evening Mail*, 26 July 1933, p. 4.

[72] Quoted in Walker, 'The Festival and the Abbey', p. 388.

[73] Cave, *Collaborations*, p. 27. See figure 8.

188 Women and Embodied Mythmaking in Irish Theatre

a different movement in a different direction. The Curtain begins to fall and has fallen before they come to rest.[74]

The 'wild and free' music unleashes an energy which has been suppressed in Ilina and expresses a chaos which contrasts with the ghosts focused gaze and encircling of Bluebeard. Despite the intense force unleashed collectively by the ghosts, breaking the connecting strings does not simply release them and result in freedom. They are now at the mercy of their environment, echoing Ilina's earlier movement when she is caught by a gust of wind. They are 'crumpled' and 'scattered' so that instead of asserting their defiance, their threat is dissipated: the climax of the play is potentially a bitter reflection on the overwhelming lack of opportunity and agency for women in 1930s Ireland. Paradoxically, enervation and stagnation animate *Bluebeard* and these states pre-empt the long-lasting impact that the decades of the Free State would have on women's cultural representation and participation. O'Neill's play offers a stark contrast to the next two plays discussed – Gore-Booth's *The Buried Life of Deirdre* and Carr's *Portia Coughlan* – in its inability to offer a more sustained and tangible sense of possibility through the creation of alternative futures and spaces for female expression. The nightmareish reality of the experiences of Ilina and the ghosts in O'Neill's *Bluebeard* exposes the illusion and violence of Bluebeard's dream-world. Their haunted bodies refuse to keep their desires in check in order to powerfully resist women's experiences of violent containment. Their songs and movement gesture towards an alternative universe, but the ghosts do not come to rest for they have nowhere to go. However, we can counter a sense of crushing defeat if we revive their defiant energies through a genealogy of performance which refutes the silencing of unhomely pasts.

Portia Coughlan: Idealization or Interrogation of the Past?

With reference to Carr's lead roles Portia Coughlan and Hester Swane, Cathy Leeney suggests that: 'Having tested what the world might offer them, they redefine "undead" as a state of becoming.'[75] *Bluebeard's* ghosts certainly attempt to unsettle the distinction between past and present but there is no sense of becoming. In the following sections I discuss Portia Coughlan's ghostliness as a strategy of subversion through Joseph Roach's concept of surrogation which reproduces cultural memory by inserting

---

[74] *Bluebeard*, MS. 21,440, p. 14. [75] Leeney, 'Ireland's "Exiled" Women Playwrights', p. 158.

Haunted Bodies and Violent Pasts 189

substitutes 'into the cavities created by loss through death or other forms of departure'.[76] In *Bluebeard* it is intended that Ilina will fill the gap left by the murdered wife who precedes her, just as the murdered wife stepped into the place of the previous wife, and so on. However, the uncanniness of Ilina's deathly performance reveals the anxiety surrounding the process of replacement and exposes Bluebeard's efforts to maintain a continuity which erases the violence of the past. I pursue the figure of the surrogate through close engagement with *Portia Coughlan* and *The Buried Life of Deirdre* in order to think further about how the haunted body might offer the opportunity to break with the past and create alternatives for the future. Roach's emphasis on embodied memory and genealogies of performance coincides with my approach to mythmaking in that he suggests that repetition can reaffirm or transform the past, just as myth can congeal past ideologies or engage with liberatory futures. First, I focus on how the unhomely surrogate enables us to engage with living memory in *Portia Coughlan*, before turning to the surrogates in Gore-Booth's play, and I then return to Carr's play in tandem with *The Buried Life of Deirdre* in order to assess how both plays offer possibility through alternative spaces which conjure a different future.

Portia Coughlan premiered in 1996 at the Peacock Theatre, Dublin,[77] and though sixty-three years had elapsed since the premiere of *Bluebeard*, the plays share some common features in the form of ghosts, melancholia and a woman living a deathly and claustrophobic existence. The play is set on Portia's thirtieth birthday which is also the fifteenth anniversary of the death of her twin, Gabriel. The relationship between the twins takes classical myth as its source and draws on stories which are all closely associated with water; in an interview, Carr stated: 'I'm fascinated by the twin motif, from Isis and Osiris to Hero and Leander.'[78] The connection between the twins takes over Portia's very being as she is haunted by the ghost of her dead brother and continues to mourn both for him and the attendant loss of identity, though this can also be attributed to her refusal

---

[76] Roach, *Cities of the Dead*, p. 2.
[77] Marina Carr, *Portia Coughlan*. Director: Garry Hynes. Cast: Derbhle Crotty, Sean Rocks, Marion O'Dwyer, Des Keogh, Don Wycherley, Bronagh Gallagher, Charlie Bonner, Stella McCusker, Pauline Flanagan, Tom Hickey, Michael Boylan, Peter Charlesworth Kelly. Set and costume design: Kandis Cook. Lighting: Jim Simmons (Peacock Theatre, Dublin, opened 27 March 1996).
[78] Victoria White, 'Twin Speak', *Irish Times*, 19 March 1996, p. 10. Additionally, in another interview (*Rage and Reason: Women Playwrights on Playwriting*, ed. Heidi Stephenson and Natasha Langridge (London: Methuen, 1997)), Carr references the influence of the story of Byblis and Caunis from Book Nine of Ovid's *Metamorphoses* which contains motifs that reinforce the link between twins, water and shifting identities.

190   Women and Embodied Mythmaking in Irish Theatre

to fulfil norms of femininity. Act One charts the early part of the day and Portia's encounters with her husband Raphael and her parents, who all criticize her for neglecting her 'duties' as a mother and wife. Portia feels trapped by the roles which society demands that she perform, that of wife and mother, and she feels suffocated in her claustrophobic home: 'the house is creakin' like a coffin [. . .] Sometimes I can't breathe anymore.'[79]

Portia's discontent in her home is made clear through conversations with lovers and friends, and so too is her strong connection with the river Belmont where Gabriel drowned. The ghost of Gabriel haunts the scenes, both visually when we see his ghost and aurally when we hear him singing. Acts Two and Three are reversed in chronological terms as Act Two opens with the recovery of Portia's drowned body from the river while Act Three returns to the hours that lead to her suicide.

Portia's need to escape the confines of her life results in her yearning to be with Gabriel once more, even in death, and she nostalgically evokes a myth of unity between them: 'Came out of the womb holdin' hands'.[80] The first version of Gabriel's death that Portia tells is of the twins' suicide pact which Portia failed to fulfil as she did not follow Gabriel into the river. Portia's description of Gabriel's final moments presents him as a helpless participant: 'the look on his face, and he tries to make it to the bank but the undertow do have him and a wave washes over him'.[81] However, the myth unravels as the play progresses and Portia's later version of Gabriel's death describes a much more malevolent character: 'and he whispered to me before he went in. "Portia," he says, "I'm goin' in now but I'll come back and I'll keep comin' back until I have you."'[82] The breakdown of Portia's romanticized notions of the siblings' relationship incorporates a destructive element, both of violence and loss of identity, and therefore of insecurity. These different versions serve to highlight Gabriel's ambivalent and uncanny presence, as well as the unreliable nature of Portia's mythmaking. Furthermore, the surrogated bodies of *Portia Coughlan* establish death as a process which continues into the present through the performed repetitions of individual and cultural memory.

As well as examining Portia's engagement with the past through Gabriel's ghost, the notion of surrogation is explored to address the living death of Portia's existence within a world she feels unaccommodated by. In order to explore key moments in the play which have the potential to break

[79] Marina Carr, *Portia Coughlan,* in *Plays 1* (London: Faber & Faber, 1999), p. 207.
[80] Carr, *Portia Coughlan,* in *Plays 1,* p. 211.   [81] Carr, *Portia Coughlan,* in *Plays 1,* p. 240.
[82] Carr, *Portia Coughlan,* in *Plays 1,* p. 250.

Haunted Bodies and Violent Pasts

down distinctions between memory and history, truth and invention, past and present, I reference two productions of *Portia Coughlan* staged on the Peacock stage of the Abbey Theatre, Dublin: the 1996 premiere directed by Garry Hynes with Derbhle Crotty in the title role and the 2004 production, directed by Brian Brady with Eileen Walsh as Portia.[83]

In *Hysteria, Trauma and Melancholia: Performative Maladies in Contemporary Anglophone Drama*, Christina Wald asserts that Portia is shaped by her experience as a melancholic. My focus on cultural memory and the perpetuation of models of femininity overlaps with Wald's proposal that 'Portia's melancholic state involves a profound failure, or refusal, to fulfil the gender expectations of her environment'.[84] However, my interpretation differs from Wald, who suggests that Portia's suicide is solely a result of her melancholic state and her obsession with a lost past. Wald's reading rests on Portia being so 'profoundly pre-occupied with the past that [she] cannot envision a non-determined, open future'.[85] Though Portia's individual memories may manifest an obsession with Gabriel, the cultural memories addressed by the play serve to conceive of the need for alternative futures as suggested in the space of the Belmont River. Carr frames Portia in a play which incorporates strategies for expression, namely an unsettling negotiation of the liminal space between life and death underpinned by the realm of myth.

Ghostly Surrogates

The surrogate broaches the space between life and death, past and present, by filling the gaps left by departure and death. Roach points to the Mardi Gras krewes of New Orleans as an example of the self-perpetuation of tradition and community through the surrogate: the roles of King Rex and King Zulu are taken on by new people each year but the apparent seamlessness of tradition is maintained through their performance. Following loss, culture reproduces itself through the incessant process of substitution or surrogacy which performs memory and defines identity. However, Roach also highlights the ways in which genealogies of performance and

---

[83] *Portia Coughlan* was performed as part of the Abbey Theatre's Centenary Programme. Director: Brian Brady. Cast: Eileen Walsh, Frank Laverty, Brid Ní Neachtain, Liam Carney, Keith McErlean, Fionnuala Murphy, Phelim Drew, Maria McDermottroe, Stella McCusker, Gerard McSorley. Set: Bláithín Sheerin. Lighting: Paul Keogan (Peacock Theatre, Dublin, opened 2 October 2004).

[84] Christina Wald, *Hysteria, Trauma and Melancholia: Performative Maladies in Contemporary Anglophone Drama* (Basingstoke: Palgrave Macmillan, 2007), p. 190.

[85] Wald, *Hysteria, Trauma and Melancholia*, p. 195.

192 Women and Embodied Mythmaking in Irish Theatre

surrogation can cast doubt on the transmission of tradition. While 'more than a century of white supremacist entitlement' stood behind King Rex, King Zulu's performance offered 'a deconstruction of that white genealogy and the veiled assertion of a clandestine countermemory in its stead'.[86] This countermemory serves to underline the risks inherent in the process of surrogacy, risks also present in the process of myth- and memory-making, when 'befuddled celebrants come to embrace desperate contingencies as timeless essentials'.[87] So do the dramaturgical choices made in the two Peacock productions of *Portia Coughlan* enable interrogation of the surrogates in the play as nostalgic performances of an elusive past, and can these surrogates reveal the limits of individual and cultural memory?

Several examples of surrogacy can be found in the play. First, Portia reveals that she married Raphael in the hope that he would 'take on the qualities'[88] of Gabriel. Raphael realizes that his substitution has failed to fulfil either of their expectations, he tells Portia in the final scene: 'I've waited thirteen year for you to talk about me the way you've just talked about him.'[89] Raphael's failure as a surrogate serves to reinforce Portia's myth of her unity with her twin. Portia's sense of a fractured identity is underlined by the process of surrogacy: she turns to Raphael to complete her identity as *Portia Coughlan*, and she also looks to Gabriel as her twin and other half. Gabriel's ghost serves as a surrogate for his absence and he is, to use Roach's term, an effigy that performs the past and 'consist[s] of a set of actions that hold open a place in memory into which many different people may step according to circumstances and occasions'.[90] Portia's sense of loss and grief for her twin is poetically expressed, and clearly links her deep emotions with the landscape:

> Forget Gabriel! He's everywhere, Daddy. Everywhere. There's not a corner of any of your forty fields that don't remind me of Gabriel. His name is in the mouths of the starlin's that swoops over Belmont hill, the cows bellow for him from the barn on frosty winter nights. The very river tells me that once he was here and now he's gone.[91]

Gabriel's surrogated presence haunts Portia through both his singing and the landscape, namely the Belmont River, and recreates memories of their doubled existence.

Gabriel's ghost therefore represents a lost past to Portia, a past which she is obsessed with recovering, through death if necessary. However, this

---

[86] Roach, *Cities of the Dead*, p. 20. [87] Roach, *Cities of the Dead*, p. 30.
[88] Carr, *Portia Coughlan*, in *Plays 1*, p. 210. [89] Carr, *Portia Coughlan*, in *Plays 1*, p. 254.
[90] Roach, *Cities of the Dead*, p. 36. [91] Carr, *Portia Coughlan*, in *Plays 1*, pp. 213–14.

Haunted Bodies and Violent Pasts 193

myth of lost union starts to break down in Act Three when we hear alternative versions of Gabriel's death and also of the violence between the twins. Portia herself starts to sense that Gabriel is functioning as a surrogate for something that has been lost:

> Suppose he's not there when I go? [. . .] Before I was always sure, was the one thing as kept me goin' – Now I don't know any more, and yet I know that somewhere he lives and that's the place I want to be.[92]

Portia's final words suggest that she remains trapped in the past: 'And though everyone and everythin' tells me I have to forget him, I cannot, Raphael, I cannot.'[93] This is reinforced by the stage directions after these lines which describe Gabriel's singing as triumphant, therefore suggesting that he has claimed her. However, is it possible to read Portia's suicide and the play as a rejection of the past rather than an embrace? Before turning to Portia's ghostly performance in Act Three as a critical engagement with cultural memory, I want to first address the uncanny aspects of Gabriel's ghost which can be utilized to undermine individual myth- and memory-making, and Portia's idealization of the past.

Portia's melancholic conjuring of Gabriel's ghost initially presents him as an idealized, though irrecoverable, presence but I want to consider the ghost's uncanny potential in performance, which undermines his idealization. Gabriel's ghost incorporates the 'undoing of ontology or repetitions of history'[94] as he jeopardizes Portia's ability to function in her world: he threatens her sense of individuated identity as well as undermining her myth of their unity. As Roach points out, the surrogate threatens to replace the author of its representation, just as Portia's identity is under threat of being subsumed by Gabriel's hold over her.[95] The stage directions for the opening scene of the play set the twins up visually as doubles: '*They mirror one another's posture and movements in an odd way; unconsciously.*'[96] As Portia's mirrored double, Gabriel questions and threatens the individuality and reliability of her identity, echoing Bhabha's suggestion that '[m]imicry is at once resemblance and menace'.[97] The 2004 production projected a flickering image of the head and shoulders of a young boy behind Portia so that the audience had the sense of being granted access into Portia's mind. However, this simply presented Gabriel as Portia's psychic creation, rather than heightening the affective and uncanny potential of his ghost. In

---

[92] Carr, *Portia Coughlan*, in *Plays 1*, p. 240.　[93] Carr, *Portia Coughlan*, in *Plays 1*, p. 255.
[94] Rayner, *Ghosts*, p. xxiii.　[95] Roach, *Cities of the Dead*, p. 6.
[96] Carr, *Portia Coughlan*, in *Plays 1*, p. 193.　[97] Quoted in Roach, *Cities of the Dead*, p. 6.

194 Women and Embodied Mythmaking in Irish Theatre

the opening scene of the 1996 production, the physical presence of the young boy who played Gabriel was more unsettling as it prompted the audience to address the fact that they too can experience the ghost and it is therefore not so easily explained away. Gabriel stood behind Portia so that he visually echoed her, not only emphasizing his importance to her individual myth- and memory-making but also highlighting her potential to question the process of reperforming cultural memory. Gabriel serves a further uncanny purpose by highlighting Portia's ability to function as a surrogate, and her living death.

As a reflection of Portia, Gabriel creates the uncanny sense that Portia is living a ghostly existence as his ghost mirrors Portia's own unfulfilled life. Her sense of deadly suffocation is clearly linked to the home which she describes as a coffin.[98] Unlike the set of the 2004 production which made no reference to Portia's domestic home, the 1996 production emphasized Portia's restrictive and isolating domestic context so that the focus was not solely on her obsession with the past and Gabriel. Kandis Cook's set design did not present the spaces of the river bank, home and bar as physically distinct, instead they were evoked more fluidly through their association with the characters which inhabit them; for example, Gabriel's presence suggested the haunting presence of the river. The emphasis was on Portia's home, intimated by a table which anchored the action and provided the battlefield across which family disputes raged. The repeated tableau of Portia sitting at the table and isolated by a spotlight highlighted her unhomely experience, and the lighting design by Jim Simmons created shadowy recesses which surrounded Portia and enhanced the claustrophobia of the space. Bhabha describes how '[t]he recesses of the domestic space become sites for history's most intricate invasions'[99] and Garry Hynes's direction exposed the cultural memory of woman's experience in the Irish home; described by Portia as 'this livin' hell'.[100] Nonetheless, the addition of Portia's final plea to Gabriel, 'Come home little brother', at the close of the 1996 production somewhat undermined the production's underscoring of cultural, rather than individual, memory. Presenting Portia as a ghostly body or surrogate that evokes cultural memory, rather than focusing solely on Gabriel's ghost as a surrogate that fills a gap in Portia's unfulfilled life, begs the question: is her life unfulfilled due to his absence or unfulfilled due to the stifling restrictions of the familial and domestic roles she is expected to perform?

---

[98] Carr, *Portia Coughlan*, in *Plays 1*, p. 207. [99] Bhabha, *The Location of Culture*, p. 9.
[100] Carr, *Portia Coughlan*, in *Plays 1*, p. 222.

Ritual and Reperformance

Roach's genealogies of performance draw on embodied memory, rather than discursively constructed memory: on the transmissions of the past through the performances of present bodies and surrogates. *Portia Coughlan* offers two revealing examples of genealogies of performance: first, in the community's reaction to Portia's death in Act Two; second, in Portia's performance in the final scene of Act Three as a ghost of a ghost. These scenes highlight the embodiment of cultural codes and the necessity of reperformance to ensure the perpetuation and adoption of genealogies of performance. However, performance of these scenes can also harness the potential that repetition offers to disrupt and interrogate this process of naturalization; thereby 'conceiving alternatives to our present condition'.[101]

The 1996 published script includes stage directions for the opening of Act Two which describe the cast's movements in reaction to the discovery of Portia's body. The directions suggest that the cast move as one body: '*Ensemble choreography, all movements in unison.*'[102] Portia's swaying body, dripping with water, is juxtaposed with the unified and controlled movements of the cast, directed to '*take a step back . . . stop . . . take another step back . . . look up at the dead Portia*'.[103] The notion of an 'ensemble choreography' was interpreted differently in the two Peacock productions. In the 2004 production, Bláithín Sheerin's set was dominated by the heavy horizontal lines of a marbled block which functioned as the riverbank and bar. Act Two opened with the company standing with their backs to the audience as they swayed gently in unison while looking up at Portia's hanging body. An eerie blue light shone from under the riverbank so that Paul Keogan's lighting design cast the swaying bodies as silhouettes. The use of these silhouettes, fog and atmospheric lighting resulted in the cast appearing more like ghosts or shadows, and therefore more dead, than Portia's swinging and uncontrollable body. The shifting boundaries

---

[101] Roach, *Cities of the Dead*, p. 25.

[102] Marina Carr, *Portia Coughlan*, in *The Dazzling Dark*, ed. Frank McGuinness (London: Faber & Faber, 1996), pp. 237–311 (p. 272). The play's first publication in *The Dazzling Dark* (1996) is marked by a strong Midlands phoneticized dialect. Subsequent publication in *Plays 1* (1999) omitted the stage directions which outline the 'ensemble choreography', as well as including some adjustments to the text and to the action, most notably in the final scene. The two productions at the Peacock, for the most part, followed the 1999 script. The 1999 script is written in a more standardized form of English.

[103] Carr, *Portia Coughlan*, in *The Dazzling Dark*, p. 272.

between life and death, and proper and improper bodies were therefore highlighted in this scene.

In the 1996 production the cast were motionless and dimly lit in a semicircle facing the audience while Portia's body, once more isolated by a spotlight, became the pivotal point between the audience and cast. The cast stood and watched as Portia's body was lowered and their silence and lack of movement jarred with the noise of the creaking pulley and Portia's swaying body. A sense of ritual was evoked in the 'ensemble choreography' of the scene change that followed as the table which Portia sat at throughout the play was carried on as if it were a coffin born by pallbearers. The 'ensemble choreography' re-enacts the past through ritual, or genealogies of performance, but repetition also creates a sense of the uncanny to suggest the deathliness of life. Moreover, reframing the table as a coffin underlined the claustrophobia of Portia's home, thereby offering reasons for her need to escape, even through death.

Portia's uncontrollable body is a 'messy visual image' which, as Maria Doyle suggests, disrupts the sense of purification and catharsis traditionally created by tragic theatre.[104] This messiness pre-empts Portia's ghostly return on stage in Act Three, after we have seen her dead body, and in the 1996 publication she describes her living death to her friend: 'Ah'm dead Maggie May, dead an' whah ya seen this long time gone be a ghost who chan't fin' her restin' place, is all.'[105] Portia therefore functions as a surrogate of the Portia we have seen in Act One: a ghost of a ghost. Acts One and Two reveal Portia's rejection of traditional models of femininity, contained within the familial and domestic sphere. Portia tells Raphael that she never wanted children and that he has failed in thinking that he could 'woo her into motherhood': 'I can't love them, Raphael. I'm just not able.'[106] Portia's relationship with her own mother is fraught and Marianne's continual berating of Portia as a bad mother eventually results in violence. The idealized model of motherhood is further undermined by Portia's grandmother Blaize Scully, whose overbearing presence in her son's life led to her banishing her daughter-in-law Marianne and the twins from her kitchen. The home becomes a site of conflict which resonates with the women's restrictions by, and complicity with, a patriarchal family model.

---

[104] Doyle, 'Dead Center: Tragedy and the Reanimated Body', p. 48.
[105] Carr, *Portia Coughlan*, in *The Dazzling Dark*, p. 293.
[106] Carr, *Portia Coughlan*, in *Plays 1*, p. 221.

Haunted Bodies and Violent Pasts

Portia's performance in Act Three, of the duties of mother and wife, mimics restrictive gender roles. Portia is coerced into performing the roles society makes available to her and this is denoted in the final scene of the play when she puts on the birthday gifts from her husband and parents – a bracelet and dress – before cooking dinner for her husband and putting the children to bed. In the premiere production the dress lay across the table like a shadow of Portia, thereby compounding her ghostliness. However, the emphasis on Portia's performance, her putting on of these traditional roles just as she dons her dress, enables her to destabilize their perpetuation in cultural memory.

Portia's mimicry in the final scene of the play evokes a genealogy of performance which suggests the cultural memory of traditional feminine roles, supporting Roach's suggestion that 'genealogies of performance document – and suspect – the historical transmission and dissemination of cultural practices through collective representations'.[107] Portia's ghostly performance highlights countermemories which are 'publicly enacted by the bodies that bear its consequences'[108] to expose the implications of both repressing and disrupting models of femininity defined within the domestic space and family unit.

Raphael tells Portia that she's 'not well' and 'not normal',[109] exposing the discrepancy between Portia's desires and the roles made available to her by society. Portia's refusal to fit traditional models of femininity is met by exclusion and denial of her subjectivity. Wald maps the 'real' and ghostly bodies of the play onto gendered norms to suggest that: '*Portia Coughlan* offers counter-fantasies to culturally accepted notions about which bodies matter and which do not in terms of life and death but also in terms of appropriately sexed and "unruly" bodies.'[110] Portia's melancholic state unhinges the borders between life and death, male and female; a sentiment echoed by Portia's mother: 'If ya passed your day like any normal woman there'd be none of this!'[111]

Portia's ghostly body in Act Three facilitates the unsettling articulation of the abject, of bodies deemed not to matter, in order to question the construction of these categories. However, unlike Wald, I do not interpret the chronology of the play as reinforcing 'the melancholic sense of the future's definiteness and inescapability'.[112] Instead, the third act enables Portia's ghostly performance to critically engage with surrogacy as a process

---

[107] Roach, *Cities of the Dead*, p. 25.   [108] Roach, *Cities of the Dead*, p. 26.
[109] Carr, *Portia Coughlan*, in *Plays 1*, p. 234.
[110] Wald, *Hysteria, Trauma and Melancholia*, p. 198.
[111] Carr, *Portia Coughlan*, in *Plays 1*, p. 211.   [112] Wald, *Hysteria, Trauma and Melancholia*, p. 196.

198   Women and Embodied Mythmaking in Irish Theatre

of self-invention which relies on reperformance and thus has the potential to keep the narrative of the past in process. As a ghost of a ghost, Portia highlights the performance of gendered roles, as well as revealing the uncanny potential of the surrogate to evoke countermemories and the unhomely past. Portia offers a critical genealogy of performance through her engagement with the repression of female subjectivities by restrictive myths of femininity; she also suggests alternative models of femininity which refuse to be contained within these limiting tropes. Gabriel's surrogacy fails to live up to Portia's expectations but her own surrogacy creates a surplus as she exceeds roles through mimicry, underlined by her associations with the river and her movement beyond the confines of her home.

Leeney draws attention to the experience of watching a performance of *Portia Coughlan*, an experience which is invigorated by Portia's energy rather than melancholia: 'In performance, despite her monstrous aspects, Portia's energy fuels the piece, overtaking the negative images of destruction, failure and suicide and enacting, in their stead, a passionate subjectivity of astonishing vigour.'[113] This is echoed in Fintan O'Toole's review of the premiere production; he remarks upon the necessity of Portia's energy, 'for if Portia once settles into any single emotional mode, the play would sink under its own weight'.[114] Senchil describes 'shadow people [who] leave ne'er a mark at all'[115] but Portia, despite being a ghost of a ghost, leaves an indelible mark on the audience. The audience are haunted by her energy and left in no doubt as to her strength of character and refusal to be silenced, as well as her refutation of confinement in her emotional expression. Her haunted body highlights the stage as an unhomely space and engages with the inherited genealogies of performance made available to her, ultimately rejecting them through her death.

Portia's final mythmaking of the twins' unity describes them 'a-twined' in the womb:

> we don't know which of us is the other and we don't want to, and the water swells around our ears, and all the world is Portia and Gabriel packed for ever in a tight hot womb, where there's no breathin', no thinkin', no seein', only darkness and heart drums and touch.[116]

Portia's impossible desire for (re)union with Gabriel asserts the failure of her fantasy 'to locate any ontological plenitude'.[117] However, the myth of their unity in the womb is also an expression of her desire for an identity

---

[113] Leeney, 'Ireland's "Exiled" Women Playwrights', p. 159.
[114] O'Toole, *Critical Moments*, p. 166.   [115] Carr, *Portia Coughlan*, in *Plays 1*, p. 246.
[116] Carr, *Portia Coughlan*, in *Plays 1*, p. 254.   [117] Wallace, *Suspect Cultures*, p. 275.

outside of the restrictions of gendered roles. The twins' fluid conception of identity, 'we don't know which of us is the other and we don't want to', echoes both Portia's and Gabriel's transgression of gendered norms. Damus's and Fintan's descriptions of Gabriel, 'DAMUS: Looked like a girl. / Fintan: Sang like one too',[118] highlights his failure to fulfil norms of masculinity. The twins' ghostly and unruly bodies fail to comply with constricting gender roles and thus are not accommodated as bodies that matter. It is to the Belmont River that they turn in their search for an undifferentiated space: a place of transformation which can accommodate unexpressed, unhomely and ghostly forms of subjectivity. Both *Portia Coughlan* and Gore-Booth's *The Buried Life of Deirdre* manifest a clear distinction between the limitations of the prevailing patriarchal model and more accommodating alternatives which are evoked through the landscape: as Melissa Sihra notes of *Portia Coughlan*, 'the close proximity of the demarcated male-owned farmlands is in stark contrast to [the] transformative potential of the ever-moving Belmont River'.[119]

The Buried Life of Deirdre

Almost ninety years separate *Portia Coughlan* and *The Buried Life of Deirdre*, but there is a clear connection in terms of the equation between land and power versus dispossession which is closely linked to Ireland's history as a colonized nation. Gore-Booth wrote *The Buried Life of Deirdre* in 1908 but she returned to it in the winter of 1916–17 to draw illustrations while she was recovering from illness.[120] Gore-Booth was working on the illustrations during a time when her sister Constance Markievicz played an active militant role in the Easter Rising, for which she was then imprisoned. The play therefore emerged from a period of conflict with the fight for Irish Independence and the First World War.

However, in contrast to *Portia Coughlan*, which is epitomized by anger and violence, *The Buried Life of Deirdre* is characterized by Deirdre's pacifist argument. Carr's play is set in the early years of the Celtic Tiger in which the national obsession with property ownership reached its zenith, whereas Gore-Booth's play arises from a period defined by struggle for an independent Irish State. Both periods aspire to very different 'freedoms': the neoliberal freedom of a market economy which would supposedly

---

[118] Carr, *Portia Coughlan*, in *Plays 1*, p. 224.
[119] Sihra, 'Renegotiating Landscapes of the Female', p. 26.
[120] See 'Note' to *The Buried Life of Deirdre* (London: Longmans, Green & Co., 1930), p. xii. There is no record of a professional production of the play.

200   Women and Embodied Mythmaking in Irish Theatre

improve everyone's lives, in contrast to freedom from colonialism; yet, both these freedoms share a uneasy relationship with feminist understandings of freedom, a discussion that has already been embarked upon in previous chapters. The surrogates in both plays embody responses to these ambitions: *Portia Coughlan* is prescient in its depiction of a world which has failed to materialize opportunity for all, whereas Gore-Booth's play holds more store in the hope that things could change for the better – an optimism which would seem more in keeping with the years in which it was written and illustrated, rather than the context of paternalist conservatism that characterized Ireland in 1930 when the play was published. Before I turn to the hope and challenge which the landscape commands in Gore-Booth's play, I want to first look at Gore-Booth's interruption of the perpetuation of inherited versions of the Deirdre myth, as well as the ways in which the reincarnated body functions as the surrogate.

In her introduction to *The Buried Life of Deirdre* Gore-Booth stresses that myth is a process which is open to reshaping: 'Free to everyone alike, these shapes of ancient beauty are ever ready to bear the brunt of new interpretations and individual experiences.'[121] Gore-Booth's play draws on the myth of Deirdre who was exiled to the woods by the king, Conor, because of a prophecy that she would bring destruction to Ulster. Deirdre falls in love with Naisi and they are forced to flee the country and Conor's jealous anger. Their exile ends when they return to Conor's court, only to be betrayed by him which results in their deaths. However, Gore-Booth brings a new dimension to the myth as she presents Deirdre as a reincarnated 'old and jealous king'.[122] The conversations in the opening act of the play make a clear and gendered distinction between those, namely Deirdre and the prophetess Lavarcam, who worship the god Mannanán who represents 'the freedom and universality of loving', and Conor who worships Angus, a god who represents 'the possessive and exclusive passion of love'.[123] A parallel is thus set up between the old king, who Deirdre was in a past life, and Conor as they are both jealous and possessive of land and women. Deirdre's description of the destructive nature of Conor's desire to possess echoes Bluebeard: 'he who could not possess, would destroy'.[124]

---

[121] Eva Gore-Booth, *The Buried Life of Deirdre* (London: Longmans, Green & Co., 1930), p. ix.
[122] Gore-Booth, *The Buried Life of Deirdre*, p. 13.
[123] Gore-Booth, *The Buried Life of Deirdre*, p. x.
[124] Gore-Booth, *The Buried Life of Deirdre*, p. 32.

The inclusion of reincarnation in the play adds an element of 'the working out of the evil we ourselves have wrought through the ages'.[125] Reincarnation shapes Deirdre's body as it is haunted by the past but this is a haunting which can be worked through and thus engages with the future. Deirdre's individual experience of reincarnation brings the buried past into the present for all to learn from and, as Cathy Leeney notes, 'in place of a tragedy of passion and jealousy building towards its catastrophic crisis, here in *The Buried Life of Deirdre* is a surprising enactment of redemption through experience'.[126] The previous chapters charted the processes of metamorphosis and death as unsettling performance strategies and in Gore-Booth's play we see Deirdre creatively rehouse herself in different bodies to explore shifting identities and to reclaim death as a liberating action and continual process which evades silence.

Gore-Booth's active resignification of the Deirdre myth undermines her representation as a passive and tragic heroine,[127] and as a temptress Eve figure, perpetuated in versions of the myth inherited from monastic scribes.[128] However, the process of rewriting is negotiated within limits as, like Gregory's *Grania*, Deirdre has to assert her position in the face of the avowed male bonds in Conor's court. As in *The Triumph of Maeve*, Gore-Booth emphasizes a female solidarity which is associated with peace and freedom; a concept which Conor's jealousy blinds him to as Deirdre remarks: 'Conor has no sister among women.'[129] Deirdre is a defiant advocate of a pacifist feminism; this stance was at odds with the militant nationalism that was developing during the period in which the play was written and illustrated. Gore-Booth draws on Greek tragedy with both the convention of the dying speech (Deirdre's) and the three act structure but the introduction of reincarnation removes the focus from the point of death and shifts it to death as process. In a similar vein to Carr's *Woman*

---

[125] Gore-Booth, *The Buried Life of Deirdre*, p. 14.

[126] Cathy Leeney, 'The Space Outside: Images of Women in Plays by Eva Gore-Booth and Dorothy Macardle', in *Women in Irish Drama: A Century of Authorship and Representation*, ed. Melissa Sihra (Basingstoke: Palgrave Macmillan, 2007), pp. 55–68 (p. 57).

[127] In her introduction to the play, Gore-Booth references Douglas Hyde's *Literary History of Ireland* in which two different endings to the myth are outlined. The first is from O'Flanagan's 1801 version in which Naisi and his brothers are killed while fighting Conor and, after her lamentation, Deirdre falls into their grave and dies. The source of the second ending is the oldest written version of the myth in the *Book of Leinster*: Deirdre is trapped like 'a ewe between two rams' on a chariot between the man who killed her lover and the King Conor so in order to escape, Deirdre throws herself from the chariot and dashes her head against a rock. See Douglas Hyde, *A Literary History of Ireland* (London: Ernest Benn; New York: Barnes & Noble, 1967), p. 317.

[128] Herbert, 'Celtic Heroine? The Archaeology of the Deirdre Story', pp. 21–2.

[129] Gore-Booth, *The Buried Life of Deirdre*, p. 38.

202   Women and Embodied Mythmaking in Irish Theatre

and Scarecrow, elements of Greek dramatic representations of death and Irish mythology are merged. The emphasis is on the possibilities of redemption and life, rather than the dying speech as the apex of a tragic narrative, and the play closes with the promise of peace enacted through Conor and Lavarcam's decision to place an offering on Mannanán's altar. Gore-Booth figures Deirdre as a woman firmly in control of her destiny, rather than one trapped within a tragic narrative, and thus is able to make a claim for the redemptive power of experience and history. This claim is made flesh through Deirdre's reincarnated body which is evocative of process and the past becoming the future.

The Reincarnated Body and the Performance of Gender

In her introduction to the play, Gore-Booth explains her incorporation of rebirth into the Deirdre myth:

> The idea of re-incarnation is not so exclusively an Eastern doctrine as many people think. Mr Douglas Hyde, in his *Literary History of Ireland*, points out its place in Irish literature, and explains that it seems to have been part of the Druidic teaching. Whether this involves some ancient little-known connection between East and West, it would be hard to say.[130]

Deirdre describes the soul as 'a wanderer, journeying again and again through many lives'.[131] Carr similarly believes in the reincarnation of souls; she stated in an interview: 'I believe in the eternal return until we get it right, that we are sent back until we get it right.'[132] Indeed, the notion of reincarnation is suggested in the 1996 published script of *Portia Coughlan* when Portia claims that '[i]n a former life ah'm sure ah war a river.'[133]

Reincarnation, as a strategy for subversion, resonates with ideas of metamorphosis and shapeshifting as explored in Chapter 3. Through reincarnation, the body is in process and can generate a transformative performance which echoes both de Beauvoir's woman as becoming and Butler's woman as site of perpetual contest. Sonja Tiernan draws attention to Gore-Booth's assertion in the journal *Urania* that 'sex was an accident and formed no essential part of an individual's nature'.[134] *The Buried Life of*

---

[130] Gore-Booth, *The Buried Life of Deirdre*, p. x.
[131] Gore-Booth, *The Buried Life of Deirdre*, p. 14.
[132] 'Marina Carr in Conversation with Melissa Sihra', p. 58.
[133] Carr, *Portia Coughlan*, in *The Dazzling Dark*, p. 255.
[134] Sonja Tiernan, '"No Measures of 'Emancipation' or 'Equality' Will Suffice": Eva Gore-Booth's Revolutionary Feminism in the Journal *Urania*', in *Women, Social and Cultural Change in*

Deirdre was written eight years before the establishment of *Urania* but in it we can see the seeds of the journal's radical arguments. In Gore-Booth's play, Deirdre rekindles the life of an old king to highlight the perpetuation of gendered models through performance: the king bears a striking resemblance to Conor in his treatment of women, thus exposing the limiting repetitions of inherited narratives and their contingent alignment of power and masculinity.

Throughout the play, Deirdre's songs foretell her death and by Act Three she is certain of the inevitability of her and Naisi's fate. However, the emphasis is firmly placed on responsibility for the deeds which bring about these deaths as Lavarcam refutes Conor's claim at the end of the play that it was the will of the gods: 'Conor, it was your evil will and your cruel deed that brought the sorrow of this terrible night.'[135] The idea of reincarnation further develops this sense of responsibility. Gore-Booth offers a reperformed identity, that of Deirdre as the old and jealous king, as a means of examining the past and learning from it. In *A Literary History of Ireland*, Hyde raises the question of whether the idea of rebirth had 'any ethical significance attached to it by the druids of Ireland, as it most undoubtedly had by their cousins the druids of Gaul'.[136] Gore-Booth certainly incorporates an ethical significance into her notion of reincarnation, namely responsibility for past crimes and violence, and the promotion of pacifism: 'that the passionate pilgrim of Angus becomes one with the mysterious light and untroubled waters of Mannanán – the Spirit of the One'.[137] The achievement of this peace and unity is only made possible through what Gore-Booth describes in the introduction as Deirdre's 'sacrifice'. Just as *The Triumph of Maeve* re-visioned narratives of sacrifice and male heroism, Deirdre's sacrifice does not see her appropriation by Conor's dominant order, 'relinquishing one's own desires in the service of a master's',[138] nor does it exonerate past crimes. Deirdre worships Mannanán who is 'the buried light in the souls of men'[139] and she believes that her death will bring forth this light: 'Pain and death are not punishment. They open the eyes of the blind.'[140]

The dual sets of imagery: light, knowledge and peace versus darkness, ignorance and violence, are embodied in Deirdre's twofold identity as both

---

Twentieth Century Ireland: Dissenting Voices?, ed. Sarah O'Connor and Christopher Shepard (Newcastle: Cambridge Scholars Press, 2008), pp. 166–82 (p. 170).
[135] Gore-Booth, *The Buried Life of Deirdre*, p. 62.   [136] Hyde, *A Literary History of Ireland*, p. 104.
[137] Gore-Booth, *The Buried Life of Deirdre*, p. x.   [138] Eagleton, *Sweet Violence*, pp. 274–5.
[139] Gore-Booth, *The Buried Life of Deirdre*, p. 9.
[140] Gore-Booth, *The Buried Life of Deirdre*, p. 57.

204   Women and Embodied Mythmaking in Irish Theatre

herself and the jealous old king. This is no simple duality: both good and evil are held within one body, and Deirdre's identity serves to suggest that the possibility of redemption is available to all. Furthermore, the experience of reincarnation enables engagement with others' embodied experiences. The myth no longer emphasizes fatalism but offers transformation and the possibility of alternative futures. The shadows of earlier times live on as restless ghosts who return to reveal crimes of the past, as Deirdre asks: 'Is not this dream the shadow of my deed, this terrible deed that has been crying out against me for a thousand years?'[141] Through her performance of the king, Deirdre reveals that these crimes are not inevitable, 'timeless essentials'[142] and that the possibility for change lies in learning from the mistakes of the past.

Reincarnation suggests a fluidity of bodies, identities and time. Time is cyclical and thus 'fulfils itself outside the teleology of tragic narrative'.[143] Like the trope of metamorphosis, reincarnation evades a tragic endpoint to offer transformation and continual process. An application of Roach's theory of surrogacy to the moment when Deirdre performs the reincarnated king offers a means of addressing the mutability of bodies and time. As the king, Deirdre is an effigy whose actions 'hold open a place in memory'.[144] Performance genealogies re-enact the past to reaffirm inherited narratives and memories but they can evoke the uncanny and undermine the certainty of our reception of the past. The moment in Act One when Deirdre reveals that she is a reincarnated king is vital in highlighting Deirdre as a 'memoried self'. Deirdre describes the king's crime:

> The King's voice is the voice of Deirdre, the King's eyes are the eyes of Deirdre, the King's heart is the heart of Deirdre. Oh, there is the sword red with blood, in the hands that are the hands of Deirdre, and the voice of the woman is crying out against the treachery of the King.[145]

Leeney points out that: 'It seems crucial that the mirroring of Deirdre in the figure of the old king be dramatized, rather than merely described, at this point.'[146] Deirdre's reincarnation needs to be embodied, not just narrated, to highlight the king as an effigy or surrogate performed through Deirdre. Deirdre's reincarnation exposes countermemories which are remembered through performance and through the bodies which bear the consequences of these repressed histories: Deirdre's body simultaneously evokes the king and the 'voice of the woman . . . crying out against

---

[141] Gore-Booth, *The Buried Life of Deirdre*, p. 13.   [142] Roach, *Cities of the Dead*, p. 30.
[143] Leeney, 'The Space Outside', p. 58.   [144] Roach, *Cities of the Dead*, p. 36.
[145] Gore-Booth, *The Buried Life of Deirdre*, pp. 12–13.   [146] Leeney, 'The Space Outside', p. 61.

the treachery of the King'. Reincarnation accordingly expresses experiences denied by the realist frame, as well as suggesting worlds beyond it; a strategy employed by Gore-Booth in her other works including *The Triumph of Maeve*.

Deirdre's re-enactment of the past has the potential to evoke the uncanny and this unsettling potential is key to staging this moment as a critical genealogy of performance, rather than a simple idealization of the past. Deirdre's uncanny performance of the king is 'at once resemblance and menace':[147] she resembles what is being narrated through her performance of the king but the king's presence is menacing in its introduction of the threat of possession and violence towards Deirdre's identity. This threat is heightened by the fact that the king mirrors Conor's possessive and jealous love, yet is embodied by his target. As the king, Deirdre describes how 'I, too, had a deep grave dug in the forest, and slew my own heart's happiness because of the jealousy of love, and buried her whom I loved in the deep grave under the trees.'[148] This pre-empts Deirdre's fate (as well as resonating with Bluebeard's murderous actions) but history does not function as inevitability in this play, instead it is in continual process and can be educative, leading to change in the future.

In discussion of Jamaican playwright Dennis Scott's *An Echo in the Bone* (1974), Roach focuses on the ceremony through which the dead are able to speak through effigies: the bodies of the living. This ritual enables the resurrection of the forgotten pasts of circum-Atlantic history and Roach highlights that spirit-world ceremonies 'tend to place catastrophe in the past, a grief to be expiated, and not necessarily in the future, as a singular fate yet to be endured'.[149] Similarly, *The Buried Life of Deirdre* evokes the spirit of the past in order to learn from it and avoids upholding a fatalistic future. The unhomely past, repressed memories and private traumas which erupt in the public realm, are embodied by the old king's reincarnation through Deirdre. The king's abuse of power and violent imposition of silence in an effort to possess a woman's love, namely the burial of the woman in a deep grave, exposes the connection between private trauma and broader structures of power. The burial of the woman represents the burial of the unhomely past and Deirdre's reincarnated body facilitates its re-emergence. Furthermore, Deirdre draws attention to Conor's resemblance to the king to reveal that the potential to repeat these crimes still lies

---

[147] Quoted in Roach, *Cities of the Dead*, p. 6.   [148] Gore-Booth, *The Buried Life of Deirdre*, p. 13.
[149] Roach, *Cities of the Dead*, p. 35.

206   Women and Embodied Mythmaking in Irish Theatre

within us. The need to acknowledge the buried light of Mannanán comes to represent the need to address our responsibility for the past.

Through her re-enactment of the past, Deirdre questions the perpetuation of unsullied memories of the king and thus holds him to account for his crimes. Her reincarnated body disrupts the continuity of cultural memory which depends upon forgetting, in this case the crimes of the king; it also reveals the limits of memory. The uncanny incorporates an element of return and it is in this process of repetition that the possibility for change lies: 'repetition is an art of re-creation as well as restoration'.[150] Deirdre tells Naisi that everyone is responsible for the past: 'You do not understand, Naisi. We have all lived so many times . . . There is not one of us young, not one of us innocent.'[151] Through Deirdre's reincarnated body, the past can be re-created in order to reshape the future as '[t]he past evermore becomes the future'.[152] Thus, the play proposes shared responsibility for the past in order to evoke a utopian future associated with the peace and freedom of Mannanán. Indeed, the ending suggests that this may be achievable as Lavarcam and Conor go together to Mannanán's altar to make an offering and Conor admits that he has much to learn: 'We none of us understood.'[153] Through bodies and the landscape, reincarnation can bring the past into critical engagement with the present. The re-creation of the past is not merely restorative: it can highlight the selective process of memory and forgetting. Moreover, in *The Buried Life of Deirdre* the reperformance of the past unloosens congealed memories to articulate unhomely narratives and provide ethical lessons.

Place and the Unhomely Past

The uncanny return and reperformance of the past is closely linked to place in both *Portia Coughlan* and *The Buried Life of Deirdre*. Carr describes her fascination with '[n]ature invested with human memory or human association'.[154] Roach's discussion of Pierre Nora's concepts of *lieux de mémoire*, 'places of memory', and *milieux de mémoire*, 'environments of memory', is particularly useful in addressing the way that place functions as a repository of recollections. Places of memory are 'a place in which everyday practices and attitudes may be legitimated, "brought out into the open", reinforced, celebrated, intensified'.[155] Roach names these spaces

---

[150] Roach, *Cities of the Dead*, p. 286.   [151] Gore-Booth, *The Buried Life of Deirdre*, p. 28.
[152] Gore-Booth, *The Buried Life of Deirdre*, p. 27.
[153] Gore-Booth, *The Buried Life of Deirdre*, p. 63.
[154] 'Interview with Marina Carr', in *Rage and Reason*, p. 154.   [155] Roach, *Cities of the Dead*, p. 28.

Haunted Bodies and Violent Pasts

'behavioural vortexes' as they perpetuate identities and modes of behaviour: 'a center of cultural self-invention through the restoration of behaviour'.[156] In contrast, environments of memory draw on memory in process and are linked to countermemories: 'the largely oral and corporeal retentions of traditional cultures'.[157] Environments of memory can therefore enable the resurfacing of repressed cultural memories, and accommodate unhomely bodies and the unhomely past.

The process of reincarnation in *The Buried Life of Deirdre* evokes 'living memory' in the moment when Deirdre embodies the king 'through the transmission of gestures, habits, and skills'.[158] Memory lives on and informs the present when we learn from the experiences of the past, a process which is very much associated with the underground passage. The distinction between places and environments of memory may run the risk of implying that the body is more 'natural' and in opposition to culture. However, both plays link nature and culture in environments of memory to de-naturalize and interrogate corporeal behaviour and genealogies of performance; both bodies and the landscape are culturally encoded. The association of Deirdre with the secret passage reshapes the simple alignment of woman with the land and nation; as Leeney contends: 'Gore-Booth appropriates the identification of the feminine with the natural world, and creates a new definition of the natural as the repository of history and culture.'[159] The buried passageway and Deirdre's reincarnated body are in process, and contain experience and living memory which can be drawn on in the present.

Both Deirdre and Portia link a violent past with the landscape; Deirdre describes how '[a] little blood shed by the wayside can stain the feet of the passersby after a thousand years'.[160] The violent eruptions of an unhomely past are articulated and experienced through the environment and the underground passage in Gore-Booth's play represents the buried past which cannot be suppressed. Deirdre and Naisi escape at the end of Act One through the passage which passes by Mannanán's altar. Naisi asks her how she knew of the route and Deirdre replies: 'I remember I saw it in dreams ... memories.'[161] The passage is therefore associated with living memory, rather than a fixed past, and also with peace and Mannanán. The underground passage is a place of reinvention and birth; as Leeney notes:

---

[156] Roach, *Cities of the Dead*, p. 28.   [157] Roach, *Cities of the Dead*, p. 26.
[158] Roach, *Cities of the Dead*, p. 26.   [159] Leeney, 'The Space Outside', p. 61.
[160] Gore-Booth, *The Buried Life of Deirdre*, p. 49.
[161] Gore-Booth, *The Buried Life of Deirdre*, p. 19.

208   Women and Embodied Mythmaking in Irish Theatre

> The underground passage begins to represent the notion of reincarnation, and of lives and fates understood through monumental time, beyond the limits of a single life. The female association of the passageway as an image of birth is emphasized by Deirdre's and Lavarcam's knowledge of it.[162]

The acknowledgement of living memory in the play leads Deirdre and Naisi to their initial escape through the passage and in Act Three they use the same route to flee from Conor. Deirdre says, '[f]ear not, Naisi, we shall escape by the secret passage',[163] before putting out all the torches and plunging the stage into darkness. The darkness symbolizes 'the buried light' of Mannanán and it results in Deirdre's failure to escape, and to her death. This is contrasted with the light which subsequently accompanies the revelation of Deirdre's dead body, yet this is a memoried and reincarnated body which brings the past to light and evokes the passageway as a place of knowledge and experience. Through acknowledgment of past memories and crimes which resurface through the secret passage as an environment of memory, the possibility for an alternative future is conceived. This alternative future is informed by the past but a past which, like Deirdre's body, identity and myth, is in process.

Landscapes of Alternative Futures

In *Portia Coughlan*, the home is a behavioural vortex which legitimates history and provides a space for the re-enactments of restrictive genealogies of performance. Portia feels confined by unaccommodating models of femininity and unable to express herself as a desiring subject in the space of the home. This experience of *déréliction* was highlighted in the 1996 production by the repeated tableau of Portia sitting trapped at the kitchen table and isolated in a spotlight. The constraining nature of this behavioural vortex was juxtaposed with Portia's corporeal freedom in the scene where she dances at the High Chaparral bar with her friends Stacia and Maggie (Act Three, Scene Four). The audience experience the release of Portia's contained energies, an exciting moment which also warns of the danger of further suppressing her frustration and rage. Portia's energy is irrepressible and violently explodes in Act Three when she leaps onto her mother and pinions her to the ground: 'You've me suffocated so I can't breathe any more!'[164] Violence is a means of resistance and expression for

---

[162] Leeney, 'The Space Outside', p. 60.   [163] Gore-Booth, *The Buried Life of Deirdre*, p. 60.
[164] Carr, *Portia Coughlan*, in *Plays 1*, p. 248.

Portia; a violence which results in her suicide as a defiant strategy for refusing genealogies of performance and the restrictive space of home.

Melissa Sihra suggests that Portia's 'plea for spaces of possibility beyond the monological discourse of home is expressed in her intimate connection with nature'.[165] The Belmont River is a free-flowing space of movement which evokes Portia's desire for self-invention and renewal. This counters Wald's argument that Portia's suicide epitomizes her general melancholic suffering and is thus linked to complete disengagement from the future as: 'The melancholic can only ever repeat the past because for him or her, everything is done and terminated.'[166] I propose that Portia's suicide can be understood as a rejection of the past and of genealogies of performance that perpetuate inherited roles of femininity, as she demands alternative expression in the river. Through the process of death, the Belmont River offers a space of transformation which can accommodate unexpressed and unhomely subjectivities, as well as facilitating the articulation of unruly bodies which are deemed to not 'matter'. If we view Portia as a melancholic, trapped in the past, then the river can be interpreted as a place of memory: a shrine to Gabriel. Conversely, the river can be construed as an environment of memory if we link it to female mythmaking, the oral tradition of storytelling and female bodily freedom; a suggestion which is in keeping with how the landscape functions in Carr's other Midlands plays. The Belmont River disrupts the imposition of fixed roles, and is therefore an environment of living memory which, like the underground passage in *The Buried Life of Deirdre*, facilitates shifting and unstable identities excluded by traditional gendered spaces.

In an interview prior to the premiere of *Portia Coughlan*, Carr remarked: 'In all of us there is a twin. That shadow part of you is often the best part of you. That identity has been fudged or subsumed in Portia, and in a sense, she's like a walking ghost herself.'[167] Portia's ghostliness questions 'what it means to live'[168] and, as in *The Mai*, there is a discrepancy between the stifling confines of the worlds these ghostly women inhabit and their desire for alternative spaces which are more accommodating. However, within existing frameworks these alternatives seem impossible and, like *The Mai*, *Portia Coughlan* functions as a negative utopia which exposes 'the contradiction between the evident possibility of fulfilment and the just as evident impossibility'.[169]

---

[165] Sihra, 'The House of Woman', p. 211.   [166] Wald, *Hysteria, Trauma and Melancholia*, p. 195.
[167] White, 'Twin Speak', p. 10.   [168] Sihra, 'Renegotiating Landscapes of the Female', p. 28.
[169] Theodor Adorno, quoted by Sue-Ellen Case in 'The Screens of Time: Feminist Memories and Hopes', p. 111.

210   Women and Embodied Mythmaking in Irish Theatre

The different approaches taken in the two Peacock productions to staging the ending illustrate how the connection between Portia and the river, and the evocation of other more accommodating spaces, is key to suggesting both possibility *and* impossibility. The 1996 production closed as it opened with Portia at the kitchen table rather than engaging with the space of the river; a decision that served to emphasize the difficulty of repudiating limiting myths of femininity and of effecting change. In contrast, in the 2004 production Portia sat on the riverbank and bright light shone out from under the marbled block to eventually blind the audience so that Portia disappeared into the space of the river. Portia's death simultaneously evokes freedom and constraint: the impossibility of making her unhomely body signify within existing structures. She is therefore doomed to ghostliness within this world but the potential of this uncertain state can be harnessed to put pressure on dominant models of femininity.

The negative utopia is illuminating in its exposure of the false promise of the Celtic Tiger period and the attendant illusion of freedom posited by a neoliberal postfeminism; Portia's rich, land-owning father describes how: 'There be nothin' the girl needs nor wants.'[170] This contrasts with the utopian possibility of *The Buried Life of Deirdre* which is associated with Mannanán, the underground passage and nature, and is made tangible through Deirdre's reincarnated body, which evokes 'the freedom of the wind blowing through the world without barriers'.[171] Leeney describes Gore-Booth's plays as 'spacious experiments'[172] which utilize the stage space to reflect the experiences of Irish women engaged in the fight for suffrage and national freedom at the start of the twentieth century. Gore-Booth wrote the play in the first decade of the twentieth century: a period of revolutionary hope in which women's activism was integral, and shaped the 1916 Proclamation which promised full and equal citizenship to all. Gore-Booth's insistence on utopia as a verb rather than a noun; on process and transformation rather than a perfected vision, indicates her acknowledgement of the various positions within contemporary feminisms and of the necessity of using dissent to invigorate, rather than close down, debate. However, *The Buried Life of Deirdre* was published in 1930 and was read by an audience contemporary with O'Neill's *Bluebeard* in which any sense of hope dissipates as the ghostly wives are scattered in all directions. Utopian possibility is wholly absent from *Bluebeard* and this highlights the vital

---

[170] Carr, *Portia Coughlan*, in *Plays 1*, p. 212.   [171] Gore-Booth, *The Buried Life of Deirdre*, p. 61.
[172] Leeney, 'The Space Outside', p. 67.

contribution that Gore-Booth's belief in an alternative future offered 1930s Ireland and the imperative of generating spaces of possibility and expression for women, which countered Ireland's 'architecture of containment'.

The Haunted Body as a Genealogy of Performance

Roach's concepts of surrogacy and genealogies of performance suggest that repetition can reaffirm or transform the past, just as myth can congeal past ideologies or engage with liberatory futures. Genealogies of performance can potentially engage with the future, highlighting the 'possibilities of restored behaviour not merely as the recapitulation but as the transformation of experience through the displacement of its cultural forms'.[173] Past actions shape our present world and though genealogies of performance attempt to forget or bury aspects of cultural memory, the haunted bodies and landscapes in *The Buried Life of Deirdre*, *Portia Coughlan* and *Bluebeard* enable these countermemories to resurface, and for private traumas to unsettle the public realm. The haunted body in these three plays offers a genealogy of performance which exposes the enduring experience of unhomeliness resulting from the perpetuation of genealogies of performance which continue to provide restrictive models of femininity. However, the haunted body also rewrites these myths and thereby enables the spectre of the past to unsettle the present, as well as gesturing towards an alternative future, for as Deirdre says: 'There is no present. It is always either the past or the future.'[174]

Bluebeard, *The Buried Life of Deirdre* and *Portia Coughlan* stage unhomely moments which, together with Roach's concept of genealogies of performance, suggest the necessity of excavating the past and articulating unspoken histories in order to imagine a different future. The ability of the past to educate us, encourage us to share responsibility and reveal alternative futures is critically engaged through these somatic countermemories; the acknowledgement in the plays of women's experiences of failure, and refusal, to fulfil limiting gender roles. The notion of the body as a repository is developed further in Chapter 6 which explores how the body retains the memory of these limiting roles and myths but also has the capacity to rewrite them. The process of disrupting a genealogy of performance through the proposition of a new body of work is central to the discussion that follows of performances by Olwen Fouéré. The possibility for transformation which flows through my discussion of the landscape

---

[173] Roach, *Cities of the Dead*, p. 29.   [174] Gore-Booth, *The Buried Life of Deirdre*, p. 26.

thus far invigorates Fouéré's *riverrun*, which explicitly links the river to an exploration of a fluid gendered identity, as well as acknowledging it as an embodied archive of countermemories. Counter to the experience of women in Ireland as one of unhomeliness, the next chapter develops discussion of the genealogy of performance as a body of work which accommodates the plays and performances considered in this book. The space of the archive and house is eschewed in favour of a more enabling and fluid space: a corpus of work which acknowledges the unhomely experience as it is felt by the bodies which bear the consequences, and is animated by the process of transforming myths of femininity.

CHAPTER 6

Olwen Fouéré's Corpus: The Performer's Body and Her Body of Work

A whispering voice emerges from the darkness: 'You pass and you do not see me.'[1] The shadowy presence of a stooped figure sitting on a bench is thus made aware to the audience in the opening moments of *Sodome, My Love* (2010).[2] This poetic monologue written by Laurent Gaudé, translated and performed by Olwen Fouéré, details the experiences of the last surviving woman of Sodome who has been buried under salt – an oblique reference to the ritual act of sowing the earth of conquered lands with salt.[3] The figure of the woman also invites comparisons with the biblical story of Lot but focuses instead on his wife's account as she emerges from her centuries-long burial under a mountain of salt.

In the opening tableau, Fouéré's physical posture is stiff, her head is bowed, she is leaning her weight on one arm, and has one leg awkwardly straightened; this tension is further compounded by the script's emphasis on the cloying atmosphere of the city of Sodome and descriptions of the sweaty clammy bodies of its inhabitants. The figure slowly materializes from this deadening space: 'I feel the bite of the salt in my veins.'[4] The sharp bite awakens her body and story, and her return to life is manifested through both narrative and corporeal presence. The salt marks the anxiety of this retelling: it both preserves and denies life, connoting the possibilities for, and limits placed on, female bodily expression.

---

[1] Laurent Gaudé, *Sodome, ma Douce*, trans. by Olwen Fouéré, unpublished script (May 2010), p. 1. The play has been published in French (Paris: Actes Sud, 2009).

[2] Laurent Gaudé, *Sodome, My Love*. Director: Lynne Parker. Cast: Olwen Fouéré. Designer: John Comiskey. Costume: Monica Frawley. Music and sound: Denis Clohessy (Rough Magic in association with TheEmergencyRoom: Project Arts Centre, Dublin, opened 16 March 2010). My performance analysis is based on my viewing of the play on 23 March, as well as the DVD recording that Rough Magic granted me access to. The company's archive is now held in the The Rough Magic Theatre Company Archive, TCD MS 11568, Manuscripts & Archives, The Library of Trinity College Dublin.

[3] Private correspondence with Olwen Fouéré, 8 November 2018.

[4] Gaudé, *Sodome, ma Douce*, p. 1.

213

214   Women and Embodied Mythmaking in Irish Theatre

The opening moments of *Sodome, My Love* encapsulate the aspects of Olwen Fouéré's substantial body of work with which this chapter is concerned: how her distinctive and vigorous physical performance style underscores the ways in which limiting myths of femininity are inscribed on, and resisted by, the embodied experiences of women. Fouéré has performed a marked number of roles which draw explicitly on myth: *Salomé* (Gate Theatre, 1988); Gregory and Yeats's *Kathleen ni Houlihan* and Yeats's *The Cuchulain Cycle* (Abbey Theatre, 1989–93); the title role in Marina Carr's *The Mai* (Peacock Theatre, 1994), Hester Swane in *By the Bog of Cats . . .* (Abbey Theatre, 1998) and Woman in *Woman and Scarecrow* (Peacock Theatre, 2007); Vincent Woods's *A Cry from Heaven* (Abbey Theatre, 2005); Fabulous Beast Dance Theatre's *The Bull* (Dublin Theatre Festival, 2005) and *The Rite of Spring* (London Coliseum, 2009); *Medea* (Dublin Fringe Festival, 2010); *Sodome, My Love* (2010); Anna Livia Plurabelle in *riverrun* (Galway Arts Festival, 2013) and, most recently, Jesse Jones's *Tremble, Tremble* (La Biennale di Venezia, 2017). Fouéré's performances intervene in a body of cultural myths which depend on repetition to achieve their force and perpetuate their meanings; meanings which are inscribed on and silence female bodies.

In this chapter I focus on *Sodome, My Love* and *riverrun* in order to explore how Fouéré's performances expose the disparity between the fixity of mythic 'woman' and the complexity of actual women by exploring how bodies undo and rewrite myths. Both performances draw on male-authored texts but I argue that Fouéré takes ownership of the text: through her exploration of the body and of the non-verbal in performance she positions herself as the author to disrupt the authority of a literary canon. However, Fouéré's status is not one of domination, instead the ongoing collaborative process which underpins *riverrun* denies the ownership of a singular literary author and posits a more fluid network of non-verbal and affective exchanges.

Touching on a Female Writing Body

Through discussion of the challenge of documenting women's bodies in theatre, Anna Cutler outlines a hierarchy of documentation: the Proper (traditional and literary forms), the Processual (which emerge from processes of production) and the Residual, 'the area of work which represents lots of doubtfully or mis-remembered memories, smells, bodily scars, and movement memory', which 'actually communicate more directly the moment of performance'.[5] Cutler argues that 'women's performance work, which uses the female body as the primary text'[6] has been excluded from the realm of the Proper and more often resides in the Residual. The differences between Cutler's Proper and Residual performance documentation are also addressed by Joseph Roach's concept of 'genealogies of performance' which focuses on how history and memory are enacted on and remembered through the body, thus shifting the emphasis from discursively documented history. These countermemories of Residual performance are traced in this book to offer a genealogy of performance that exposes how women's bodies bear the consequences of the imposition of myths of femininity. Though working from male-authored texts with her translation of Gaudé's script in *Sodome, My Love* and her adaptation of Joyce's novel in *riverrun*, I would argue that Fouéré is the author who uses the female body as the primary text in order to uncover the inscription of bodies, as well as the bodily meanings which exceed inscription.

Cutler looks to the ways in which the Residual elements of performance may be attended to through address of a Potential Body which 'holds the many histories and inscriptions of ourselves but is also open to new possibilities.'[7] Fouéré's performances in *Sodome, My Love* and *riverrun* offer a Potential Body: inscribed by an archive of myths of femininity but also generating other possibilities. Cutler advocates *écriture féminine* as a means of documenting the Potential Body, whereby 'the written landscape becomes the performance landscape'.[8] Through the process of 'writing the body', *écriture féminine* aims to return ownership of female bodies to women, as Hélène Cixous describes: 'it will give her back her goods, her pleasures, her organs, her immense bodily territories which have been kept under seal'.[9]

In *Sodome, My Love*, the last surviving woman of Sodome returns to her body in order to author her story and articulate an embodied subjectivity. *Écriture féminine* risks advocating a return to an originary female body, prior to inscription, unless it addresses the economic and historical conditions which shape the cultural inscription of gender. In order to avoid reasserting an inflexible idealized representation of woman which fails to acknowledge how sexual difference is reinscribed through biological discourse, the body needs to be understood as a 'site of contestation':

---

[5] Anna Cutler, 'Abstract Body Language: Documenting Women's Bodies in Theatre', *New Theatre Quarterly*, 14:2 (May 1998), 111–18 (p. 113).
[6] Cutler, 'Abstract Body Language', p. 113.   [7] Cutler, 'Abstract Body Language', p. 115.
[8] Cutler, 'Abstract Body Language', p. 117.   [9] Cixous, 'Laugh of the Medusa', p. 880.

216   Women and Embodied Mythmaking in Irish Theatre

a Potential Body which is inscribed, yet also in process and thus exceeds inscription.

In the opening section of *Sodome, My Love* the audience witness the slow revival of the residues of the woman's life, and thus attention is drawn to the ways in which bodies come to life and are full of potential, yet are simultaneously fragmented, limited and inscribed. The figure's whispered voice and body emerge from the darkened stage to mark her presence and following these initial moments, a large close-up of her face is projected onto the mirrors stage left: a face which echoes the stillness of Lot's wife as its eyes remain closed. She asks us, 'Do you feel?'[10] as raindrops start to fall, slowly at first, on the projected face whose mouth opens in response. Then the figure starts to move, almost imperceptibly, as she is revived by the sensuousness and fertility of the rain: 'The first drop is for me. / It falls on my lips with the weight of a cherry.'[11] Her physical and onscreen presence draws our attention to the ways in which our bodies are inscribed by our experiences: the falling rain leaves tracks on the projected face as she tells us, 'I let the rain scar my face.'[12] This section of the play closes with the sound of falling rain becoming increasingly loud, almost threatening to drown out her assertion that 'I am coming back to life.'[13] She tilts her head back and releases the hand which she has been sitting on; lifting her claw-like hand to catch the raindrops. Her bodily tension conveys the traces of her petrification, frozen in salt and time, but now she is revived by the rain and we witness her gradual release.

The inability to fully articulate the bodily meanings generated in performance, of only touching on their residues and of exceeding inscription, corresponds to Jean-Luc Nancy's sense of the withdrawal connoted by touch. Susan Leigh Foster discusses the 'possibility of a scholarship that addresses a writing body as a well as a body written upon'[14] and Nancy's work in *Corpus* broaches the gap between body and text through his exploration of the tactility of writing: the creation of a corpus of tact and the attendant anxiety. We can explore this anxiety through the encounter of performance; of the tactful and tactile negotiations required of the audience and performers. Furthermore, within the context of my reading of the feminist potential of Nancy's work, this anxiety underlines the impossibility of fully touching on another's embodied experiences and thus of the difficulties of documenting the material complexities of

[10] Gaudé, *Sodome, ma Douce*, p. 1.   [11] Gaudé, *Sodome, ma Douce*, p. 2.
[12] Gaudé, *Sodome, ma Douce*, p. 2.   [13] Gaudé, *Sodome, ma Douce*, p. 3.
[14] Foster, *Choreographing History*, p. 12.

women's embodied experiences through myth. Nancy's understanding of the anxious relationship between body and discourse has huge potential for feminist critique of performance, particularly in his notion of exscription which addresses that which is beyond inscription.

The Performing Female Body as a Lived Body

The physicality of Fouéré's performance is crucial in highlighting how limiting myths of femininity are not just discursively imposed but viscerally lived, and thereby interrogated. Olwen Fouéré is described as an actor who 'has been a creative force in Irish theatre, bringing a keen physicality to her work inside and outside the mainstream'.[15] This 'keen physicality' is central to Fouéré's radical contribution to Irish theatre in its engagement with corporeal and non-verbal means of expression; with reference to her 1999 collaboration with composer Roger Doyle, *Angel/Babel*, Fouéré describes how: 'My own need to dissolve disciplinary boundaries and articulate a performance-based theatrical language was growing, in resistance to the inherent traditions of a predominantly literary Irish theatre.'[16] Furthermore, Fouéré intervenes in a literary theatre tradition which marks women's contribution by iconicity and associates her with the body, thereby excluding the creativity of the female body. The discussion of *Sodome, My Love* and *riverrun* which follows, focuses on how a creative female corporeality is brought into play by understanding the performing female body as a lived body which is fundamental to experience and the production of knowledge.

Attending to the female body as a site of struggle facilitates consideration of the ways in which limiting myths of femininity are inscribed on and through the body, and of the body as a 'site of contestation, in a series of economic, political, sexual, and intellectual struggles'.[17] Chapter 1 redresses the neglect of the creativity of the performing female body: my analysis of the tensions of the tableaux vivants performed by the Inghinidhe na hÉireann counters the elision of non-literary forms from a history of Irish literary theatre through the assertion of the female body as maker of meaning. Counter to the dominance of the writer's text in histories of Irish theatre, Anna McMullan highlights Yeats's and Beckett's awareness of the

---

[15] Sweeney, *Performing the Body in Irish Theatre*, p. 45.
[16] Olwen Fouéré, 'Operating Theatre and *Angel/Babel*', in *The Dreaming Body: Contemporary Irish Theatre*, ed. Paul Murphy and Melissa Sihra (Gerrard's Cross: Colin Smythe, 2009), pp. 115–24 (p. 115).
[17] Grosz, *Volatile Bodies*, p. 19.

218   Women and Embodied Mythmaking in Irish Theatre

'expressive potential of the actor's body'.[18] McMullan also draws attention to the importance of the Irish independent theatre sector in developing practices that highlight the visual, kinesic and the corporeal as major means of expression and signification.[19] Fouéré's work highlights the creative agency of the body: alerting the audience to the expressive potential and creativity of the corporeal. It is perhaps no surprise that Fouéré has engaged with dance theatre, most recently with choreographer-director Michael Keegan-Dolan (Fabulous Beast), as dance offers: '[t]he possibility of a body that is written upon but that also writes. It asks scholars to approach the body's involvement in any activity with an assumption of potential agency to participate in or resist whatever forms of cultural production are underway.'[20] Susan Leigh Foster's 'claim for a writing-dancing body'[21] enables examination of Fouéré's corporeal intervention in the cultural production of myths of femininity.

My analysis of *Sodome, My Love*, and of the unnamed woman's writing body, is developed in tandem with discussion of Jean-Luc Nancy's notion of exscription in *Corpus* which addresses an outer edge beyond language which exceeds inscription. Nancy's project is not a feminist one; indeed, in *Corpus* Nancy evokes the womb–tomb matrix that I discuss in Chapter 4 with reference to sacrifice and dying bodies, and which I argue *Sodome, My Love* resists: 'skulls with staring eye-holes, castrating vaginas, not openings, but evacuations, enucleations, collapses'.[22] However, drawing on Nancy facilitates discussion of the possibilities for, and difficulties of, documenting the body. Like the myths of femininity which are invoked only to be critiqued, feminist theory can draw on Nancy in order to explore alternative critical frameworks which articulate that which has been excluded: women and their bodies. Nancy's exploration of the anxious relationship between body and discourse enables examination of that which is beyond inscription: the excluded creative female body as the other edge of signification. In *riverrun* the revolutionary body of the river generates a fearless exploration of the space between body and representation to undo the fixity of myth and present the exscribed body.

Nancy develops his examination of the exscribed body through his conception of a corpus or body of work; I turn to analysis of *riverrun* in order to explore how between-bodies and spaces extend towards each other to form a corpus. Much of Fouéré's work explores the terrain between two

---

[18] McMullan, 'Reclaiming Performance', p. 32.   [19] McMullan, 'Reclaiming Performance', p. 30.
[20] Foster, *Choreographing History*, p. 15.   [21] Foster, *Choreographing History*, p. 19.
[22] Jean-Luc Nancy, *Corpus*, trans. by Richard A. Rand (New York: Fordham University Press, 2008), p. 75.

states, identities or worlds, and she puts this down to her childhood experience of growing up in a bilingual household: 'I certainly experienced as a child, being in between two languages, and that was the true place, not the English or the French – the in between.'[23] This is reflected in her work which refuses easy categorization and resists text-based performance. In an interview, Fouéré reflects that 'what fascinated me about theatre was what was underneath the text; the whole things about presence and performance and the whole non-verbal world'.[24]

This non-verbal world is a threshold between music, voice and body as evidenced in Fouéré's work with Operating Theatre (1980–2006), as well as *riverrun* (2013).[25] Operating Theatre was a 'music-theatre company' and, as such, music was integral to the performances; this is illustrated by *Angel/Babel* (1999) in which Fouéré was wired up with several sensors on parts of her body so that her movements triggered or transformed sound from different sources.[26] In *riverrun*, Fouéré is 'composer, musician and conductor'[27] of her version of the final section of James Joyce's *Finnegan's Wake* in which she embodies the voice of Anna Livia Plurabelle, the river Liffey or Life. Alma Kelliher's sound design is mixed live to seamlessly merge with Fouéré's own articulate and inarticulate soundscape to create a language that extends between, and beyond, Joyce's text. *Sodome, My Love* offers a more traditionally recognizable narrative and verbal world than *riverrun*, yet Denis Clohessy's sound design also utilizes an affective soundscape of city noise and atmospheric electronic reverberations, while Fouéré's performance delights in the sensuous nature of language through bodily movement. Rather than thinking about the non-verbal as what is 'underneath the text', implying a hierarchy, we can look to the expressive potential of the actor's body in *Sodome, My Love* and *riverrun* in order to access what performance conveys and which language cannot articulate: the excluded creative female body as the other edge of signification. This enables exploration of the possibilities for female

---

[23] Susan Conley, 'riverrun: Olwen Fouéré on the voice of the river', *Irish Theatre Magazine*, 7 July 2013.

[24] 'Olwen Fouéré in Conversation with Melissa Sihra', in *Theatre Talk: Voices of Irish Theatre Practitioners*. ed. Lilian Chambers, Ger Fitzgibbon, and Eamonn Jordan (Dublin: Carysfort Press, 2001), pp. 155–66 (p. 155).

[25] James Joyce, *riverrun*. Adapted, directed and performed: Olwen Fouéré. Co-Director: Kellie Hughes. Sound Design: Alma Kelliher. Lighting design: Stephen Dodd. Costume: Monica Frawley (TheEmergencyRoom and Galway Arts Festival: Druid Theatre, Galway, opened 18 July 2013).

[26] Olwen Fouéré, 'Operating Theatre and *Angel/Babel*', p. 117.

[27] Kellie Hughes, 'In the *Wake* of Olwen Fouéré's *riverrun*', in *The Palgrave Handbook of Contemporary Irish Theatre and Performance*, ed. Eamonn Jordan and Eric Weitz (Basingstoke: Palgrave Macmillan, 2018), pp. 415–19 (p. 418).

220 Women and Embodied Mythmaking in Irish Theatre

authorship which question the dominance of a text-focused performance tradition. Furthermore, shifting the emphasis from the body as bearer to maker of meaning rewrites the corporeal realm which woman has traditionally been aligned with; resisting the inscription of silence and passivity on woman and the body.

Sodome, My Love and the Inscription of Myths of Death and Femininity

Chapter 4 looks at the ambivalent status of the virgin–whore dichotomy, and how cultural myths of death and femininity function as a means of effacing the threat of death and desiring female bodies by removing female autonomy of expression. *Sodome, My Love* intervenes in this body of cultural myths: throughout the play, Fouéré's postures and movements veer between seduction and petrification to create an uncertainty and instability which is heightened by the central motif of the salt, which both strips life away and preserves it. Sodome is a city characterized by profligate passions and bodies, and the surviving woman is the threatening remains of that excess; as she warns us in the opening section of the play: 'I am here, / Amongst you. I am the last daughter of Sodome.'[28]

The contagion which ravages the city is introduced by a male ambassador from Gomorrhe but culpability is shifted to the women of Sodome: the woman reveals that the armies of Gomorrhe wanted to destroy 'Us, the women . . . Our smiles of seduction.'[29] Thus, the women of Sodome, and the last surviving daughter of Sodome, epitomize the fearful union of death and femininity. The ambivalent representation of the surviving woman is compounded by her decision to wreak a 'voluptuous revenge'[30] on those who inflicted her punishment. She will employ an arsenal of contagion and sexuality, as made clear when she places an opened lipstick on the bench and states: 'That is the weapon I will use.'[31] However, woman's sexuality as weapon, wreaking revenge and asserting agency, reads ambiguously within a postfeminist and neoliberal context; an issue to which I return (in section 'The Exscribed Body, "Outside the Text"') through discussion of the ending of the play.

In the biblical story, Genesis 19, the city of Sodome's enjoyment of sinful pleasures results in disaster so angels help Lot and his family to flee. They are warned not to look back but Lot's wife does so, and she is turned into

---

[28] Gaudé, *Sodome, ma Douce*, p. 2. [29] Gaudé, *Sodome, ma Douce*, p. 12.
[30] Gaudé, *Sodome, ma Douce*, p. 20. [31] Gaudé, *Sodome, ma Douce*, p. 20.

Olwen Fouéré's Corpus

a pillar of salt, thus it is possible to read this as punishment for her desiring backwards glance at the iniquitous city. The myth of Lot's wife silences the desiring female body and she is stabilized as mythic icon. In *Sodome, My Love* she is reawakened; Lot's wife tells her story through the revival of the surviving woman of Sodome's body. The exploration of the threshold between death and life, which in turn explores the body in the process of representation, is familiar terrain for Fouéré who, in 2007, played Woman in the Irish premiere of Marina Carr's *Woman and Scarecrow*; a performance in which (as I argue in Chapter 4), the sculptural qualities of the staging highlighted Woman's reshaping of her dying body to refuse the fixed moment of idealization. The limits inflicted on the surviving daughter of Sodome's corporeal being and expression are felt throughout the opening sections of the play when we see her tense body slowly, and almost imperceptibly at first, return to life. Fouéré has described the importance of 'finding your stillness so that movement can come out of stillness'.[32] In *Sodome, My Love* this stillness intensifies the audience's awareness of every movement she makes and thereby heightens the expressive and interrogatory potential of the body: 'The still *acts* because it interrogates the possibility of one's agency within controlling regimes of capital, subjectivity, labor and mobility.'[33]

Like the Inghinidhe na hÉireann tableaux vivants performed in 1901 (Chapter 1), *Sodome, My Love* highlights the constraints placed on the articulation of an embodied female subjectivity, and the tension between the reality of women's lives and limiting myths of femininity. There is the potential for the woman of Sodome, as an echo Lot's wife, to revive and reinscribe her story, but the limits placed on corporeal expression reveal how agency, autonomy and choice are reframed within postfeminist and neoliberal discourse. The 'still acts' that structure *Sodome, My Love* contrast with the fluidity of *riverrun*'s form, yet in both performances Fouéré draws on stillness as means of signalling her control of her body, non-verbal registers and of her authorship of the work.

'The Law of Touching Is Separation'

Nancy's philosophy of the body in *Corpus* potentially resonates with a feminist project of reclaiming the female body; a body which inhabits

---

[32] 'Olwen Fouéré in Conversation with Melissa Sihra', p. 156.
[33] André Lepecki, *Exhausting Dance: Performance and the Politics of Movement* (Oxford and New York: Routledge, 2006), p. 15.

222   Women and Embodied Mythmaking in Irish Theatre

the space outside of the symbolic and is therefore denied representation: 'We lose our footing at "the body". Here, non-sense doesn't mean something absurd, or upside-down, or somehow contorted. ... It means, instead: no sense, or a *sense* whose approach through any figure of "sense" is absolutely ruled out. Sense making sense where sense meets its limit.'[34] Thus, for Nancy, 'the fragmentation of writing ... responds to the ongoing protest of bodies in – against – language.'[35]

The body which Nancy offers is defined by uncertainty; a crucial point for a feminist reading of Potential Bodies that offer a non-essentialist *écriture féminine*. In the opening sentence of *Corpus*, Nancy invokes the Eucharistic phrase *Hoc est enim corpus meum* ('This is my body') to invoke the performative of Christian ritual which brings the body and God into presence. However, crucially for Nancy, this presence is also marked by the absence that is felt: 'The presentified "this" of the Absentee par excellence: incessantly, we shall have called, convoked, consecrated, policed, captured, wanted, absolutely wanted it.'[36] Just as the body invokes presence and absence, touch is, for Nancy, defined by anxiety, namely between contact and separation: 'From one singular to another, there is contiguity but not continuity. There is proximity, but only to the extent that extreme closeness emphasises the distancing it opens up. All being is in touch with all being, but the law of touching is separation.'[37]

The repetition of the surviving woman's reawakening, as she relives her story and her salty incarceration in the final sections of the play, underlines the anxiety of fully touching on another's embodied experiences. As her narrative comes full circle, she is petrified before our eyes, 'I had become a statue',[38] and she adopts the same posture which closed the opening section of the play: seated with one arm outstretched to catch the rain, while the projected face appears once more and opens its mouth to taste the raindrops. The reassertion of the myth through its cyclical retelling, and its inhibition of Lot's wife's corporeal expression, ensures that the audience are acutely aware of the ways in which myths are repeatedly inscribed on, and lived through, the body. The tall screens that surround the performance space create a proliferation of images of, and different perspectives on, the woman in the process of representation: the close-ups of Fouéré highlight the re-inscription of myth, as well as the potential for its disruption, and thus the anxiety of searching for an authentic body. The surviving

[34] Nancy, *Corpus*, p. 13.   [35] Nancy, *Corpus*, p. 21.   [36] Nancy, *Corpus*, p. 3.
[37] Jean-Luc Nancy, *Being Singular Plural* (Stanford: Stanford University Press, 2000), p. 5.
[38] Gaudé, *Sodome, ma Douce*, p. 8.

daughter resists the imposition of silence and she reminds us that while her killers grew old and died, she lived on: 'I was nothing more than a salty residue of life / But I endured.'[39] Her enduring presence is marked not just by her verbal retelling of her experiences but by the recreation of her embodied experience. She may have been merely a residue, but her traces cannot be erased and the repetition of her opening posture and gestures serves as a countermemory which reasserts her presence. However, though the figure's performative writing of her body and life strives to bring her presence into being, it simultaneously marks the felt absence: 'But we certainly feel some formidable anxiety: "here it is" is in fact not so sure, we have to seek assurance for it.'[40]

We seek this assurance through touch which 'challenges, allays all our doubts about appearances'.[41] Nancy utilizes the notion of tactility through writing, 'the page itself is a touching (of my hand while it writes, and your hands while they hold the book.) . . . you read me, and I write you'.[42] If we extend this tactile relationship to performance, we can address how the writing body touches the performance space and audience. Nancy's touch confers distance, thereby addressing the limits of our ability to share another's embodied experiences, and the impossibility of fully returning an authentic body to these female mythic icons: 'Writing touches upon bodies *along the absolute limit* separating the sense of the one skin from the skin and nerves of the other. Nothing *gets through*, which is why it touches.'[43] In the context of a discussion of the appropriation of women as mythic icons, understanding the anxiety of Nancy's sense of touch offers the possibility of exploring how female bodies resist silence through the reassertion of their materiality.

The Exscribed Body, 'Outside the Text'

In order to address the limits of touch and the withdrawal connoted, Nancy introduces his concept of exscription: 'We have to begin by getting through, and by means of, the *exscription* of our body: its being inscribed-outside, its being placed *outside the text* as the most *proper* movement of its text; the text *itself* being abandoned, left at its limit.'[44] Cutler's Potential Body can be thought of as exscribed: the cultural inscriptions on the body are acknowledged, but so too is that which is on the outer edge of language and the body. The Potential and exscribed body is turned outside, to reveal

---

[39] Gaudé, *Sodome, ma Douce*, p. 19.   [40] Nancy, *Corpus*, p. 5.   [41] Nancy, *Corpus*, p. 5.
[42] Nancy, *Corpus*, p. 51.   [43] Nancy, *Corpus*, p. 11.   [44] Nancy, *Corpus*, p. 11.

224   Women and Embodied Mythmaking in Irish Theatre

the body as 'being-exscribed'.[45] This broaches the gap between the narrative of *Sodome, My Love* and the bodily meanings generated by Fouéré's performance; her movements indicate how myth is not just inscribed on the body, but how bodies open out to undo myth. Attending to the bodily meanings generated in performance exposes myth's apparent fixity and authority, and enables us to touch on the exscribed edge of Lot's wife's body, beyond the limits and silence of mythic iconicity.

Prior to the woman's second reawakening at the end of the play, she describes how she hid herself in an attempt to survive the city's massacre. She is discovered by the last of the enemy and she begs him to kill her, but instead is condemned to her fate: to be buried alive in salt. It is through the very limits of Fouéré's corporeality that she expresses the surviving woman's and Lot's wife's experiences: she lies on her front on the bench with one arm trailing on the floor, however her splayed hand pushes against the ground, her tension pre-empting the pain of her incarceration in salt, subject to the exertion of this man's power: 'I can still remember his hand gripping my arm, / The vice of power in his hand. / I knew the agony that was to come.'[46] Stark white light drenches the stage as the woman describes how she could hear the mountains of salt being dragged into the city. She describes her screams as she feels the 'bite' of the salt as each shovelful is poured on her. However, she is soon exhausted, and her presence is silenced by the salt, 'no sound of a pulse in my veins'.[47] The section closes with the words, 'Nothing else. / Nothing',[48] and she once more adopts the seated, and still, position of the opening of the play. Her incarceration imposes silence and language collapses temporarily, yet her body presents her exscribed-being: 'And a twofold failure is given: a failure to speak about the body, a failure to keep silent about it. A double-bind.'[49] Her exscribed-being embodies resistance to the death imposed by female iconicity.

Fouéré's performance in *Sodome, My Love* realizes the potential of the anxiety of touch: of the instability and possibility of the space between touch/separation and presence/absence. The last daughter of Sodome's body resides in this between space: 'The created body is there, meaning *between* here and there.'[50] The tension and danger of navigating between spaces is made explicit by the ending of the play in which Fouéré walks out past the audience and through their exit to enter the 'real' world.

---

[45] Nancy, *Corpus*, p. 19.   [46] Gaudé, *Sodome, ma Douce*, p. 15.
[47] Gaudé, *Sodome, ma Douce*, p. 17.   [48] Gaudé, *Sodome, ma Douce*, p. 17.
[49] Nancy, *Corpus*, p. 57.   [50] Nancy, *Corpus*, p. 99.

The blurring of boundaries was heightened in a special performance of the play in Macedonia on 31 July 2010: it was staged on the ancient site of the Church of St Sophia. The open-air site meant that the voices of passers-by, playing children and the sounds of traffic merged with the play's soundscape.[51] The historical resonance of the site with its ruins and Byzantine architecture underlined the woman's situation as a survivor of Sodome, moving between the past and present. The play draws on contagion, both in the script and staging, which, as Fintan Walsh notes in his review of the Project production: 'juxtaposed against projections of swirling blood, makes us think not only of the curtailment of female sexuality, but more pointedly of illnesses such as HIV/AIDS and the rightist religious rhetoric that imagines it as a curse from God'.[52] The ending serves to express an uncontainable sexuality and an unruly female body: just as the surviving daughter of Sodome intends to spread the contagion in revenge for her fate, she warns that her corporeal presence will be embodied by all who come into contact with her: 'I will be carried by the breath, / By the hand, / By the eyes.'[53]

The play closes with her refusal to be silenced as mythic statue; however, there is an ambiguity to the ending of the play. Following this vengeful declaration, Fouéré puts on lipstick, sunglasses, trench-coat and high heels, and departs in the guise of a femme fatale. This highly sexualized figure draws on tropes of death and femininity, as well as illustrating the complex intertwinement of feminism and antifeminism within postfeminism. Fouéré delivers her final lines in front of a montage of images which flashes up on the screen behind her, including images circulating within popular culture of runway models and pop singers such as Beyoncé.[54] These images, like the knowing adoption of the figure of the femme fatale, acknowledge the entanglement of female desirability with feminist versions of agency which, as Rosalind Gill argues, defines a new femininity: 'Femininity here is powerful, playful and narcissistic – less desiring of a sexual partner than empowered by the knowledge of her own sexual attractiveness.'[55] However, evoking a postfeminist sensibility risks wielding

---

[51] *Sodome, My Love.* Director: Lynne Parker. Cast: Olwen Fouéré. Designer: John Comiskey. Costume: Monica Frawley. Music and sound: Denis Clohessy (Rough Magic in association with TheEmergencyRoom: Ohrid Festival, St Sophia, Macedonia, 31 July 2010). DVD recording held in the The Rough Magic Theatre Company Archive, TCD MS 11568, Manuscripts & Archives, The Library of Trinity College Dublin.
[52] Fintan Walsh, Review in *Irish Theatre Magazine*, 16 March 2010 www.irishtheatremagazine.ie/Re views/Current/Sodome–My-Love [Accessed 20 August 2013].
[53] Gaudé, *Sodome, ma Douce*, p. 22.   [54] The screens were not used in the Macedonia performance.
[55] Gill, 'Culture and Subjectivity', p. 438.

226   Women and Embodied Mythmaking in Irish Theatre

the avenging woman's weapons, her sexuality and contagion, against her in a move that pathologizes her desires.

Though the ending is problematic in its evocation of a postfeminist femininity, Fouéré's self-sculpting throughout the play serves to counter how 'neoliberalism requires individuals to narrate their life story as if it were the outcome of deliberative choices';[56] instead her performance attends to the visceral effects of myths of femininity and their inscriptions on the female body, as well as the risks of inhabiting, and the possibilities for questioning, these myths. It is the contagion of these corporeal traces that is unsettling: 'I am entering your cities and I will leave the unknown scent of Sodome in my wake. / First it will intrigue you, then it will disturb you.'[57] We, the audience, will bear the bodily traces and residues of performance, and facilitate the contagion's spread; a contagion which enables the re-emergence of a female corpus that has been repressed by myth and Proper theatre documentation: her embodied subjectivity, and her body of work.

Between-bodies and Potential Bodies are marked by process and occupy the space of the Residual; they are haunted by that which is unnameable: that is, the 'intimate self-texture'[58] of the body. Thus what is exscribed through the performance of *Sodome, My Love* is the embodied experience of a mythic icon, Lot's wife – a statue who comes to life to assert her presence and story, and in this process articulates the tensions of female embodied experience within patriarchal society, as both mythic object and embodied subject, as well as the anxiety of touching upon this experience. Furthermore, the postfeminist femme fatale of the ending highlights, as Cathy Leeney notes, 'the difficulty of finding strategies to image women's sexual desire alongside resistance to hegemonic gender iteration'.[59] In both *Sodome, My Love* and *riverrun*, the female body is not silent and inscribed but is the author of its own representation and documentation. However, where Fouéré's performance of the surviving woman of Sodome explores the tension generated by the 'still-act' to evoke the space between petrification and freedom from the imposition of myth; *riverrun* embraces movement, fluidity and transformation.

---

[56] Gill, 'Culture and Subjectivity', p. 436.   [57] Gaudé, *Sodome, ma Douce*, p. 19.
[58] Nancy, *Corpus*, p. 75.
[59] Cathy Leeney, 'Second Skin: Costume and Body: Power and Desire, in *Radical Contemporary Theatre Practices by Women in Ireland*, ed. Miriam Haughton and Mária Kurdi (Dublin: Carysfort Press, 2015), pp. 41–54 (p. 53).

Olwen Fouéré's Corpus 227

Re-embodying Anna Livia Plurabelle

In *Finnegan's Wake*, Anna Livia Plurabelle's transformative journey, as the River Liffey flows through Dublin to join the Irish Sea in Dublin Bay, is invigorated by the rhythms, and inventive play, of language. Joyce's text verges on the non-verbal realm; a space which *riverrun* further explores through performance to generate the potential for disturbance and transformation: of myth, the performer and the audience. Fouéré's adaptation *riverrun* reworks the final chapter, Book IV, of *Finnegan's Wake*, 'skipping chunks of text, inserting a couple of short passages from earlier in the book'.[60] The process of adaptation, as well as the collaborative way in which the work was developed and is performed, positions the icon as author of meaning as Fouéré gains control of the male-authored frame. The collaboration of a tight creative team was fundamental to the development of a performance where text, voice, movement, sound design and lighting, all respond organically to one another to evoke the fluid body of the river. Fouéré initially collaborated with sound designer/composer Alma Kelliher for six months, before Stephen Dodd joined the team as lighting designer and Kellie Hughes brought her expertise in physical theatre to the work as co-director.

Each performance sees Fouéré and Kelliher embarking on the journey anew as the sound design is mixed live.[61] *riverrun* is composed of six sections, connected by five transitions or 'knee-plays' – an idea that Fouéré drew from Robert Wilson's theatre.[62] An immersive experience of being in, and subsequently part of, the river is created through the interaction of sound, movement and lighting. We are submerged deeper in the river as we move through each 'knee-play', until the voice of Anna Livia Plurabelle emerges and we resurface in the final section. The transitionary space of the 'knee-play' counteracts the dizzying play of Joyce's text and the immersive nature of the performance, to provide a breathing space for Fouéré and to allow the audience to orient themselves as we navigate our way *through* the river.

The energy of the river pulses through Fouéré's body: from her vigorous sweeping and swaying gestures, to the almost imperceptible lulling rhythms which seem to rise up through her. Her weight is almost

---

[60] Olwen Fouéré, 'Following the flow of the "Wake" to its Source', *Irish Times*, 13 July 2013.

[61] My analysis of the production draws on my attendance of the performance at the Project Arts Centre, Dublin, on 3 October 2013, as well as my viewing of the recording made during the premiere run at the Druid Theatre, Galway Arts Festival, 18–27 July 2013.

[62] Hughes, 'In the *Wake* of Olwen Fouéré's *riverrun*', p. 418.

228   Women and Embodied Mythmaking in Irish Theatre

constantly shifting as her feet appear to respond to a rippling surface beneath. In contrast to this vigorous re-embodiment of Anna Livia Plurabelle, most Dubliners are more familiar with her as the statue which resided in the middle of O'Connell Street, the city's main thoroughfare, until 2001.[63] She was affectionately nicknamed 'The Floozie in the Jacuzzi' (a Floozie is a colloquial word for a sexually promiscuous woman) as she lay naked in her stone basin with water bubbling past. The process of casting the figure into sculpture functions, as Ailbhe Smyth argues, 'to erase the untidy realities of fleshy women'.[64] Fouéré describes the impulse behind her work as 'a very strong feeling, from a very young age, that there was a whole chunk of existence that was incommunicable with the reality we live in, and that it takes a revolutionary force to break through that'.[65] Fouéré's skilful use of her body, its physical and vocal capacities, enables a rewriting of Anna Livia Plurabelle's experiences which opens out to express her exscribed-being.

The opening words of the performance serve as a clarion call for the reclaiming of female embodied experience, as *riverrun* begins in a moment of transition which evokes dusk and dawn:

> Sandhyas! Sandhyas! Sandhyas!
> Calling all downs. Calling all downs to dayne. Array! Surrection.[66]

Fouéré's intonation of these opening words draws on meditative chanting: Sandhyas is a Sanskrit word for morning or evening prayers. The sounds-cape reverberates and swells to evoke a strange atmosphere suggestive of a watery world or celestial space. This sonic environment is simultaneously natural and unfamiliar: sound designer Alma Kelliher describes her palette of sounds as drawing on sources as diverse as womb sounds, water sounds and NASA sound recordings.[67] The lighting design by Stephen Dodd is equally atmospheric and in the opening moments of the performance the stage is bathed in an indigo hue that means we can only discern Fouéré's dim figure; we witness the attempts by this figure to assert herself and emerge from this eerie, cosmic vastness.

Key to the struggle for articulation of the writing body is the responsive interaction between sound, lighting and movement. Co-director Kellie

---

[63] It was relocated to the Croppies Memorial Park in 2011, following the erection of the spire on O'Connell Street. 'The Floozie in the Jacuzzi' was the only female statue amidst the historical male figures on O'Connell Street.

[64] Smyth, 'The Floozie in the Jacuzzi', p. 8.

[65] Conley, '*Riverrun*: Olwen Fouéré on the voice of the river'.   [66] Joyce, *Finnegan's Wake*, p. 593.

[67] Personal Interview with Alma Kelliher, 17 May 2017.

Hughes explains how they played with a sense of expansion and contraction throughout the performance: 'We expanded and contracted Olwen's vocal impulses into physical echoes.'[68] The opening lines of the performance capture the ebb and flow of diminishment and growth: as Fouéré voices the first lines, the lighting changes from the indigo hue which envelops the whole space to contract to a white spot on Fouéré. Against the darkness of the surrounding stage space, and counter to the contracting movement, this heralds Anna Livia's 'Array Surrection', or resurrection – the focus of the final section of the performance. Kelliher strove to capture the pressure of the water as we dive down and this heightens the sense of release when Anna Livia surfaces in the final section.[69] The soundscape is echoed by Fouéré who, in the moments of the performance where we are at the deepest depths of the river, holds her head still between the palms of her hands while she delivers her lines in a rapid whisper to suggest the intense pressure. The opposing movements of expansion and contraction evoke the experiences of the female body: of birth and of orgasm.

In the final section Anna Livia's expression of her desiring body is made explicit through her increasing sexual arousal as signalled by a sharp intake of breath and the escalation of the rhythm of Fouéré's delivery of the text until: 'And she is coming. Swimming in my hindmoist. ... One two moremens more.'[70] As she comes to orgasm, she shouts 'Avelaval', holding the final syllable before letting it trail off and then pausing to catch her breath. Throughout this final section, the audience is focused on Fouéré as she is front lit from the waist up, against a dark stage. However, the space once more starts to contract as the spot shrinks to illuminate only Fouéré's shoulders and head, and we are reminded of Anna Livia's struggle to assert her desiring body: 'I am passing out. O bitter ending! I'll slip away before they're up. They'll never see. Nor know. Nor miss me.'[71] Through the process of remaining in flux, the female body strives to make its presence felt and to resist definition by essentialized myths of femininity. The circularity that structures both Joyce's text and *riverrun* ensures that the anxiety that underpins this process, of both disappearing and defiantly remaining, is marked.

Smyth describes the monumental statue of O'Connell Street's '"Riverrun" Woman through whom meanings flow':[72] '[e]ssentially vacuous, receptacle without individual identity, mute spectacle, silent cipher,

---

[68] Hughes, 'In the *Wake* of Olwen Fouéré's *riverrun*', p. 417.
[69] Personal Interview with Alma Kelliher, 17 May 2017. [70] Joyce, *Finnegan's Wake*, p. 628.
[71] Joyce, *Finnegan's Wake*, p. 627. [72] Smyth, 'The Floozie in the Jacuzzi', p. 11.

Women and Embodied Mythmaking in Irish Theatre

the symbolic female figure is incapable of *conferring* meaning.'[73] Fouéré's performance disrupts the silencing of women's bodies through the figure of iconic Woman by re-embodying the voice of Anna Livia Plurabelle. Her transformative journey generates possibility, as well as registering the anxiety surrounding the loss of self and denial of embodied expression. Fouéré resists the definitive expression of mythic Woman as her performance revels in the capacity of female corporeality to generate meaning. Smyth's article draws on *écriture féminine* to open up the myth of Anna Livia Plurabelle, striving to reclaim her plurability: 'Uncertain, risky, feeling inappropriate because, place of passage, of becoming, beyond (mis)appropriation. Evolving, open, spacious, unfixed.'[74] Fouéré's embodiment of Anna Livia similarly embraces process as the form and content of *riverrun* are invigorated by a desire to remain 'unstable, unfixed, on the cusp of something rather than at its destination'.[75] Furthermore, *riverrun* is invigorated and shaped by female embodied experiences. This risks reinscribing sexual difference biologically, but both *Sodome, My Love* and *riverrun* reveal the female body as a Potential Body which is inscribed, yet also exceeds inscription. The daughter of Sodome's resistance to her petrification as mythic woman embodies her refusal to be stilled, but *riverrun* explores the space of process in a more sustained manner as it is embedded in the structure of the performance.

Journey and Process

The organic and collaborative process of *riverrun*'s development flows from the rehearsal space into the live show as Fouéré's performance and the live sound design mutually respond to one another and therefore continue to shift through the performance run. The responsive and flexible nature of the performance also embraces interaction with the venue: both the space and the audience. Hughes describes it as a 'site-responsive' work which is continually changing as the residues of previous performances and venues are accrued and carried forward. This ensures that *riverrun* is in constant evolution, a daunting prospect for Fouéré as a performer for whom the danger of the work lies in the risk of 'learning to swim again, diving off a cliff'.[76]

---

[73] Smyth, 'The Floozie in the Jacuzzi', p. 9.   [74] Smyth, 'The Floozie in the Jacuzzi', p. 23.
[75] Hughes, 'In the *Wake* of Olwen Fouéré's *riverrun*', p. 417.
[76] Hughes, 'In the *Wake* of Olwen Fouéré's *riverrun*', p. 415.

Olwen Fouéré's Corpus

The audience also have to be open to diving into the river and surrendering to the experience of being swept along. The set is deliberately sparse to invite the audience to 'creatively engage and author their own journey down the river'.[77] The set consists solely of a microphone stand which curves to Fouéré's right and some scattered natural sea salt. The sea salt is deposited in waves created by the microphone lead; echoing both the sinuous shape of the lead as it winds its way across the stage, as well as Fouéré's movements. The stand is inspired by the fluid curves of the river; a bespoke design by sound engineer Benny Lynch, which avoids placing a physical, vertical obstacle between Fouéré's body and the audience, potentially disrupting their connection. In the moments prior to the beginning of the performance, Fouéré stands by the audience seating, acknowledging audience members with a quiet smile as they enter. This invitation to engage with the world of *riverrun* is crucial: the performance begins as Fouéré moves into the performance space, takes off her shoes and steps over the microphone lead. It is clear that she has stepped into the river and the audience are on board with her.

Fouéré describes the experience of *riverrun* in an *Irish Times* article: 'It's an amazing journey to embark on, through an ever-changing universe, unbound by so-called reality, narrative or character, all those fixed ideas that can tyrannise the boundaries of our imagination.'[78] Part of this process of unloosing boundaries in *riverrun* is the presentation of the gendered body. Joyce's Anna Livia is presented as an essential femininity: life-giving, mysterious, uncontainable, disembodied. Fouéré's costume deliberately positions Anna Livia more ambiguously: she wears a dark suit with a metallic pale-gold V-neck sleeveless top underneath, and her long silver-white hair is tied back. She is costumed with attributes that can be simultaneously read as masculine and feminine, or in effect neither. In an interview, Fouéré recalls her performance as Antonin Artaud in the 2005 installation, *Here Lies . . .*, which was based on his experiences in Ireland in 1937; Fouéré describes how she met the eyes of a boy in the audience: 'he looked back at me like, what are you? He was fascinated, he didn't know if I was an animal, a man, a woman, what was I? And that made the whole thing worthwhile.'[79]

---

[77] Hughes, 'In the *Wake* of Olwen Fouéré's *riverrun*', p. 418.

[78] Fouéré, 'Following the flow of the "Wake" to its source'.

[79] *Olwen Fouéré: The Works*, RTE One, aired 28 February 2014, www.youtube.com/watch?v=nFy62 CrTL14 [Accessed 17 May 2017]. The installation *Here Lies . . .* was first performed at the Galway Arts Festival in 2005.

232 Women and Embodied Mythmaking in Irish Theatre

She clearly delights in these unsettling affects which her muscular and lithe physique and deep voice contribute to. The first five sections of *riverrun* draws on an array of identities and voices, as Fouéré describes: 'Finn MacCool and Foyn MacHooligan, cartoon-like heroes, music-hall gags, a giant body and its cosmic counterpart, the constellation of Orion, Ursa Major, the Egyptian book of the dead, various characters – celestial, human, animal, vegetal and mineral – hover.'[80] The cumulative effect of their ebb and flow paves the way for the radical unfixing of myth's gendered essentialism in the final section. Anna Livia's body is released from ideals of Irish femininity, of 'Mater-reality',[81] which are bound up within an impossible contradiction of maternity and de-sexualization to explore a more fluid, non-binary conception of the gendered body.

There is a shift in the final section in which we hear Anna Livia's voice emerge: both the sound design which fades to silence and the accessibility of Anna Livia's lines, 'It is the softest morning that ever I can ever remember me',[82] create an intimacy with the audience. Furthermore, Fouéré removes her jacket in the last 'knee-play' so there is a sense of Anna Livia being laid bare and of a more natural presentation. On the one hand, this apparent simplicity focuses our attention on *her* authorship of her journey, as well as her refusal to reinforce existing myths of an essential fluid femininity which is threatening and unknowable. Yet, conversely, the silence of the final section has a very strange effect in that it surrounds Fouéré's voice and renders it uncanny: it serves as an alienation effect which forces us to question what indeed is 'natural'.

The 'Sound-Dance' of Between-Bodies

Fouéré has described *Finnegan's Wake* as 'a seam of dark matter, somewhere between energy and form, music and language'.[83] The between space of *riverrun* is reflected in Fouéré's performance which playfully and skilfully orchestrates the text, her voice and movement, Kelliher's sound design, and the lighting, to access those unarticulated and dark expressions which refuse to be pinned down. Her body generates meaning as: 'The river leads the way, a sound-dance of revolutionary energy which is impossible to surf like an expert.'[84] Joyce's notion of a 'sound-dance' is suggestive of a writing body and articulates the terrain which Anna Livia

---

[80] Fouéré, 'Following the flow of the "Wake" to its source'.
[81] Smyth, 'The Floozie in the Jacuzzi', p. 8.   [82] *Finnegan's Wake*, p. 621.
[83] Fouéré, 'Following the flow of the "Wake" to its source'.
[84] Fouéré, 'Following the flow of the "Wake" to its source'.

Olwen Fouéré's Corpus

Plurabelle traverses, between body and language. Nancy's evocation of the uncertainty and (im)possibility of the space between touch/separation and presence/absence evokes Anna Livia's state of 'disembodied embodiment to embodied disembodiment.'[85] We can link the between space of the 'sound-dance', and Anna Livia's between-body, to Nancy's exploration of the creative space between which generates a corpus, or body, of work. Nancy looks to between-bodies and between spaces as anxious realms of touch and separation, and applies this to the body of language:

> Exscription is produced in the loosening of unsignifying spacing: it detaches words from their senses, always again and again, abandoning them to their extension. A word, so long as it's not absorbed without remainder into a sense, *remains* essentially extended between other words, stretching to touch them, though not merging with them: that's language as *body*.[86]

The creation of a body of language that extends 'between other words' suggests the fragmentary assemblage that defines Nancy's understanding of a corpus; it also evokes the haunting 'remains' of female embodied experience, or indeed, as Fouéré suggests, 'the voice of Lucia, Joyce's incarcerated daughter, with her silenced rage, her dancer's brilliance and the multilingual fire of her wit'.[87]

In *riverrun*, the animation of the joints of the 'knee-play' fleshes out the bones of the performance. Hughes describes the 'knee-plays' as transitions where 'the breath ... brings us deeper into the subconscious of the giant body of *Finnegan's Wake*'.[88] The movement of the breath expands and contracts the body of the work. During the 'knee-plays' Fouéré blows on the microphone in a rhythmic manner which suggests heartbeats and enables us to feel the rhythms of the body, as well as creating the rhythms of the performance. The final 'knee-play' which precedes Anna Livia's rebirth deploys these corporeal rhythms much more vigorously as Fouéré removes her jacket and starts to swing it in circles, timing the movement with the rhythm of her breathing onto the microphone. In the 'knee-plays' the lighting shifts back to the atmospheric indigo hue of the opening of the performance and Fouéré's delivery of her lines draws on whispers, echoes and even whistling, so that we are affectively enveloped between body and language. The soundscape comes to the fore in the 'knee-plays' – both Fouéré's use of the microphone and Kelliher's sound design – so that it is primarily a non-verbal world which extends between the body of language

---

[85] Smyth, 'The Floozie in the Jacuzzi', p. 7.   [86] Nancy, *Corpus*, p. 71.
[87] Fouéré, 'Following the flow of the "Wake" to its source'.
[88] Hughes, 'In the *Wake* of Olwen Fouéré's *riverrun*', p. 418.

234 Women and Embodied Mythmaking in Irish Theatre

and of Joyce's text. *riverrun*'s fluid, non-binary between-bodies, and the between spaces – of a river, a womb, an interplanetary cosmos – extend towards one another to produce a body of work which heralds the resurfacing of Anna Livia Plurabelle's corporeal expression. Nancy's corpus is invigorated by the traces of bodily meanings which extend between one another. Nancy's writing catalogues 'A corpus of tact: skimming, grazing, squeezing, thrusting, pressing, smoothing, scraping, rubbing, caressing . . . ',[89] and the list continues. The creative space between-bodies generates a body, just as the tactility of the page, of the hands that wrote on it and the hands that hold it, creates the tactile body of work: 'you read me, and I write you.'[90]

This corpus of tact is relational in its circulation of intensities that pass between bodies; illustrating Gregg and Seigworth's description of how affect is 'born in in-between-ness and resides as accumulative beside-ness'.[91] The joints of the 'knee-play' sections assemble a corpus of tact which touches on the audience so that the transformation of the river into the body of the sea is echoed by the audience transformation into an experiential body. Resonating with the contagion generated by *Sodome, My Love*, the immersive experience of *riverrun* depends upon the circulation of affects generated by the exscribed edge of female embodied experience.

Corpus: A Genealogy of Women in Irish Theatre

Between the bodies of Fouéré's performances, a body of work is created which serves as a document of corporeal resistance to myths of femininity. The mythic women of Fouéré's performances touch on and write one another to suggest a 'corpus of tact' which creates resonances and residues that attend to the visceral experience of female embodiment in tension with limiting myths of femininity. Fouéré's description of her performance as *Kathleen ni Houlihan* speaks to the other mythic women which she has played, from Salomé, through Carr's work, to *Sodome, My Love* and *riverrun*, who counter the feminine ideal with their desiring bodies: Fouéré states that it is: '[f]ascinating to subvert the long-suffering image we have inherited of her [Kathleen ni Houlihan]. To unleash the seductive, manipulative queen with predatory desires running through the country of

---

[89] Nancy, *Corpus*, p. 93.   [90] Nancy, *Corpus*, p. 51.
[91] Gregory J. Seigworth and Melissa Gregg, 'Introduction: An Inventory of Shimmers', in *The Affect Theory Reader* (Durham and London: Duke University Press, 2010), pp. 1–25 (p. 2).

Olwen Fouéré's mythic women become powerful forces as she explores their exscribed-being, their writing body, and intervenes in the performative reassertion of limiting myths of femininity which silence a desiring and creative female corporeality. Fouéré's corpus draws attention to the transformative process of writing the body and of self-sculpting, thereby exploring the inscription of meaning on the body, as well as the potential for resistance.

Fouéré's corpus spreads further – between the other performances explored in this book – to contribute to a corpus of mythmaking generated by women in Irish theatre. This genealogy reaches across the decades to create a giant corpus of work which troubles the canon of a male-dominated Irish literary theatre. Counter to the stifling of women's expression in Ireland, both publicly and theatrically, this corpus enables this silence to eloquently express their absent presence. 'Absent flesh *does* ghost bones'[93] and this corpus embodies the rejection of women in Irish theatre, of their exclusion wrought by a linear history of performance, as we trace their histories 'within chains of reinterpretation that bring them into complex filiations with one another'.[94] The fragments and residues of the corpus that this book offers attest to the potential of the exscribed body to open out these mythic icons and, in the process, to undo the inheritance of an idealized Irish femininity: 'the place of residue is arguably *flesh* in a network of body-to-body transmission of affect and enactment – evidence across generations, of impact'.[95]

The resistance to linearity and fixity which shapes this corpus of myth-making is embodied by *riverrun*. The salt in *Sodome, My Love* corroborates women's experiences within Irish culture as it violently silences the figure who echoes Lot's wife, yet preserves the traces of her embodied experiences, and thus her struggle for expression. However, the salty residues of *riverrun* mark a more radical refusal to conform to traditional, and patriarchal, structures, whether narrative and theatrical forms, or society's ideological configurations and material edifices. Anna Livia Plurabelle's repudiation of containment is expressed by the circularity of Joyce's text which famously ends with the first part of the sentence which is completed in the opening line of the novel. The final moments of *riverrun* also return us to the beginning: as the soundscape swells, the reverberations incorporate an echo

---

[92] Olwen Fouéré, 'Afterword: The Act and The Word', in Melissa Sihra, *Women in Irish Drama*, pp. 219–20 (p. 220).
[93] Schneider, *Performing Remains*, p. 102.   [94] Stone, 'On the Genealogy of Women', p. 93.
[95] Schneider, *Performing Remains*, p. 100.

of Fouéré's opening chant. However, the concluding tableau heightens the uncertainty of both ending and beginning, and of touching on the embodied experiences of Anna Livia: after delivering the final suspended line, Fouéré looks into the distance, transfixed, and an ecstatic smile spreads across her face to suggest Anna Livia's entry into the sea and her transformation. Her frozen expression is sculpted by the glacial white spotlight: it is both a death mask and the generation of a new beginning. The ambiguity of this uncontainable ending refuses the imposition of petrifying myths of Woman, of 'the beauty of Woman ... conceived as a mask for decay, and the sexual relation with her as a form of death rather than conception'.[96]

Echoing the shape of *Finnegan's Wake* to reveal how a genealogy of women's mythmaking defers in multiple directions, this disruptive 'still-act' also returns us to the opening chapter of this book and the 'still remains' of the revolutionary bodies of the Inghinidhe na hÉireann's tableaux vivants. Echoing through the bones of this corpus of women's mythmaking in Irish theatre is the exscribed edge of women's corporealities: their unhomeliness; their revolutions; their metamorphic transformations; their deaths and resurrections; and their haunting remains, all of which refuse to be contained within, and thus rewrite, myth.

[96] Bronfen, *Over Her Dead Body*, p. 67.

Bibliography

Plays

Burke-Kennedy, Mary Elizabeth, *Women in Arms*, in *Seen and Heard: Six New Plays by Irish Women*, ed. Cathy Leeney (Dublin: Carysfort Press, 2001).

Women in Arms, unpublished script for 2002 production, ITA/258/01/11 (Storytellers Theatre Company Archive, Dublin City Library and Archive).

Carr, Marina, *Ariel* (Oldcastle: The Gallery Press, 2002).

On Raftery's Hill (London: Faber & Faber, 2000).

Plays 1: Low in the Dark; The Mai; Portia Coughlan; By the Bog of Cats ... (London: Faber & Faber, 1999).

Plays 3: Sixteen Possible Glimpses; Phaedra Backwards; The Map of Argentina; Hecuba; Indigo (London: Faber & Faber, 2015).

Portia Coughlan, in *The Dazzling Dark*, ed. Frank McGuinness (London: Faber & Faber, 1996).

The Cordelia Dream (Oldcastle: The Gallery Press, 2008).

Woman and Scarecrow (Oldcastle: The Gallery Press, 2006).

Gaudé, Laurent, *Sodome, ma Douce*, trans. Olwen Fouéré, unpublished script (May 2010).

Gonne, Maud, *Dawn*, in *Lost Plays of the Irish Renaissance*, ed. Robert Hogan and James Kilroy (California: Proscenium Press, 1970).

Gore-Booth, Eva, *Poems of Eva Gore-Booth: Complete Edition* (London: Longmans, Green & Co., 1929).

The Buried Life of Deirdre (London: Longmans, Green & Co., 1930).

The Death of Fionavar (London: E. MacDonald, 1916).

Gregory, Lady Augusta, *Grania*, in *Selected Plays*, ed. Mary Fitzgerald (Gerrard's Cross: Colin Smythe, 1983).

Meehan, Paula, *Mrs Sweeney*, in *Rough Magic: First Plays*, ed. Siobhan Bourke (Dublin: New Island, 1999).

Milligan, Alice, *The Last Feast of the Fianna*, in *Maeve: A Psychological Drama in Two Acts by Edward Martyn, The Last Feast of the Fianna: A Dramatic Legend by Alice Milligan* (Chicago: De Paul University Press, 1967).

O'Brien, Edna, *Triptych and Iphigenia* (New York: Grove Press, 2003).

O'Neill, Mary Devenport, *Bluebeard*, in *Prometheus and Other Poems* (London: Jonathan Cape, 1929).

238   *Bibliography*

Bluebeard, MS. 21,440, Abbey Theatre Papers, National Library of Ireland, July 1933.

Yeats, W.B., *Cathleen ni Houlihan*, in *Selected Plays*, ed. Richard Allen Cave (London: Penguin, 1997).

Secondary Sources

Aeschylus, *The Oresteia*, trans. Alan Shapiro and Peter Burian (Oxford: Oxford University Press, 2003).

Ap Hywel, Elin, 'Elise and the Great Queens of Ireland: "Femininity" as Constructed by Sinn Fein and the Abbey Theatre, 1901–1907', in *Gender in Irish Writing*, ed. David Cairns and Toni O'Brien Johnson (Milton Keynes: Open University Press, 1991), pp. 23–39.

Arrington, Lauren, *Revolutionary Lives: Constance and Casimir Markievicz* (Princeton and Oxford: Princeton University Press, 2016).

Bakhtin, Mikhail, *Rabelais and His World* (Cambridge: MIT Press, 1968).

Barnes, Ben, *Plays and Controversies: Abbey Theatre Diaries 2000–2005* (Dublin: Carysfort Press, 2008).

Barthes, Roland, *Mythologies*, revised edn (Paris: Editions du Seuil, 1957; repr. London: Vintage, 2009).

Becket, Fiona, 'A Theatrical Matrilineage? Problems of the Familial in the Drama of Teresa Deevy and Marina Carr', in *Ireland in Proximity: History, Gender, Space*, ed. Scott Brewster, Virginia Crossman, Fiona Becket and David Alderson (London: Routledge, 1999), pp. 80–93.

Bhabha, Homi K., *The Location of Culture* (London: Routledge, 1994).

Blumenberg, Hans, *Work on Myth*, trans. Robert M. Wallace (Cambridge: MIT Press, 1985).

Boland, Eavan, *Object Lessons: The Life of the Woman and the Poet in our Time* (Manchester: Carcanet, 1995).

Bourke, Angela, 'Lamenting the Dead', in *The Field Day Anthology of Irish Writing Volume IV: Women's Writing and Traditions*, ed. Angela Bourke, Siobhán Kilfeather, Maria Luddy, Margaret Mac Curtain, Gerardine Meaney, Máirín Ní Dhonnchadha, Mary O'Dowd, and Clair Wills (Cork: Cork University Press, 2002), pp. 1365–7.

Breathnach, Proinnsias, 'Occupational Change and Social Polarisation in Ireland: Further Evidence', *Irish Journal of Sociology*, 16:1 (2007), 22–42.

Brecht, Bertolt, *Brecht on Theatre: The Development of an Aesthetic*, ed. and trans. John Willett (London: Methuen, 1978).

Bronfen, Elisabeth, *Over Her Dead Body: Death, Femininity and the Aesthetic* (Manchester: Manchester University Press, 1992).

Bronfen, Elisabeth and Sarah Webster Goodwin (eds), *Death and Representation* (Baltimore and London: The John Hopkins University Press, 1993).

Bibliography

Butler, Judith, *Bodies That Matter: On the Discursive Limits of Sex* (London: Routledge, 1993).

Gender Trouble: Feminism and the Subversion of Identity (Abingdon: Routledge, 1990; repr. 2007).

Case, Sue-Ellen, *Feminism and Theatre* (London: Macmillan, 1988).

'The Screens of Time: Feminist Memories and Hopes', in *Feminist Futures? Theatre, Performance, Theory*, ed. Elaine Aston and Geraldine Harris (Basingstoke: Palgrave Macmillan, 2006), pp. 105–17.

Cave, Richard Allen, *Collaborations: Ninette de Valois and William Butler Yeats* (Alton: Dance Books, 2011).

'The Dangers and Difficulties of Dramatising the Lives of Deirdre and Grania', in *Perspectives of Irish Drama and Theatre*, ed. Jacqueline Genet and Richard Allen Cave (Gerrard's Cross: Colin Smythe, 1991), pp. 1–16.

Chapman, Mary, '"Living Pictures": Women and *Tableaux Vivants* in Nineteenth-Century American Fiction and Culture', *Wide Angle* 18:3 (July 1996), 22–52.

Cixous, Hélène, 'Aller à la Mer', in *Twentieth Century Theatre: A Sourcebook*, ed. Richard Drain (London: Routledge, 1995), pp. 133–5.

'Laugh of the Medusa', *Signs*, 1:4 (Summer, 1976), 875–93.

Clark, Rosalind, *The Great Queens: Irish Goddesses from the Morrígan to Cathleen ni Houlihan* (Gerrard's Cross: Colin Smythe, 1991).

Clune, Anne, 'Mythologising Sweeney', *Irish University Review*, 26:1 (1996), 48–60.

Collins, Lucy, *Poetry by Women in Ireland: A Critical Anthology 1870–1970* (Liverpool: Liverpool University Press, 2012).

Condren, Mary, 'Notes on Eva Gore-Booth's *A Psychological and Poetic Approach to the Study of Christ in the Fourth Gospel*', in *The Field Day Anthology of Irish Writing Volume IV: Women's Writing and Traditions*, ed. Angela Bourke, Siobhán Kilfeather, Maria Luddy, Margaret Mac Curtain, Gerardine Meaney, Máirín Ní Dhonnchadha, Mary O'Dowd and Clair Wills (Cork: Cork University Press, 2002), pp. 659–63.

The Serpent and the Goddess: Women, Religion and Power in Celtic Ireland (New York: HarperCollins, 1989).

Connolly, Linda, *The Irish Women's Movement: From Revolution to Devolution* (Basingstoke: Palgrave Macmillan, 2002).

Costera Meijer, Irene and Baukje Prins, 'How Bodies Come to Matter: An Interview with Judith Butler', *Signs*, 23:2 (Winter 1998), 275–86.

Coupe, Laurence, *Myth* (London: Routledge, 1997).

Cutler, Anna 'Abstract Body Language: Documenting Women's Bodies in Theatre', *New Theatre Quarterly*, 14:2 (May 1998), 111–18.

De Beauvoir, Simone, *The Second Sex*, trans. H.M. Parshley (Paris: Gallimard, 1949; repr. London: Vintage, 1997).

De Valois, Ninette, *Come Dance with Me* (London: Hamish Hamilton, 1959).

Diamond, Elin, *Unmaking Mimesis: Essays on Feminism and Theatre* (London: Routledge, 1997).

240 *Bibliography*

Dolan, Jill, *The Feminist Spectator as Critic* (Ann Arbor: The University of Michigan Press, 1991; repr. 1998).

Donoghue, Emma, '"How Could I Fear and Hold Thee by the Hand?": The Poetry of Eva Gore-Booth', in *Sex, Nation and Dissent in Irish Writing*, ed. Eibhear Walshe (Cork: Cork University Press, 1997), pp. 16–42.

Doyle, Maria, 'Dead Center: Tragedy and the Reanimated Body in Marina Carr's *The Mai* and *Portia Coughlan*', *Modern Drama*, 49:1 (Spring 2006), 41–59.

Eagleton, Terry, *Sweet Violence: The Idea of the Tragic* (Oxford: Blackwell Publishing, 2003).

Euripides, *The Bacchae and Other Plays*, trans. John Davie (London: Penguin, 2005).

Ferriter, Diarmaid, *Occasions of Sin: Sex and Society in Modern Ireland* (London: Profile, 2009).

The Transformation of Ireland 1900–2000 (London: Profile Books, 2005).

Fitzpatrick, Lisa, 'Taking Their Own Road: The Female Protagonists in Three Irish Plays by Women', in *Women in Irish Drama: A Century of Authorship and Representation*, ed. Melissa Sihra (Basingstoke: Palgrave Macmillan, 2007), pp. 69–86.

Foley, Imelda, *The Girls in the Big Picture: Gender in Contemporary Ulster Theatre* (Belfast: The Blackstaff Press, 2003).

Forte, Jeanie, 'Realism, Narrative, and the Feminist Playwright – A Problem of Reception', in *Feminist Theatre and Theory*, ed. Helene Keyssar (Basingstoke: Macmillan, 1996), pp. 19–34.

Foster, Susan Leigh, *Choreographing History* (Bloomington: Indiana University Press, 1995).

Fouéré, Olwen, 'Afterword: The Act and The Word', in *Women in Irish Drama: A Century of Authorship and Representation*, ed. Melissa Sihra (Basingstoke: Palgrave Macmillan, 2007), pp. 219–20.

'Journeys in Performance: On Playing in *The Mai* and *By the Bog of Cats . . .* ', in *The Theatre of Marina Carr: 'Before Rules Was Made'*, ed. Cathy Leeney and Anna McMullan (Dublin: Carysfort Press, 2003), pp. 160–71.

'Operating Theatre and *Angel/Babel*', in *The Dreaming Body: Contemporary Irish Theatre*, ed. Paul Murphy and Melissa Sihra (Gerrard's Cross: Colin Smythe, 2009), pp. 115–24.

Freud, Sigmund, 'The "Uncanny"', in *Art and Literature: Vol. 14* (Harmondsworth: Penguin, 1990), pp. 335–76.

Gill, Rosalind, 'Culture and Subjectivity in Neoliberal and Postfeminist Times', *Subjectivity*, 25 (2008), 432–45.

Girard, René, *Violence and the Sacred* (London: The Athlone Press, 1995).

Gore-Booth, Eva, *Rhythms of Art*, Peace and Freedom Pamphlet No. 12, League of Peace and Freedom, D/4131/L/4, Lissadell Papers, Public Record Office of Northern Ireland, 1917.

Gregory, Augusta, *Our Irish Theatre: A Chapter of Autobiography* (New York and London: G.P. Putnam's Sons, 1913).

Grosz, Elizabeth, *Volatile Bodies: Towards a Corporeal Feminism* (Bloomington: Indiana University Press, 1994).

Bibliography

Hall, Edith, 'Iphigenia and her Mother at Aulis: A Study in the Revival of a Euripidean Classic', in *Rebel Women: Staging Ancient Greek Drama Today*, ed. John Dillon and S.E. Wilmer (London: Methuen, 2005), pp. 3–33.

Harris, Susan Cannon, *Gender and Irish Drama* (Bloomington: Indiana University Press, 2002).

Hayes, Alan (ed.), *Hilda Tweedy and the Irish Housewives' Association: Links in the Chain* (Galway: Arlen House, 2012).

Heaney, Seamus, *Sweeney Astray* (Derry: Field Day, 1983).

Hearne, Dana, '*The Irish Citizen*, 1914–1916: Nationalism, Feminism and Militarism', *The Canadian Journal of Irish Studies*, 18:1 (July 1992), 1–14.

Herbert, Maire, 'Celtic Heroine? The Archaeology of the Deirdre Story', in *Gender in Irish Writing*, ed. David Cairns and Toni O'Brien Johnson (Milton Keynes: Open University Press, 1991), pp. 13–22.

Hogan, Robert and James Kilroy, *The Irish Literary Theatre, 1899–1901* (Dublin: The Dolmen Press, 1975).

Hughes, Kellie, 'In the *Wake* of Olwen Fouéré's *riverrun*', in *The Palgrave Handbook of Contemporary Irish Theatre and Performance*, ed. Eamonn Jordan and Eric Weitz (Basingstoke: Palgrave Macmillan, 2018), pp. 415–19.

Hyde, Douglas, *A Literary History of Ireland* (London: Ernest Benn; New York: Barnes & Noble, 1967).

Innes, C.L., *Woman and Nation in Irish Literature and Society, 1880–1935* (Athens: The University of Georgia Press, 1993).

Irigaray, Luce, 'The Bodily Encounter with the Mother', in *The Irigaray Reader*, ed. Margaret Whitford (Oxford: Basil Blackwell, 1991), pp. 34–46.

'When Our Lips Speak Together', trans. Carolyn Burke, *Signs*, 6:1 (1978), 69–79.

'Women-Mothers, the Silent Substratum of the Social Order', in *The Irigaray Reader*, ed. Margaret Whitford (Oxford: Basil Blackwell, 1991), pp. 47–52.

Joyce, James, *Finnegan's Wake* (London: Faber & Faber, 1939; repr. London: Penguin, 1992).

Kearney, Richard, 'Between Tradition and Utopia: The Hermeneutical Problem of Myth', in *On Paul Ricoeur: Narrative and Interpretation*, ed. David Wood (London: Routledge, 2002), pp. 55–73.

'Editorial – Mythology', in *The Crane Bag Book of Irish Studies (1977–1981)*, ed. Mark Patrick Hederman and Richard Kearney (Dublin: Blackwater Press, 1982), pp. 155–7.

Myth and Motherland (Derry: Field Day, 1984).

'Myth as the Bearer of Possible Worlds: Interview with Paul Ricoeur', in *The Crane Bag Book of Irish Studies (1977–1981)*, ed. Mark Patrick Hederman and Richard Kearney (Dublin: Blackwater Press, 1982), pp. 260–6.

On Stories (London: Routledge, 2002).

Strangers, Gods and Monsters: Interpreting Otherness (London: Routledge, 2003).

242 *Bibliography*

Kiberd, Declan, 'Introduction', in *Amid our Troubles: Irish Versions of Greek Tragedy*, ed. Marianne McDonald and Michael J. Walton (London: Methuen, 2002), pp. VII–XIII.

Kinsella, Thomas, *The Táin* (Oxford: Oxford University Press, 1970).

Kirby, Peadar, *Celtic Tiger in Collapse: Explaining the Weaknesses of the Irish Model* (Basingstoke: Palgrave Macmillan, 2010).

Kohfeldt, Mary Lou, *Lady Gregory: The Woman Behind the Irish Renaissance* (London: Deutsch, 1985).

Kristeva, Julia, *Powers of Horror* (New York: Columbia University Press, 1982).

Kurdi, Mária, 'Updating Male Texts, Humour and Theatricality: The Representation of Marginalised Irish Womanhood in Paula Meehan's *Mrs Sweeney*', *EPONA: E-Journal of Ancient and Modern Celtic Studies*, 1;2 (2007), 1–9, www.epona-journal.hu/epona_languages/English/files/issue_0712/Kurdi_final.pdf.

Leeney, Cathy, 'Interchapter 1: 1900–1939', in *Women in Irish Drama: A Century of Authorship and Representation*, ed. Melissa Sihra (Basingstoke: Palgrave Macmillan, 2007), pp. 23–7.

'Ireland's "Exiled" Women Playwrights: Teresa Deevy and Marina Carr', in *The Cambridge Companion to Twentieth-Century Irish Drama*, ed. Shaun Richards (Cambridge: Cambridge University Press, 2004), pp. 150–63.

Irish Women Playwrights, 1900–1939: Gender and Violence on Stage (New York: Peter Lang, 2010).

'Marina Carr: Violence and Destruction: Language, Space and Landscape', in *A Companion to Modern British and Irish Drama 1880–2005*, ed. Mary Luckhurst (Oxford: Blackwell Publishing, 2006), pp. 509–18.

'Second Skin: Costume and Body: Power and Desire', in *Radical Contemporary Theatre Practices by Women in Ireland*, ed. Miriam Haughton and Mária Kurdi (Dublin: Carysfort Press, 2015), pp. 41–54.

'The New Woman in a New Ireland?: *Grania* after Naturalism', *Irish University Review*, 34:1 (2004), 157–70.

'The Space Outside: Images of Women in Plays by Eva Gore-Booth and Dorothy Macardle', in *Women in Irish Drama: A Century of Authorship and Representation*, ed. Melissa Sihra (Basingstoke: Palgrave Macmillan, 2007), pp. 55–68.

'Women and Irish Theatre before 1960', in *The Oxford Handbook of Modern Irish Theatre*, ed. Nicholas Grene and Chris Morash (Oxford: Oxford University Press, 2016), pp. 269–85.

Lepecki, André, *Exhausting Dance: Performance and the Politics of Movement* (Oxford and New York: Routledge, 2006).

Lewis, Gifford, *Eva Gore-Booth and Esther Roper: A Biography* (London: Pandora Press, 1988).

Lonergan, Patrick, *Theatre and Globalization: Irish Drama in the Celtic Tiger Era* (Basingstoke: Palgrave Macmillan, 2009).

Lysaght, Patricia, 'Traditional Storytelling in Ireland in the Twentieth Century', in *Traditional Storytelling Today: An International Sourcebook*, ed. Margaret Read MacDonald (London: Fitzroy Dearborn, 1999), pp. 264–72.

Bibliography

Macintosh, Fiona, *Dying Acts: Death in Ancient Greek and Modern Irish Tragic Drama* (Cork: Cork University Press, 1994).

Matthews, Ann, *Renegades: Irish Republican Women 1900–1922* (Cork: Mercier Press, 2010).

McCoole, Sinéad, *No Ordinary Women* (Dublin: O'Brien Press, 2004).

McDonald, Ronan, 'Sean O'Casey's Dublin Trilogy: Disillusionment to Delusion', in *The Cambridge Companion to Twentieth-Century Irish Drama*, ed. Shaun Richards (Cambridge: Cambridge University Press, 2004), pp. 136–49.

McGrath, Aoife, *Dance Theatre in Ireland: Revolutionary Moves* (Basingstoke: Palgrave Macmillan, 2013).

McMullan, Anna, 'Gender, Authorship and Performance in Contemporary Irish Women Playwrights', in *Theatre Stuff: Critical Essays on Contemporary Irish Theatre*, ed. Eamonn Jordan (Dublin: Carysfort Press, 2000), pp. 34–46.

'Marina Carr's Unhomely Women', *Irish Theatre Magazine*, 1:1 (1998), 14–16.

'Reclaiming Performance: The Contemporary Irish Independent Theatre Sector', in *The State of Play: Irish Theatre in the 'Nineties*, ed. Eberhard Bort (Trier: Wissenschaftlicher Verlag Trier, 1996), pp. 29–38.

'Unhomely Bodies and Dislocated Identities in the Drama of Frank McGuinness and Marina Carr', in *Indeterminate Bodies*, ed. Roger Cook, Naomi Segal and Lib Taylor (Basingstoke: Palgrave Macmillan, 2003), pp. 181–91.

'Unhomely Stages: Women Taking (a) Place in Irish Theatre', in *Druids, Dudes and Beauty Queens*, ed. Dermot Bolger (Dublin: New Island, 2001), pp. 72–90.

McRobbie, Angela, *The Aftermath of Feminism: Gender, Culture and Social Change* (London: Sage, 2009).

Meehan, Paula, Eavan Boland and Mary O'Malley, *Three Irish Poets: An Anthology*, ed. Eavan Boland (Manchester: Carcanet, 2003).

Merleau-Ponty, Maurice, *The World of Perception* (Paris: Gallimard, 1945; repr. Oxford: Routledge, 2004).

Milligan, Alice, 'The Last Feast of the Fianna', *Beltaine*, 2 (February 1900), 18–21.

Morris, Catherine, *Alice Milligan and the Irish Cultural Revival* (Dublin: Four Courts Press, 2012).

'Alice Milligan: Republican Tableaux and the Revival', *Field Day Review*, 6 (2010), 132–65.

Murphy, Paul, 'Woman as Fantasy Object in Lady Gregory's Historical Tragedies', in *Women in Irish Drama: A Century of Authorship and Representation*, ed. Melissa Sihra (Basingstoke: Palgrave Macmillan, 2007), pp. 28–41.

Murray, Christopher, *Twentieth-Century Irish Drama: Mirror up to Nation* (New York: Syracuse University Press, 2000).

Nancy, Jean-Luc, *Being Singular Plural* (Stanford: Stanford University Press, 2000).

Corpus, trans. Richard A. Rand (New York: Fordham University Press, 2008).

Nic Shiubhlaigh, Máire, *The Splendid Years: Recollections of Máire nic Shiubhlaigh as Told to Edward Kenny* (Dublin: James Duffy, 1955).

O'Brien, Edna, *Mother Ireland* (London: Weidenfeld & Nicolson, 1976).

O'Brien, Victoria, *A History of Irish Ballet from 1927 to 1963* (Bern: Peter Lang, 2011).

O'Connor, Pat, *Emerging Voices: Women in Contemporary Irish Society* (Dublin: Institute of Public Administration, 1998).

O'Keeffe, J.G. (trans.), *Buile Suibhne* (London: Irish Texts Society, 1913).

O'Rahilly, Cecile (trans.), *Táin Bó Cúailnge: Recension I* (Dublin: Dublin Institute for Advanced Studies, 1976).

O'Toole, Fintan, *Critical Moments: Fintan O'Toole on Modern Irish Theatre*, ed. Julia Furey and Redmond O'Hanlon (Dublin: Carysfort Press, 2003).

Ovid, *Metamorphoses*, trans. David Raeburn (London: Penguin, 2004).

Pašeta, Senia, *Irish Nationalist Women, 1900–1918* (Cambridge: Cambridge University Press, 2013).

Pethica, James, '"Our Kathleen": Yeats's Collaboration with Lady Gregory in the Writing of *Cathleen ni Houlihan*', *Yeats Annual*, No. 6 (Basingstoke: Macmillan Press, 1988), pp. 3–31.

Pierse, Michael, *Writing Ireland's Working Class: Dublin after O'Casey* (Basingstoke: Palgrave Macmillan, 2011).

Preston, Carrie J., *Modernism's Mythic Pose: Gender, Genre, Solo Performance* (Oxford: Oxford University Press, 2011).

Price, Janet and Margaret Shildrick (eds), *Feminist Theory and the Body: A Reader* (Edinburgh: Edinburgh University Press, 1999).

Quinn, Antoinette, 'Cathleen ni Houlihan Writes Back: Maud Gonne and Irish Nationalist Theater', in *Gender and Sexuality in Modern Ireland*, ed. Anthony Bradley and Maryann Gialanella Valiulis (Amherst: University of Massachusetts Press, 1997), pp. 39–59.

Rayner, Alice, *Ghosts: Death's Double and the Phenomena of Theatre* (Minneapolis: University of Minnesota Press, 2006).

Reynolds, Paige, *Modernism, Drama and the Audience for Irish Spectacle* (Cambridge: Cambridge University Press, 2007).

Ricoeur, Paul, 'Myth as the Bearer of Possible Worlds', in *A Ricoeur Reader: Reflection and Imagination*, ed. Mario J. Valdés (Hemel Hempstead: Harvester Wheatsheaf, 1991), pp. 482–90.

Roach, Joseph, *Cities of the Dead: Circum-Atlantic Performance* (New York: Columbia University Press, 1996).

Rockett, Kevin and Emer Rockett, *Magic Lantern, Panorama and Moving Picture Shows in Ireland, 1786–1909* (Dublin: Four Courts Press, 2011).

Schneider, Rebecca, *Performing Remains: Art and War in Times of Theatrical Reenactment* (London and New York: Routledge, 2011).

Seigworth, Gregory J. and Melissa Gregg, 'Introduction: An Inventory of Shimmers', in *The Affect Theory Reader* (Durham and London: Duke University Press, 2010), pp. 1–25.

Sihra, Melissa, 'Renegotiating Landscapes of the Female: Voices, Topographies and Corporealities of Alterity in Marina Carr's *Portia Coughlan*', *Australasian Drama Studies*, 43 (October 2003), 16–31.

Bibliography

'The House of Woman and the Plays of Marina Carr', in *Women in Irish Drama: A Century of Authorship and Representation*, ed. Melissa Sihra (Basingstoke: Palgrave Macmillan, 2007), pp. 201–18.

'The Unbearable Darkness of Being: Marina Carr's *Woman and Scarecrow*', *Irish Theatre International*, 1:1 (2008), 22–37.

Silverman, Kaja, *The Acoustic Mirror: The Female Voice in Psychoanalysis and Cinema* (Bloomington: Indiana University Press, 1988).

Singleton, Brian, *Masculinities and the Contemporary Irish Theatre* (Basingstoke: Palgrave Macmillan, 2011).

Sophocles, *The Theban Plays*, trans. E.F. Watling (Harmondsworth: Penguin, 1974).

Smith, James M., *Ireland's Magdalen Laundries and the Nation's Architecture of Containment* (Indiana: University of Notre Dame Press, 2007).

Smyth, Ailbhe, 'The Floozie in the Jacuzzi', *The Irish Review*, No. 6 (Spring 1989), 7–24.

Stallybrass, Peter and Allon White, *The Politics and Poetics of Transgression* (Ithaca: Cornell University Press, 1995).

Stam, Robert, 'Mikhail Bakhtin and Left Cultural Critique', in *Postmodernism and Its Discontents*, ed. E. Ann Kaplan (London: Verso, 1989), pp. 116–45.

Stone, Alison, 'On the Genealogy of Women: A Defence of Anti-Essentialism', in *Third Wave Feminism: A Critical Exploration*, ed. Stacy Gillis, Gillian Howie and Rebecca Munford (Basingstoke: Palgrave Macmillan, 2004), pp. 85–96.

Sweeney, Bernadette, *Performing the Body in Irish Theatre* (Basingstoke: Palgrave Macmillan, 2008).

Taylor, Diana, *The Archive and the Repertoire: Performing Cultural Memory in the Americas* (Durham and London: Duke University Press, 2003).

Taylor, Lib, 'The "Unhomely" Stage', *Studies in Theatre and Performance*, 26:3 (2006), 205–20.

Tiernan, Sonja, '"Engagements Dissolved": Eva Gore-Booth, *Urania* and the Radical Challenge to Marriage', in *Tribades, Tommies and Transgressives; Histories of Sexualities: Volume I*, ed. Mary McAuliffe and Sonja Tiernan (Newcastle: Cambridge Scholars, 2008), pp. 128–44.

Eva Gore-Booth: An Image of such Politics (Manchester: Manchester University Press, 2012).

'"No Measures of 'Emancipation' or 'Equality' Will Suffice": Eva Gore-Booth's Revolutionary Feminism in the Journal *Urania*', in *Women, Social and Cultural Change in Twentieth Century Ireland: Dissenting Voices?*, ed. Sarah O'Connor and Christopher Shepard (Newcastle: Cambridge Scholars Press, 2008), pp. 166–82.

(ed.), *The Political Writings of Eva Gore-Booth* (Manchester: Manchester University Press, 2015).

Trotter, Mary, *Ireland's National Theaters: Political Performance and the Origins of the Irish Dramatic Movement* (New York: Syracuse University Press, 2001).

Turner, Cathy and Synne K. Behrndt, *Dramaturgy and Performance* (Basingstoke: Palgrave Macmillan, 2008).

Bibliography

Wald, Christina, *Hysteria, Trauma and Melancholia: Performative Maladies in Contemporary Anglophone Drama* (Basingstoke: Palgrave Macmillan, 2007).

Wallace, Clare, *Suspect Cultures: Narrative, Identity and Citation in 1990s New Drama* (Prague: Litteraria Pragensia, 2006).

'Tragedy and Abjection in Three Plays by Marina Carr', *Irish University Review*, 31:2 (2001), 431–49.

Walker, Kathrine Sorley, 'The Festival and the Abbey: Ninette de Valois' Early Choreography, 1925–34, Part One', *Dance Chronicle*, 7:4 (1984–5), 379–412.

Walsh, Fintan, 'Homelysexuality and the "Beauty" Pageant', in *Crossroads: Performance Studies and Irish Culture*, ed. Sara Brady and Fintan Walsh (Basingstoke: Palgrave Macmillan, 2009), pp. 196–209.

Walsh, Ian R., *Experimental Irish Theatre: After W.B. Yeats* (Basingstoke: Palgrave Macmillan, 2012).

Wandor, Michelene, *Carry On, Understudies: Theatre and Sexual Politics* (London and New York: Routledge, 1986).

Ward, Margaret, *Maud Gonne: Ireland's Joan of Arc* (London: Pandora, 1990).

Unmanageable Revolutionaries: Women and Irish Nationalism (London: Pluto Press, 1989).

Warner, Marina, *Alone of All Her Sex: The Myth and Cult of the Virgin Mary* (London: Picador, 1985).

Fantastic Metamorphoses, Other Worlds (Oxford: Oxford University Press, 2002).

Managing Monsters: Six Myths of Our Time (London: Vintage, 1994).

Monuments and Maidens: The Allegory of the Female Form (London: Vintage, 1996).

No Go the Bogeyman: Scaring, Lulling and Making Mock (London: Vintage, 2000).

Waters, Maureen, 'Lady Gregory's *Grania*: A Feminist Voice', *Irish University Review*, 25:1 (1995), 11–24.

Welch, Robert, *The Abbey Theatre, 1899–1999: Form and Pressure* (Oxford: Oxford University Press, 1999).

Whitford, Margaret, *Luce Irigaray: Philosophy in the Feminine* (London and New York: Routledge, 1991).

Worth, Katherine, *The Irish Drama of Europe from Yeats to Beckett* (London: Athlone Press, 1978).

Yeats, W.B., *Collected Poems* (London: Vintage, 1992).

Young, Ella, *Flowering Dusk* (London: Longmans, Green and Co., 1945).

Young, Iris Marion, *On Female Body Experience: 'Throwing Like a Girl' and Other Essays* (Oxford: Oxford University Press, 2005).

Zipes, Jack (trans. and ed.), *The Complete First Edition. The Original Folk and Fairy Tales of the Brothers Grimm* (Oxford: Princeton University Press, 2014).

Interviews

'Interview with Marina Carr', in *Rage and Reason: Women Playwrights on Playwriting*, ed. Heidi Stephenson and Natasha Langridge (London: Methuen, 1997), pp. 146–55.

'Interview with Marina Carr', RTE Radio One 'Playwrights in Profile', 23 September 2007.

'Marina Carr in Conversation with Melissa Sihra', in *Theatre Talk: Voices of Irish Theatre Practitioners*, ed. Lilian Chambers, Ger Fitzgibbon and Eamonn Jordan (Dublin: Carysfort Press, 2001), pp. 55–63.

'Olwen Fouéré in Conversation with Melissa Sihra', in *Theatre Talk: Voices of Irish Theatre Practitioners*. ed. Lilian Chambers, Ger Fitzgibbon and Eamonn Jordan (Dublin: Carysfort Press, 2001), pp. 155–66.

Susan Conley, 'riverrun: Olwen Fouéré on the voice of the river', *Irish Theatre Magazine*, 7 July 2013.

Programme Notes

Carr, Marina, Programme Note for *Iphigenia at Aulis*, Abbey Theatre Dublin. Directed by Katie Mitchell, opened 28 March 2001.

Hederman, Mark Patrick, 'Musings on Ariel', Programme Note for *Ariel*, Abbey Theatre Dublin. Directed by Conall Morrison, opened 2 October 2002.

Leeney, Cathy, Programme Note for *Women in Arms*, Civic Theatre, Tallaght, Dublin. Directed by Mary Elizabeth Burke-Kennedy, opened 9 April 2002.

Macintosh, Fiona, Programme Note for *Woman and Scarecrow*, Peacock Theatre Dublin. Directed by Selina Cartmell, opened 10 October 2007.

Newspaper Articles

'An Irishman's Diary', *Irish Times*, 14 October 1943, p. 3.

'At the Children's Matinee', *United Irishman*, 7 September 1901, p. 3.

'Ballets at the Abbey', *Dublin Evening Mail*, 26 July 1933, p. 4.

'Beautiful Ballets', *Irish Independent*, 26 July 1933, p. 11.

Bean na hÉireann, 1:3 (February 1909), p. 1.

Fouéré, Olwen, 'Following the flow of the "Wake" to its source', *Irish Times*, 13 July 2013.

'Irish Women's Franchise League: Daffodil Fete', *Irish Times*, 25 April 1914, p. 9.

'Lyric Theatre Company', *Irish Times*, 6 November 1948, p. 6.

'Lyric Theatre Programme at the Abbey', *Irish Independent*, 17 November 1948, p. 3.

McGarry, Patsy, 'Catholic Church Resembles "a Male Bastion of Patronising Platitudes", McAleese Says', *Irish Times*, 8 March 2018.

'Mixed Bill at the Abbey Theatre', *Irish Press*, 26 July 1933.

'Patriotic Children's Treat', *United Irishman*, 7 July 1900, p. 7.

248 *Bibliography*

'Payne School of Dance: Pleasing Programme in Father Mathew Hall', *Irish Times*, 20 June 1938, p. 2.
The Evening Herald, 20 November 1948, p. 5.
'The Gaelic Tableaux', *United Irishman*, 13 April 1901, p. 5.
The Irish Citizen, 9 May 1914, p. 401.
The Irish Citizen, 6 September 1913, p. 127.
'The Lyric Theatre', *Irish Times*, 4 June 1945, p. 3.
The New York Times Magazine, 10 September 1916, p. 2.
United Irishman, 24 August 1901, p. 2.
United Irishman, 7 September 1901, p. 4.
United Irishman, 4 October 1902, p. 1.

Reviews

Bassett, Kate, 'Anyone Got a Stain-Remover?', *Independent*, 25 June 2006.
Billington, Michael, 'Review of *Iphigenia*', *Guardian*, 12 February 2003.
Callaghan, David, 'Performance Review: The Mai', *Theatre Journal*, 49:3 (1997), 373–5.
Hall, Edith, 'Barbarism with Beatitude', *Times Literary Supplement*, 21 February 2003.
Marlowe, Sam, 'Reviews: First Night', *The Times*, 23 June 2006, p. 22.
O'Brien, Harvey, 'Review of *Ariel*, 10 October 2002, https://culturevulture.net/theater/ariel-marina-carr/ [Accessed 17 June 2017].
Walsh, Fintan, Review in *Irish Theatre Magazine*, 16 March 2010, www.irishtheatremagazine.ie/Reviews/Current/Sodome–My-Love [Accessed 20 August 2013].
White, Victoria, 'Twin Speak', *Irish Times*, 19 March 1996, p. 10.

Webpages

Constitution of Ireland – Bunreacht Na hÉireann, www.taoiseach.gov.ie/DOT/eng/Historical_Information/The_Constitution/Constitution_of_Ireland_-_Bunreacht_na_h%C3%89ireann.html [Accessed 1 March 2018].
Gender Counts: An Analysis of Gender in Irish Theatre, 2006–2015, Commissioned by #WakingTheFeminists. Funded by The Arts Council. Researched by Dr Brenda Donohue, Dr Ciara O'Dowd, Dr Tanya Dean, Ciara Murphy, Kathleen Cawley and Kate Harris, http://www.wakingthefeminists.org/research-report/ [Accessed 15 January 2018].
The Irish Family Planning Association, www.ifpa.ie/Hot-Topics/Abortion/Statistics [Accessed 8 March 2018].
Lizzie Clachan, www.lizzieclachan.co.uk/WomanandScarecrow47.html [Accessed 21 August 2017].
Mary Devenport O'Neill, http://marydevenportoneill.org [Accessed 10 August 2017].
Monica Frawley, www.monicafrawley.com/#/by-the-bog-of-cats/ [Accessed 17 November 2016].

Mothers Artists Makers, https://mamsireland.wordpress.com/ [Accessed 13 June 2018].

Olwen Fouéré: The Works, RTE One, Aired 28 February 2014, www.youtube.com/watch?v=nFy62CrTL14 [Accessed 17 May 2017].

Proclamation of Independence, www.taoiseach.gov.ie/eng/Historical_Information/State_Commemorations/Proclamation_of_Independence.html [Accessed 22 November 2018].

Referendum of 6 March 2002, http://electionsireland.org/results/referendum/refresult.cfm?ref=200225 [Accessed 21 April 2010].

RTE Archives, 'The Ireland that We Dreamed of', 1943, www.rte.ie/archives/exhibitions/eamon-de-valera/719124–address-by-mr-de-valera/ [Accessed 4 October 2017].

Storytellers Theatre Company, www.storytellerstheatrecompany.com/artistic.html [Accessed 27 October 2008].

#WakingTheFeminists, www.wakingthefeminists.org/about-wtf/how-it-started/ [Accessed 13 March 2018].

Archival Material

Druid Theatre Archive, Hardiman Library, National University of Ireland, Galway.

Holloway, Joseph, *A Dublin Playgoer's Impressions 1901*, Microfilm P8517, National Library of Ireland.

Holloway, Joseph, *A Dublin Playgoer's Impressions 1902*, Microfilm P8518, National Library of Ireland.

Letters to Alice Milligan, MS 5048, National Library of Ireland.

O'Brien, Edna, *Trojan Women/ Greek Men*, OB/522 (June 2002) and OB/526 (10 November 2002), Edna O'Brien Papers, University College Dublin Library Special Collections.

The Rough Magic Theatre Company Archive, TCD MS 11568, Manuscripts & Archives, The Library of Trinity College Dublin.

Storytellers Theatre Company Archive, Dublin City Library and Archive.

Performances Seen

Burke-Kennedy, Mary Elizabeth, *Women in Arms*. Directed: Mary Elizabeth Burke-Kennedy. Cast: Cathy Belton, Iseult Golden, Simone Kirby, Síle Nic Chonaonaigh, Ciaran McIntyre, Aidan Kelly, Simon O'Gorman. Set Design: Bláithín Sheerin. Costume Design: Catherine Fay. Lighting Design: Nick McCall (Storytellers Theatre Company and Cork Opera House: The Civic Theatre, Tallaght, Dublin, opened 8 April 2002).

Carr, Marina, *Ariel*. Director: Conall Morrison. Cast: Des Cave, Ingrid Craigie, Siobhan Cullen, Mark Lambert, Barry McGovern, Elske Rahill, Dylan Tighe, Eileen Walsh. Lighting: Rupert Murray. Costume: Joan O'Clery.

250 *Bibliography*

Set Design: Frank Conway (Abbey Theatre, Dublin, opened 1 October 2002).

Portia Coughlan. Director: Brian Brady. Cast: Eileen Walsh, Frank Laverty, Brid Ní Neachtain, Liam Carney, Keith McErlean, Fionnuala Murphy, Phelim Drew, Maria McDermottroe, Stella McCusker, Gerard McSorley. Set: Bláithín Sheerin. Lighting: Paul Keogan (Peacock Theatre, Dublin, opened 2 October 2004).

Woman and Scarecrow. Director: Selina Cartmell. Cast: Olwen Fouéré, Barbara Brennan, Bríd Ní Neachtain, Simon O'Gorman. Set and costume design: Conor Murphy. Lighting: Paul Keogan. Sound: Denis Clohessy (Peacock Theatre, Dublin, opened 10 October 2007).

Fouéré, Olwen (Adapted from James Joyce's *Finnegan's Wake*), *riverrun.* Directed and Performed: Olwen Fouéré. Co-Dir: Kellie Hughes. Sound Design: Alma Kelliher. Lighting Design: Stephen Dodd. Costume: Monica Frawley (TheEmergencyRoom and Galway Arts Festival: Druid Theatre, Galway, opened 18 July 2013).

Gaudé, Laurent, *Sodome, My Love.* Trans: Olwen Fouéré. Director: Lynne Parker. Cast: Olwen Fouéré. Designer: John Comiskey. Costume: Monica Frawley. Music and sound: Denis Clohessy (Rough Magic in association with TheEmergencyRoom: Project Arts Centre, Dublin, opened 16 March 2010).

Recordings of Performances

Burke-Kennedy, *Women in Arms.* Directed: Mary Elizabeth Burke-Kennedy. Cast: Cathy Belton, Iseult Golden, Simone Kirby, Síle Nic Chonaonaigh, Ciaran McIntyre, Aidan Kelly, Simon O'Gorman. Set Design: Bláithín Sheerin. Costume Design: Catherine Fay. Lighting Design: Nick McCall (Storytellers Theatre Company and Cork Opera House: The Civic Theatre, Tallaght, Dublin, opened 9 April 2002). Storytellers Theatre Company Archive.

Carr, Marina, *Ariel.* Director: Conall Morrison. Cast: Des Cave, Ingrid Craigie, Siobhan Cullen, Mark Lambert, Barry McGovern, Elske Rahill, Dylan Tighe, Eileen Walsh. Lighting: Rupert Murray. Costume: Joan O'Clery. Set Design: Frank Conway (Abbey Theatre, Dublin, opened 1 October 2002). Abbey Theatre Archive.

By the Bog of Cats . . .. Director: Patrick Mason. Cast: Olwen Fouéré, Siobhan Cullen, Pauline Flanagan, Tom Hickey, Eamon Kelly, Pat Kinevane, Ronan Leahy, Pat Leavy, Fionnuala Murphy, Conor McDermottroe, Joan O'Hara, Kerrie O'Sullivan, Conan Sweeny. Lighting: Nick Chelton. Set and Costume: Monica Frawley (Abbey Theatre, Dublin, opened 7 October 1998). Abbey Theatre Archive.

Hecuba. Director: Erica Whyman. Cast: David Ajao, Nadia Albina, Derbhle Crotty, Ray Fearon, Edmund Kingsley, Amy Mcallister, Chu Omambala, Lara Stubbs, Marcus Acquari/Nilay Sah/Luca Saraceni, Sebastian Luc Gibb/

Christopher Kingdom/Daniel Vicente Thomas/Yiannis Vogiaridis. Designer: Soutra Gilmour. Lighting: Charles Balfour. Composer: Isobel Waller-Bridge. Sound: Andrew Franks (Royal Shakespeare Company: Swan Theatre, Stratford-upon-Avon, opened 17 Sept, 2015). Royal Shakespeare Company Archive.

The Mai. Director: Brian Brady. Cast: Olwen Fouéré, Derbhle Crotty, Owen Roe, Michele Forbes, Maire Hastings, Stella McCusker, Bríd Ní Neachtain, Joan O'Hara. Music: Michael O'Suilleabhain. Lighting: Aedin Cosgrove. Set and Costume: Kathy Strachan (Peacock Theatre Dublin, opened 5 October 1994). Abbey Theatre Archive.

The Mai. Director: Brian Brady. Cast: Olwen Fouéré, Catherine Mack, Robert O'Mahony, Maire Hastings, Stella McCusker, Bríd Ní Neachtain, Joan O'Hara, Joan Sheehy. Music: Michael O'Suilleabhain. Lighting: Aedin Cosgrove. Set and Costume: Kathy Strachan (Abbey Theatre Production: Abbey Centre, Ballyshannon, opened 24 April, 1995). Abbey Theatre Archive.

On Raftery's Hill. Director: Garry Hynes. Cast: Mary Murray, Michael Tierney, Cara Kelly, Valerie Lilley, Tom Hickey, Kieran Ahern, Keith McErlean. Designer: Tony Walton. Lighting: Richard Pilbrow. Costume: Monica Frawley (Druid Theatre Company/ Royal Court co-production: Town Hall Theatre, Galway, opened 9 May 2000). Druid Theatre Archive.

Portia Coughlan. Director: Garry Hynes. Cast: Derbhle Crotty, Sean Rocks, Marion O'Dwyer, Des Keogh, Don Wycherley, Bronagh Gallagher, Charlie Bonner, Stella McCusker, Pauline Flanagan, Tom Hickey, Michael Boylan, Peter Charlesworth Kelly. Set and costume design: Kandis Cook. Lighting: Jim Simmons (Peacock Theatre, Dublin, opened 27 March 1996). Abbey Theatre Archive.

Portia Coughlan. Director: Brian Brady. Cast: Eileen Walsh, Frank Laverty, Brid Ní Neachtain, Liam Carney, Keith McErlean, Fionnuala Murphy, Phelim Drew, Maria McDermottroe, Stella McCusker, Gerard McSorley. Set: Bláithín Sheerin. Lighting: Paul Keogan (Peacock Theatre, Dublin, opened 2 October 2004). Abbey Theatre Archive.

Woman and Scarecrow. Directed by Selina Cartmell. Cast: Olwen Fouéré, Barbara Brennan, Bríd Ní Neachtain, Simon O'Gorman. Set and costume design: Conor Murphy. Lighting: Paul Keogan. Sound: Denis Clohessy (Peacock Theatre, Dublin, opened 10 October 2007). Abbey Theatre Archive.

Fouéré, Olwen (adapted from James Joyce's *Finnegan's Wake*), *riverrun*. Directed and Performed: Olwen Fouéré. Co-Dir: Kellie Hughes. Sound Design: Alma Kelliher. Lighting Design: Stephen Dodd. Costume: Monica Frawley (TheEmergencyRoom and Galway Arts Festival: Druid Theatre, Galway, opened 18 July 2013).

Gaudé, Laurent, *Sodome, My Love*. Trans: Olwen Fouéré. Director: Lynne Parker. Cast: Olwen Fouéré. Designer: John Comiskey. Costume: Monica Frawley. Music and sound: Denis Clohessy (Rough Magic in association with

TheEmergencyRoom: Project Arts Centre, Dublin, opened 16 March 2010).
Rough Magic Archive. Trinity College Dublin, Special Collections.
Gaudé, Laurent, *Sodome, My Love*. Trans: Olwen Fouéré. Director: Lynne Parker.
Cast: Olwen Fouéré. Designer: John Comiskey. Costume: Monica Frawley.
Music and sound: Denis Clohessy (Rough Magic in association with
TheEmergencyRoom: Ohrid Festival, Saint Sophia, Macedonia, 31 July
2010). Rough Magic Archive, Trinity College Dublin, Special Collections.
Meehan, Paula, *Mrs Sweeney*. Director: Kathy McArdle. Cast: Ger Ryan, Mick
Nolan, Anto Nolan, Neilí Conroy, Gina Moxley, Tim Ruddy, Emmet
Dowling, Barry White. Lighting: Paul Keogan. Designer: Barbara
Bradshaw (Rough Magic Theatre Company: Project@ The Mint, opened
7 May 1997). Rough Magic Theatre Company Archive.

Index

abjection, 106, 108, 114, 116, 119, 121, 126, 127, 132, 146, 148, 170
abortion, 5
  See also referenda, and, Eighth Amendment
  X Case, the (1992), 111
Aeschylus
  Agamemnon, 150, 151
  The Eumenides, 187
  The Oresteia, 152
affect, 33, 36, 43, 47, 80, 98, 132, 133, 234
aisling, the figure, 4, 44, 57
Allgood, Sara, 107
Antigone, 135
architecture of containment, 12, 65, 175, 211
archive, the, 23, 212

Bakhtin, Mikhail, 74
banshee, 39, 158, 165
Barthes, Roland, 18
  Mythologies, 11
Bean na hÉireann, 50
Beckett, Samuel, 74, 217
Bhabha, Homi, 14, 66, 69, 71, 159, 173, 194
Bible, The
  Genesis 19, 220
  Isaiah 29, 143, 147
Binski, Paul, 166
Blunt, Wilfred Scawen, 107
Boland, Eavan, 1, 10
bourgeois feminism, 130
Breathnach, Proinnsias, 99
Brecht, Bertolt
  Mother Courage and Her Children, 93
Brechtian theatre, 66, 85, 89–98, 101, 102
Brian Boru, 38
Brigit, Saint and Mother Goddess, 29, 30, 38, 39
Bronfen, Elisabeth, 136, 138, 159, 162, 164
Burke-Kennedy, Mary Elizabeth, 3, 42
  Women in Arms, 9, 20, 65–67, 85–103, 150
Butler, Judith, 23, 105, 126, 138, 161, 202
  Bodies That Matter, 106, 114

Gender Trouble, 106
  materialization, 118
  performativity, 16

Calor Housewife of the Year, 109
canon of Irish theatre, the, 2, 10, 23, 24, 25, 74, 235
Caravaggio
  Death of the Virgin, 164
carnivalesque, 72, 74–78
Carr, Marina, 3, 13, 202
  Ariel, 9, 23, 135, 138, 139, 141–144, 146–150, 155–157, 160, 165, 170–171, 185
  By the Bog of Cats . . ., 15, 19, 23, 130, 149, 214
  Hecuba, 153–154
  On Raftery's Hill, 15–17, 19, 160, 170
  Phaedra Backwards, 163
  Portia Coughlan, 9, 19, 23, 119, 146, 149, 160, 165, 173, 174, 183, 188–199, 208–210, 211
  The Cordelia Dream, 142
  The Mai, 9, 19, 23, 109–114, 115, 117–120, 126–134, 142, 146, 160, 164, 165, 170, 214
  Woman and Scarecrow, 9, 129, 135, 138, 154, 157–171, 202, 214, 221
Cartmell, Selina, 120, 142, 157
Case, Sue-Ellen
  negative utopia, 132–133, 170, 209, 210
catharsis, 119, 154, 157, 158, 167, 169, 196
Catholic Church, the, 4, 12, 39, 111, 155
  and misogyny, 5
Cave, Richard Allen, 107, 179
ceilidh, 29, 30, 39
Celtic Literary Society, The, 28, 34
Celtic Tiger, the, 15, 25, 67, 69, 72, 83, 98–100, 111, 136, 141, 155, 199
Children's Treat, the (1900), 28
Churchill, Caryl
  Top Girls, 100
Cinderella, 115
Cixous, Hélène, 10, 18, 128, 215
Clark, Rosalind, 40

253

Index

254

class
  and feminism, 24
  working-class, 67, 69, 70, 71, 72, 78
Clohessy, Denis, 219
coalitional politics, 2, 23, 24, 63
Collins, Lucy, 176
Condren, Mary, 29
Constitution of Ireland, the (1937), 41, 109, 172
  Article 41.2, 13
contraceptive train, the, 110
Corless, Catherine, 175
corporeality, a creative female, 1, 3, 6, 10, 21, 106,
  114, 118, 126, 129
Council of the Status of Women, the, 110
Coupe, Laurence, 11
Criminal Law Amendment Act, the (1935), 175
crucifixion of Christ, 59
Cumann na mBan, 40
Curran, Sarah, 30, 39
Cutler, Anna, 214, 223

danse macabre, the, 166
Dark Rosaleen. *See* Inghean Dubh
de Beauvoir, Simone, 5, 104, 135, 202
de Valera, Éamon, 13, 109
de Valois, Ninette, 176–178, 182, 187
  choreography of the Furies, 187
  influences on, 177
death and femininity, tropes of, 125, 135–171,
  220–221, 225, 236
Deevy, Teresa, 180
  Katie Roche, 130
Descartes, René, 6
Devlin, Anne, 30, 35, 38, 39, 40
Diamond, Elin, 41, 46, 89, 102
Dodd, Stephen, 227, 228
Dolan, Jill, 8
Donoghue, Emma, 58
dramaturgy, 8
drug addiction, 67, 71, 83
dystopian, 17

Eagleton, Terry, 139
Early Christian Ireland, 88
Easter Rising, The (1916), 11, 52, 61, 199
écriture féminine, 215, 222, 230
Eighth Amendment, the, 5, 98, 110
  Repeal of, 5, 111
Electra, 115
Elizabeth, Queen, 39
embodied mythmaking, 6, 8, 9, 21, 23, 24, 25, 37,
  42, 47, 64, 102
emigration (1980s), 98
Employment Equality Act, the (1977), 110
employment, women's, 111, 136

equal pay, 110
Euripides
  Hecuba, 154
  Iphigenia at Aulis, 139, 141, 143, 144, 149, 156
European Economic Community, 110
exile, 69
  exiled artist, 74
expressionism, 176, 187

Fay Brothers, the, 31
female corpse, the, 9, 113, 120, 134, 136, 148, 162,
  169, 172, 186
feminine eroticism, 57, 58, 62
feminist spectator, the. *See* Dolan, Jill
First Commission on the Status of Women,
  the, 109
First World War, 52, 199
Fitzpatrick, Lisa, 113
Foster, Susan Leigh, 218
  writing-dancing body, 8
Fouéré, Olwen, 1, 3, 10, 131, 157, 167
  Angel/Babel, 217, 219
  Here Lies . . ., 231
  riverrun, 1, 10, 21, 84, 150, 211, 214, 219, 221,
  227–236
  Sodome, My Love, 10, 18, 42, 213–226, 230, 235
Freud, Sigmund, 14, 71, 136, 137, 166

Gaudé, Laurent, 213
gaze, the male, 95
Gender Counts Report, 85
genealogies of performance, 173, 189, 191, 195–198,
  204–205, 208, 209, 211–212, 215
genealogy, a feminist, 2, 10, 15, 23–24, 25, 42, 235, 236
gestic feminist criticism, 90, 101
Gill, Rosalind, 7, 140, 225
Girard, René, 151, 152
globalization, 3, 137
Gonne, Maud, 3, 27, 28, 29, 34, 43
  Dawn, 9, 27, 43, 47–51, 64
  influence of tableaux vivants, 47
  performance in *Kathleen ni Houlihan*, 45–47
'good death', the, 9, 135, 138, 163, 169
Gore-Booth, Eva, 3, 20, 24, 86
  'To Maeve', 86
  *A Psychological and Poetic Approach to the Study
  of Christ in the Fourth Gospel*, 59
  The Buried Life of Deirdre, 9, 56, 59, 96, 173,
  174, 188, 199–208, 210–211
  The Death of Fionavar, 52, 59–63
  The Triumph of Maeve, 9, 27, 51–64, 123
Gormlai, 38, 39
Gregory, Lady Augusta, 3, 62
  'Our Irish Theatre', 12
  Gods and Fighting Men, 116, 122

Index

Grania, 9, 20, 107–108, 115–117, 121–123, 126, 130–133
Kathleen ni Houlihan, 9, 16, 31, 43–47 56, 60, 64, 92, 119, 120, 135, 163, 165, 214, 234
Kincora, 39, 165
Grosz, Elizabeth, 5, 6, 105

Hall, Edith, 140, 147, 150, 156
Hamilton, Emma Lyon, 32, 36
Harris, Susan Cannon, 120, 148, 163
Haughey, Charles, 110
haunted body, the, 9
Health and Family Planning Act, the (1979), 110
Heaney, Seamus
  Sweeney Astray, 68
Hearne, Dana, 26
Herbert, Maire, 96
HIV/AIDS, 67, 71, 72, 75, 225
Holloway, Joseph, 35–36, 46
Home Rule Crisis (1912–14), 26
home, institutional, 175
home, the domestic, 13, 14, 15, 69, 70, 75, 78, 81, 83, 174, 175, 190, 194, 196, 208
homoerotic, 108
Houston, Kathleen, 58
Hughes, Kellie, 227, 229, 233
Hynes, Garry, 191, 194

Ibsen, Henrik, 48, 133
  Hedda Gabler, 46
imaginary, a female, 105, 106, 129, 133
incest, 16, 17
industrial schools, 13
Inghean Dubh, the, 30, 39
Inghinidhe na hÉireann
  tableaux vivants, 3, 9, 17, 21, 27–43, 48, 87, 98, 165, 217, 221, 236
Innes, C.L., 94, 97
interrogative myth, 20
Iraq War, the second, 139, 156
Ireland Fettered and Ireland Free, tableau of, 30, 36, 38, 39–41, 43
Irigaray, Luce, 18, 23, 41, 105, 106, 152
  déréliction, 14, 115, 117, 208
Irish Citizen, The, 29
Irish Free State, the, 4, 12, 25, 41, 64, 174, 179, 180, 188
Irish Housewives' Association, the, 41
Irish literary theatre tradition, 7, 217
Irish Literary Theatre, the, 12, 49, 124
Irish Women's Franchise League, the, 37
  tableaux vivants, 40, 58
Irish Women's Liberation Movement, the, 110

Joan of Arc, 40
John Paul II, Pope, 98
Johnston, Anna, 34, 40
Joyce, James, 74
  Finnegan's Wake, 1, 21, 219, 227, 232, 236
  Ulysses, 21
Juries Bill, the (1927), 174

Kearney, Richard, 11, 18, 21, 63, 87, 120, 184
Keegan-Dolan, Michael, 218
keening (caoineadh), 48
Kelliher, Alma, 227, 228, 232
Keogan, Paul, 77, 161, 195
Kiberd, Declan, 12
Kinsella, Thomas
  The Táin, 91, 93
Kirby, Peadar, 67, 136
Kohfeldt, Mary Lou, 107
Kristeva, Julia, 114, 119, 139

Lady Godiva, tableau of, 32
Leeney, Cathy, 2, 31, 39, 54, 85, 107, 116, 121, 130, 180, 185, 188, 198, 207
lesbian, 54, 58
lighting, 47, 53, 56, 76–77, 91, 97, 144, 161, 194, 195, 227, 228, 232, 233
lived body, the, 1, 6, 105, 217
Lovett, Ann, 111
Lyric Theatre Players, 178, 180, 181

MacGinley, P.T.
  Eilís agus an Bhean Dhéirce, 30
Macintosh, Fiona, 144, 158
Maeve, Queen, 29, 30, 38, 39, 40, 97
Magdalene laundries, 13
Markievicz, Constance, 29, 52, 58, 63, 199
marriage bar, the, 110
masculinity, 17, 72, 81, 82, 199, 203
matrilineal tradition, 23
McAleese, Mary, 5
McDonald, Ronan, 66
McGee, Mary, 110
McGrath, Aoife, 179
McMullan, Anna, 7, 13, 65, 93
McRobbie, Angela, 99, 100
Medusa, 164, 187
Meehan, Paula, 3, 24
  'Home', 84
  'Mrs Sweeney', 70
  'My Father Perceived as a Vision of St Francis', 73
  Mrs Sweeney, 9, 20, 65–84
melancholy, 209
  and gender, 191, 197
melodrama, 32

Index

memory, 9, 168–169, 206
  countermemory, 183, 192, 197, 198, 204, 207,
    211, 215, 223
  cultural memory, 149, 173, 185, 188, 190–194,
    197, 206, 211
  embodied memory, 22, 189, 195
  living memory, 207, 209
Merleau-Ponty, Maurice, 6
metamorphosis, 9, 70, 72–74, 104–134, 138, 201,
  204, 236
Millais, John Everett
  Ophelia, 157
Milligan, Alice, 3, 31, 34
  tableaux vivants, 34, 36
  The Deliverance of Red Hugh O'Donnell, 30
  The Last Feast of the Fianna, 124–126
mimesis, feminist, 41, 54
Miss Ireland, 109
modernism, 37
Molony, Helena, 29
Mooney, Ria, 177, 182
Morrígan, 39, 158, 165
Morris, Catherine, 36
mother and baby homes, 13, 175
Mothers Artists Makers (MAM), 13
Murray, Christopher, 122, 181
Murray, Rupert, 144
myth
  and ideology, 11
  and violence, 11, 15

Nancy, Jean-Luc, 216, 221–223, 233–234
  exscription, 10, 217, 218–219, 223–224, 228, 233,
    234, 235, 236
nationalism, 3, 12, 27–29, 31, 33, 35, 38, 40, 43, 48,
  51, 53, 60, 64, 97, 107, 108, 116, 201
neoliberalism, 3, 7, 98, 100, 137, 140, 162, 199, 210,
  220, 226
New Woman, the, 108
Nic Shiubhlaigh, Maire, 26, 27, 46
Nightingale, Florence, 40
Nora, Pierre
  places of memory, and environments of
    memory, 206–209
Northern Ireland, conflict in, 102

O'Brien, Edna, 3
  Iphigenia, 9, 135, 138, 139–141, 144–146, 150–152,
    155, 171
  Mother Ireland, 144
  Trojan Women/ Greek Men, 154
O'Casey, Sean, 66, 71, 74, 81
O'Connor, Pat, 99, 111
O'Leary, Margaret, 180
  The Woman, 113, 128, 135

O'Malley, Grace, 29, 30, 39
O'Neill, Mary Devenport, 3
  Bluebeard, 9, 17, 18, 64, 172–188, 189, 205,
    210, 211
  Cain, 178
O'Toole, Fintan, 66, 155, 156, 198
Ovid, 104, 117, 129, 131
Oxford Handbook of Modern Irish Theatre, The, 2

pacifism, 27, 51–63, 199, 201
Pašeta, Senia, 28
pastoral, the, 17
Payne School of Ballet, the, 177
Payne, Sara (Sara Patrick), 177
Penelope (*The Odyssey*), 115
Pierse, Michael, 69
pietà, 120, 161, 164
Poe, Edgar Allan, 162
poses plastiques, 32, 35
postcolonialism, 12, 136, 137, 179
postfeminism, 7, 25, 98–101, 112, 137, 141, 153, 162,
  210, 220, 225, 226
Power, Jennie Wyse, 31
Preston, Carrie J., 37
Proclamation of Independence, the, 41, 210
Pro-Life Amendment Campaign, the (PLAC), 98

Quinn, Antoinette, 47
Quinn, Maire, 34

realism, 9, 19, 20, 45, 46, 47, 48, 50, 53, 65, 66, 70,
  71, 73, 77, 78, 79, 83, 89, 133, 156, 166, 167,
  170, 185, 187, 205
recession (1980s), 25, 98, 110
referenda
  abortion (1983), 98, 110
  abortion (1992), 111
  abortion (2002), 136
  abortion (2018), 5
  Article 41 (2019), 14
  divorce (1986), 98, 111
  divorce (1995), 111
repertoire, the. *See* Diana Taylor
revivalism, 37
Reynolds, Paige, 33
Ricoeur, Paul, 19, 20
Roach, Joseph, 173
  surrogation, 173, 188, 190, 191–194, 200,
    204, 211
Robinson, Mary, 111
Roper, Esther, 51, 57
Rose of Tralee, The, 109

sacrifice, 170, 203
  and men, 44

Index

and women, 49, 120, 135–157, 163
blood sacrifice, 44, 60, 145, 148, 151, 154
Sappho, 40
Schneider, Rebecca, 2, 21, 22, 42
set design, 17, 155, 165, 166, 194, 195, 231
Shakespeare, William
Hamlet, 148
The Tempest, 143
Shan Van Vocht, The (magazine), 34, 40
Shan Van Vocht, the (The Poor Old Woman),
4, 40
Sheehy-Skeffington, Francis, 38, 61
Sheehy-Skeffington, Hanna, 37, 40
Sihra, Melissa, 3, 129
Silverman, Kaja, 147
Smith, James M., 12, 174
Smyth, Ailbhe, 4, 228, 229
sound design, 127, 149, 219, 227, 228, 230, 232, 233
sovereignty, the figure, 4, 57, 62, 108, 117
Stone, Alison, 2, 23
storytelling, 11, 15, 17, 87, 89, 209
suffrage, women's, 26, 28, 30, 38, 51, 107
voting rights granted, 41
suicide, 113, 118, 130, 170, 191, 193, 209
Sweeney, Bernadette, 8
symbolic, a female, 19, 131
symbolism, 20, 45, 46, 48, 50, 53, 176, 181
Synge, J.M., 94, 107
In the Shadow of the Glen, 49

tableaux vivants, nineteenth-century, 184
Taylor, Diana, 22
Taylor, Lib, 69
Tiernan, Sonja, 52, 58, 202
tragedy, 169, 171, 204
and women, 126, 130, 135, 138, 170
Greek, 144, 146, 156, 201
trauma, 66, 72–75, 81, 82–83, 149, 205
Trotter, Mary, 31

uncanny, the, 137, 146, 157, 164, 165, 167, 171, 173,
190, 193–194, 196, 198, 205, 232
unemployment, 98
unheimlich, 46–47
unhomely, the, 14, 22, 23, 43, 64, 66, 70–80, 115,
137, 149, 159, 167, 169, 205, 207, 210, 212, 236
Urania, 58, 202
utopian, 20, 56, 63, 132, 206, 210

Venus Rising, tableau of, 32
Victoria, Queen, 28, 44
Virgin Mother, the, 4, 40, 44, 111, 120, 145,
164
voice-off, the, 147

Waking The Feminists, 11
Wald, Christina, 191
Wallace, Clare, 168
Walton, Tony, 17
Ward, Margaret, 28
Warner, Marina, 107, 164, 166, 187
Wilson, Robert, 227
woman-as-nation, the figure of, 3–4, 10, 16, 30, 35,
36, 39, 40–41, 43–51, 66, 86, 108, 144
womb-tomb matrix, the, 39, 44, 135, 157, 164,
175, 218
writing body, the, 9, 10, 218, 228, 235

Yeats, W.B., 31, 94, 128, 217
'In Memory of Eva Gore-Booth and Con
Markievicz', 63
'Leda and the Swan', 70
At the Hawk's Well, 179
Four Plays for Dancers, 176, 181
Kathleen ni Houlihan. See Gregory, Lady
Augusta
The Only Jealousy of Emer, 178
Young, Ella, 28
Young, Iris Marion, 6, 7